THE HANDBOOK OF BRAND MANAGEMENT SCALES

The Handbook of Brand Management Scales is a concise, clear and easy-to-use collection of scales in brand management. Scales are critical tools for researchers measuring consumer insights, emotions and responses. Existing handbooks of marketing scales do not include (or include very few) scales related to brand management constructs. This book is the first to meet this need.

Sample scales include brand personality, brand authenticity, consumer–brand relationships and brand equity. Each scale is included with a clear definition of the construct it is designed to benchmark, a description of the scale itself, how to use it and examples of possible applications in managerial and academic contexts.

A much-needed reference point, this is a unique, vital and convenient volume that should be within reach of every marketing scholar's and manager's desk.

Lia Zarantonello (PhD) is Senior Lecturer (Associate Professor) in Marketing at the University of Bath School of Management. Her previous appointments include IÉSEG School of Management, France, and Bocconi University, Italy. She was also visiting scholar at Columbia Business School, USA. Dr Zarantonello's research interests are in the field of brand management, with a focus on brand experience, consumers' emotions toward brands and brand equity. She has published in international peer-reviewed journals, including the *Journal of Marketing*, the *Journal of Consumer Psychology*, the *International Journal of Research in Marketing*, the *Journal of Advertising Research*, the *International Journal of Advertising* and the *Journal of Brand Management*.

Véronique Pauwels-Delassus (PhD) is Associate Professor of Marketing and Academic Director of the MSc in Digital Marketing and CRM at IÉSEG School of Management (LEM-CNRS), part of the Catholic University of Lille in France. Prior to entering the academic world, Dr Pauwels-Delassus was the marketing director for an international food company. Her strong experience in strategic marketing across different countries contributes to the pragmatic approach adopted in her publications and teaching in the field of brand management, brand name substitution, brand equity and consumer resistance toward brand strategies. She has published in international peer-reviewed journals such as the *Journal of Brand Management*, the *Journal of Product and Brand Management* and the *Journal of Consumer Marketing*.

Brands are a magic and fascinating world. But so many studies, surveys and researches have been conducted on brands that travelling through the Brand world is a difficult journey. To find a path in the jungle of concepts, the variety of theories and the large array of metrics, guidance is needed. With a theoretical background and methodological properties as well as relevant scales this handbook provides that help. In the name of all the future students and young searchers, facing for the first time the complexity of brands and brand management, we have to thank Lia Zarantonello and Véronique Pauwels-Delassus for their useful handbook.

Professor Marie-Hélène Fosse-Gomez, *University of Lille, Executive Director in charge of Research, French Marketing Association, France*

This handbook contains robust, testable, reliable and valid branding scales developed by well recognised academics. It is a tool that can help all brand management researchers, both practitioners and academics, to conduct rigorous survey research, save time and produce quality research output.

Dr Cleopatra Veloutsou, *Senior Lecturer, University of Glasgow, UK*

The Handbook of Brand Management Scales will serve as a wonderful resource for anyone interested in conducting research on brands.

David E. Sprott, *Boeing / Scott & Linda Carson Chaired Professor of Marketing, Washington State University, USA*

This handbook is an impressive and up-to-date compilation of brand management scales dealing with all core themes such as brand personality, brand authenticity and consumers' emotions toward the brand. No doubt this book will quickly become a must-have for any practitioners or researchers involved in the branding management research field.

Professor Pierre Valette-Florence, *IAE de Grenoble & CERAG, Université Grenoble Alpes, France*

The last two decades have seen many exciting new areas of branding research; authenticity, attachment/love and experience, to name a few. Yet researching these new (and older) topics calls for well validated scales. This book is indispensable for anyone doing branding research today.

Rajeev Batra, *S.S. Kresge Professor of Marketing, University of Michigan, USA*

Appropriate metrics are increasingly more important in order to properly manage brands in markets characterized by growth in technological, relational and competitive complexity. This handbook provides a detailed description of relevant scales useful to address a variety of branding issues; from brand knowledge analysis to brand emotions and relationship management. This is a remarkable example of relevance both for academic and managerial communities.

Bruno Busacca, *Dean, SDA Bocconi School of Management and Professor, Department of Marketing, Università Luigi Bocconi, Italy*

Wonderful! The handbook that was missing in brand management is finally here. I found all the measure scales for answering managerial brand issues. It is my new reference book: relevant, helpful, easy to use and thorough.

Géraldine Michel, *Professor, IAE of Paris, University of Paris 1 Panthéon-Sorbonne, and Director of Brands & Values Chair, France*

The 13 thematic sections of this handbook are very clearly organized; with an overview, extensive and rigorous presentation of the scales development, and a strong academic and managerial focus. The scales included come mainly from journals belonging to the two highest tiers of UK/French Journal rankings, a selection procedure that ensures the highest quality throughout the book.

Christian Derbaix, *Professor Emeritus, Louvain School of Management, Belgium*

THE HANDBOOK OF BRAND MANAGEMENT SCALES

*Lia Zarantonello and
Véronique Pauwels-Delassus*

LONDON AND NEW YORK

First published 2016
by Routledge
2 Park Square, Milton Park, Abingdon, Oxon OX14 4RN

and by Routledge
711 Third Avenue, New York, NY 10017

Routledge is an imprint of the Taylor & Francis Group, an informa business

© 2016 Lia Zarantonello and Véronique Pauwels-Delassus

The right of Lia Zarantonello and Véronique Pauwels-Delassus to be identified as authors of this work has been asserted by them in accordance with sections 77 and 78 of the Copyright, Designs and Patents Act 1988.

All rights reserved. No part of this book may be reprinted or reproduced or utilised in any form or by any electronic, mechanical, or other means, now known or hereafter invented, including photocopying and recording, or in any information storage or retrieval system, without permission in writing from the publishers.

Trademark notice: Product or corporate names may be trademarks or registered trademarks, and are used only for identification and explanation without intent to infringe.

British Library Cataloguing in Publication Data
A catalogue record for this book is available from the British Library

Library of Congress Cataloging in Publication Data
Zarantonello, Lia.
  The handbook of brand management scales / Lia Zarantonello and Véronique Pauwels-Delassus. — First Edition.
    pages cm
  Includes bibliographical references and index.
  1. Marketing research—Statistical methods—Handbooks, manuals, etc.
2. Consumer behavior—Research. 3. Scaling (Social sciences)—
Handbooks, manuals, etc. I. Pauwels-Delassus, Véronique. II. Title.
  HF5415.3.Z37 2015
  658.8'27—dc23
  2015004069

ISBN: 978-0-415-74295-5 (hbk)
ISBN: 978-0-415-74296-2 (pbk)
ISBN: 978-1-315-81399-8 (ebk)

Printed and bound by CPI Group (UK) Ltd, Croydon, CR0 4YY

To my parents and my sister, who are far but always in my heart;
To my husband Marcello, for his immense love;
To my son Giulio, for the joy and the meaning he has brought into my life.
Lia Zarantonello

To my parents for their affection and for teaching me the meaning of courage.
To my husband Fabien and my children Marie and Charles
for their love and the happiness they bring me every day.
To my family and my friends for all their encouragement.
To you, dear readers: be creative, passionate,
try to learn something new every day and share it with others!
Véronique Pauwels-Delassus

CONTENTS

List of tables xii
List of boxes xiv
Acknowledgments xv
Foreword by K. L. Keller xvi
Foreword by S. Sthanunathan xviii

Introduction 1

1 Brand identity and brand image 6
  1.1 Overview 6
  1.2 Brand image (Hsieh, 2002) 7
  1.3 Online corporate brand image (Da Silva & Syed Alwi, 2008) 10
  1.4 Political candidate's brand image (Guzmán & Sierra, 2009) 13
  1.5 B2B service brand identity (Coleman, de Chernatony & Christodoulides, 2011) 15
  1.6 Non-profit brand image (Michel & Rieunier, 2012) 18
  1.7 Academic focus 21
  1.8 Managerial focus 22
       References 24

2 Brand associations 26
  2.1 Overview 26
  2.2 Brand associations (Low & Lamb, 2000) 27
  2.3 Team brand associations in professional sport (Ross, James & Vargas, 2006) 30
  2.4 Corporate brand associations (Mann & Ghuman, 2014) 34
  2.5 Academic focus 38

2.6	Managerial focus	39
	References	40

3 Brand personality   43
3.1	Overview	43
3.2	Dimensions of brand personality (Aaker, 1997)	44
3.3	Japanese and Spanish brand personality constructs (Aaker, Benet-Martínez & Garolera, 2001)	48
3.4	*Personnalité humaine et de marque*/Human and brand personality (Ferrandi & Valette-Florence, 2002)	53
3.5	Brand personality in charitable giving (Venable, Rose, Bush & Gilbert, 2005)	56
3.6	Destination personality (Ekinci & Hosany, 2006)	59
3.7	Gender dimensions of brand personality (Grohmann, 2009)	62
3.8	New measure of brand personality (Geuens, Weijters & De Wulf, 2009)	66
3.9	Brand personality applied to cities (Kaplan, Yurt, Guneri & Kurtulus, 2010)	70
3.10	Industrial brand personality (Herbst & Merz, 2011)	73
3.11	*Baromètre de la personnalité de la marque*/Brand personality barometer (Ambroise & Valette-Florence, 2010a, 2010b)	77
3.12	Brand personality appeal (Freling, Crosno & Henard, 2011)	80
3.13	Brand masculine patterns (Azar, 2013)	84
3.14	Academic focus	87
3.15	Managerial focus	88
	References	89

4 Brand authenticity   92
4.1	Overview	92
4.2	Brand authenticity (Bruhn, Schoenmüller, Schäfer & Heinrich, 2012)	93
4.3	Brand extension authenticity (Spiggle, Nguyen & Caravella, 2012)	96
4.4	Consumer-based brand authenticity (Napoli, Dickinson, Beverland & Farrelly, 2014)	100
4.5	Consumer–brand relational authenticity (Ilicic & Webster, 2014)	104
4.6	Academic focus	107
4.7	Managerial focus	108
	References	110

5 Perceived brand differentiation   112
5.1	Overview	112
5.2	Brand parity (Muncy, 1996)	113
5.3	Perceived brand globalness (Steenkamp, Batra & Alden, 2003)	116

5.4	Perceptions of brand luxury (Vigneron & Johnson, 2004)	118
5.5	Brand leadership (Chang & Ko, 2014)	122
5.6	Academic focus	126
5.7	Managerial focus	126
	References	128

6 Attitudes toward the brand 130

6.1	Overview	130
6.2	Attitude toward private-label brands (Burton, Lichtenstein, Netemeyer & Garretson, 1998)	131
6.3	Children's attitude toward the brand (Pecheux & Derbaix, 1999)	134
6.4	Adolescents' attitude toward the brand (Derbaix & Leheut, 2008a, 2008b)	137
6.5	Academic focus	140
6.6	Managerial focus	140
	References	142

7 Experiential consumption with brands 144

7.1	Overview	144
7.2	Brand community (McAlexander, Schouten & Koenig, 2002)	145
7.3	Brand experience (Brakus, Schmitt & Zarantonello, 2009)	148
7.4	Brand experience in services organizations (Nysveen, Pedersen & Skard, 2013)	151
7.5	Brand tribalism (Taute & Sierra, 2014)	154
7.6	Academic focus	157
7.7	Managerial focus	158
	References	160

8 Consumers' emotions toward the brand 162

8.1	Overview	162
8.2	The feeling of love toward a brand (Albert, Merunka & Valette-Florence, 2009)	163
8.3	Brand romance (Patwardhan & Balasubramanian, 2011)	166
8.4	Brand love (Batra, Ahuvia & Bagozzi, 2012)	169
8.5	A new C-OAR-SE–based measure of brand love (Rossiter, 2012)	175
8.6	Negative emotions toward brands (Romani, Grappi & Dalli, 2012)	176
8.7	Romantic brand jealously (Sarkar & Sreejesh, 2014)	180
8.8	Academic focus	182
8.9	Managerial focus	183
	References	185

9 Attachment to the brand 187

9.1	Overview	187
9.2	*Attachement à la marque*/Attachment to the brand (Lacœuilhe, 2000)	188

x Contents

9.3	Brand detachment (Perrin-Martinenq, 2004)	190
9.4	Consumers' emotional attachment to brands (Thomson, MacInnis & Park, 2005)	192
9.5	Brand attachment (Park, MacInnis, Priester, Eisingerich & Iacobucci, 2010)	195
9.6	Academic focus	199
9.7	Managerial focus	200
	References	202

10 Consumer–brand relationships 204

10.1	Overview	204
10.2	Brand loyalty (Odin, Odin & Valette-Florence, 2001)	205
10.3	*Mesure multidimensionnelle de la confiance dans la marque*/ Multi-dimensional measure of brand trust (Gurviez & Korchia, 2002)	207
10.4	Brand trust (1) (Delgado-Ballester, Munuera-Alemán & Yagüe-Guillén, 2003)	210
10.5	Brand relationship quality (Kim, Lee & Lee, 2005)	213
10.6	Dimensions of the product-brand and consumer relationship (Veloutsou, 2007)	215
10.7	Brand trust (2) (Li, Zhou, Kashyap & Yang, 2007)	217
10.8	Academic focus	221
10.9	Managerial focus	222
	References	224

11 Brand equity 227

11.1	Overview	227
11.2	Multi-dimensional consumer-based brand equity (Yoo & Donthu, 2001)	228
11.3	Consumer-based brand equity (Vázquez, del Río & Iglesias, 2002)	233
11.4	Facets of customer-based brand equity (Netemeyer *et al.*, 2004)	237
11.5	Customer-based brand equity in the team sports industry (Bauer, Sauer & Schmitt, 2005)	242
11.6	The equity of online brands (Christodoulides, de Chernatony, Furrer, Shiu & Abimbola, 2006)	245
11.7	Cross-national consumer-based brand equity (Buil, de Chernatony & Martínez, 2008)	248
11.8	Employee-based brand equity (King, Grace & Funk, 2012)	252
11.9	Academic focus	255
11.10	Managerial focus	256
	References	258

12	**Consumer dispositions toward brands**		**260**
	12.1 Overview		260
	12.2 Brand dependence (Bristow, Schneider & Schuler, 2002)		261
	12.3 Meanings of branded products (Strizhakova, Coulter & Price, 2008)		263
	12.4 Brand engagement in self-concept (Sprott, Czellar & Spangenberg, 2009)		268
	12.5 Brand relevance in category (Fischer, Völckner & Sattler, 2010)		271
	12.6 Brand schematicity (Puligadda, Ross & Grewal, 2012)		275
	12.7 Academic focus		279
	12.8 Managerial focus		280
	References		282
13	**Brand orientation**		**284**
	13.1 Overview		284
	13.2 Multi-dimensional non-profit brand orientation (Ewing & Napoli, 2005)		285
	13.3 Brand orientation in the business-to-business sector (Baumgarth, 2010)		289
	13.4 Brand orientation in the context of destination branding (Hankinson, 2012)		291
	13.5 Academic focus		294
	13.6 Managerial focus		295
	References		297

Author index   *299*
Scale index   *306*

TABLES

1.1	Brand image scale	8
1.2	Online corporate brand image scale	10
1.3	Political candidate's brand image scale	13
1.4	B2B service brand identity scale	16
1.5	Non-profit brand image scale	19
2.1	Brand associations scale	28
2.2	Team brand associations scale	31
2.3	Corporate brand associations scale	34
3.1	Brand personality scale	45
3.2	Japanese brand personality scale	49
3.3	Spanish brand personality scale	50
3.4	*Personnalité humaine et de marque*/Human and brand personality scale	54
3.5	Non-profit brand personality scale	57
3.6	Destination personality scale	60
3.7	Masculine and feminine brand personality scale	62
3.8	The new measure of brand personality	66
3.9	City brand personality scale	70
3.10	Industrial brand personality scale	74
3.11	*Baromètre de la personnalité de la marque*/Brand personality barometer	77
3.12	Brand personality appeal scale	80
3.13	Brand masculinity dimensions scale	84
4.1	Brand authenticity scale	93
4.2	Brand extension authenticity scale	97
4.3	Consumer-based brand authenticity scale	101
4.4	Consumer-brand relational authenticity scale	104
5.1	Brand parity scale	113

5.2	Perceived brand globalness scale	116
5.3	Brand luxury index scale	119
5.4	Brand leadership scale	123
6.1	Attitude toward private-label brands scale	131
6.2	Children's attitude toward the brand scale	134
6.3	Adolescents' attitude toward the brand scale	137
7.1	Integration in brand community scale	146
7.2	Brand experience scale	148
7.3	Service brand experience scale	152
7.4	Brand tribalism scale	154
8.1	Brand love feeling scale	163
8.2	Brand romance scale	167
8.3	Brand love prototype scales	170
8.4	The contrastive measure of brand love	175
8.5	Negative emotions toward brands scale	177
8.6	Romantic brand jealousy scale	180
9.1	*Attachement à la marque*/Attachment to the brand scale	188
9.2	Brand detachment scale	190
9.3	Emotional attachment scale	192
9.4	Brand attachment scale	195
10.1	Brand loyalty scale	205
10.2	*Mesure multidimensionnelle de la confiance dans la marque*/ Multi-dimensional measure of brand trust	208
10.3	Brand trust scale	210
10.4	Brand relationship quality scale	213
10.5	Brand relationship scale	216
10.6	Global measure of brand trust	218
10.7	Multi-dimensional scale of brand trust	218
11.1	Multi-dimensional consumer-based brand equity scale	229
11.2	Consumer-based brand equity scale	234
11.3	Customer-based brand equity scale	237
11.4	Brand equity in team sports scale	242
11.5	Online retail/service brand equity scale	246
11.6	Cross-national consumer-based brand equity	249
11.7	Employee brand equity scale	252
12.1	Brand dependence scale	261
12.2	Meanings of branded products scale	264
12.3	Brand engagement in self-concept scale	268
12.4	Brand relevance in category and antecedents scales	271
12.5	Brand schematicity scale	275
13.1	Multi-dimensional non-profit brand orientation scale	286
13.2	B2B brand orientation scale	289
13.3	Destination brand orientation scale	292

BOXES

Brand attitude	64
Purchase intention of the brand	64
Likelihood of recommendation of the brand	64
Brand extension fit	98
Cognitive brand loyalty	114
Price sensitivity	114
Perceived usefulness of market information	115
Brand as icon of local culture	117
Brand familiarity	117
Brand attitude	149
Brand trust	165
Word-of-mouth	166
Brand loyalty	166
Overall brand love	173
Purchase intention	230
Attitude toward the brand	230
Brand and product category experience	230
Overall brand equity (OBE)	232
Brand image consistency	239
Brand disparity	262
Brand leadership	293

ACKNOWLEDGMENTS

We would like to express our sincere gratitude to all of the people that have contributed, directly or indirectly, to the development of this handbook. First and foremost, we would like to thank our supervisors, mentors, current and former colleagues at University of Bath School of Management, IÉSEG School of Management, Catholic University of Lille, Bocconi University in Milan and IULM University in Milan, as well as co-authors and members of the different marketing associations such as AFM (Association Française du Marketing) and AMS (Academy of Marketing Science), who have inspired us in our branding research and have shared our interest and passion for brand-related topics.

In addition, we would like to thank all the students we have met over the years, those who attended our courses as well as those who wrote their dissertations under our supervision. They have been an important stimulus to work on this handbook, having realized, thanks to them, the need for systematizing and organizing measurement scales in the field of brand management. We should also not forget all the managers with whom we have interacted over the years for our insightful discussions on brand-related topics and speculations about future developments of brand management and measurements in companies. These managers have been a constant source of exchange and inspiration to the handbook.

Last but not least, we are extremely grateful to the editors at Routledge for having supported us in this project, to the authors of the scales included in the handbook who gave us feedback on our work and to Kevin L. Keller and S. Sthanunathan, who accepted writing the forewords to the handbook – respectively, one with a more academic focus, the other one with a more managerial focus. Their point of view on brand measurement is a further cause for reflection on the topic.

FOREWORD

Branding, without question, is a complex subject to study and master. There are so many different issues to consider, so many different perspectives to adopt, and so many different objectives to achieve. Like any challenging social science subject, there is not always agreement as to how to best address all the various concerns. With branding, perhaps too much energy and effort has been expended at times trying to stake out turf and establish singular positions at the expense of accommodating other points of view and ways of thinking. The fact is that multiple vantage points and approaches are almost invariably more helpful for learning and lead to better conclusions and better decisions than a more restrictive treatment or examination.

Because of the complexity and diversity of thinking with branding, metrics are critical to help managers and researchers understand what is working and what is not and, most importantly, how and why. Metrics are vital to successfully managing a brand and helping it to thrive and grow. Yet, in part because of the many issues, perspectives and objectives involved, developing a small number of simple metrics to capture the wide range of branding effects of interest is extremely difficult, if not impossible.

Fortunately, with *The Handbook of Brand Management Scales* (2015), Lia Zarantonello and Véronique Pauwels-Delassus provide a comprehensive, critical and up-to-date view of academic efforts to design scales to achieve a deeper understanding of various facets of brands, branding and brand management. This project was undoubtedly a hugely difficult – but crucially important – undertaking. Such a detailed exposition of relevant scales and measures improves our understanding of the "lay of the land" of what we know and don't know about brand metrics that will aid academics, students and practitioners alike.

One of the real advantages of such a thorough examination of branding scales, however, is the in-depth comparisons it affords. Assembling relevant scales in one place, it is easier to understand similarities and differences, strengths and weaknesses, and applicability to different situations. With a solid foundation in the form of a pool of potentially relevant measures, scales can be revised, combined, tested and used to suit the particular needs of different marketers and researchers.

The 13 chapters in this handbook cover a varied set of branding topics related to brand image, brand intangibles, brand emotions, brand value and so on. Recognizing the geographical and disciplinary diversity of academics developing scales to study branding, relevant research is sourced from a wide range of journals across Europe and North America. Scales are carefully analysed in terms of their methodological, theoretical and managerial properties. Although such reviews are necessarily subjective in nature, they provide much insight and a basis for readers to draw their own conclusions depending on their personal values, experiences and goals.

Lia Zarantonello and Véronique Pauwels-Delassus should be congratulated on their accomplishment. This handbook is certainly a must-read for any brand researcher or strategist interested in brand performance, value and diagnostics. It is a handbook in the truest sense of the word, providing invaluable and practical help, insight and guidance.

Kevin Lane Keller
E. B. Osborn Professor of Marketing
Dartmouth College
Hanover, NH
December 2014

FOREWORD

In my 28 years as an insight professional, the most fascinating question has always been "What differentiates brands that grow from those that don't?" While market forces like distribution and pricing have an impact in the short run, the long-term success of a brand depends on consumers' perceptions and engagement with the brand.

Marketers and market researchers have been bombarded with a plethora of constructs and theories. However, there is universal acknowledgement of the presence of a relationship between consumers and the brand they consume. Indeed, many of such constructs originated from the J. Dewey framework – 1910: Problem/need recognition, Information search, Evaluation of alternatives, Purchase decision, Post-purchase behaviour. Through these stages, consumers form associations of the brand with benefits (functional and emotional), imagery and personality. They develop perceptions about how relevant and different brands are relative to other offerings and judge how authentic the brand really is. All this creates resonance for the brand with its consumers. Stronger resonance in turn will trigger a higher likelihood of gaining their loyalty – behaviourally by purchasing more, being advocates for the brand and even willingness to pay a premium.

This handbook will be of great help to market researchers and marketers to understand and integrate measures to assess and manage consumers' experience with a brand. This handbook has also the merit of casting some light on conceptual frontiers of consumers' emotions, brand love and attachment and relationship with a brand.

The fundamental constructs of how consumers form an engagement with the brand has survived the test of time and still represent the foundation of good brand management. However, the world of brand building has become more complex because consumers these days are not always following a linear journey as outlined by Dewey. For instance, from relying on the neighbour for an opinion on the new washing powder being advertised, now consumers have the power of Google and Amazon at their fingertips. People decide on which hotel they would stay at while on vacation based on Trip Advisor reviews. The advent of the digital era has transformed the nature of interaction between the brand and the consumers from a one-way broadcast to a two-way engagement. Instances of people buying what they don't even need are not uncommon these days. Some brands have created a strong relationship with their consumers underpinned by emotions such as love. While there are several tablets that look like the iPad and have similar functionality, consumers are willing to pay a premium for an iPad. The new Coke formulation experience of 1985 showed the world clearly that the engagement of consumers went well beyond just the product.

Consumers are more than ever influenced in their choices by their online friends. In this virtual world, what consumers can share with peers may change their own perception of the brand. Even though managers can communicate more directly to consumers and have at their disposal huge sets of data allowing them to have better consumer knowledge, consumers are increasingly playing a bigger role in how brands are shaped. While brands can become more powerful and get real fans, they are also becoming more vulnerable. It is therefore more important for managers to keep the control on actively managing their brands and understanding what is really happening with their brands. The interest of the handbook is to provide a broader picture of instruments which can inspire market researchers and managers with complementary measurements to their current tools in order to have a better understanding of consumers' perceptions, emotions and relationships with the brands.

Academics are a divided house on whether there are parallels between consumers' relationship with a brand and relationships among human beings (particularly with your spouse or partner). On the other hand, for senior marketers, having a numeric target makes it possible to focus a large organization behind a goal. The Holy Grail has been to find one number to summarize equity as well as consumers' engagement with the brand. The purists cringe at this as "you can't measure your marriage in one number or describe it in one word".

Nevertheless, the love that a person has for a brand has a lot of similarities with the love the same person has for a real person. With this handbook, you can find insight in order to measure the intensity and the quality of the relationship between the consumer and the brand to keep it hot!

Stan Sthanunathan
Senior Vice President – Consumer &
Market Insights, Unilever
London, December 2014

INTRODUCTION

Measure what is measurable,
And make measurable what is not so.
                              Galileo Galilei

I. Rationale of the handbook

We both started this *Handbook of Brand Management Scales* coming from different backgrounds and with different perspectives on branding but with one common belief: the field of brand management has grown so much over the last few decades that brand concepts, dimensions and related measurement scales have multiplied. Today, the field of brand management appears rich in concepts, dimensions and related measurement scales, but still fragmented and unstructured. Existing handbooks of marketing scales, despite providing valuable support for general marketing and consumer research issues, offer limited help to academics and practitioners working in the field of brand management, as they have included only a few brand-related scales. As a result, getting a clear idea or a "big picture" of brand concepts, dimensions and related measurement scales is a challenge that many academics and practitioners have to face nowadays.

With this handbook, we provide a collection of the major brand-related measurement scales that have been developed in the field of brand management over the last two decades. We have selected these scales from marketing and consumer research literature and have organized them in thematic sections in the handbook. Each section contains an overview which introduces the general concept and then presents the scales in a concise and clear way. By so doing, we aim to provide quality assistance to academics and practitioners working on brand-related projects and wishing to adopt valid and reliable measures in their research. Moreover, the handbook offers a complementary approach to both the academic and managerial world. We leveraged our experiences and backgrounds, both inside and outside academia, and created a handbook that can be useful to the marketing community. At the end of each section, we have included both an academic and a managerial focus, where we provide food for thought. This way, we also aim to inspire academics and practitioners in their brand-related projects, as well as to question them about possible new applications and implications of the brand-related measures included in the handbook.

As Galileo Galilei's quote tells us, trying to measure phenomena has always been a major task. We recognise the importance of measurement, which helps us better understand brand-related phenomena and, ultimately, allows us to manage them. This is something we deal with every day in all our brand-related research and consulting activities. We hope that our handbook will be a valuable reference to you in your work, whether you are an academic or a practitioner.

II. Targets of the handbook

The Handbook of Brand Management Scales is addressed to both academic and managerial communities who are looking for qualified help or inspiration in their brand-related research. In particular, we believe that the handbook will be useful to:

- *University students* of all levels, attending business schools and faculties, who are starting to work or are already working on a project or dissertation on brand-management topics. The handbook represents a fundamental reference for them. It will provide suggestions about possible work as a starting point for their own projects and dissertations. It will also make the search for brand-related measurement scales easier.
- *Academics* working on brand-related topics. The handbook will support them in their research. It will give them the possibility to quickly check available scales on a given topic or evaluate the possibilities they have with respect to a given topic. The handbook will give them the chance to quickly familiarize themselves with new measurement scales in the field of brand management. The handbook will therefore provide an easy and quick way to find the scales they need.
- *Professionals* wishing to complement their knowledge of industry-related brand measurement scales with others from academia. Without our handbook, professionals will hardly have access to brand-related scales from academic resources. The handbook wants to give them the possibility to learn about these scales. It will also give them insights about possible uses of the scales.

III. Criteria for scale selection

The Handbook of Brand Management Scales includes major measurement scales in the field of brand management. With "major scales", we refer to scales that have been developed through a rigorous and well-documented process reported in a published article.[1] In order to identify these scales, we have consulted a broad range of marketing journals. Our selection of scales is guided by official journal rankings used in the UK and France, the countries where we currently work, as well as our qualitative judgments. Specifically, we searched for brand-management scales in the journals belonging to the two highest tiers of journal rankings used in UK and France:

- grade four and grade three journals as reported in *Version 4 of the Association of Business School (ABS) Academic Journal Quality Guide*, used in the UK;
- category 1 and 2 journals of the French *Categorization of Journals in Economy and Management* list, Section 37 du Comité National de la Recherche Scientifique, October 2011, version 3.01.

Although the two journal ranking lists overlap to a great extent, some differences between the two are present. Overall, the journals that we included in our search are the following (alphabetical order): *European Journal of Marketing, Industrial Marketing Management, International Journal of Research in Marketing, International Marketing Review, Journal of Advertising, Journal of Advertising Research, Journal of Business Research, Journal of Consumer Psychology, Journal of Consumer Research, Journal of International Marketing, Journal of Marketing, Journal of Marketing Management, Journal of Marketing Research, Marketing Science, Journal of Retailing, Journal of Service Research, Journal of the Academy of Marketing Science, Marketing Letters, Marketing Science, Psychology and Marketing,* and *Recherche et Application en Marketing.*

Based on our qualitative judgment, we also consulted the following journals:

- *Journal of Brand Management* and *Journal of Product and Brand Management* because of the focus of these journals on brand-management issues.
- *International Journal of Market Research* because of the focus of the journal on methodological issues, including scale-development papers.
- Top journals from specific fields including: *Journal of Sport Management* (sports); *Journal of Travel Research* (tourism); *Journal of Personality and Social Psychology* (psychology); and *Journal of International Business Studies* (international management). These fields are often chosen by our students in their dissertations, and we believe that other students may benefit from our selection of scales within these fields. Moreover, some of these fields (sports, tourism) represent fields in which the logic of brand management is expanding, too. The scales in this handbook may stimulate ideas for future research and applications, and may also interest academics and practitioners.
- *Advances in Consumer Research*, one of the top conferences for consumer and marketing researchers. The conference has proceedings in which full-length papers are included, where the methodology of the studies conducted is well documented. Scale-development papers focusing on brand-related issues have been therefore selected if a full-length paper was available.

We did our best to identify the major brand-related measurement scales within these journals. We apologize for any major scale we may have forgotten. We welcome comments and feedback for future versions of the handbook.

IV. Organization and contents of the handbook

The Handbook of Brand Management Scales collects nearly 70 measurement scales. In addition to these scales that are presented extensively, several other scales are recalled in the handbook. We reference all the other measures taken from literature and used by researchers to develop their scale. We also report in boxes additional brand-related measures created by researchers in order to examine the validity of their scale. In total, the handbook contains more than a hundred brand-related scales. Although the majority of these scales are in English, scales in other languages are presented in the handbook, including French, Spanish, Japanese and Turkish.

Scales in the handbook are organized in 13 chapters. Chapter 1 covers the pillar topics of brand identity and brand image and presents five scales about either topics. Moving from identify and image, the handbook presents four scales on brand associations in Chapter 2. In a link with brand associations, Chapter 3 includes 12 scales capturing the personality of brands in general or with a focus on a country or sector. The next chapter, Chapter 4, covers scales related to the increasingly important topic of brand authenticity, whereas Chapter 5 includes scales related to perceived brand differentiation. Chapter 6 covers another pillar topic in brand management, that of brand attitudes, and presents three scales which capture attitudes toward a specific type of brand or specific targets of consumers. Chapter 7 consists of four scales about the experiential consumption with brands, and Chapter 8 includes six scales on consumers' emotions toward brands, most of which, but not all, pertain to positive emotions toward brands. Chapter 9 includes but also goes beyond emotions and presents four scales about consumers' attachment to or detachment from brands. Going from emotions to relationships, Chapter 10 is about consumer–brand relationships and comprises six scales measuring some aspects of these relationships. Chapter 11 deals with the important topic of brand equity and presents seven scales assessing brand equity in general terms or with a focus on a specific industry or sector. Chapter 12 comprises five scales on consumers' dispositions, that is, scales assessing orientations, inclinations and tendencies of consumer toward brands Finally, Chapter 13 includes three scales on brand orientation in specific contexts.

Within each chapter, the contents of the handbook are organized as follows. The introduction to the chapter provides an overview of the chapter, as well as key references on the topic. We then present the scales following their order of publication. Each scale is presented as follows:

- *Definition of construct*, where we provide an explanation of the construct to which the scale is related.
- *Scale description*, where we describe how the scale is structured and how it should be used.

- *Scale development*, where we provide a clear and concise summary of the scale-development process that was followed to develop the scale.
- *Samples*, where we provide descriptions of the samples used in the scale-development process.
- *Reliability and validity*, where we give details about the psychometric properties of the scale.
- *Managerial applications*, where we illustrate the uses of the scale as suggested by the researchers who developed it.

At the end of each chapter, we include an academic focus and a managerial focus. In the academic focus, we offer suggestions of possible dissertations that may be pursued on the chapter's topic and that are based on the conceptualizations and measurements provided in the chapter. We then include a managerial focus, whose objective is to question managers about possible applications of the measurement scales presented previously. Finally, we include a reference section with all references mentioned in the chapter.

Bath and Lille, December 2014

Lia Zarantonello & Véronique Pauwels-Delassus

Note

1. Key references on scale development include: Bergkvist, L. & Rossiter, J. R. (2007). The predictive validity of multiple-item versus single-item measures of the same constructs. *Journal of Marketing Research*, 44 (2), 175–184; Churchill, G. A., Jr. (1979). Paradigm for developing better measures of marketing constructs. *Journal of Marketing Research*, 16 (1), 64–73; DeVellis, R. F. (2011). *Scale development: theory and applications* (3rd ed.). Thousand Oaks, CA: Sage; Gerbing, D., & Anderson, J. (1988). An updated paradigm for scale development incorporating unidimensionality and its assessment. *Journal of Marketing Research*, 25 (2), 186–192; Netemeyer, R. G., Bearden, W. O., & Sharma, S. (2003). *Scaling procedures. Issues and applications*. Thousand Oaks, CA: Sage; Nunnally, J. C., & Bernstein, I. H. (1994). *Psychometric theory* (3rd ed.). New York, NY: McGraw-Hill; Rossiter, J. R. (2002). The C-OAR-SE procedure for scale development in marketing. *International Journal of Research in Marketing*, 19 (4), 305–335; Steenkamp, J., & Baumgartner, H. (1998). Assessing measurement invariance in cross-national consumer research. *Journal of Consumer Research*, 25 (1), 78–90.

1
BRAND IDENTITY AND BRAND IMAGE

1.1 Overview

In marketing literature, great attention has been given to brand image from either company or consumer perspectives. Brand image can be defined as the perception about a brand which is reflected by the brand associations held in the consumer's memory (Keller, 1993). The brand image consists of the consumer's perception of the brand identity and positioning defined by the company. Brand image is not a simple understanding of the communication activity of the company but corresponds to the consumer interpretation of the total set of brand-related activities developed by a company (Park, Jaworski & MacInnis, 1986). The positive meanings consumers associate with a brand serve as drivers of future purchase behaviour (Aaker, 1991). The importance of a brand in a market is therefore influenced by a company's ability to evaluate the consumer perception of the brand and the company's ability to manage the strategy of brand positioning, adequately revealing brand values to a consumer (Kotler, Armstrong, Harris & Piercy, 2013). According to Park, Jaworski and MacInnis (1986), brand success in the market depends on the choice of brand identity, the usage of identity-developing image and the guarantee that image adequately transfers the brand identity chosen by a company with the aim of differentiating it from competitors and responding to a desired consumer value.

Because of the relevance of brand image for both consumers and companies, researchers have dedicated a lot of attention to developing measures to capture this concept (cf. Bruner, Hensel & James, 2005). Among these measures, some have been developed by following a rigorous and well-documented process. Five scales have been identified and reported in the current chapter. Three of them consider brand image from a business-related perspective, whereas two of them extend the concept outside the business sphere. Specifically, the brand image scale developed by

Hsieh (2002) aims at measuring a brand image across nations and allows researchers to evaluate if consumers perceive brand similarly in the light of the differences in the cultural and business environments. The scale developed by Da Silva and Syed Alwi (2008) aims at measuring the corporate brand image in an online environment. This is particularly interesting: first, considering the growth of online business and, second, because the virtual environment reduces the physical contact with the company and people. As brand image and brand identity are key concepts for consumers and companies driving performance in the market, Coleman, de Chernatony and Christodoulides (2011) examine this concept in the business-to-business sector and suggest a scale enabling researchers to measure the brand identity of a company in a service sector.

The other two brand image scales included in the chapter go beyond the business sphere. Michel and Rieunier (2012) examine brand image in relation to non-profit organizations, in the light of the importance that the non-profit world represents nowadays and the characteristics of this sector. Their non-profit brand image scale allows researchers to measure the brand image of charities and provides a better understanding of which dimensions of brand image influence donation behaviour. Guzmán and Sierra (2009) apply the concept of brand image to political candidates. Their political candidate's brand image scale can evaluate the perception of the candidate and which dimensions are taken into consideration by voters when making an electoral decision.

1.2 Brand image (Hsieh, 2002)

Definition of construct

Brand image is conceptualized by the researcher from an associative network perspective (Farquhar & Herr, 1993): "In associative networks, what differentiate one brand from another in memory are brand image dimensions and the strength and the uniqueness of associations that constitute image dimensions" (Hsieh, 2002, p. 50). Brand image is defined as a cross-national, benefit-oriented, multi-dimensional construct consisting of a set of benefit-based brand associations which help consumers understand how the brand can answer their needs symbolically, economically, sensorily or as a utility. The *symbolic* dimension reflects emotional motives. The *economic* dimension is related to value for needed characteristics. The *sensory* dimension reflects experiential benefits. The *utility* dimension corresponds to functional attributes.

Scale description

The brand image scale is developed with specific reference to the car industry and contains four benefit-based brand image dimensions, namely *sensory, symbolic, utilitarian* and *economic*. The *sensory* dimension includes five associations/items, some of them being closely linked with the car industry such as "good acceleration"

8 Brand identity and brand image

and "fun to drive". The *symbolic* dimension contains two associations/items: "luxury features" and "prestige". The *utilitarian* dimension is measured with three associations/items which are also specific to the sector of activity ("made to last", "reliability" and "safe in accident"). The *economic* dimension contains two associations/items related to car specificities such as "good fuel economy" and "good dealer service". The 12 items composing the scale are measured through nominal variables (yes/no), as respondents are asked to evaluate a given car brand by saying which of the provided items applies to the car brand investigated.

The brand image scale can also be used to compute a global brand image cohesiveness index based on the difference of brand image perceptions between the initial country and the foreign ones.

TABLE 1.1 Brand image scale

Scale dimension	Scale item
Sensory	• Exciting
	• Fun to drive
	• Good acceleration
	• Styling
	• Sporty
Symbolic	• Luxury features
	• Prestige
Utilitarian	• Made to last
	• Reliability
	• Safe in accident
Economic	• Good fuel economy
	• Good dealer service

Scale development

The development of the scale starts with exploratory research based on focus-group discussions. Participants are asked to evaluate the desirability and the importance of various attributes, which allows identifying 14 benefit-oriented associations (items) mentioned as salient beliefs about automobiles by the majority.

The main survey is conducted in 20 countries by trained interviewers. A total of 53 car brands are selected for the survey. Brands are read to participants, and those known to them are evaluated on the 14 identified items. A correspondence analysis (CA) approach is employed to explore the dimensionality of the scale, because nominal scales are used in the data collection. Five dimensions are extracted in the analysis, and cumulatively they explain more than 95% of the variance. The analysis reveals three major dimensions, namely the economic-symbolic dimension, the sensory dimension and the utilitarian dimension. Two items are eliminated at this stage, "perceived high quality" and "latest technology". The former item is dropped because the dimension to which it refers, *quality*, is in question. The latter item is eliminated because it is included in the fifth dimension along with "styling", because the link between the two is not clear according to the researcher, and "styling" could be combined with the sensory dimension; this decision is supported by the smallest inertia (0.008) of the "latest technology" item, suggesting a limited contribution in explaining variance.

To confirm the dimensionality of brand image, a confirmatory factor analysis (CFA) is performed on the 12 items. Both the three-factor model derived from the CA and a four-factor model presenting separate economic and symbolic dimensions are estimated through LISREL VII. The tetrachoric correlation matrix and weighted least squares are employed in the analysis because of the dichotomous nature of the variables. The results indicate that the four-factor model has a better fit ($\chi^2 = 2,585.68$, $df = 48$, $p = 0.0000$, GFI = 1.00, RMSR = 0.05, RMSEA = 0.018, NFI = 0.87, NNFI = 0.82, CFI = 0.87) than the three-factor model ($\chi^2 = 3,298.82$, $df = 51$, $p = 0.0000$; RMSR = 0.06, RMSEA = 0.02, NFI = 0.83; NNFI = 0.79; CFI = 0.83). Validity tests are performed next.

Samples

The sample is composed of 200 respondents from each of the 20 countries with the exception of Japan (300 respondents) and the United States (370 respondents) because of the large sales volume in these two countries. The survey is conducted by trained interviewers in the major commercial centres of 70 metropolitan areas. In total, the sample includes 4,320 international respondents.

Reliability and validity

The reliability of the brand image scale is assessed by analysing the R^2 associated with the parameter estimates in the measurement model. The 12 items indicate a modest satisfactory reliability of the measurement model, with R^2 value ranging from 0.12 to 0.48 except for the "styling" association, which has the lowest R^2 value of 0.03 and suggests a poor measure and a lack of internal consistency.

The convergent and the discriminant validities of the four-factor brand image scale are established by comparing the four-factor model with the three-factor model. The higher loadings of the items in the four-factor model indicate a better fit in terms of convergent validity. The factor loadings of each association range from 0.17 for "styling" to 0.70 for "exciting". The estimated χ^2 statistics are significantly smaller in the four-factor model than in the three-factor model, suggesting a better discriminant validity for the four-factor model.

Managerial applications

This brand image scale can be used to measure and manage brand image across countries in the automobile industry. This scale helps managers build brand image and clarify the promise of the brand in satisfying consumers' symbolic, economic, sensory, and utilitarian needs. This scale also allows managers to assess the degree of brand globalization in terms of brand image cohesiveness. Country clusters that share similar brand image perceptions have been identified in this study, which can be useful for international marketers in managing their brand globally.

1.3 Online corporate brand image (Da Silva & Syed Alwi, 2008)

Definition of construct

Corporate brand image (CBI) can be seen as "the additional brand values that are inherent in or associated with the corporation and its products and services" (Balmer & Gray, 2003, p. 973). CBI is considered the consumer's emotional response to a brand based on their repeated experiences that leads to the personification of brand attributes which differentiate it from competitors (Patterson, 1999). Building on these contributions, Da Silva and Syed Alwi define online CBI as an affective and emotional construct, resulting from experience with the company over time. They use the corporate character framework proposed by Davies et al. (2004) to further conceptualize online CBI as a multi-dimensional construct, in particular as consisting of the dimensions of *agreeableness, enterprise, informality, chic* and *competence*.

Scale description

The online CBI scale includes five dimensions and 20 items. *Agreeableness* and *informality* are assessed with four items, *enterprise* with seven items, *chic* with three items and *competence* with two items. All items are measured using a 5-point Likert-type scale anchored by 1 = "strongly disagree" to 5 = "strongly agree".

TABLE 1.2 Online corporate brand image scale

Scale dimension	Scale item
Agreeableness	• Pleasant
	• Friendly
	• Agreeable
	• Supportive
Enterprise	• Daring
	• Trendy
	• Exciting
	• Cool
	• Imaginative
	• Innovative
	• Technical

(Continued)

TABLE 1.2 (Continued)

Scale dimension	Scale item
Informality	• Open • Easygoing • Simple • Straightforward
Chic	• Refined • Prestigious • Elegant
Competence	• Secure • Reliable

Scale development

To develop the online CBI scale, the researchers propose to use the corporate character scale advanced by Davies *et al.* (2004), including seven dimensions and 49 items. The first step of the online CBI scale development consists, therefore, in testing the appropriateness and validity of the corporate character scale. Following a reliability analysis conducted in SPSS 12, the researchers decide to adopt the full corporate character scale without any alternation.

A survey studying the empirical context of an online retail bookstore is conducted as main study. The questionnaire contains the corporate character scale and measures on customer satisfaction (adapted from Oliver, 1997) and loyalty intention (adapted from Zeithmal, Berry & Parasuraman, 1996).

Data analysis is conducted using AMOS 4. The 49 corporate character scale items are subjected to a CFA specifically performing a first-order measurement model. The results of this initial analysis show a poor fit. The model is therefore revised until it attains acceptable values in the goodness-of-fit indices. A first-order measurement model with five dimensions and 20 items provides a satisfying solution ($\chi(160)^2 = 337.84$, $p < 0.001$; $\chi^2/df = 2.1$; GFI = 0.936; CFI = 0.937; RMSEA = 0.047). A reliability analysis is therefore conducted. A second-order measurement model is then tested, where a second-order overall online CBI variable is introduced being explained by the five first-order dimensions. The second-order model performs very similarly on all fit indexes ($\chi(165)^2 = 372.44$, $p < 0.001$; $\chi^2/df = 2.3$; GFI = 0.931; CFI = 0.926; RMSEA = 0.05). Therefore, online corporate brand image can be modelled either as a five-factor model (first order) or as a latent variable construct (second/higher order). Online CBI explains 95%, 31%, 49%, 25% and 69% of the variance associated with the dimensions of *agreeableness, enterprise, competence, chic* and *informality*, respectively. Tests of convergent and discriminant validities are conducted.

The impact of online CBI on customer satisfaction and loyalty is analysed in a full structural model. The results show a good fit to the data ($\chi(316)^2 = 686.452$, $p < 0.001$; $\chi^2/df = 2.2$; GFI = 0.905; CFI = 0.926; RMSEA = 0.048). The scale's nomological validity is verified.

Samples

The sample used for the pilot study is obtained using a drop-off/pick-up methods in the Manchester Business School and other schools in the University of Manchester. One hundred eighty-seven questionnaires are distributed, resulting in 53 usable questionnaires.

The sample used for the main study is obtained through a convenience sample of customers from a bookstore. Before leaving the store, these customers are asked to participate in a survey on an online bookstore. Participants are screened to ensure they have sufficient experience with the online bookstore being studied. The final sample consists of 511 experienced customers of the online bookstore.

Reliability and validity

The reliability of the scale is first evaluated in the pilot study and further assessed in the main study. Cronbach's coefficient alpha obtained in the pilot study indicates a high level of internal consistency for *agreeableness* (0.80), *enterprise* (0.89) and *competence* (0.92) and a weaker coefficient for *ruthlessness* (0.67), *chic* (0.61), *informality* (0.54) and *machismo* (0.59). Composite reliabilities calculated in the main study are all above the recommended level (*agreeableness* = 0.77; *enterprise* = 0.79; *competence* = 0.63; *chic* = 0.76; *informality* = 0.63), which confirms the reliability of the online CBI scale.

Convergent validity is assessed in the main study and supported, with all items being statistically significant at $p < 0.001$. The discriminant validity is also supported; correlation results are low for all dimensions (ranging from 0.26 to 0.67) except between *agreeableness* and *informality* dimensions (0.81). Nevertheless, the results of the chi-square differences test confirm that those two factors are separate factors ($\chi(1)^2 = 34.7$, $p < 0.001$).

The nomological validity is also confirmed. Indeed, the corporate brand image is indicated as a strong predictor of both satisfaction and loyalty. The total effect of online CBI on loyalty intention is the sum of its direct effect (standardized path coefficient = 0.22) and the indirect effect via consumer satisfaction (standardized path coefficient = 0.34), giving a total effect of 0.56.

Managerial applications

The online CBI scale offers managers the possibility of measuring the perceived brand image in a virtual environment. Furthermore, this measure provides a better understanding and the possibility of tracking the key dimensions of the corporate brand image. As the online CBI has a direct and indirect impact on brand loyalty, managers can develop marketing strategies in order to enhance some dimensions of the brand image as well as to improve the satisfaction and loyalty of their customers.

1.4 Political candidate's brand image (Guzmán & Sierra, 2009)

Definition of construct

Political candidates' image seems to be critical to electoral success (Funk, 1999), as it can be used by voters as shortcut that helps them to decide how to vote (Shabad & Andersen, 1979). Political candidates can be viewed as brands (Nakanishi, Cooper & Kassarijian, 1974) and examined in terms of the brand image they have. The construct of political candidate's brand image advanced by Guzmán and Sierra takes its roots from Aaker's (1997; see Chapter 3, pp. 44–48) brand personality framework and Caprara, Barbaranelli and Zimbardo's (2002) political candidate personality framework. The construct contains five dimensions, namely: *capability*, which is described by the level of perceived competence issued from Aaker's brand personality framework and the energy of the candidate issued from Caprara *et al.*'s candidate personality framework; *openness*, which is similar to the openness factor described in the candidate personality framework; *empathy*, which includes traits from the brand personality framework ("cheerful", "sentimental", "friendly", "cool" and "young"); *agreeableness*, which contains four traits of the candidate personality framework, three coming from the agreeableness facet ("generous", "loyal" and "sincere") and one coming from the conscientiousness facet ("reliable"); and finally *handsomeness*, which is a new dimension described with three traits issued from the sophistication factor in the brand personality framework ("glamorous", "good-looking" and "charming").

Scale description

The political candidate's brand image scale contains 26 traits and five dimensions. The first dimension, the candidate's perceived *capability*, is constituted by two facets: the candidate's perceived competence (six items) and the candidate's perceived energy (three items). The second and the third dimensions, namely *openness* and *empathy*, both contain five items. The fourth dimension corresponds to the candidate's *agreeableness*, which is configured by four items. The last dimension is *handsomeness*, which contains three items. All the traits used are positively balanced. Traits are evaluated using a 5-point Likert scale ranging from 1 ("not at all descriptive") to 5 ("extremely descriptive").

TABLE 1.3 Political candidate's brand image scale

Scale dimension	Scale facet	Scale item
Capability	Competence	• Hardworking • Intelligent • Leader • Successful • Constant • Responsible

(*Continued*)

14 Brand identity and brand image

TABLE 1.3 (Continued)

Scale dimension	Scale facet	Scale item
	Energy	• Dynamic • Energetic • Enterprising
Openness	–	• Sharp • Creative • Innovative • Modern • Original
Empathy	–	• Cheerful • Sentimental • Friendly • Cool • Young
Agreeableness	–	• Generous • Loyal • Sincere • Reliable
Handsomeness	–	• Glamorous • Good-looking • Charming

Scale development

In order to develop the candidate's brand image scale, the researchers first combine the 42 traits from Aaker's brand personality scale (1997) and the 25 adjectives used to measure politicians' personalities by Caprara *et al.* (2002). After eliminating four traits which are common to both lists and five which are perceived by the researchers as irrelevant or redundant when translated into Spanish, a list of 58 items is retained. All items need to be positively balanced, as negative descriptors in electoral surveys are not admitted in Mexico. In a following survey taking place during the 2006 election, Mexican respondents evaluate the three principal political candidates on the 58 selected items.

Data are subjected to a series of principal component analyses using oblique rotation. After checking the internal consistency of the factors, all items with communalities < 0.40 are excluded from the scale; in case of cross-loadings, items are assigned to the factor with a larger loading. This process results in a five-factor solution including 26 traits with an explained variance of 60.358%. Factor correlations range from 0.198 to 0.624. Confirmatory factor analysis using a structural equation modelling procedure is then performed for each individual candidate, and results support the five-factor solution previously identified. The fit of the three models is as follows: $\chi^2 = 1{,}288.50$ (candidate 1), 1,307.58 (candidate 2) and 1,333.05 (candidate 3); $df = 289$ (all three candidates); IFI = 0.98 (all three); CFI =

0.98 (all three); GFI = 0.92 (all three); AGFI = 0.90 (all three); NFI = 0.98 (candidate 1), 0.98 (candidate 2) and 0.97 (candidate 3); and RMSEA = 0.055 (candidate 1), 0.056 (candidate 2) and 0.056 (candidate 3).

Samples

The sample is composed of 1,144 Mexican registered voters over the age of 18 years and is selected thanks to the Mexican Federal Electoral Institute list of voters in each state. The questionnaire is administered in all 32 states in Mexico and in 88 locations. Respondents are selected by random sample based on age and gender. The questionnaire is administered using a door-to-door survey method, which results in 1,089 valid responses.

Reliability and validity

The candidate's brand image scale has a good level of internal consistency with Cronbach's alphas coefficients being above 0.80 for the five dimensions. The authors use CFA fit indices obtained for each of the three candidates to prove the scale's reliability as well as convergent and discriminant validities.

Managerial applications

The political candidate's brand image scale can find application for future political campaigns in Mexico. Even if the scale has not been validated in an international environment, it can serve as a basis for understanding which element may form candidates' image in other countries.

1.5 B2B service brand identity (Coleman, de Chernatony & Christodoulides, 2011)

Definition of construct

B2B (business-to-business) service brand identity is defined by the researchers as "the strategist's vision of how a B2B service brand should be perceived by its stakeholders" (Coleman, de Chernatony & Christodoulides, 2011, p. 1064). According to this view, brand identity emanates from the organization and integrates internal and external perspectives holistically. B2B service brand identity is a second-order multi-dimensional construct comprising five dimensions, namely *employee and client focus*, which measures how well the organization considers employees and integrates client needs; *corporate visual identity*, which evaluates the recognition of the organization through different visual elements; *brand personality*, which measures the favourability and the strength of the brand personality; *consistent communication*, which indicates the degree to which marketing communications are integrated as well as the consistency and the clarity of the message conveyed to the stakeholders; and finally *human resource initiatives*, which measures the relevance of employee training programs and the monitoring of the employees' performance.

Scale description

The B2B service brand identity scale contains five dimensions and 15 items. The *employee and client focus* dimension contains five items. The *corporate visual identity* and the *brand personality* dimensions each contain three items. The *consistent communication* and the *human resource initiatives* dimensions each contain two items. Each item is measured on a 7-point Likert scale where 1 = "strongly agree" to 7 = "strongly disagree".

TABLE 1.4 B2B service brand identity scale

Scale dimension	Scale item
Employee and client focus	• Our organization treats each employee as an essential part of the organization • Our employees will help clients in a responsive manner • Our organization makes an effort to discover our clients' needs • Our organization responds to our clients' needs • Our top management is committed to providing quality service
Corporate visual identity	• The font we use is an important part of our visual identity • Our logo is an important part of who we are • The corporate visual identity is helpful in making our organization recognizable
Brand personality	• The associations making up our brand personality are extremely positive • Our clients have no difficulty describing our brand personality • Our brand personality has favourable associations
Consistent communications	• The people managing the communications program for our organization have a good understanding of the strengths and weaknesses of all major marketing communications tools • Our organization's advertising, PR and sales promotion all present the same clear consistent message to our stakeholders
Human resource initiatives	• Our employee training programs are designed to develop skills required for acquiring and deepening client relationships • Our organization regularly monitors employees' performance

Scale development

The development of the B2B service brand identity scale is guided by the extant scaling literature (Anderson & Gerbing, 1988; Churchill, 1979; DeVellis, 1991; Gerbing & Anderson, 1988; Netemeyer, Bearden & Sharma, 2003). The scale is developed through an item-generation phase and one round of quantitative data collection.

The initial pool of 119 items is generated based on a literature review and then subjected to an expert panel. Pre-tests and a pilot survey are conducted, resulting in a selection of 50 items for the final survey, which is sent by postal mail. The completed sample is randomly split into a calibration sample, used to develop the scale, and a validation sample, used to verify the scale dimensionality and establish its psychometric properties.

The calibration sample is subjected to principal components analysis with promax rotation and allows the researchers to identify five dimensions and 20 items for the B2B service brand identity scale. This analysis explains 56.2% of the variance.

The confirmatory factor analysis using AMOS V16.0.1 supports the five dimensional model with 15 items, which demonstrates satisfactory levels of fit across all samples. Across the calibration, validation and full samples, GFI and CFI are 0.93, 0.92, 0.95 and 0.96, 0.96 and 0.97, respectively. The RMSEA is 0.05 for all samples.

Composite reliability and construct validity tests are finally performed.

Samples

In the item-generation phase, the sample of experts is composed of three brand academics (two in the United States and one in Germany) and three senior consultants working at global brand agencies in the UK. The pre-tests are conducted with MBA students working in the IT service sector. The sample used for the pilot survey is composed of 50 executives randomly selected from the sampling frame.

The sample used for the final survey consists of 2,200 senior marketing executives working in the UK's B2B IT service sector which, after postal mail, results in a completed sample of 421 individuals (19% response rate). This sample is then split into calibration ($n = 211$) and validation ($n = 210$) samples.

Reliability and validity

The reliability of the B2B service brand identity scale is tested using the validation sample. All composite reliabilities exceed the recommended level of 0.6, which confirms the internal consistency of the scale: *employee and client focus* (alpha = 0.89), *corporate visual identity* (alpha = 0.77), *brand personality* (alpha = 0.75), *consistent communication* (alpha = 0.73) and *human resource initiatives* (alpha = 0.75).

Face validity of B2B service brand identity items is examined in the item-generation phase, thanks to the experts.

Convergent validity is demonstrated through three tests. All average variance extracted values are greater than 0.5, the smallest item test statistic is greater than 1.96 ($t = 6.7$; $\alpha = 0.001$) and all standardized factor loadings are greater than 0.5 (ranging from 0.62 to 0.95, 0.50 to 0.98 and 0.55 to 0.97, respectively, for the calibration, validation and full samples).

Discriminant validity is demonstrated in three ways. First, the χ^2 for the unconstrained five-factor model is significantly lower than the χ^2 of each constrained model. Second, all estimated confidence intervals (+/− two standard errors) for each dimension correlations do not contain the value 1. Third, with the exception of the brand personality and consistent communications correlation, the variance extracted estimates are greater than the square of the correlations for each pair of dimensions. Although only two of the three tests support the discriminant validity of the scale, there are no theoretical reasons to combine brand personality and marketing communication-related items. Furthermore, forcing a four-factor model results in a deterioration of model fit. For these reasons, the scale containing the five dimensions is considered to possess discriminant validity.

Managerial applications

The B2B service brand identity scale provides managers with a practical tool to audit and track their service brand identity. By assessing the different dimensions of their service brand identity, managers can identify areas of strength and weakness and take corrective action where necessary. The parsimony of the scale facilitates such practical applications. This scale presents the advantage of containing varied and cross-functional dimensions. Thus, it can indicate to managers that they should coordinate actions among various departments within the organization in order to optimise B2B service brand identity.

1.6 Non-profit brand image (Michel & Rieunier, 2012)

Definition of construct

Giving the importance of fundraising in the non-profit sector and considering that favourable brand image results in higher numbers of donations (Bennett & Gabriel, 2003), the researchers develop a specific scale to measure non-profit brand image, taking into account the peculiarities of the non-profit world. In so doing, they differentiate from the non-profit brand image framework developed by Bennett and Gabriel (2003), which is predominantly based on concepts used in commercial rather than non-profit branding. Non-profit brand image is a multi-dimensional construct containing four dimensions, namely *usefulness, efficiency, affect* and *dynamism*.

Scale description

The non-profit brand image scale contains four dimensions and 14 items. *Usefulness* is measured with three items ("indispensable", "useful" and "civic-minded"), *efficiency* is assessed with five items ("efficient", "serious", "well-managed", "provides an excellent service to beneficiaries" and "the charity uses its assets wisely"), *affect* is evaluated with four items ("friendly", "generous", "warm" and "engaging") and *dynamism* is assessed with two items ("modern" and "innovative"). The strength of association with the non-profit brands is measured using a 5-point Likert scale where 1 = "strongly disagree" and 5 = "strongly agree".

TABLE 1.5 Non-profit brand image scale

Scale dimension	Scale item
Usefulness	• Indispensable • Useful • Civic-minded
Efficiency	• Efficient • Serious • Well-managed • Provides an excellent service to beneficiaries • Uses assets wisely
Affect	• Friendly • Generous • Warm • Engaging
Dynamism	• Modern • Innovative

Scale development

The scale development process consists of three data collections, that is, a preliminary qualitative study to generate the items and test their content validity (study 1) followed by two surveys to test the validity and reliability of the scale (study 2).

Study 1 consists of in-depth interviews conducted face to face with both donors and non-donors. Interviews cover the themes of individual donor behaviour, the image of charities to which the interviewees donate or do not donate their money and the image of a specific French non-profit charity. The data collected are subjected to a thematic content analysis, which results in the generation of 144 non-profit brand image items. A pool of fundraising professionals is then asked to evaluate this initial set of items in order to select the most relevant one for measuring non-profit brand image. The 37 retained items are the ones which are selected as relevant by all judges.

Study 2 consists of two surveys, one conducted face to face (FtoF) and one distributed via Internet (I) in order to determine whether the scale produces comparable and reliable results via these two means of administration. Respondents are provided with five non-profit organizations and are asked to assess the one they know the most; they are excluded from the sample if they do not know any of the five non-profit organizations. In addition to the 37 non-profit brand image items, the questionnaire includes a measure of donation intentions developed by the researchers and a measure of the typicality of the non-profit organization in the field of humanitarian aid adapted from the literature (Rosch & Mervis, 1975).

The data collected are subjected to a CFA. A four-factor model is identified, but the overall model fit emerges as relatively low. Thus, items with significant factor cross-loadings and which do not load higher on their intended factor are eliminated from the scale. Another CFA is performed with the 14 remaining items. The

14-item, four-factor model exhibits better fit indexes for both the face-to-face and internet samples. The CFI is 0.94 for both samples and the RMSEA is 0.07 for both samples. The chi-square value for the face-to face model is 276 with 70 degrees of freedom ($p < 0.01$) and 1,057.7 with 70 degrees of freedom ($p < 0.01$) for the Internet model.

The non-profit brand image scale reliability and validity are checked next. Multiple regressions with SPSS are then performed in order to analyse the influence of non-profit brand image on intention to give money and time. Simple regressions related to the typicality of a non-profit organization are finally performed and indicate that the typicality of a non-profit organization significantly explains the intention to give money ($\beta = 0.54$, $p < 0.01$, $R^2 = 0.29$) and time ($\beta = 0.48$, $p < 0.01$, $R^2 = 0.23$).

Samples

The sample used in study 1 to generate the items consists of an *ad hoc* sample of 15 donors and 15 non-donors. The sample of 15 professionals used to select the items is composed of fundraisers, charity communication managers, market survey managers and employees from communication agencies specializing in non-profit.

Two samples are used in study 2: one face-to-face sample and one Internet sample. The response rate obtained for the face-to-face study is 60% (484 respondents) compared to 8.6% for the Internet study (1,727 answered questionnaires out of 20,000 contacts; of the answered ones, 1,192 questionnaires are correctly completed). The face-to-face sample is representative of the French population for age, gender and employment.

Reliability and validity

The reliability and validity of the non-profit brand image scale are established in study 2. With respect to construct reliability, all four non-profit brand image dimensions demonstrate sufficient reliability. Construct reliability estimates are based on the standardized loadings for the four-factor correlated model. Coefficient alpha reliability estimates obtained for each dimension are respectively for *usefulness* 0.79 (FtoF) and 0.80 (I), *efficiency* 0.83 (FtoF) and 0.87 (I), *affect* 0.81 (FtoF) and 0.83 (I) and *dynamism* 0.76 (FtoF) and 0.81 (I). Furthermore, all *t*-values are significant ($p < 0.01$) and all standardized estimates exceed 0.50.

The scale's discriminant validity is established by examining the variance-extracted statistics. These are equal to 57% (FtoF) and 59% (I) for *usefulness*, 63% (FtoF) and 55% (I) for *efficiency*, 61% (FtoF) and 54% (I) for *affect* and 62% (FtoF) and 69% (I) for *dynamism*. Furthermore, discriminant validity is assessed by comparing the variance extracted within constructs with the square of the bivariate correlation between factors. All variance-extracted estimates exceed the square of the between-factor correlations, except for the face-to-face sample, where square bivariate correlation between affect and efficiency (0.67) is higher than the variance explained by efficiency (0.63) and affect (0.60).

Furthermore, the results obtained with the multiple regression analysis indicate that the four dimensions of non-profit brand image influence the giving behaviour. The four dimensions of non-profit brand image globally explain 31% of intentions to give money: *efficiency* ($\beta = 0.30$, $p < 0.01$), *usefulness* ($\beta = 0.13$, $p < 0.01$), *affect* ($\beta = 0.13$, $p < 0.01$) and *dynamism* ($\beta = 0.09$, $p < 0.01$). Similarly, the four dimensions of non-profit brand image globally explain 24% of intentions to give time: *affect* ($\beta = 0.21$, $p < 0.01$), *efficiency* ($\beta = 0.18$, $p < 0.01$), *usefulness* ($\beta = 0.12$, $p < 0.01$), and *dynamism* ($\beta = 0.08$, $p < 0.01$).

Managerial applications

Considering the importance of fundraising in the non-profit sector, this scale provides non-profit organizations with a tool enabling them to trace their brand image over time and compare it with other organizations. This scale allows managers to identify the performance of the brand on each dimension and can indicate which dimension to improve by specific communication actions in order to increase the giving behaviour. As the scale can be used online, it provides an affordable tool for non-profit organizations to trace their brand image and to monitor their actions.

1.7 Academic focus

- In a dissertation, one may investigate the impact of one unsuccessful marketing activity on brand image. Examples of activities may include a brand extension that does not meet consumers' needs or a television advertising campaign that is not appealing and does not communicate the benefits of a product in a clear way. Brand users versus non-users (Romaniuk, Bogoloma & Riley, 2012) could be compared to better understand the effects on brand image.
- A dissertation may examine the relationship between corporate brand associations (Mann & Ghuman, 2014; see Chapter 2, pp. 34–37) and corporate brand image (Da Silva & Syed Alwi, 2008). Such a dissertation could try to understand how brand associations contribute to brand image in the context of a corporate brand. Online and/or offline organizations could be taken into account.
- A dissertation may investigate the antecedents and outcomes of the brand image of political candidates (Guzmán & Sierra, 2009). It could be interesting, for example, to examine the extent to which political party membership influences the brand image of political candidates and to which extent the brand image of a political candidate influences consumers' intentions to vote and electoral choices.
- A dissertation may investigate the relationship between B2B service brand identity (Coleman, de Chernatony & Christodoulides, 2011) and

22 Brand identity and brand image

> the brand orientation of a given B2B organization (Baumgarth, 2010; see Chapter 13, pp. 289–291). On a general level, one may hypothesize a positive relationship between the two constructs. However, the dissertation may examine which dimensions of B2B service brand identity are more central to the organization's brand orientation.
>
> - Focusing on the non-profit sector, a dissertation could compare the predictive power of a general non-profit brand image scale (Michel & Rieunier, 2012) versus a more specific brand image scale, such as that of non-profit brand personality (Venable, Rose, Bush & Gilbert, 2005; see Chapter 3, pp. 56–59). Outcomes such as donor intentions and donor behaviours could be studied.

1.8 Managerial focus

> - **Are you sure that your brand image is not confusing because it stands for something different in every market?**
>   Consumers tend to prefer global brands because they associate the global image with a perception of brand superiority (Shocker et al., 1994). Therefore, it is important that brand managers evaluate if the brand image is coherent across countries. To illustrate, Mercedes is perceived everywhere as a luxury brand and associated with excellent engineering, performance and styling. In the United States, Nissan is more associated with a performance car challenging rugged landscapes, whereas in Japan, it is more perceived as a compact car easily manoeuvrable in town. Renault corresponds to a low-cost brand in Russia, whereas this positioning is held by Dacia, another brand from Renault Company, in many other countries. Even though there may be a country-specific strategy in place, if a brand stands for something different in every market, it can confuse the consumer perception regarding these global brands. The brand image scale developed by Hsieh (2002) for the car industry could be adapted to other markets and used to study the extent to which brands are perceived differently across international markets. The knowledge resulting from this assessment may be useful in developing a global branding strategy and enhancing some specific brand image dimensions which should be common across countries.
> - **Have you checked that your brand image is not eroding internationally?**
>   Even though a brand can be strong and global, the performance of the brand can decrease in some countries due to local competition or due to a change of positioning over time. To avoid losing this brand superiority, it is necessary to check that this positive image is associated with real benefits. Scales such as the brand image scale developed by

Hsieh (2002) for the car industry offer an interesting perspective, measuring the image with a benefit-based approach. Hsieh's scale allows managers to have a clear understanding of what the brand provides to consumers, symbolically, economically, sensorily or as a utility, in order to make sure that the brand is not eroding and represents much more than just a name or a symbol on packaging.

- **Are you sure that you are not putting your corporate brand image at risk when developing your sales online?**
The development of the Internet has completely changed marketing practices and has allowed consumers to have more interactivity and experiences with brands. Therefore, it is really important for managers to track the online corporate brand image to make sure that it remains consistent across channels. Indeed, the corporate brand image may have the potential to impact consumer preferences for the company and for the products of the company (Mann & Ghuman, 2014). The online corporate brand image scale provides a useful tool to track different dimensions of the corporate brand image which may impact the satisfaction and the loyalty of their customers. The corporate brand image scale could also, to some extent, be used to study the image of online brands.
- **Is your employees' brand perception coherent with your customers' brand image?**
The best ambassadors of your brands are your employees, but have you checked if your employees have a clear understanding of your brand promise? Are they aware of the last campaign which has been aired? Do they know how the brand is perceived by their customers? The B2B service brand identity scale (Coleman, de Chernatony & Christodoulides, 2011) allows companies to evaluate the image of the brand among stakeholders and identify dimensions which could be enhanced in order to improve the coherence between the internal and external perception of the brand.
- **How can you improve the image of your charity in order to influence donor behaviour?**
As with any other brand, it is really important that non-profit organizations evaluate the positioning of their brand compared to other non-profit organizations. The non-profit image scale developed by Michel and Rieunier (2012) enables non-profit organizations to track the evolution of their brand image over time and to identify the influence of communication or specific mailing on the different dimensions of the brand. According to Michel and Rieunier (2012), by reinforcing the usefulness and efficiency dimensions of the brand, it is possible to influence donation behaviour. A transparent communication explaining the accounts of the organization or providing information about donation equivalencies enhances charitable giving.

References

Aaker, D. A. (1991). *Managing brand equity. Capitalizing on the value of a brand name*. New York, NY: Free Press.

Aaker, J. L. (1997). Dimensions of brand personality. *Journal of Marketing Research*, 34 (3), 347–356.

Anderson, J. C., & Gerbing, D. W. (1988). Structural equation modeling in practice: a review and recommended two step approach. *Psychological Bulletin*, 103, 411–423.

Balmer, J.M.T., & Gray, E. R. (2003). Corporate brands: what are they? What of them? *European Journal of Marketing*, 37, 972–997.

Baumgarth, C. (2010). "Living the brand": brand orientation in the business-to-business sector. *European Journal of Marketing*, 44 (5), 653–671.

Bennett, R., & Gabriel, H. (2003). Image and reputational characteristics of UK charitable organizations: an empirical study. *Corporate Reputation Review*, 6 (3), 276–289.

Bruner, G. C., II, Hensel, P. J., & James, K. E. (2005). *Marketing scales handbook: A compilation of multi-item measures*. Chicago, IL: American Marketing Association.

Caprara, G. V., Barbaranelli, C., & Zimbardo, P. G. (2002). When parsimony subdues distinctiveness: simplified public perceptions of politicians' personality. *Political Psychology*, 23 (1), 77–95.

Churchill, G. A., Jr. (1979). A paradigm for developing better measures of marketing constructs. *Journal of Marketing Research*, 16 (February), 64–73.

Coleman, D., de Chernatony, L., & Christodoulides, G. (2011). B2B service brand identity: scale development and validation. *Industrial Marketing Management*, 40, 1063–1071.

Da Silva, R. V., & Syed Alwi, S. F. (2008). Online corporate brand image, satisfaction and loyalty. *Brand Management*, 16 (3), 119–144.

Davies, G., Chun, R., da Silva, R., & Roper, S. (2004). Corporate character scale to assess employee and customer views of organisation reputation. *Corporate Reputation Review*, 7, 125–146.

DeVellis, R. F. (1991). *Scale development: theory and applications*. Thousand Oaks, CA: Sage.

Farquhar, P. H., & Herr, P. M. (1993). The dual structure of brand associations. In D. A. Aaker & A. L. Biel (eds.), *Brand equity & advertising's role in building strong brands*. Hillsdale, NJ: Lawrence Erlbaum Associates, 263–279.

Funk, C. L. (1999). Bringing the candidate into models of candidate evaluation. *Journal of Politics*, 61 (3), 700–722.

Gerbing, D. W., & Anderson, J. C. (1988). An updated paradigm for scale development incorporating unidimensionality and its assessment. *Journal of Marketing Research*, 25, 186–192.

Guzmán, F., & Sierra, V. (2009). A political candidate's brand image scale: are political candidates brands? *Journal of Brand Management*, 17 (3), 207–217.

Hsieh, M. H. (2002). Identifying brand image dimensionality and measuring the degree of brand globalization: a cross national study. *Journal of International Marketing*, 10 (2), 46–67.

Keller, K. L. (1993). Conceptualizing, measuring, and managing customer-based brand equity. *Journal of Marketing Research*, 29, 1–22.

Kotler, P., Armstrong, G., Harris, L., & Piercy, N. F. (2013). *Principles of marketing European edition* (6th ed.). London: Pearson.

Mann, B. J. S., & Ghuman, M. K. (2014). Scale development and validation for measuring corporate brand associations. *Journal of Brand Management*, 21 (1), 43–62.

Michel, G., & Rieunier, S. (2012). Nonprofit brand image and typicality influences on charitable giving. *Journal of Business Research*, 65, 701–707.

Nakanishi, M., Cooper, L. G., & Kassarijian, H. H. (1974). Voting for a political candidate under conditions of minimal information. *Journal of Consumer Research*, 1 (2), 36–43.

Netemeyer, R. G., Bearden, W. O., & Sharma, S. (2003). *Scaling procedures: issues and applications*. Thousand Oaks, CA: Sage.

Oliver, R. L. (1997). *Satisfaction: a behavioural perspective on the consumer*. Boston, MA: McGraw-Hill.

Park, C. W., Jaworski, B., & MacInnis, D. J. (1986). Strategic brand concept-image management. *Journal of Marketing*, 50 (October), 135–145.

Patterson, M. (1999). Re-appraising the concept of brand image. *Journal of Brand Management*, 6, 409–426.

Romaniuk, J., Bogoloma, S., & Riley, F. (2012). Brand image and brand usage. *Journal of Advertising Research*, 52 (2), 243–251.

Rosch, E., & Mervis, C. (1975). Family resemblances: studies in the internal structures of categories. *Cognitive Psychology*, 7 (4), 573–605.

Shabad, G., & Andersen, K. (1979). Candidate evaluations by men and women. *Public Opinion Quarterly*, 43 (1), 18–35.

Shocker, A. D., Srivastava, R. K., & Rueckert, R. W. (1994). Challenges and opportunities facing brand management: an introduction to the special issue. *Journal of Marketing Research*, 31 (May), 149–158.

Venable, B. T., Rose, G. M., Bush, V. D., & Gilbert, F. W. (2005). The role of brand personality in charitable giving: An assessment and validation. *Journal of the Academy of Marketing Science*, 33, 295–312.

Zeithmal, V. A., Berry, L. L., & Parasuraman, A. (1996). The behavioural consequences of service quality. *Journal of Marketing*, 60, 31–46.

2
BRAND ASSOCIATIONS

2.1 Overview

Brand associations are defined as anything in memory linked to a brand (Aaker, 1991), as informational nodes linked to the brand node in memory that contains the meaning of the brand for consumers (Keller, 1998). The way consumers perceive brands through communication and experience forges brand associations in their minds (Keller, 1998; Oliver, 1997; Reicheld, 1996). Brand associations help consumers to process information and differentiate the brand from its competitors, and they influence consumer purchase behaviour. Brand associations can be seen as signals of quality or have unique significance for the consumer, promoting a favourable attitude and behaviour toward the brand, leading to a strong relationship and customer-based brand equity (Aaker, 1991; Keller, 1993). In this sense, brand associations represent the basis for brand loyalty and are a key determinant of long-term relationships (Fournier, 1998). The major aim of branding is therefore to create strong, unique and favourable brand associations in the minds of consumers (Keller, 1993, 1998).

Keller's (1998) and Aaker's (1991) conceptualizations of brand associations have been the basis of subsequent contributions trying to operationalize this construct. This chapter collects three scales on brand associations. Low and Lamb (2000) develop a general brand associations scale which can be applied to examine any brand. The scale allows researchers to measure functional and symbolic perceptions (brand image) as well as overall brand evaluations (brand attitude and perceived quality), which are fundamental elements in brand success.

The other two brand associations scales included in the chapter refer to specific contexts of application. Mann and Ghuman (2014) extend the brand associations framework to corporate brands and elaborate a scale to assess corporate brand associations defined as the set of associations that a person hold in minds toward a company. Their corporate brand associations scale measures emotional and functional facets which may impact consumer preferences for the company and its products.

Ross, James and Vargas (2006) extend the concept of brand associations even further. They apply the concept of brand associations to the sport sector, and they propose to measure brand associations that consumers hold in mind in the specific case of a sport team, which can be considered a brand for different stakeholders in the sport industry. Taking its roots from the team association model (TAM) developed by Gladden and Funk (2002), their team brand associations scale contains a wide range of dimensions derived from consumers' perceptions toward their favourite sport team, which concern not only the brand but also the organization and the performance of the club.

2.2 Brand associations (Low & Lamb, 2000)

Definition of construct

The researchers refer to Aaker's (1991) and Keller's (1998) frameworks to define brand associations. Based on Aaker (1991), brand associations are considered anything linked in memory to a brand. Similarly, Keller (1998) defines brand associations as informational nodes linked in memory to a brand that contain the meaning of the brand for consumers. Brand associations are conceptualized by the researchers as a multi-dimensional construct consisting of three dimensions: *brand image*, which consists of functional and symbolic perceptions of a brand; *brand attitude*, which corresponds to an overall evaluation of the brand; and *perceived quality*, which is considered the consumer's judgments about the overall excellence or superiority of the brand.

Scale description

The brand associations scale consists of the dimensions of brand image, perceived quality and brand attitude. The *brand image* dimension is product category specific and includes a variable number of customized items for the brand one wants to investigate; these items are introduced by the lead-in statement "I think that the (product Y) in this advertisement is/has . . .". The *perceived quality* dimension is measured with three items, based on the lead-in statement "I think that the advertised (product Y) is . . .". The *brand attitude* dimension is measured using three items, based on the lead-in statement "I think that (brand X) brand (product category Y) is . . .". All items are measured using a semantic differential scale.

TABLE 2.1 Brand associations scale

Scale dimension	Scale item
Brand image	I think that the (product Y) in this advertisement is/has: • List of customized items selected for the product category[1]
Perceived quality	I think that the advertised (product Y) is: • Inferior/Superior • Low quality/High quality • Excellent/Poor*
Brand attitude	I think that (brand X) brand (product category Y) is: • Bad/Good • Unpleasant/Pleasant • Valuable/Worthless*

Note: *indicates the item is reverse coded.

[1]Brand image items used: unfriendly/friendly, outdated/modern, not useful/useful, popular/unpopular*, harsh/gentle and natural/artificial* (shampoo brand), an attractive package/an unattractive package*, exciting/boring*, not fun/fun (soft drink brand), an attractive package/an unattractive package*, bad colour/good colour, an unattractive appearance/an attractive appearance, not creamy/creamy (mustard brand), a good reputation/a bad reputation*, an attractive appearance/an unattractive appearance, good style/bad style*, low quality/high quality, unreliable/reliable, uncomfortable/comfortable (wristwatch brand), good taste/bad taste*, unattractive packaging/attractive packaging, unappetizing/appetizing (cereal brand), low quality/high quality, unreliable/reliable, durable/not durable* (washing machine brand), good ingredients/bad ingredients*, soft/hard*, nutritious/not nutritious*, dry/moist, fresh/stale* (raisin bread brand), a good reputation/a bad reputation*, poor quality materials/good quality materials, good performance/poor performance*, durable/not durable* (golf clubs brand), low quality/high quality, outdated/modern, challenging/not challenging*, fun/not fun* (computer game brand).

Scale development

The brand associations scale is developed through three studies, in accordance with the suggestions of Churchill (1979) and Zaichkowsky (1985).

The first study tests a protocol for generating category-specific items for brand image, as this construct requires items that are specifically related to a product category. In a pre-test, respondents are asked to write down any ideas, feelings, or attitudes that they associate with a specific product (handheld calculator). Responses to these open-ended questions are tabulated, and the most frequently mentioned terms are used to generate semantic differential items. This pre-test results in a set of 17 items. In the main study, respondents are shown an advertisement describing basic features and benefits of a fictitious brand of handheld calculator. Then they are asked to rate such a brand using the 17 items and a scale on purchase intention. Coefficient alpha and exploratory factor analysis allow the researchers to retain five items on brand image. A predictive validity test is conducted.

Study 2 checks whether the protocol tested in study 1 can be used to measure brand image in another product category and investigates the dimensionality of the brand associations construct. A pre-test is used to identify a new product category (shampoo) based on usage rate and frequency of purchase scores. Following the protocol tested in study 1, the pre-test is also used to generate a set of brand image items for a shampoo brand. Scale items for perceived quality (Keller & Aaker, 1992) and brand attitude (Zinkhan, Locander & Leigh, 1986) are derived from the marketing literature. In the main study, respondents are asked to complete the questionnaire consisting of six brand image items, three brand attitude items and three perceived quality items after watching an advertisement for a fictitious shampoo. After checking the reliability of the three constructs, the dimensionality of the scale is assessed by comparing three-dimensional and one-dimensional confirmatory factor analysis measurement models using LISREL VII. The results indicate that the three-dimensional model fit the data better (GFI = 0.88 instead of 0.81, AGFI = 0.82 instead of 0.72, RMR = 0.06 instead of 0.07), and the chi-squared difference test for the two models is significant (delta chi-square = 101.42, df = 3, p < 0.001).

Study 3 further assesses the dimensionality of the scale under different conditions of brands' familiarity using real brands. Two pre-tests are used to select eight brands with different degrees of familiarity from different product categories. In the main study, respondents are randomly exposed to an advertisement for each of the eight brands and are asked to indicate their level of familiarity with each brand using a 7-point semantic differential scale anchored with "familiar" and "unfamiliar". Then, respondents are asked to evaluate each brand on the three constructs of the brand associations scale. Two confirmatory factor analysis models (three-dimensional and one-dimensional) are estimated for each of the eight brands using LISREL VII. For all the brands, the three-dimensional model provides better results than the one-dimensional model (AGFIs for the three-dimensional models range from 0.75 to 0.94 for the different brands) based on chi-squared difference tests. Discriminant validity tests are conducted.

Samples

The samples used for the three studies are composed of undergraduate students. Study 1 uses a sample of 35 students in the pre-test and a sample of 533 students in the main study. Studies 2 and 3 are respectively based on samples of 105 and 100 students.

Reliability and validity

The reliability of the five-item *brand image* dimension is checked in study 1 using coefficient alpha (equal to 0.71), whereas the reliability of the six-item *brand image* dimension is checked in study 2 (alpha equal to 0.78). In study 2, the reliability of the other two constructs is also checked, with coefficient alphas equal to 0.77 for the *perceived quality* dimension and 0.87 for the *brand attitude* dimension.

With regard to validity, predictive and discriminant validities tests are conducted. The predictive validity of the five-item *brand image* dimension is checked in study 1 by computing the correlation with purchase intention (r = 0.48, p < 0.01). The discriminant validity of the brand associations scale is checked in study 3. The study first checks the phi coefficient for each pair of constructs in a two-latent-constructs model (*brand image* and *brand attitude*, *brand image* and *perceived quality* or *brand attitude* and *perceived quality*); all phi coefficients are significantly less than 1.00. The researchers then carry out a comparison between the phi coefficient squared for each of the 24 pairs of constructs with the variance extracted for each latent construct in the same two-latent-constructs model. None of the brands passes this test of discriminant validity for all the comparisons. The number of paired discriminant validity tests passed by each brand is expressed as percentage and ranges from 33.3% to 88.9%. This percentage is correlated with brand familiarity ($r = 0.77$, $p = 0.025$), thus indicating that more familiar brands are more likely to satisfy discriminant validity tests for the three constructs.

Managerial applications

The brand associations scale offers managers a tool easy to include in regular tracking studies to evaluate and benchmark consumers' brand perception over time. Managers can develop customized scale items to measure *brand image* by selecting consumers' unique associations for a particular product category according to the protocol suggested by the researchers and combine this measure with the general *perceived quality* and *brand attitude* scales.

2.3 Team brand associations in professional sport (Ross, James & Vargas, 2006)

Definition of construct

Brand associations are defined as anything linked in memory to a brand (Aaker, 1991). The team brand association scale (TBAS) measures brand associations that consumers hold for a sport team. TBAS takes its root from the team association model (TAM) developed by Gladden and Funk (2002). Compared to TAM, the TBAS presents the advantage of being developed from sport consumers' perceptions regarding their favourite sport team, which correspond to the conceptual definition of brand associations. The TBAS contains 11 dimensions which explore various associations people hold in mind for a sport team brand such as *brand mark* (associations identifying the team brand), *rivalry* (thoughts regarding the competition among teams), *concessions* (associations linked with eating and consuming beverage at the stadium), *social interaction* (the idea of associating with others), *team history* (thoughts regarding the history of success and the history of the team's personnel), *commitment* (evaluation of the individual affiliation to a sport team), *organizational attributes* (thoughts regarding fans' relationship management), *non-player personnel* (thoughts regarding the team management), *stadium community* (perception of the team's home stadium), *team success* (associations linked with the success of the players and perceived quality of the team itself) and *team play* (specific characteristics that may be ascribed to the team's play).

Scale description

The TBAS is composed of sport team brand associations collected from consumers and regrouped under 11 identified factors: *brand mark* (three items), *rivalry* (three items), *concessions* (four items), *social interaction* (two items), *team history* (five items), *commitment* (two items), *organizational attributes* (three items), *non-player personnel* (five items), *stadium community* (seven items), *team success* (five items) and *team play* (two items). All 41 items are measured on 7-point Likert-type scales with response categories anchored by never (1) and always (7).

TABLE 2.2 Team brand associations scale

Scale dimension	Scale item
Brand mark	• The symbol of the team • The team's logo • The team colour
Rivalry	• Beating the team's main rival • The team's biggest opponent • The team's conference
Concessions	• Eating a specific food at the stadium/arena • Eating at the stadium/arena • Concessions at the stadium/arena • Consuming beverages at the stadium/arena
Social interaction	• Other fans of the team • Going to games with my friends
Team history	• A specific era in the team's history • Game winning plays in the team's history • Championships the team has won • The most recent championship the team won • The success of the team in the past
Commitment	• Being a fan of the team since childhood • Regularly following the team
Organizational attributes	• An organization committed to its fans • A team loyal to its fans • The team giving back to the community
Non-player personnel	• The head coach • A current coach on the team • Excellent coaches • The team's management • Owners of the team
Stadium community	• The area surrounding the stadium/arena • The community surrounding the stadium/arena • The location of the stadium/arena • The city that the team is from • What stadium/arena the team plays its home games in • The team's home stadium/arena • Unique characteristics of the team's stadium/arena
Team success	• A winning team • The performance of the team • Quality players • The quality of the team • A great team
Team play	• How the team scores its points • Specific team characteristics (e.g., lucky, exciting)

Scale development

The TBAS scale is developed in a four-phase research design according to Churchill's suggested procedure (1979).

Phase 1 consists of a thought-listing procedure in order to generate specific sport team items corresponding to associations held in mind by individuals relative to their favourite professional sports team. Respondents are asked to list their favourite professional sport team and then write down their first thoughts regarding this team. Two hundred and eighteen individual thoughts regarding their favourite professional sport teams are provided by respondents and are content analysed by the researchers with the help of two coders. The analysis results in the identification of 15 broad categories (coefficient of agreement = 81.7%) and in the generation of 70 refined items.

Phase 2 consists of a quantitative phase. Respondents are asked to rate the extent to which they think of each of the 70 associations when they have their favourite professional sport team in mind. They are also asked for how long they have been a fan of their favourite team in order to assess the viability of the sample as sport consumers. An exploratory factor analysis using maximum likelihood extraction with oblique direct quartimin rotation is performed with the comprehensive exploratory factor analysis program in order to identify brand association dimensions. Different numbers of factors to retain are suggested in the output: the Kaiser criterion suggests retaining 13 factors, whereas the scree test suggests only 3; the examination of the RMSEA indicates 4 or more factors and the parallel analysis suggests retaining 7, although the interpretability of factor loadings suggests the retention of 10 factors. Therefore, models with 3, 7, 10 and 13 factors are examined in order to determine which one provides the best fit. The item loadings for each model are assessed to ensure that the items load significantly on the respective factors. The 10-factor solution is accepted, and 50 items are retained. The 10-factor solution accounts for 64.7% of the total variance and has an RMSEA of 0.061.

Phase 3 corresponds to the review of the 50 items by expert judges for face and content validities. This phase results in the retention of 41 items, the renaming of one factor and the division of one factor into two distinct factors, bringing to 11 the total number of factors.

Phase 4 consists of a second data collection. Respondents are instructed to list their favourite professional team and to complete the questionnaire containing the scale with 41 items, a question to indicate the number of years the respondent has been a fan, and the 24 items from Gladden and Funk's (2002) TAM. A confirmatory factor analysis using LISREL 8.54 is performed in order to estimate the TBA model and assess the reliability and the validity of the scale. The results of the confirmatory factor analysis indicate a reasonable fit for the 11-factor model (χ^2 = 2318.66; RMSEA = 0.074; ECVI = 6.19; TLI = 0.93; CFI = 0.95). Tests of convergent, discriminant and construct validities (using the TAM scale) are conducted.

Samples

The sample in phase 1 is composed of 40 undergraduate students at a large Midwestern university who are significant consumers or users of sport. Thirty-seven forms are completed (92.5% effective response rate). The sample of phase 2 is a convenience sample of 395 students from a large Midwestern university; 367 completed and usable questionnaires are collected from them. The sample in phase 3 consists of three experts who are faculty members with PhDs from three different universities and with expertise in sport brand management. The sample in phase 4 is composed of 467 students from the same university as phase 2 (resulting in 447 completed and usable questionnaires).

Reliability and validity

The internal scale reliability is verified in phase 4 and emerges as acceptable for eight dimensions. The Cronbach's alphas range from 0.76 to 0.90 for eight dimensions but are equal to 0.56 for *social interaction* and *team play* and equal to 0.62 for *concessions*. The AVE values exceed the recommended 0.50 cut-off for the eight dimensions, but are below for *social interaction* (0.40), *commitment* (0.46) and *team play* (0.40).

Validity is checked with respect to content validity (phases 1 and 3), convergent validity, discriminant validity and criterion validity (phase 4). The content and face validities are assured in phase 1 by collecting sport team associations from consumers and by asking experts to review the items in phase 3.

Evidence of convergent validity is provided based on t-values (ranging from 11.03 to 24.30), the values of the factor loadings and the residual values (only 8.1% of residuals are greater than 0.15).

The discriminant validity is examined with two tests. The first test examines the correlations among latent constructs and their standard errors. Although the correlations between some of the constructs are high (ranging from 0.022 up to 0.889), no relationship fails this first test. The second, more rigorous test evaluates the AVE for each construct, which should be greater than the square correlation between that construct and any other. The results indicate a lack of discrimination for two factors (*team play* and *commitment*).

The criterion validity is examined using concurrent validity. Seven factors identified in the current study are correlated with eight factors from Gladden and Funk's (2002) TAM. Evidence of concurrent validity is strong, each of the seven factors being significantly correlated with at least five of the factors of the TAM scale (correlation coefficients ranging from 0.108 to 0.552 at $p < 0.05$ significance level).

Managerial applications

Given the increasing importance of the sport industry and the management of professional sport teams, it becomes necessary for sport marketers to understand what associations spectators and fans hold in mind in order to attract or retain consumers. TBAS is a useful tool to measure the brand associations and identify which dimensions should be enhanced to reinforce the positive brand associations that already exist. Therefore, the TBAS helps sport marketers better understand how to adapt marketing activities by promoting specific attributes in order to reinforce brand team image and improve brand equity.

2.4 Corporate brand associations (Mann & Ghuman, 2014)

Definition of construct

Consistent with literature (e.g., Spears, Brown & Dacin, 2006), corporate brand associations are defined as the set of mental linkages about a company or an organization that a person holds. Corporate brand associations correspond to the perception that stakeholders have in mind through communication and experience over time. Corporate brand associations is a multi-dimensional construct representing both functional and emotional facets of corporate brand associations from a customer-based perspective. The construct captures seven dimensions: *corporate ability and growth* (the company's perceived performance), *symbolic benefits* (the way the company would enhance the consumers' personality), *perceived external prestige* (the prestigious image of the company), *corporate ethics* (the ethical behaviour of the company), *corporate social responsibility* (perception of the social activities of the company), *visual identity* (the physical appearance of the company) and *corporate communications* (perception of the company's communication actions).

Scale description

The corporate brand associations scale consists of seven dimensions with 28 items. The *corporate ability and growth* dimension is measured with five items. The *symbolic benefits* and the *corporate ethics* are both evaluated with six items. *Corporate social responsibility* and *corporate communications* are measured with two items each. The *perceived external prestige* dimension is captured with four items. The *visual identity* is evaluated with three items, of which one is reverse coded. All items are measured on 5-point Likert scales ranging from "strongly agree" to "strongly disagree".

TABLE 2.3 Corporate brand associations scale

Scale dimension	Scale item
Corporate ability and growth	• This company has potential for future growth • This company is always improving • This company has a clear vision about its future • This is a successful company • This company recognises and takes advantage of market opportunities

(Continued)

TABLE 2.3 (Continued)

Scale dimension	Scale item
Symbolic benefits	• Products of this company express youthful spirit • If I purchase a product of this company, I would feel that I made a smart choice • If I purchase a product of this company, I would feel that I stand out in a crowd • Products of this company help to get admiration in society • If I purchase a product of this company, I would be able to express my personality • This company helps to display status symbol
Perceived external prestige	• This company is recognised world wide • This company is well established in (specific country) • This company is looked upon as a prestigious company in society overall • This company successfully retains a prestigious place in various rankings
Corporate ethics	• This is a good company to work for • This company has a fair attitude toward its competitors • This company does not mislead people • This company is very honest • This company does its business in an ethical way • If a consumer encounters a problem, this company shows sincere interest in solving his/her problem
Corporate social responsibility	• This company is doing a lot for the welfare of society • This company supports good causes
Visual identity	• This company is an old-fashioned company* • I like the physical appearance of this company (logo, colour, buildings, branch offices, etc.) • This is a stylish company
Corporate communications	• This company always provides the required information to the public • This company communicates clearly about its products

Note: *indicates the item is negatively phrased and reverse coded.

Scale development

The corporate brand associations scale is developed through a four-step process following Churchill's (1979) suggested procedure.

Step 1 corresponds to item generation and selection. An initial pool of scale items is generated based on existing literature and consists of 70 items related to the various hypothesized dimensions of corporate brand associations. These items are evaluated for content and face validity by scholars in the marketing field. A selection of 56 items is retained based on their suggestions, reworded when required and then pretested in a pilot survey. Forty-nine items are retained to be used for the final survey.

36 Brand associations

Step 2 consists of a data collection. Respondents are asked to evaluate one company on the 49 items related to the different types of corporate brand associations and to state their degree of familiarity with such company using a 5-point scale ranging from 1 = "not at all familiar" to 5 = "very much familiar"; only respondents who are familiar with the assigned company are considered in the analysis. Data are collected for a service category (insurance services), a durable sector (automobile) and fast-moving consumer goods (FMCG) sector (soaps, shampoos, and toothpastes). Two companies per sector are selected through a screening survey based on top-of-mind awareness among respondents.

Data collected in step 2 are analysed in step 3, which consists of the scale purification through exploratory factor analysis (EFA) using principle axis factoring and varimax rotation and confirmatory factor analysis (CFA). A first EFA identifies an eight-factor solution explaining 62.52% of total variance; items with a factor loading below 0.50 are dropped. A second EFA suggests a seven-factor solution accounting for 63.11% of total variance, with all the 37 remaining items having a clear loading on the seven factors. A CFA is performed by running factor models separately for the three sectors. The results show low loadings for nine items and an unacceptable overall model fit. After dropping these nine items, a modified CFA model with seven factors and 28 items is performed. The results indicate that the seven-factor, 28-item model provides better fit indices (insurance: $\chi^2(df = 329) = 2179.09$, RMSEA = 0.13, CFI = 0.92, IFI = 0.92, NFI = 0.90, NNFI = 0.90; automobiles: $\chi^2(df = 329) = 1515.56$, RMSEA = 0.11, CFI = 0.89, IFI = 0.89, NFI = 0.87, NNFI = 0.87; FMCG: $\chi^2(df = 329) = 1454.87$, RMSEA = 0.11, CFI = 0.86, IFI = 0.87, NFI = 0.85, NNFI = 0.86).

Reliability, validity and measurement invariance tests are conducted in step 4.

Samples

The sample used in step 1 is composed of a convenience sample of 50 respondents and two marketing scholars. Data are collected in step 2 from 665 respondents from three major cities of a northern state of India and results in 588 usable questionnaires. The sample is a representative sample of the population, in terms of age and gender, thanks to quota sampling. A convenience sample of 150 consumers is used to select the companies tested in the screening survey.

Reliability and validity

The reliability of the corporate brand associations scale is tested for the three sectors using coefficient alpha, composite reliability (CR), and average variance extracted (AVE). All the alphas are above the recommended level of 0.70 except for the *visual identity* dimension in the automobile sector (alpha equal to 0.68) and the *corporate social responsibility* and *visual identity* dimensions in the FMCG sector (alphas equal to 0.64 and 0.62 respectively). CR values are above the recommended level of 0.70 except for the *corporate social responsibility* and *visual identity* dimensions in the FMCG sector (CR values equal to 0.69 and 0.63, respectively). AVE scores are above the recommended level of 0.50 expect in the case of the *visual identity* dimension, which has one of 0.39. The validity of the corporate brand associations scale is checked with respect to content validity, convergent validity and discriminant validity.

The scale's content validity is assured in step 1 thanks to the item-generation and selection process based on the literature review and the pre-test.

Convergent validity is established through the use of exploratory and confirmatory factor analyses. With respect to EFA, an eigenvalue of 1 and factor loading of 0.50 are taken as criteria for significance of a factor and an item in a factor, respectively. With respect to CFA, convergent validity is established if item loadings are equal to or above the recommended cutoff of 0.60. Out of a total of 84 factor loadings obtained in the three sectors, only 5 factor loadings in the FMCG sector do not meet this criterion. Convergent validity is further assessed using the Bentler-Bonett coefficient (NFI), which is equal to or above 0.85 in the three sectors. The discriminant validity of the corporate brand associations scale is assessed for the three sectors by comparing the square root of the AVE with the correlation coefficient (phi coefficient) between two constructs of interest. All the square roots of AVE values are greater than the corresponding phi coefficients except for one case (*visual identity* in the FMCG sector). For this case, the discriminant validity is further checked by examining whether the correlation between two of the constructs (*visual identity* and *corporate ability and growth*) in the FMCG sector is different from unity, The result shows that the two constructs are significantly different at $p < 0.01$ (for 1 df, delta $\chi^2 = 8.02$).

The measurement invariance of the scale across the three sectors is demonstrated with respect to metric invariance only. Two analyses are conducted: unconstrained model ($\chi^2 = 5149$, $df = 987$, RMSEA = 0.12, CFI = 0.90, IFI = 0.90, RFI = 0.86, NFI = 0.88, and NNFI = 0.88), where the factor loadings of the models for the three sectors are not constrained to be equal, and constrained model ($\chi^2 = 5958$, $df = 1029$, RMSEA = 0.13, CFI = 0.88, IFI = 0.88, RFI = 0.84, NFI = 0.86, and NNFI = 0.878), where the factors loadings of the three sectors are constrained to be equal. Even though the increase in chi-square between the two models is significant (delta $\chi^2 = 809$, $df = 42$, $p < 0.001$), the remaining goodness-of-fit indices show considerably less marked decrease in fit (ranging between 0.01 and 0.02).

Managerial applications

The corporate brand associations scale provides a useful tool for planning, assessment and tracking purposes. Managers can use the scale to track the corporate brand associations over time and identify strengths and weaknesses toward competitors considering the various dimensions. The brand association scale can therefore help managers better position the organisation and identify the dimensions to be focused on, while communicating with consumers or implementing marketing actions.

2.5 Academic focus

- A recent contribution shows that the mismatch between intended brand associations and perceived brand associations does not always result in negative consumer responses (Koll & von Wallpach, 2014). These findings have been obtained in a European context. To check the extendibility of the findings, a dissertation may replicate the study in a different context: a non-European country, scoring higher on the uncertainty/avoidance cultural dimension (Hofstede, 2001), may be considered. Consumers with different degrees of tolerance to ambiguous information (Kirton, 1981) and/or preference for consistency (Cialdini, Trost & Newsom, 1995) could be considered as well.
- Building on Ross, James and Vargas (2006), a dissertation could focus on their scale about team brand associations in professional sports. This dissertation could investigate the extent to which team brand associations in professional sport formed through attending events differentiate from team brand associations in professional sport formed via media consumption (e.g., television). How do the dimensions of team brand associations in professional sport differentiate? Are they always present? How do their weights differentiate?
- In another dissertation focusing on team brand associations in professional sports (Ross, James & Vargas, 2006), one could examine the relationship between brand associations and brand equity in professional sports (Bauer, Sauer & Schmitt, 2005; see Chapter 11, pp. 242–244). More specifically, one could investigate how brand associations contribute to brand equity in professional sports and how this relationship varies across different types of sports fan behaviour (Hunt, Bristol & Bashaw, 1999) and sports involvement (Shank & Beasley, 1998; Wann, Schrader & Wilson, 1999).
- Mann and Ghuman (2014) developed their scale on corporate brand associations taking into account consumers' perspective only. However, as these researchers have pointed out, it would be useful to understand to what extent these associations change if other stakeholders are considered (e.g., employers). When considering these stakeholders, can the same dimensions of corporate brand associations be found?
- In a dissertation, one may focus on the antecedents, moderators and/or outcomes of corporate brand associations for consumers (Mann & Ghuman, 2014). Examples of possible antecedents are brand awareness (Holden, 1993) and brand salience (Romaniuk & Sharp, 2009). Examples of possible moderators include consumer involvement in product category (Zaichkowsky, 1985) and consumer knowledge of the product (Aurier & Ngobo, 1999; Guo & Meng, 2008). Example of possible outcomes include brand trust (Delgado-Ballester, Munuera-Allemán & Yagüe-Gillén, 2003; Li, Zhou, Kashyap & Yang, 2008; see Chapter 10) and brand loyalty (Odin, Odin & Valette-Florence, 2001; see Chapter 10).

2.6 Managerial focus

- **Why is important to have a clear and deep understanding of your brand associations?**
  Brand managers should have a clear and deep understanding of the associations that consumers have in mind for their brands, especially nowadays, as part of brand meanings can also be created online by other consumers. A lack of knowledge of brand associations can have serious consequences and lead to less effective communication campaigns because the campaigns do not convey the intended message and image. Furthermore, the existence of negative associations could alter the brand image and should lead to corrective actions. By tracking the evolution of brand associations using the scale developed by Low and Lamb (2000), managers can optimize their communication strategies by reinforcing some positive associations and minimizing negative ones or inducing some new associations which could help create a clear and distinctive positioning against competitors.
- **Why should a company measure corporate brand associations?**
  Corporate communication and marketing communication are in general handled by two different departments within companies. Nevertheless, corporate brand associations may have the potential to impact consumer preferences for the company and for the products of the company (Mann & Ghuman, 2014). Therefore, it can be interesting for managers to evaluate the impact of both the corporate and marketing initiatives on corporate brand associations. Companies are, for instance, investing in publicizing their corporate social responsibility programs in order to create favourable associations and positive reputation with both internal and external stakeholders. The corporate brand associations scale (Mann & Ghuman, 2014) can be useful in evaluating the impact of such actions on the corporate brand.
- **Have you identified which favourable associations are key in the case of brand extension or brand alliance strategy?**
  Brand extension or brand alliance can offer interesting opportunities. They can enhance brand equity by facilitating and reducing the cost of introduction of new products. Nevertheless, it is really important to identify the associations of the parent brand and the perception of the extended product. Indeed, if the brand extension's associations are not coherent with the core associations of the parent brand, this strategy can alter the brand equity of the parent brand (Michel, 1999). Furthermore, it is important to check that the associations of the parent brand are relevant in the new category of product to facilitate the acceptance of the brand extension. On the other hand, important opportunities for brand extensions and brand alliances are missed

because managers are not aware of favourable associations that are relevant in other product categories and could allow successful development there.
- **In the case of a brand name change strategy, do you know which associations should be transferred to the new brand?**
Many marketing managers are confronted with brand name substitutions in order to optimise their brand's portfolio. Nevertheless, replacing a brand with a stronger brand can fail if the two brands are not perceived as similar for consumers (Pauwels-Delassus & Mogos Descotes, 2012). To successfully manage a brand change, it is also really important to be able to transfer the associations from the abandoned brand to the new brand in order to transfer the brand equity of the replaced brand (Pauwels-Delassus & Fosse-Gomez, 2012). Therefore, before thinking of brand change, managers should identify the associations of each brand in order to check the coherence between the two brands and define a strategy allowing the transfer of brand associations.
- **In order to develop an efficient global campaign, have you got a clear understanding of your brand associations in each country?**
International companies tend to develop global marketing strategies in order to optimize their investment and find economies of scale by developing the same advertising campaign across countries. Nevertheless, developing a global campaign can be risky, as consumers may locally perceive the message and interpret the meaning of brands in different ways. International managers should have a clear identification of brand associations across countries and also a clear understanding of their meanings, which can vary due to cultural issues. The brand associations scale developed by Low and Lamb (2000) can be useful to measure the brand associations in each country, as the scale offers the possibility to use customized items for evaluating the brand image. By including some global associations which are similar across countries and specific local items, managers can have a better understanding of the consumers' brand perception and evaluate the capacity of the global campaign in enhancing some key associations.

References

Aaker, D. A. (1991). *Managing brand equity: capitalizing on the value of a brand name*. New York, NY: Free Press.

Aurier, P., & Ngobo, P.-V. (1999). Assessment of consumer knowledge and its consequences: a multi-component approach. *Advances in Consumer Research*, 26 (1), 569–575.

Bauer, H. H., Sauer, N. E., & Schmitt, P. (2005). Customer-based brand equity in the team sport industry: Operationalization and impact on the economic success of sport teams. *European Journal of Marketing*, 39 (5/6), 496–722.

Churchill, G. A., Jr. (1979). A paradigm for developing better measures of marketing constructs. *Journal of Marketing Research*, 16 (February), 64–73.

Cialdini, R. B., Trost, M. R., & Newsom, J. T. (1995). Preference for consistency: the development of a valid measure and the discovery of surprising behavioral implications. *Journal of Personality & Social Psychology*, 69, 318–328.

Delgado-Ballester, E., Munuera Alemán, J. L., & Yagüe-Guillén, M. J. (2003). Development and validation of a brand trust scale. *International Journal of Market Research*, 45 (1), 35–53.

Fournier, S. (1998). Consumers and their brands: developing relationship theory in consumer research. *Journal of Consumer Research*, 24 (March), 343–373.

Gladden, J., & Funk, D. (2002). Developing an understanding of brand associations in team sport: empirical evidence from consumers of professional sport. *Journal of Sport Management*, 16, 54–81.

Guo, L., & Meng, X. (2008). Consumer knowledge and its consequences: an international comparison. *International Journal of Consumer Studies*, 32 (3), 260–268.

Hofstede, G. (2001). *Culture's consequences: Comparing values, behaviors, institutions, and organizations across nations* (2nd ed.). Thousand Oaks, CA: Sage.

Holden, S. (1993). Understanding brand awareness: let me give you a C(l)ue! *Advances in Consumer Research*, 20 (1), 383–388.

Hunt, K. A., Bristol, T., & Bashaw, R. E. (1999). A conceptual approach to classifying sports fans. *Journal of Services Marketing*, 13 (6), 439–452.

Keller, K. L. (1993) Conceptualizing, measuring and managing customer-based brand equity. *Journal of Marketing*, 1, 1–22.

Keller, K. L. (1998). *Strategic brand management: building, measuring, and managing brand equity*. Upper Saddle River, NJ: Prentice Hall.

Keller, K. L., & Aaker, D. A. (1992). The effects of sequential introduction of brand extensions. *Journal of Marketing Research*, 29 (February), 35–50.

Kirton, M. A. (1981). Reanalysis of two scales of tolerance of ambiguity. *Journal of Personality Assessment*, 45 (4), 407–414.

Koll, O., & von Wallpach, S. (2014). Intended brand associations: Do they really drive consumer response? *Journal of Business Research*, 67 (7), 1501–1507.

Li, F., Zhou, N., Kashyap, R., & Yang, Z. (2008). Brand trust as a second-order factor. An alternative measurement model. *International Journal of Market Research*, 50 (6), 817–839.

Low, G. S., & Lamb, C. W. (2000). The measurement and dimensionality of brand associations, *Journal of Product & Brand Management*, 9 (6), 350–368.

Mann, B.J.S., & Ghuman, M. K. (2014). Scale development and validation for measuring corporate brand associations. *Journal of Brand Management*, 21 (1), 43–62.

Michel, G. (1999). L'évolution des marques: approche par la théorie du noyau central. *Recherche et Applications en Marketing*, 14 (4), 33–53.

Odin, Y., Odin, N., & Valette-Florence, P. (2001). Conceptual and operational aspects of brand loyalty: An empirical investigation. *Journal of Business Research*, 53, 75–84.

Oliver, R. L. (1997). *Satisfaction: a behavioral perspective on the consumer*. Boston, MA: McGraw-Hill.

Pauwels-Delassus, V., & Fosse-Gomez, M. H. (2012). Les enjeux de l'abandon d'une marque locale: la question du transfert d'image. *Décisions Marketing*, 67, 11–22.

Pauwels-Delassus, V., & Mogos Descotes, R. (2012). Brand name substitution and brand equity transfer. *Journal of Product & Brand Management*, 21 (2), 117–125.

Reicheld, F. (1996). *The loyalty effect: the hidden force behind growth, profits, and lasting value*. Boston, MA: Harvard Business School Press.

Romaniuk, J., & Sharp, B. (2009). Conceptualizing and measuring brand salience. *Marketing Theory*, 4 (4), 327–342.

Ross, S. D., James, J. D., & Vargas, P. (2006). Development of a scale to measure team brand associations in professional sport. *Journal of Sport Management*, 20, 260–279.

Shank, M. D., & Beasley, F. M. (1998). Fan or fanatic: refining a measure of sports involvement. *Journal of Sport Behavior*, 21 (4), 435–443.

Spears, N., Brown, T. K. J., & Dacin, P. A. (2006). Assessing the corporate brand: the unique corporate association valence (UCAV) approach. *Journal of Brand Management*, 14 (1/2), 5–19.

Wann, D. L., Schrader, M. P., & Wilson, A. M. (1999). Sport fan motivation: questionnaire validation, comparisons by sport, and relationship to athletic motivation. *Journal of Sport Behavior*, 22 (1), 114–139.

Zaichkowsky, J. L. (1985). Measuring the involvement construct. *Journal of Consumer Research*, 12 (December), 341–352.

Zinkhan, G. M., Locander, W. B., & Leigh, J. H. (1986). Dimensional relationships of aided recall and recognition, *Journal of Advertising*, 15, 38–46.

3
BRAND PERSONALITY

3.1 Overview

The notion of brand personality is based on the assumption that brands can be seen as human by consumers, as part of their daily lives. Brands, therefore, can be described in terms of their personality, as if they were people. Brand personality is usually considered as part of the imagery associated with a brand (Keller, 1993, 1998).

Scales on brand personality allow researchers to measure consumers' perceptions of a personality of a brand. This perceived brand personality can be more or less aligned with the brand personality planned by the company. Brand personality, in fact, is one of the elements that should be taken into account when planning the identity of a brand (Kapferer, 2012). Scales on brand personality started to be developed at the end of the 1990s, thanks to the contribution of Aaker (1997), and have become extremely popular over the years, although some criticism about their usefulness has been raised (Romaniuk & Ehrenberg, 2012). Aaker's scale has been followed by several other scales which either adopt a different perspective, focus on one of the aspects of Aaker's brand personality or investigate brand personality in specific contexts.

Some researchers move away from Aaker's definition of brand personality as a set of "human characteristics" and define brand personality as a set of "personality traits"; this alternative view implies that they leave out elements such as age or gender, which, according to them, are not strictly related to brand personality. That is the case of the new measure of brand personality by Geuens, Weijters and De Wulf (2009) and the brand personality barometer by Ambroise and Valette-Florence (2010a; 2010b). Moreover, Ferrandi and Valette-Florence (2002) develop a human and brand personality scale in French that allows researchers to measure both personalities using the same measurement tool.

In addition to these general scales on brand personality, the literature offers scales that are focused on one of the characteristics highlighted by Aaker (1997). There are two scales that allow researchers to investigate in depth the gender that is associated with a brand. That is the case of the masculine and feminine brand personality scale by Grohmann (2009) and the brand masculinity dimensions scale by Azar (2013).

Brand personality scales related to specific contexts are available, too. For studies in Japan or in Spanish-speaking countries, Japanese and Spanish brand personality scales (Aaker, Benet-Martínez & Garolera, 2001) have been developed. The literature also offers brand personality scales which are applicable to non-profit sectors (Venable et al., 2005), business-to-business (Herbst & Merz, 2011), city branding (Kaplan et al., 2010) and destination branding (Ekinci & Hosany, 2006).

Finally, the chapter includes one brand personality scale which does not measure the type of personality a brand is associated with, but the extent to which a given brand personality is or is not appealing for consumers. That is the case of the brand personality appeal scale proposed by Freling, Crosno and Henard (2011).

3.2 Dimensions of brand personality (Aaker, 1997)

Definition of construct

Aaker (1997, p. 347) defines brand personality as "the set of human characteristics associated with a brand". Brand personality is defined as a multi-dimensional and multi-faceted construct that enables consumers to express themselves along several dimensions. Similar to the "big five" model of human personality, brand personality is measured along five dimensions, that is, *sincerity, excitement, competence, sophistication* and *ruggedness*.

Scale description

The brand personality scale includes five dimensions, 15 facets and 42 personality traits (items). The *sincerity* dimension includes the four facets "down-to-earth", "honest", "wholesome" and "cheerful", which include, respectively, three, three, two and three items. The *excitement* dimension includes the four facets "daring", "spirited", "imaginative" and "up-to-date", which include, respectively, three, three, two and three items. The *competence* dimension includes the three facets "reliable", "intelligent" and "successful", which include three items each. The *sophistication* dimension includes the two facets "upper class" and "charming", which include three items each. The *ruggedness* dimension includes the two facets "outdoorsy" and "tough", which include three and two items respectively.

All personality traits are measured using a 5-point scale ranging from 1 = "not at all descriptive" to 5 = "extremely descriptive". Traits can be summed and averaged within each dimension to form dimension scores (e.g., *sincerity* score).

TABLE 3.1 Brand personality scale

Scale dimension	Scale facet	Scale item
Sincerity	Down-to-earth	• Down-to-earth • Family-oriented • Small-town
	Honest	• Honest • Sincere • Real
	Wholesome	• Wholesome • Original
	Cheerful	• Cheerful • Sentimental • Friendly
Excitement	Daring	• Daring • Trendy • Exciting
	Spirited	• Spirited • Cool • Young
	Imaginative	• Imaginative • Unique
	Up-to-date	• Up-to-date • Independent • Contemporary
Competence	Reliable	• Reliable • Hard working • Secure
	Intelligent	• Intelligent • Technical • Corporate
	Successful	• Successful • Leader • Confident
Sophistication	Upper class	• Upper class • Glamorous • Good-looking
	Charming	• Charming • Feminine • Smooth
Ruggedness	Outdoorsy	• Outdoorsy • Masculine • Western
	Tough	• Tough • Rugged

Scale development

The brand personality scale is developed through a process consisting of preliminary studies of personality trait generation and stimuli selection and three subsequent studies.

Two stages are conducted in the personality trait generation. In stage 1, a set of 309 personality traits is generated based on psychology and marketing literature, as well as qualitative research (free-association task). Here, respondents are asked to write down the personality traits that come to mind when thinking about two brands in three types of product categories (symbolic, utilitarian and both). In stage 2, the set of 309 personality traits is reduced to 114 based on a study in which respondents are asked to rate the extent to which each trait is descriptive of brands in general using a 7-point scale (1 = "not at all descriptive" and 7 = "extremely descriptive"). A scale rating of 6 corresponding to "very descriptive" is used as the cutoff for reducing the set of personality traits.

To select the stimuli, the 1992 EquiTrend study is used. Criteria of brand salience, representativeness of different brand personality and a range of product categories (symbolic, utilitarian and both) are used to identify 37 brands. These brands are then divided into four groups of 10 each, with one brand (Levi's) in all groups.

The first study identifies the brand personality dimensions. Respondents are asked to rate the extent to which the 114 personality traits describe each of the 10 brands using a 5-point scale where 1 = "not at all descriptive" and 5 = "extremely descriptive". Exploratory factor analysis using principal component analysis with varimax rotation allows the researcher to identify a five-factor solution based on eigenvalues (greater than 1.0), scree plot, interpretability criteria, variance explained (equal to 92%) and stableness/robustness of the solution across sub-samples (males versus females, younger versus older respondents). Three items with a loading < 0.40 are dropped. Five individual exploratory factor analyses are conducted to identify the facets within each dimension. Principal component analysis, varimax rotation and unconstrained number of factors to be extracted are used in the analysis. The results reveal a total of 15 facets: 4 each for *sincerity* and *excitement*, 3 for *competence* and 2 each for *sophistication* and *ruggedness*. A clustering procedure is adopted to identify the best personality traits in each of the 15 facets. The analysis shows three clusters for each facet; the trait with the highest item-to-total correlation in each cluster is retained, leaving 45 traits in the scale.

The second study is a test-retest and is conducted to check the reliability of the scale. The test-retest questionnaire is sent two months after the original questionnaire. Respondents are provided with all 114 personality traits to avoid systematic bias. Correlation between time 1 and time 2 is checked for all the traits; those with a correlation < 0.60 between time 1 and time 2 are dropped, leaving 42 traits in the scale.

The third study confirms the brand personality dimensions using a different sample of brands and respondents. A new sample of 20 brands is derived from the 1992

EquiTrend study by selecting brands with the highest salience within the product categories that are discarded in the first study. Exploratory factor analysis using varimax rotation and an unconstrained number of factors to be extracted supports the five-factor solution previously identified. Confirmatory factor analysis estimating a five-factor model for the 42 traits reports satisfying indexes when factors are allowed to correlate: CFI = 0.98, GFI = 0.91, AGFI = 0.86, RMSEA = 0.07, χ^2 = 9216.80 (with 809 degrees of freedom, $p < 0.01$).

Samples

The personality trait generation uses 16 respondents in stage 1 and 25 respondents in stage 2. The three subsequent studies are based on samples of respondents representing the U.S. population with respect to gender, age, household income, ethnicity and geographic location. In the first study, 1,200 questionnaires are mailed and 631 are returned (approximately 55% return rate). A test-retest sample is used in the second study, whereby a random subset of 200 respondents is selected from the original sample of respondents; 81 questionnaires are returned (41% return rate). In the third study, 250 questionnaires are mailed and 180 are returned (72% response rate).

Reliability and validity

Reliability tests are carried out throughout the scale development process with respect to the scale's stability, test–retest reliability and internal consistency. The stability of the five-factor solution is checked in the first and third studies. In the first study, separate factor analyses using principal component analysis, varimax rotation and unrestricted numbers of factors to be extracted are conducted on four sub-samples (males versus females, younger versus older respondents). Similar factor structures are found in the four sub-samples as in the total-sample factor analysis, and factor congruence correlations range from 0.92 to 0.95. In the third study, a factor analysis using principal component analysis, varimax rotation and unrestricted numbers of factors to be extracted shows, again, similar factor structures and factor congruence correlations between 0.97 and 0.99.

The test-retest reliability and the internal consistency of the scale are checked in the second study. The test-retest correlation between time 1 and time 2 for the five factors is 0.75 (*sincerity*), 0.74 (*excitement*), 0.76 (*competence*), 0.75 (*sophistication*) and 0.77 (*ruggedness*). The Cronbach's alpha is 0.93 (*sincerity*), 0.95 (*excitement*), 0.93 (*competence*), 0.91 (*sophistication*) and 0.90 (*ruggedness*). Item-to-total correlations are higher than 0.55 (average = 0.85).

With regard to validity, the content validity of the brand personality scale is established in the preliminary studies of personality trait generation and stimuli selection. External validity and generalizability are ensured through the use of a sample of consumers that are representative of the national population.

Managerial applications

The brand personality scale represents a valid, reliable and generalizable scale that practitioners can use as an alternative to the *ad hoc* measures typically used in practical research. It can be applied across different product categories, and it enables the identification of benchmark personality brands.

3.3 Japanese and Spanish brand personality constructs (Aaker, Benet-Martínez & Garolera, 2001)

Definition of construct

To define Japanese and Spanish brand personalities, Aaker, Benet-Martínez and Garolera (2001) rely on the conceptualization of brand personality provided by Aaker (1997) on the basis of several studies in the United States (see this chapter, pp. 44–48). The Japanese brand personality consists of four dimensions which are shared with the U.S. brand personality (*excitement, competence, sincerity* and *sophistication*) and one dimension which is culture specific (*peacefulness*). Similarly, the Spanish brand personality includes three dimensions which overlap with the U.S. brand personality (*excitement, sincerity* and *sophistication*) and two dimensions which are culture specific (*peacefulness* and *passion*). Whereas the shared dimensions of brand personality capture more universal meanings, the culture-specific dimensions are indicative of orientations that can be found only in given cultures: the *peacefulness* dimension reflects the greater weight on cooperation and harmony in East Asian and Latin cultures, and the *passion* dimension is reflective of higher levels of felt and communicated emotions in Latin cultures.

Scale description

Both Japanese and Spanish brand personality scales include five dimensions which, in turn, include several facets measured by three items each. Specifically, the Japanese brand personality scale consists of five dimensions and 12 facets: *excitement*, containing the facets "talkativeness", "freedom", "happiness" and "energy"; *competence*, which comprises "responsibility", "determination" and "patience"; *peacefulness*, which covers "mildness" and "naivety"; *sincerity*, which includes one facet only, that is, "warmth"; and *sophistication*, containing "elegance" and "style". In total, the scale presents 36 items.

The Spanish brand personality scale consists of five dimensions and 11 facets: *excitement*, which covers "happiness", "youth" and "independence"; *sincerity*, containing "thoughtfulness" and "realness"; *sophistication*, which comprises "style" and "confidence"; *peacefulness*, which embraces "affection" and "naivety"; and *passion*, which consists of "intensity" and "spirituality". The scale presents 33 items in total.

Brand personality traits in both scales are measured using a 5-point scale ranging from 1 = "not at all descriptive" to 5 = "extremely descriptive". Traits can be summed and averaged within each dimension to form dimension scores (e.g., *sincerity* score).

TABLE 3.2 Japanese brand personality scale

Scale dimension	Scale facet	Scale item (English translation)	Scale item (original Japanese term)
Excitement	Talkativeness	• Talkative • Funny • Optimistic	• 話好きな • ユーモアがある • 楽観的な
	Freedom	• Positive • Contemporary • Free	• 積極的な • 現代的な • 自由な
	Happiness	• Friendly • Happy • Likeable	• 人なつっこい • ほがらかな • 愛想のよい
	Energy	• Youthful • Energetic • Spirited	• 若々しい • 元気な • 快活な
Competence	Responsibility	• Consistent • Responsible • Reliable	• 一貫した • 責任感がある • しっかりした
	Determination	• Dignified • Determined • Confident	• 堂々とした • 意志の強い • 自信に満ちた
	Patience	• Patient • Tenacious • Masculine	• 忍耐強い • 粘り強い • 男性的な
Peacefulness	Mildness	• Shy • Mild-mannered • Peaceful	• 内気な • おっとりした • 平和な
	Naivety	• Naïve • Dependent • Childlike	• ナイーブな • 寂しがり屋な • 子供っぽい
Sincerity	Warmth	• Warm • Thoughtful • Kind	• 暖かい • 気が利く • 優しい
Sophistication	Elegance	• Elegant • Smooth • Romantic	• 上品な • 素敵な • ロマンチックな
	Style	• Stylish • Sophisticated • Extravagant	• おしゃれな • 洗練された • 贅沢な

TABLE 3.3 Spanish brand personality scale

Scale dimension	Scale facet	Scale item (English translation)	Scale item (original Spanish term)
Excitement	Happiness	• Happy • Outgoing • Fun	• *Alegre* • *Extrovertida* • *Divertida*
	Youth	• Daring • Young • Spirited	• *Atrevida* • *Joven* • *Viva*
	Independence	• Unique • Imaginative • Independent	• *Única* • *Creativa* • *Independiente*
Sincerity	Thoughtfulness	• Considerate • Thoughtful • Well-mannered	• *Considerada* • *Atenta* • *Correcta*
	Realness	• Real • Sincere • Down-to-earth	• *Real* • *Sincera* • *Realista*
Sophistication	Style	• Good-looking • Glamorous • Stylish	• *Elegante* • *Glamorosa* • *Moderna*
	Confidence	• Confident • Persistent • Leader	• *Segura de sí misma* • *Persistente* • *Dirigente*
Peacefulness	Affection	• Affectionate • Sweet • Gentle	• *Cariñosa* • *Dulce* • *Amable*
	Naivety	• Naïve • Mild-mannered • Peaceful	• *Ingenua* • *Apacible* • *Pacífica*
Passion	Intensity	• Fervent • Passionate • Intense	• *Fervorosa* • *Apasionada* • *Intensa*
	Spirituality	• Spiritual • Mystical • Bohemian	• *Espiritual* • *Mística* • *Bohemia*

Scale development

The scale development process follows a combined emic-etic approach (Hui & Triandis, 1985). It includes two studies for the Japanese brand personality (studies 1 and 2) and other two studies for the Spanish brand personality (studies 3 and 4).

With respect to the Japanese brand personality, study 1 identifies the Japanese brand personality dimensions. The brands to be used as stimuli in the study are selected within 24 product categories serving both symbolic and utilitarian functions. Through a preliminary study, the most well-known brands in each of these categories are identified. Brands are then divided into six sets of four brands each, and one brand (Coca-Cola) is added to all of them. The selection of the personality attributes to be used in the study is based on a free-association task (number of attributes = 138), brand personality research in Japan (number of attributes = 71) and Aaker's brand personality framework (number of attributes = 44). Items which are redundant ($n = 61$), ambiguous ($n = 25$) or irrelevant to the context ($n = 67$) are dropped, leaving a set of 100 personality attributes. In the study, participants are asked to evaluate one group of brands on these 100 attributes. Data analysis is conducted using all brands after checking that the mean rating of Coca-Cola across the groups does not present significant differences. Exploratory factor analysis, conducted using principal component analysis with varimax rotation, reveals a five-factor solution. Each of these factors is then factor analysed separately. This allows the researchers to identify the facets for each factor, for a total of 12 facets. Within each facet, the three attributes with the highest item-to-total correlation (from 0.80 to 0.94) are retained. The final list of personality attributes is translated from Japanese into English through a back-translation process. A test-retest study is conducted after about eight weeks in order to show the stability of the scale over time.

Study 2 assesses the overlap between the Japanese and U.S. brand personality dimensions and the robustness of the Japanese brand dimensions using a different sample of respondents and brands. The questionnaire is now written in English and is administered to bilingual participants. Participants are asked to rate 10 brands, randomly selected from those used in study 1, on U.S. and Japanese brand personality attributes. A correlational analysis is conducted. Correlations between conceptually related dimensions range from 0.63 (between U.S. and Japanese *sincerity*) to 0.81 (between U.S. and Japanese *sophistication*). Correlations between culture-specific dimensions (*ruggedness* for U.S. and *peacefulness* for Japan) and all other dimensions are stronger between U.S. *ruggedness* and Japanese *competence* ($r = 0.39$) and between Japanese *peacefulness* and U.S. *sincerity* ($r = 0.41$). A confirmatory joint factor analysis is also performed. A model with six latent components, representing the four components of brand personality shared by Japan and the United States and two culture-specific components, is first estimated. Adequate fit indexes are reported: $\chi^2(20, N = 900) = 163$, $p < 0.001$, CFI = 0.91 and GFI = 0.92. A second model with four components, which does not include the culture-specific ones (U.S. *ruggedness* and Japanese *peacefulness* are represented as variations of *competence* and *sincerity* respectively) is also estimated: $\chi^2(26, N = 900) = 325$, $p < 0.001$, CFI = 0.71 and GFI = 0.79. This latter model is not satisfactory and reports a significant decrease in the overall fit (delta $\chi^2(6) = 626$).

Study 3 identifies the Spanish brand personality dimensions, similarly to study 1. The brands to be used in the study are selected following the same criteria as study 1; six brand groups are forms, and one brand (Coca-Cola) is added to all of them. The selection of the personality attributes is based on a free-association task (number of attributes = 128), brand personality research in Spain (number of attributes = 64), Aaker's brand personality (number of attributes = 44) and Spanish brand personality (number of attributes = 30) frameworks. Items which are redundant ($n = 79$), ambiguous ($n = 16$) or irrelevant to the context ($n = 94$) are removed, leaving a set of 77 personality attributes. In the study, participants are asked to rate a group of brands on these attributes. Exploratory factor analysis using principal component analysis with varimax rotation is conducted and reveals five factors. Analysis within each factor allows the researchers to identify 11 facets. Three attributes with the highest item-to-total correlation (from 0.70 to 0.84) are kept within each facet. The final list of personality attributes is translated from Spanish into English through a back-translation process. A test-retest study is conducted after about seven weeks.

Similarly to study 2, study 4 assesses the overlap between the Spanish and the U.S. brand personality dimensions and the robustness of the Spanish brand dimensions using a different sample of respondents and brands. The questionnaire is now written in English and is administered to bilingual participants. Participants are asked to rate 10 brands, randomly selected from those used in study 1, on U.S. and Spanish brand personality attributes. A correlational analysis is conducted. Correlations between conceptually related dimensions range from 0.83 (between U.S. and Spanish *sophistication*) to 0.87 (between U.S. and Spanish *excitement*). The correlation between Spanish and Japanese *peacefulness* is equal to 0.78. Correlations between culture-specific dimensions (*ruggedness* for the U.S. and *passion* for Spain) and all other dimensions are stronger between U.S. *ruggedness* and Spanish *sophistication* ($r = 0.42$) and between Spanish *passion* and U.S. *sophistication* ($r = 0.51$). A confirmatory joint factor analysis is also performed. A model with the three dimensions of brand personality shared by Spain and the United States, one dimension shared between by Spain and Japan and two culture-specific dimensions (*passion* and *ruggedness*) is estimated. Adequate fit indexes are reported: $\chi^2(23, N = 870) = 111$, $p < 0.001$, CFI = 0.92 and GFI = 0.91. A second model is tested, where the dimensions not shared by the United States and Spain load as follows: *ruggedness* and *competence* on *sophistication*, *passion* on *sophistication* and *peacefulness* on *sincerity*. This model is unsatisfactory ($\chi^2(43, N = 870) = 392$, $p < 0.001$, CFI = 0.55 and GFI = 0.74) and reports a significant decrease in the overall fit (delta $\chi^2(20) = 281$).

Samples

Study 1 employs various samples: 46 Japanese participants in the stimuli selection; 50 Japanese participants in the personality attribute selection; 1,495 Japanese participants who are representative of the Japanese population in terms of gender, age, marital status, education level and occupation in the main study; and 60 Japanese participants in the retest. Study 2 involves a sample of 114 Japanese participants, of whom 56 are Japanese students enrolled at a large Japanese university and 58 are Japanese exchange students at a large U.S. university.

Study 3 utilizes samples of 36 Spanish undergraduate and graduate students in the personality attribute selection; 692 Spanish participants who are representative of the Spanish population in terms of gender, age, marital status, education level and occupation in the main study; and 58 Spanish participants in the retest. Study 4 uses a sample of 110 Spanish participants, of whom 42 are Spanish students enrolled at a large Spanish university and 59 are Spanish individuals living in the United States affiliated with a Spanish cultural institution.

Reliability and validity

With regard to the Japanese brand personality, its reliability is examined in study 1. Cronbach's alpha is computed for each of the five dimensions and ranged from 0.80 (*peacefulness*) to 0.90 (*excitement*). Test-retest correlations for the five dimensions range from 0.81 (*peacefulness*) to 0.88 (*sophistication*). Convergent and discriminant validities are examined in study 2. The correlation matrix shows that the convergent correlation between conceptually related dimensions ($M = 0.75$) is higher than the average off-diagonal correlations ($M = 0.29$).

The reliability of the Spanish brand personality is examined in study 3. The Cronbach's alpha for the five dimensions ranges from 0.80 (*sophistication*) to 0.91 (*excitement*). Test-retest correlations for the five dimensions range from 0.77 to 0.83. Convergent and discriminant validities are examined in study 4. The correlation matrix shows that the convergent correlation between conceptually related dimensions ($M = 0.83$) is higher than the average off-diagonal correlations ($M = 0.32$).

Managerial applications

The Japanese and Spanish brand personality scales can be used for the same purposes as the brand personality scale developed in the United States (see this chapter, pp. 44–48), but in specific geographic contexts (Japan and Spain).

3.4 *Personnalité humaine et de marque*/Human and brand personality (Ferrandi & Valette-Florence, 2002)

Definition of construct

Ferrandi and Valette-Florence (2002) propose that consumer and brand personalities share the same semantic structure – that is, the same personality traits and the corresponding dimensions that are used to describe human personality can be used to describe brand personality. They propose that both human and brand personalities consist of the following dimensions: *introversion* (introversion), which is characterized by being more interested and focused on internal rather than external activities; *amabilité* (agreeableness), which describes the tendency to be oriented toward others; *consciencieux* (conscientiousness), which describes the tendency to be scrupulous, unflinching and orderly; *neurotisme* (neuroticism), which is characterized by anxious and nervous behaviours; and *ouverture* (openness), which describes the openness to new experiences.

Scale description

The human and brand personality scale includes five dimensions (*introversion, amabilité, consciencieux, neurotisme* and *ouverture*), measured through three unipolar items each. Respondents are asked to say to which extent they agree or disagree that each item is descriptive of themselves (for human personality) or a brand (for brand personality). To express their evaluations, respondents are given 9-point Likert scales ranging from 1 = "strongly disagree" to 9 = "strongly agree". Items within each dimension can be averaged to form dimension scores (for example, *ouverture* score).

TABLE 3.4 *Personnalité humaine et de marque*/Human and brand personality scale

Scale dimension (Translation in English)	Scale item (Translation in English)
Introversion (introversion)	• *Réservé* (bashful) • *Timide* (shy) • *Renfermé* (withdrawn)
Amabilité (agreeableness)	• *Chaleureux* (warm) • *Compatissant* (sympathetic) • *Gentil* (kind)
Consciencieux (conscientiousness)	• *Organisé* (organized) • *Efficace* (efficient) • *Méthodique* (systematic)
Neurotisme (neuroticism)	• *Envieux* (envious) • *Susceptible* (touchy) • *Jaloux* (jealous)
Ouverture (openness)	• *Imaginatif* (imaginative) • *Créatif* (creative) • *Malin* (deep)

Scale development

The human and brand personality scale is developed in accordance with Churchill (1979) and common practices in intercultural research (e.g., Marchetti & Usunier, 1990). The scale development process starts with the back-translation from English to French of Saucier's (1994) 40-item scale on human personality. This scale is chosen because of its brevity compared to other human personality scales and because of its consistency with the dominant "big five" model of personality. Two data collections follow: the first consists in a survey and tests the structure of the scale, reduces its items and examines its reliability and validity; the second comprises semi-structured interviews and tests the semantic equivalence of human and brand personality scales.

In the survey, respondents are asked to evaluate their own personality and the personality of four brands using Saucier's (1994) scale. Brands are selected based on their familiarity and representativeness of different personality traits; 16 brands are used in total (four groups of four brands each). An exploratory factor analysis using principal component analysis with promax rotation is conducted for human and brand personality separately after constraining to five the number of factors to be extracted. Twenty-five items are discarded because of low commonalities (< 0.40). The final solution explains 62.33% and 63.88% of total variance for human and brand personalities, respectively. Confirmatory factor analyses support this solution: RMSEA = 0.050 (human personality) and 0.051 (brand personality); GFI = 0.975 (human personality) and 0.974 (human personality); AGFI = 0.955 (human personality); and 0.951 (brand personality). A test of structural similarity between the human personality scale and the brand personality scale is also performed through a congruence analysis with Procrustes rotation. The correlation coefficients between any two dimensions are higher than 0.90 (between 0.995 and 0.999). Reliability and validity tests are conducted.

In the interviews, respondents are asked about their associations on both human and brand personality. A content analysis is conducted, and interviewees' associations are coded using the scheme 1 = "inverse relation", 2 = "absence of relation" and 3 = "positive relation" between human and brand personalities. The associations are analysed through a nonlinear principal components analysis. The analysis reveals five dimensions which account for 52.54% of total variance and present high similarity with the human and brand personality scale: three dimensions are identical (*introversion, neurotisme* and *consciencieux*); two dimensions are grouped into one (*ouverture* and *amabilité*); and one new dimension emerges (*chaleureux*). A typological analysis is conducted on the words within these dimensions. The analysis shows that the meaning associated with these dimensions is consistent with that of the human and brand personality scales.

Samples

The survey is based on a sample of 537 university students. The interviews are conducted with 12 university students. Both studies are conducted in France.

Reliability and validity

The reliability and validity of the human and brand personality scales are tested using data from the survey.

The scale's reliability is examined through the Jöreskog's rho associated with each dimension. The coefficient is equal to 0.82 (human personality) and 0.70 (brand personality) for *introversion*; to 0.67 (human personality) and 0.67 (brand personality) for *amabilité*; to 0.71 (human personality) and 0.75 (brand personality) for *consciencieux*; to 0.57 (human personality) and 0.66 (brand personality) for *neurotisme*; and to 0.71 (human personality) and 0.79 (brand personality) for *ouverture*.

Validity is tested with respect to convergent and predictive validity. Convergent validity is checked by computing the average variance extracted (AVE). AVE is equal to 0.61 (human personality) and 0.44 (brand personality) for *introversion*; to 0.43 (human personality) and .41 (brand personality) for *amabilité*; to 0.47 (human personality) and 0.50 (brand personality) for *consciencieux*; to 0.33 (human personality) and 0.40 (brand personality) for *neurotisme*; to 0.47 (human personality) and 0.56 (brand personality) for *ouverture*.

The predictive validity of the human and brand personality scale is examined as the scale's ability to differentiate between the personality of different brands. An analysis of variance is performed to that aim. The analysis shows that each of the 16 brands is characterized by a different personality and that dimensions are statistically different from one another: *introversion* ($F = 15.385$, $p < 0.0001$), *amabilité* ($F = 8.948$, $p < 0.0001$), *consciencieux* ($F = 15.114$, $p < 0.0001$), *neurotisme* ($F = 3.650$, $p < 0.0001$) and *ouverture* ($F = 22.879$, $p < 0.0001$). Predictive validity is also tested through a nonlinear generalized canonical analysis in order to understand the interaction among brands, human personality factors and brand personality factors. The analysis shows that the five axis corresponding to the five scale dimensions account for the 47% of the total variance. Brands and brand personality explain the phenomenon more than human personality does, as their loss index is weaker (loss index equal to 2.322 for brands, to 2.120 for brand personality and to 3.554 for human personality), and the portion of the variance explained is higher (brand personality explains 58%; human personality explains 29%).

Managerial applications

The human and brand personality scale represents an instrument that managers can use to understand the personality of their brand, the personality of their consumers and if there is a correspondence between the two. It therefore represents an instrument that managers can use in their brand strategies to improve the positioning of their brand, as well as to attract potential consumers who are sensitive to the brand personality traits presented.

3.5 Brand personality in charitable giving (Venable, Rose, Bush & Gilbert, 2005)

Definition of construct

Non-profit brand personality is conceptualized as an extension of brand personality, as defined by Aaker (1997; see this chapter, pp. 44–48), to the non-profit sector. The need for such a scale is necessitated by the differences in perceptions of non-profit brands as compared to for-profit brands, that is, the intangible character, the social nature and the importance of trust-related aspects to perceptions of non-profits. Non-profit brand personality comprises four dimensions. Two of these dimensions, *sophistication* and *ruggedness*, are the same as those included in Aaker's original brand personality scale. The other two are new: *integrity* and *nurturance*. The *integrity* dimension refers to the extent to which a non-profit brand is perceived as reputable, honest and reliable, whereas the *nurturance* dimension focuses on the extent to which a non-profit brand is considered loving, compassionate and caring.

Scale description

The non-profit brand personality scale includes four dimensions and 15 items, that is, *integrity* (five items), *ruggedness* (four items), *sophistication* (three items) and *nurturance* (three items). Items are evaluated on a 5-point scale where 1 = "not at all descriptive" and 5 = "very descriptive". Items can be summed and averaged within each dimension to form dimension scores (i.e., *integrity, ruggedness, sophistication* and *nurturance* scores).

TABLE 3.5 Non-profit brand personality scale

Scale dimension	Scale item
Integrity	• Honest • Reputable • Reliable • Positive influence • Committed to the public good
Ruggedness	• Masculine • Outdoorsy • Tough • Western
Sophistication	• Glamorous • Upper-class • Good-looking
Nurturance	• Compassionate • Loving • Caring

Scale development

The non-profit brand personality scale is developed through a six-study, multi-method design.

Studies 1 to 3 are qualitative and are used to test whether non-profit organizations have personalities and what contents and dimensions characterize these personalities. These studies are preceded by a phase of stimuli selection in which the set of brands to be used is identified. The *National taxonomy of exempt entities* serves as a basis to identify the brands, which are reviewed by a faculty panel; this process results in the identification of 18 brands, that is, 6 brands for three different categories (health, environment/rights and arts/humanities).

In study 1, a focus group with students is conducted. Students are asked to describe two non-profit brands of their choice within each of the three categories using five adjectives; an open discussion follows. In study 2, the same procedure is adopted, but non-student participants are involved. In study 3, in-depth interviews with donors and non-profit professionals are conducted following a semi-structured protocol. These studies result in the generation of 12 brand personality items regarding the thoughtfulness, integrity and reliability of the non-profit brand, which are specific to the non-profit context and are not included in Aaker's brand personality scale.

Studies 4 to 6 are quantitative and are used to examine empirically the dimensions of non-profit brand personality and to assess the reliability and validity of these dimensions. In study 4, respondents (university faculty/staff) are asked to evaluate one of three brands using 54 brand personality items, including Aaker's (1997) original 42 items and the 12 items derived from the qualitative studies. The three brands used (one per category) represent the most mentioned ones in the qualitative part. Study 5 follows a similar procedure but uses students as respondents and employs a different set of brands (i.e., one from each of the top five categories of non-profit organizations from the *National taxonomy of exempt entities*). Exploratory factor analysis using principal component analysis with varimax rotation is conducted separately for study 4 and study 5 and allows the researchers to identify a four-factor solution with 15 items. Data collected in study 4 are also subjected to a multivariate analysis of variance in order to show that the mean scores for the three non-profit brands differ across the dimensions of brand personality ($p < 0.05$).

In study 6, participants are asked to evaluate one of three brands using the 15 non-profit brand personality items and a three-item measure of likelihood to contribute to a non-profit organization. The three brands used are identified through previous studies and are checked in pre-test. A confirmatory factor analysis supports a correlated four-factor solution ($\chi^2 = 370.3$, $df = 84$, GFI = 0.947, IFI = 0.962, CFI = 962, RMSEA = 0.060). This solution performs better than alternative models, including a one-dimensional model (delta $\chi^2 = 1,826.5$, $df = 6$), uncorrelated four-factor model (delta $\chi^2 = 1,026.2$, $df = 6$) and three-factor model (delta $\chi^2 = 438.2$, $df = 3$).

Samples

Study 1 uses nominal focus groups with junior and senior undergraduate students enrolled in the business school of a large, public, southeastern university in the United States. Study 2 uses 16 non-student respondents who are contributors to non-profit organizations; respondents are recruited through a notice in an office complex in a medium-size city and an announcement in a newsletter of a retirement community in a smaller city. Study 3 involves 18 non-student participants who are donors or non-profit professionals. Study 4 uses full-time faculty and staff from a large, public, southeastern university in the United States. A total of 1,380 surveys is distributed through campus mail, and 403 are returned (approximately 29% response rate). Study 5 is based on a sample of 355 undergraduate business majors from two large public universities in the United States. Study 6 uses 94 respondents for the brand selection and 1,029 completed interviews (7,952 eligible telephone numbers; 12.9% response rate) from a sample representative of the U.S. population in terms of gender, household income, age, ethnicity and geographic location.

Reliability and validity

The reliability of the non-profit brand personality scale is checked in studies 4, 5 and 6. In study 4, the coefficient alpha is equal to 0.91 (*integrity*), 0.84 (*ruggedness*), 0.84 (*sophistication*) and 0.81 (*nurturance*). In study 5, the coefficient alpha is equal to 0.86 (*integrity*), 0.87 (*ruggedness*), 0.84 (*sophistication*) and 0.82 (*nurturance*). To support construct reliability, study 6 reports coefficient alpha of 0.92 (*integrity*), 0.75 (*ruggedness*), 0.72 (*sophistication*) and 0.88 (*nurturance*), significant t-values ($p < 0.001$) and all standardized estimates > 0.50.

Tests of validity are conducted in study 6. With regard to discriminant validity, it is shown that the average variance extracted for each factor (0.70 for *integrity*, 0.42 for *nurturing*, 0.46 for *sophistication* and 0.71 for *nurturance*) exceeds the square of bivariate correlation between factors (< 0.01 for *integrity/ruggedness*; 0.02 for *ruggedness/nurturance*; 0.33 for *ruggedness/sophistication*; 0.13 for *sophistication/nurturance*; 0.19 for *integrity/sophistication*; and 0.66 for *integrity/nurturance*). The discriminant validity between *integrity* and *nurturance* is also demonstrated through a chi-square test. The model in which the correlation between *integrity* and *nurturance* is set to 1 performs worse than the correlated four-factor model (delta $\chi^2 = 12.2$, $df = 1$).

Predictive validity is tested with respect to the likelihood to contribute to a non-profit organization. The correlation between this measure and the scale's four factors is checked for each of the three brands surveyed. Correlation coefficients range from 0.104 to 0.432 and are all significant ($p < 0.01$) with the exception of *sophistication* and *ruggedness* and the likelihood to contribute to a non-profit organization for one of the three brands surveyed.

Managerial applications

Brand personality is a concept that should be taken into account by non-profit organizations, as it can help them build a more specific and unique image by communicating their personality dimensions in a clear way. The non-profit brand personality scale offers these organizations the opportunity to understand their existing brand personality and, based on that, define the positioning strategies to adopt across key stakeholder groups (e.g., donors and non-profit practitioners). The non-profit brand personality scale should be used in non-profit contexts instead of for-profit brand personality scales, as it includes dimensions which are specific to this field (*nurturance* and *integrity*).

3.6 Destination personality (Ekinci & Hosany, 2006)

Definition of construct

Ekinci and Hosany (2006) build on the work of Aaker (1997; see this chapter, pp. 44–48) and extend the concept of brand personality outside the sphere of commercial brands in relation to tourism destinations. They define destination personality as "the set of human characteristics associated with a destination" (Ekinci and

60 Brand personality

Hosany, 2006, p. 127). As commercial brands, in fact, tourism destinations are rich in terms of the symbolic value they provide and can be described in terms of their personality. The construct of destination personality includes three dimensions: two of them, *sincerity* and *excitement*, are the same as Aaker's brand personality, whereas one, *conviviality*, is specific to the tourism context.

Scale description

The destination personality scale includes three dimensions for a total of 12 items: *sincerity* (five items), *excitement* (four items) and *conviviality* (three items). Items are evaluated by respondents on a 5-point Likert-type scale ranging from 1 = "not at all descriptive" to 5 = "extremely descriptive".

TABLE 3.6 Destination personality scale

Scale dimension	Scale item
Sincerity	• Reliable
	• Sincere
	• Intelligent
	• Successful
	• Wholesome
Excitement	• Exciting
	• Daring
	• Original
	• Spirited
Conviviality	• Friendly
	• Family-oriented
	• Charming

Scale development

To develop the destination personality scale, a pre-test and a study are conducted.

In the pre-test, respondents are asked to indicate which of the Aaker's 42 personality traits can be used to describe tourism destinations. Personality traits that are chosen by at least 70% of the respondents are retained, leaving 27 items split across Aaker's five dimensions to be used in the study.

The study is based on two data collections. Respondents are asked to recall the last tourism destination they visited outside the UK in the past three months (sample 1) or few hours after their holiday (sample 2) and to evaluate this destination using items on destination personality, affective destination image (Russell, 1980), cognitive destination image (derived from Ong & Horbunluekit, 1997) and intention to recommend (Cronin & Taylor, 1992).

Exploratory factor analysis using principal component analysis with varimax rotation is run. Items with low factor loadings (< 0.45), high cross-loadings (> 0.40) or low commonalities (0.3) are dropped, and the analysis is re-run until items display satisfying values. The final solution, which accounts for about 62%

of total variance, includes three factors and 12 items with commonalities ranging from 0.46 to 0.82. This model reports a poor fit in the confirmatory factor analysis run next. Based on modification indexes, an additional item is removed, and a better fit is achieved after the analysis is re-run (χ^2 = 52.97, df = 41, GFI = 0.91, NNFI = 0.94, CFI = 0.95, SRMR = 0.07, RMSEA = 0.05).

Reliability and validity tests are conducted, and a post-hoc analysis shows that one destination personality dimension (*conviviality*) moderates the relationship between destination image and intention to recommend (t-value > 2.00).

Samples

The pre-test is conducted with 20 native British respondents. In the study, 275 questionnaires are collected across samples, but 25 of them are excluded because respondents are non-British. Sample 1 includes 155 responses (148 usable) from respondents who are approached at high streets, around shopping complexes and train stations in three cities in the UK. Sample 2 comprises 120 responses (102 usable) from respondents approached in a European airport waiting for their flight to go back to the UK.

Reliability and validity

Content validity is checked in the pre-test, based on which items that are relevant in the tourism context are retained. Reliability and other types of validities are examined in the study. With regard to reliability, composite reliability scores are equal to 0.71 for *sincerity*, 0.70 for *excitement* and 0.70 for *conviviality*. Item-to-total correlations range from 0.40 to 0.67. For discriminant validity, it is shown that the squared correlations between any two factors are lower than the average variance extracted of each factor (equal to 0.51 for *sincerity*, 0.50 for *excitement* and 0.52 for *conviviality*). For convergent validity, it is shown that all factor loadings are equal to 0.35 or higher and are significant, with t-values between 3.17 and 5.54. Predictive validity is proved with respect to affective image, cognitive image and intention to recommend through a series of ordinary least squares regressions. *Sincerity* and *conviviality* are significant predictors of affective image: betas are equal to 0.209 (p = 0.0002) and 0.313 (p < 0.0001), respectively. *Excitement* and *conviviality* are significant predictors of cognitive image: betas are equal to 0.141 (p < 0.05) and 0.220 (p = 0.001) respectively. *Conviviality* is a significant predictor of the intention to recommend, with beta = 0.243 (p < 0.0001).

Managerial applications

Destination marketers should concentrate not only on the image of a destination but also on its personality. The destination personality scale can be used by destination marketers in their positioning and differentiation strategies in order to develop a distinctive and attractive personality for their places. To develop strong destination personality characteristics, marketers could use advertising, communication methods and other destination management tactics.

3.7 Gender dimensions of brand personality (Grohmann, 2009)

Definition of construct

Consistent with Aaker's (1997; see this chapter, pp. 44–48) definition of brand personality, gender dimensions of brand personality are defined by Grohmann (2009, p. 105) as "the set of human personality traits associated with masculinity and femininity applicable and relevant to brands". *Masculine* brand personality (MBP) and *feminine* brand personality (FBP) are unidimensional and independent dimensions.

Scale description

The MBP/FBP scale includes two dimensions, *masculinity* and *femininity*, which are captured by six items each. Items are measured on 9-point scales ranging from 1 = "not at all descriptive" to 9 = "extremely descriptive". Items can be summed and averaged within each dimension to form dimension scores for both MBP and FBP.

TABLE 3.7 Masculine and feminine brand personality scale

Scale dimension	Scale item
Masculine brand personality (MBP)	• Adventurous • Aggressive • Brave • Daring • Dominant • Sturdy
Feminine brand personality (FBP)	• Expresses tender feelings • Fragile • Graceful • Sensitive • Sweet • Tender

Scale development

The MBP/FBP scale is developed following a process consisting of an item-generation phase and seven following studies.

In the item-generation phase, a first set of items is derived from a task in which respondents are asked to list words they associate with MBP and FBP. This set of items is integrated with others from scales on masculine and feminine human personality such as Bem sex role inventory (BSRI; Bem, 1974), the personal attributes questionnaire (Spence, Helmreich & Stapp, 1974) and the masculinity trait index/femininity trait index (Barak & Stern, 1986). The revision performed by a group of consumer researchers results in a set of 72 items.

In study 1, the items are administered to a sample of respondents, who rate them in relation to four brands identified through a pre-test. Exploratory factor analysis using principal components analysis reveals a two-factor solution. Ten items with high cross-loading are removed, and a two-factor confirmatory analysis is performed (NFI = 0.92, NNFI = 0.93, CFI = 0.93, GFI = 0.31, SRMR = 0.17, RMSEA = 0.19, CN = 60.44). Additional items are dropped based on individual reliabilities < 0.50, modification indexes > 3.84 and chi-square difference tests between the CFA of resulting solutions and the CFA of the full scale. The final solution includes 12 items (6 for each dimension) and reports a good fit in the CFA (NFI = 0.98, CFI = 0.99, NNFI = 0.98, GFI = 0.95, SRMR = 0.03, RMSEA = 0.06, CN = 251.86).

Study 2 examines the generalizability of the MBP/FBP scale in relation to symbolic, utilitarian and utilitarian-symbolic product categories. Each respondent rates the scale in relation to one group of brands identified through the Equi Trend study (in total, two groups of 22 brands each are created). A two-factor measurement model is estimated (χ^2(53) = 1942.68, p < 0.001, CN = 136, NFI = 0.96, NNFI = 0.95, CFI = 0.96, GFI = 0.91, SRMR = 0.08, RMSEA = 0.11). The two-factor model shows good fit across utilitarian, symbolic and mixed product categories, except for the RMSEA, which is > 0.06.

Study 3 examines the predictive validity of the MBP/FBP scale. The scale is applied to a set of 16 brands (four groups of four brands each), for which *a priori* expectations are established through a pre-test. The pre-test identifies four product categories with one brand in each category perceived as relatively high on masculinity and one perceived relatively high on femininity. In the study, each respondent rates one group of four brands on the 12 MPB/FBP items. A measurement model is estimated (χ^2(53) = 553.38, p < 0.01, CN = 149.03, NFI = 0.96, NNFI = 0.96, CFI = 0.96, GFI = 0.92, SRMR = 0.07, RMSEA = 0.09). Mean values of the brands on the MBP and FBP dimensions are computed and confirm the expectations for all product categories.

Study 4 establishes the scale's discriminant validity. In study 4a, respondents rate one of four sets of brands on MBP/FBP and BSRI scales; each set includes six brands from different product categories. In study 4b, respondents rate four brands from different product categories in terms of MBP/FBP and Aaker's (1997) ruggedness/ sophistication dimensions. Various tests are conducted for discriminant validity purposes.

Studies 5, 6 and 7 test the nomological validity of the MBP/FBP scale through ANOVA and/or MANOVA. Study 5 examines whether the presence of spokespeople in an advertisement influences consumers' perceptions of MBP and FBP. Respondents are asked to judge the personality of a fictitious brand after being exposed to a print advertisement in a 3 (spokesperson: masculine, feminine, none) × 2 (participants' gender: male, female) between-subject experiment. Brand's fictitious name and product categories are derived from a pre-test.

Study 6 examines the influence of brand personality and self-concept congruence on various brand responses. Respondents are asked to evaluate one of three brands on scales of brand trust, brand affect, attitudinal brand loyalty and behavioural brand loyalty (Chaudhuri & Holbrook, 2001), brand preference (Sirgy *et al*., 1997), word of mouth (Kim, Han & Park 2001), brand attitude, purchase intention and likelihood of recommendation of the brand (new measures; see boxes below). Respondents also rate their sex role identity (Barak & Stern, 1986) and the brand's MBP and FBP.

Brand attitude

What is your global evaluation of the brand?

- Negative/Positive
- Dislike/Like
- Favourable/Unfavourable

Purchase intention of the brand

How likely are you to purchase this brand in the future?

- Unlikely/Likely
- Improbable/Probable

Likelihood of recommendation of the brand

How likely are you to recommend this brand to a friend?

- Unlikely/Likely
- Improbable/Probable

Study 7 examines whether brand personality lends itself to the creation of brand fit in a brand extension context. Pre-tests are used to identify parent brands and extension categories. In the study, which is designed as a 2 (parent brand personality: masculine, feminine) × 2 (extension category: masculine, feminine) mixed design, respondents provide answers on extension evaluation, purchase likelihood of the extension and brand fit (Bhat & Reddy, 2001).

Samples

The item-generation phase uses 60 undergraduate students in the exploratory task and four consumer researchers. Study 1 is based on a sample of 369 undergraduate students and uses another sample of 60 students in the pre-test. Study 2 uses a sample of 281 students. Study 3 uses a sample of 280 undergraduate students after running a pre-test with 36 students. Study 4 uses a sample of 544 undergraduate students in study 4a and a sample of 461 undergraduate students in study 4b. Study 5 utilizes a sample of 292 undergraduate students after running a pre-test with 75 students. Study 6 employs a sample of 371 students. Study 7 employs a sample of 112 undergraduate students after running two pre-tests with, respectively, 28 and 88 respondents.

Reliability and validity

The MBP/FBP scale's content validity is established in the item-generation phase through the evaluation of the scale items by consumer researchers.

Details about the reliability and convergent validity of the scale are given in studies 1 to 4 and 6. For MBP, coefficient alpha is equal to 0.91 (study 1), 0.89 (study 2), 0.90 (study 3), 0.91 (study 4) and 0.91 (study 6). For FBP, coefficient alpha is equal to 0.90 (study 1), 0.90 (study 2), 0.91 (study 3), 0.93 (study 4) and 0.90 (study 6). For MBP, composite reliability is equal to 0.92 (study 1), 0.90 (study 2), 0.92 (study 3), 0.92 (study 4) and 0.92 (study 6). For FBP, composite reliability is equal to 0.92 (study 1), 0.88 (study 2), 0.93 (study 3), 0.94 (study 4) and 0.94 (study 6). For MBP, item-to-total correlations are > 0.67 (study 1), > 0.51 (study 2), > 0.50 (study 3), > 0.52 (study 4) and > 0.52 (study 6). For MBP, item-to-total correlations are > 0.60 (study 1), > 0.58 (study 2), > 0.53 (study 3), > 0.78 (study 4) and > 0.73 (study 6). For MBP, AVE is equal to 0.67 (study 1), 0.63 (study 2), 0.66 (study 3), 0.67 (study 4) and 0.65 (study 6). For FBP, composite reliability is equal to 0.75 (study 1), 0.56 (study 2), 0.70 (study 3), 0.74 (study 4) and 0.69 (study 6).

Evidence of discriminant validity of the MBP/FBP scale is provided in study 4. In study 4a, to prove discriminant validity between MBP and BSRI/masculinity and FBP and BSRI/femininity, chi-square difference tests between relevant one and two-factor CFA models are performed. Results show that the two-factor models present a significantly reduced chi-square value (MBP and BSRI/masculinity: delta χ^2 = 5811.27, df = 1, p < 0.00001; ϕ = 0.82, SE = 0.01; FBP and BSRI/femininity: delta χ^2 = 2820.35, df = 1, p < 0.00001; ϕ = .89, SE = 0.01). In addition, confidence intervals around the correlation estimates do not include ±1. However, AVE does not exceed the squared correlation of MBP and BSRI/masculinity (AVE$_{MBP}$: 0.65 < 0.66) and FBP and BSRI/femininity (AVE$_{FBP}$: 0.62 < 0.64).

The same criteria are used in study 4b to prove discriminant validity between MBP and BSRI/masculinity and FBP and BSRI/femininity. Chi-square difference tests between relevant one- and two-factor CFA models are conducted (MBP and ruggedness: delta χ^2 = 5811.27, df = 1, p < 0.00001; ϕ = 0.57, SE = 0.02; FBP and sophistication: delta χ^2 = 3657.26, df = 1, p < 0.00001; ϕ = 0.64, SE = 0.02). These results are supported by confidence intervals around the correlation estimates, which do not include ±1 and AVE statistics, which exceed the squared correlation (AVE$_{MBP}$: 0.67 > 0.30; AVE$_{FBP}$: 0.74 > 0.41).

The nomological validity of the MBP/FBP scale is tested in studies 5 to 7. Study 5 shows that masculine and feminine spokespeople can shape perceptions of MBP and FBP: masculine (or feminine) spokesperson is associated with stronger perceptions of MBP (or FBP) compared with FBP (or MBP). Study 6 demonstrates that brand personality/self-concept congruence is associated with more favourable brand responses. Finally, study 7 shows that, in a brand extension context, the fit between gender dimensions of brand personality and extension category perceptions results in more positive extension evaluations and higher purchase likelihood.

Managerial applications

The suggested use for the MBP/FBP scale is in the evaluation of positioning strategies. Three uses, in particular, are identified: analysing consumers' perceptions of MBP/FBP after the brand has gone through positioning, repositioning and brand extension strategies; mapping consumers' perceptions of MBP/FBP of competing brands; and exploring alternative positioning strategies for one's brand. To create MBP/FBP perceptions, managers can utilize spokespeople in advertisements.

3.8 New measure of brand personality (Geuens, Weijters & De Wulf, 2009)

Definition of construct

The new measure of brand personality (NMBP) relies on the conceptualization of brand personality as "the set of *human personality traits* that are both *applicable to* and *relevant for* brands" (Geuens, Weijters and De Wulf, 2009, p. 97). Geuens, Weijters and De Wulf (2009) contrast this definition of brand personality with Aaker's (1997; see this chapter, pp. 44–48) which, according to them, suffers from a too-broad/loose conceptualization. Defined as "the set of human characteristics associated with a brand" (Aaker, 1997, p. 347), Aaker's brand personality not only embraces perceived brand personality, but also comprises perceived user characteristics such as age and gender. By adopting a narrower definition, Geuens, Weijters and De Wulf focus on personality traits only. Their construct of brand personality includes the dimensions of *responsibility, activity, aggressiveness, simplicity* and *emotionality*.

Scale description

The NMBP consists of five dimensions and 12 items. The *responsibility* and *activity* dimensions are measured by three items each, whereas the *aggressiveness, simplicity* and *emotionality* dimensions are measured by two items each. Items are rated using 7-point scales where 1 = "not characteristic of the brand" and 7 = "very characteristic of the brand".

TABLE 3.8 The new measure of brand personality

Scale dimension	Scale item
Responsibility	• Down-to-earth • Stable • Responsible

(Continued)

TABLE 3.8 (Continued)

Scale dimension	Scale item
Activity	• Active • Dynamic • Innovative
Aggressiveness	• Aggressive • Bold
Simplicity	• Ordinary • Simple
Emotionality	• Romantic • Sentimental

Scale development

The scale-development process starts with the selection of personality traits, where Churchill's (1979) method of scale development is complemented with Rossiter's (2002) C-OAR-SE procedure. To accomplish that, items are derived from the literature on brand/human personality and two focus groups, where participants are asked to imagine brands as persons and to describe the personality of some brands in their own words. The resulting set of 244 unique items is then assessed by a panel of expert judges and another panel of marketing researchers. Forty items that are considered most appropriate for brands are kept from this initial pool. A set of five studies follows.

Study 1 consists of a pre-test of the 40 items using a set of 20 brands representing different purchase motivations (functional, experiential, symbolic and emotional). Each respondent rates one brand on each of the 40 items. Principal component analysis with varimax rotation results in five factors with eigenvalues > 1. Items with a loading < 0.60 on their focal factor and a cross-loading > 0.35 are eliminated, leaving a set of 18 items. Then the sample is split into two sub-samples and a confirmatory factor analysis is conducted on each sub-sample. The five-factor solution is supported by both sub-samples: respectively, $\chi^2(125) = 461.490$ and 413.594, CFI = 0.927 and 0.930, TLI = 0.910 and 0.914, RMSEA = 0.066 and 0.061; all factor loadings are significant ($p < 0.001$).

Study 2 validates the five-factor solution using a wider array of 193 brands from 20 product categories. Each respondent rates one brand. The sample is split into two sub-samples: the first sub-sample is used to check the five-factor, 18-item solution, whereas the second sub-sample is used for validity purposes. Data for each sub-sample are aggregated on the brand level (on average, each brand is rated by 30 respondents). Using the first sub-sample, a CFA reveals an unsatisfactory fit; six items are therefore eliminated based on modification indexes. A satisfactory fit is then obtained in both sub-samples: respectively, $\chi^2(44) = 110.119$ and 117.102, CFI = 0.969 and 0.965, TLI = 0.954 and 0.948 and RMSEA = 0.088 and 0.093. The second sub-sample is used to verify the scale's reliability and discriminant validity.

Study 3 checks the test-retest reliabilities of the five dimensions for 84 brands over a period of one year. The second data collection is conducted using an independent sample with similar demographic characteristics as the sample in the first data collection (see what follows for details). Each respondent uses the 12-item scale for evaluating three brands. Eighty-four of the 193 brands used in study 1 are included. Correlation analysis is performed to check the test-retest reliability of the scale.

Study 4 tests the cross-cultural validity of the scale with regard to the U.S. population and its nomological validity with regard to the contribution of the brand personality dimensions to brand attitudes for two groups of consumers adhering different values (conservation and self-transcendence). Twenty brands reflecting functional, image, experiential and hedonic purchase motivations are used. Respondents evaluate brands on the brand personality scale and the short Swartz's value survey (Lindeman & Verkasalo, 2005). CFA and multi-group analyses are performed.

Study 5 further assesses the cross-cultural validity of the scale using one brand (Coca-Cola) and consumers from nine European countries (France, Germany, Italy, the Netherlands, Poland, Romania, Spain, Switzerland and Turkey). The translation of the brand personality scale is obtained through a translation and back-translation process; adaptations are made on scale items in the translation process. Data analysis is run on the individual level. CFA and G-theory analysis are conducted to verify the brand personality scale's validities.

Samples

The selection of the brand personality items is obtained through two focus groups with eight junior researchers in the marketing domain and 10 graduate students in general/marketing management; eight judges including marketing professors at a business school or marketing managers in a company; and 20 marketing researchers of a university or a business school. Study 1 uses an online Belgian consumer panel, which generates 1,235 usable responses (41.7% response rate). Study 2 uses online questionnaires from 12,789 Belgian consumers (19.2% response rate). Study 3 uses the sample of study 2 as a test sample and a new one of 4,500 consumers (14.3% response rate) as the re-test sample. Study 4 is based on 401 U.S. consumers (2.8% response rate). Study 5 involves multiple samples which are representative of the national population with regard to age and gender: 284 respondents from France, 250 from Germany, 231 from Italy, 265 from the Netherlands, 198 from Poland, 251 from Romania, 250 from Spain, 225 from Switzerland and 250 from Turkey.

Reliability and validity

The reliability of the final NMBP scale is tested in study 2. All factor loadings exceed 0.59 and have a $p < 0.001$. Composite reliabilities of the five factors are 0.95 (*activity*), 0.95 (*responsibility*), 0.93 (*aggressiveness*), 0.95 (*simplicity*) and 0.79 (*emotionality*). The test-retest reliability of the scale is tested in study 3. Correlations between time 1 and time 2 are 0.85 (*activity*), 0.90 (*responsibility*), 0.84 (*aggressiveness*), 0.93 (*simplicity*) and 0.90 (*emotionality*).

The scale's discriminant validity is tested in study 2 by comparing the average variance extracted (AVE) for the five dimensions with the square of the bivariate correlations between factors. The AVE for the five dimensions, equal to 0.86 (*activity*), 0.85 (*responsibility*), 0.87 (*aggressiveness*), 0.67 (*simplicity*) and 0.90 (*emotionality*), is higher than the between-factor squared correlations (between 0.00 and 0.43).

The nomological validity of the NMB's scale is partially demonstrated in study 4. Respondents are classified in low versus high conservation group and low versus high self-transcendence group based on a median split. A multi-group analysis is performed for each of the two groups; the model tested, in both analyses, includes brand attitudes as a function of the five brand personality dimensions. The first multi-group analysis shows that there is no difference between the low versus high conservation group ($\chi^2 = 6.864$, $df = 5$, $p = 0.231$). On the contrary, the second multi-group analysis shows that the brand personality dimensions have a differential impact on the low versus high self-transcendence group ($\chi^2 = 17.444$, $df = 5$, $p = 0.004$).

The cross-cultural validity of the NMBP is tested in studies 4 (U.S.) and 5 (European countries). In study 4, the five-factor, 12-item model reports: $\chi^2 = 482.878$, $df = 44$, TLI = 0.903, CFI = 0.935 and RMSEA = 0.091. It also reports that factor loadings are positive and significant ($p < 0.001$) and composite reliabilities are higher than 0.70.

In study 5, a multi-group analysis is used to test the configural invariance of the five-factor model of brand personality. The results show a good fit of the model across countries ($\chi^2 = 1,095.5$, $df = 396$, TLI = 0.936, CFI = 0.957, RMSEA = 0.028), as well as in each country. Composite reliabilities are equal to or exceed 0.86 (*activity*), 0.62 (*responsibility*), 0.60 (*aggressiveness*), 0.78 (*simplicity*) and 0.64 (*emotionality*), except for *aggressiveness* in Germany, which is equal to 0.55. In study 5, G-theory is applied to cross-cultural data so that sources of variance and generalizability coefficients (GC) are computed for each factor. The analysis shows that GC for the brand personality dimensions range from 0.70 to 0.91 and that the major source of variance is the individual (variance components between 44% and 75.3%); country or the country by item interaction explain smaller portion of the variance (variance components between 2.6% and 9.2% and 0.1% and 2.7%, respectively).

Managerial applications

According to Geuens, Weijters and De Wulf, the NMBP offers several advantages. First, the five-factor, 12-item NMBP is short and easy to administer, considering that surveys on brand personality typically include several other scales. Second, the NMBP proved to be generalizable across various different countries including Belgium, France, Germany, Italy, the Netherlands, Poland, Romania, Spain, Switzerland, Turkey and the United States. This can be an advantage for companies which are conducting multi-country studies. The use of the same measurement instrument across countries allows companies to achieve economies of scale and makes comparisons between countries more manageable. Third, the scale can be used for studies on an aggregate level across multiple brands of different product categories or for studies across different competitors within a specific product category, as well as for studies on an individual brand level.

3.9 Brand personality applied to cities (Kaplan, Yurt, Guneri & Kurtulus, 2010)

Definition of construct

By developing the construct of city brand personality, the authors extend the brand personality framework to place branding. Referring to Aaker's (1997; see this chapter, pp. 44–48) original definition of brand personality, city brand personality is conceptualized as "the set of human characteristics associated with the city brand" (Kaplan, Yurt, Guneri & Kurtulus, 2010, p. 1293), where *human characteristics* can include utilitarian, symbolic and experiential attributes, and *city brand* can be any city, irrespective of the fact that this city is or is not a tourist destination. The construct of city brand personality includes the following six dimensions: *excitement, malignancy, peacefulness, competence, conservatism* and *ruggedness*. Whereas four of these dimensions (*excitement, peacefulness, competence* and *ruggedness*) are consistent with previous studies on brand personality, two of them (*malignancy* and *conservatism*) are new; they cover negative aspects of personality not included in previous frameworks.

Scale description

The city brand personality scale includes six dimensions and 78 items: *excitement* (30 items), *malignancy* (20 items), *peacefulness* (12 items), *competence* (6 items), *conservatism* (5 items) and *ruggedness* (5 items). Five of the six scale dimensions are divided into facets: "passionate", "outgoing", "feminine" and "sympathetic" (for *excitement*); "unreliable", "arrogant" and "self-seeking" (for *malignancy*); "calm" and "domestic" (for *peacefulness*); "authoritarian" and "sophisticated" (for *competence*); and "religious" and "uneducated" (for *conservatism*). It is not reported, however, which items belong to which facet.

All items are measured using a 5-point Likert-type scale ranging from 1 = "absolutely disagree" to 5 = "absolutely agree". The scale is originally developed in Turkish; an English translation is provided by the authors.

TABLE 3.9 City brand personality scale

Scale dimension	Scale facet	Scale item (English translation)	Scale item (Original Turkish term)
Excitement	• Passionate • Outgoing • Feminine • Sympathetic	• Amusing • Enthusiastic • Attractive • Exhilarated • Energetic • Sexy • Sympathetic • Passionate • Cheerful • Popular	• Eğlenceli • Heyecan verci • Çekici • Coşkulu • Enerjik • Seksi • Sempatik • Tutkulu • Neşeli • Popüler

(Continued)

TABLE 3.9 (Continued)

Scale dimension	Scale facet	Scale item (English translation)	Scale item (Original Turkish term)
		• Feminine	• Kadınsı
		• Witty	• Esprituel
		• Chatty	• Konuşkan
		• Independent	• Özgür
		• Creative	• Yaratıcı
		• Friendly	• Canayakın
		• Stylish	• Şık
		• Flexible	• Esnek
		• Emotional	• Duygusal
		• Extraordinary	• Sıradışı
		• Mystical	• Gizemli
		• Risk taker	• Risk alan
		• Enthusiastic	• Hevesli
		• Self-indulgent	• Ehlikeyif
		• Tender	• Narin
		• Fanciful	• Hayalperest
		• Optimistic	• İyimser
		• Self-confident	• Kendine güvenli
		• Curious	• Meraklı
		• Elite	• Seçkin
Malignancy	• Unreliable	• Tactless	• Densiz
	• Arrogant	• Trickster	• Entrikacı
	• Self-seeking	• Fickle	• Maymun iştahlı
		• Arrogant	• Küstah
		• Selfish	• Bencil
		• Snob	• Ukala
		• Unreliable	• Güvenilmez
		• Self-seeking	• Çıkarcı
		• Greedy	• Açgözlü
		• Inconsistent	• Tutarsız
		• Barefaced	• Yüzsüz
		• Shrewd	• Kurnaz
		• Immoderate	• Dengesiz
		• Ungrateful	• Nankör
		• Callous	• Vurdumduymaz
		• Spoilt	• Şımarık
		• Irresponsible	• Sorumsuz
		• Arriviste	• Sonradan görme
		• Malevolent	• Kötüniyetli
		• Stingy	• Cimri
Peacefulness	• Calm	• Peaceful	• Huzurlu
	• Domestic	• Tolerant	• Hoşgörülü
		• Benevolent	• Yardımsever
		• Good-natured	• İyi huylu
		• Realistic	• Mantıklı

(Continued)

TABLE 3.9 (Continued)

Scale dimension	Scale facet	Scale item (English translation)	Scale item (Original Turkish term)
		• Gentle	• Kibar
		• Decent	• Ahlaklı
		• Sincere	• Samimi
		• Loyal	• Sadık
		• Fastidious	• Titiz
		• Modern	• Çağdaş
		• Homebody	• Evcimen
Competence	• Authoritarian	• Strong	• Güçlü
	• Sophisticated	• Leader	• Lider ruhlu
		• Mature	• Olgun
		• Clever	• Zeki
		• Authoritarian	• Otoriter
		• Charismatic	• Karizmatik
Conservatism	• Religious	• Poor	• Yoksul
	• Uneducated	• Uneducated	• Eğitimsiz
		• Villager	• Köylü
		• Devout	• Yobaz
		• Religious	• İnançlı
Ruggedness	–	• Jealous	• Kıskanç
		• Rebellious	• Asi
		• Nervous	• Asabi
		• Rough	• Sert
		• Harsh	• Haşin

Scale development

The city brand personality scale is developed following a two-stage research design.

The first stage generates a list of personality traits (items) that can be used to describe cities. In a pilot study, participants are asked to write down five human personality traits that they find appropriate to characterize 10 given cities reflecting different attributes (symbolic, utilitarian and both). The resulting list is enriched with personality traits derived from the literature. The combined list is revised by an expert panel who rate how descriptive each trait is when attributed to cities. The resulting list includes 87 personality traits.

The second stage of the research consists of a quantitative study. Respondents are asked to rate one of three cities (Istanbul, Ankara or Izmir) on the 87 items. An exploratory factor analysis using principal component analysis with varimax rotation reveals a six-factor structure (total variance explained = 51.3%). Seventy-eight items are retained based on factor loadings (at least 0.40 on one factor). It follows a facet identification step, in which each factor is individually factor analysed using principal component analysis with varimax rotation. The analyses reveal a total of 13 facets.

Samples

Stage 1 uses a sample of 195 university students in the pilot test and five professionals to judge the city brand personality scale items. Stage 2 is based on 898 questionnaires of students from public and private universities in three Turkish cities (Izmir, Ankara and Istanbul), with a similar number of participants for each city (297 in Izmir, 305 in Ankara and 296 in Istanbul).

Reliability and validity

The reliability of the city brand personality scale is reported in stage 2. The six factors have a coefficient alpha that ranges from 0.63 to 0.94. The overall reliability of the scale is 0.95.

Managerial applications

The city brand personality scale offers practical implications for urban policy makers. The scale represents a positioning and differentiation tool that could be used to establish a distinct city brand personality. The scale also highlights the peculiarities of brand personality associated with cities compared to products, having two dimensions (*malignancy* and *conservatism* dimensions) that are unique to this context.

3.10 Industrial brand personality (Herbst & Merz, 2011)

Definition of construct

Industrial brand personality (IBP) is conceptualized similarly to Aaker's brand personality (see this chapter, pp. 44–48), but with a focus on industrial or business-to-business brands. IBP is defined as "the set of human characteristics associated with a B2B brand" (Herbst and Merz, 2011, p. 1074). It includes three dimensions: *performance, sensation* and *credibility*. *Performance* refers to functional brand associations, which are particularly important for B2B brands; this dimension covers an aspect that is not included in Aaker's brand personality scale. *Sensation* relates to the self-expressive reasons behind consumers' adoption of a given brand and overlaps with Aaker's original *excitement* and *sophistication* dimensions. *Credibility* is centred on trust-related aspects and overlaps with Aaker's *sincerity* dimension.

Scale description

The IBP scale includes three dimensions, five facets and 39 personality traits (items). Specifically, the *performance* dimension includes three facets and 19 items: "achievement-oriented" (7 items), "competent" (7 items) and "leading" (5 items). The *sensation* dimension includes two facets and 13 items: "exciting" (9 items) and "charming" (4 items). The *credibility* dimension includes seven items and no facet. All items are evaluated on a 6-point scale from 1 = "not at all descriptive" to 6 = "very descriptive". Items can be summed and averaged within each dimension to form dimension scores (i.e., *performance*, *sensation* and *credibility* scores).

TABLE 3.10 Industrial brand personality scale

Scale dimension	Scale facet	Scale item
Performance	Achievement-oriented	• Achievement-oriented • Professional • Analytical • Hard-working • Intelligent • Proactive • Educated
	Competent	• Competent • Proper • Careful • Experienced • Rational • Problem-oriented • Diligent
	Leading	• Leading • Innovative • International-oriented • Scientific • Creative
Sensation	Exciting	• Exciting • Young • Glamorous • Cool • Trendy • Daring • Good-looking • Adventurous • Imaginative
	Charming	• Charming • Cheerful • Feminine • Tempered
Credibility	–	• Sincere • Real • Reliable • Down-to-earth • Honest • Original • Trustworthy

Scale development

Following Aaker's (1997; see this chapter, pp. 44–48) development of a brand personality scale and Venable et al.'s (2005; see this chapter, pp. 56–59) development of a brand personality scale for non-profit brands, the IBP scale is developed through a multi-method design including two qualitative studies (studies 1 and 2) and three quantitative studies (studies 3 to 5).

Studies 1 and 2 investigate if industrial brands have a personality and generate personality traits that are relevant to industrial brands. Study 1 uses in-depth interviews with practitioners from leading German B2B firms. Twenty-four companies are identified based on the typology of Backhaus, Plinke and Rese (2003); the selection of companies is validated by a faculty panel. For each of these companies, a marketing/sales executive is interviewed. Interviewees are asked to list at least three adjectives to describe the personality of their own company and that of two competing brands of their choice. Additional items are derived in study 2, which consists of a content analysis of the mission statements of the industrial firms listed on the German stock exchange ($N = 18$). Overall, studies 1 and 2 result in 78 items, of which 72 are new and 6 overlap with Aaker's brand personality scale.

Studies 3 to 5 examine quantitatively the dimensionality of the IBP scale. Study 3 reduces the set of IBP items. Each respondent is asked to evaluate two out of four brands on the 72 new personality traits using a 6-point scale (1 = "not at all descriptive", 6 = "very descriptive"). The four brands are selected in line with Backhaus, Plinke and Rese's (2003) industrial company systematization; this selection is validated by academic experts. Mean computation allows the researchers to retain 31 new personality traits (only those with a mean > 4.0).

Study 4 identifies the structure of the IBP scale. A survey is conducted using the same four brands used in the previous study. Each participant rates two randomly assigned brands on 73 personality traits (the 31 new items plus the 42 items from Aaker's scale). Exploratory factor analysis (EFA) reveals a three-factor solution explaining 67% of the total variance. Thirty-nine items are retained, based on their loadings (> 0.55) and cross-loadings (< 0.40). Another EFA within each factor allows the researchers to identify the scale facets. It follows a comparison of the mean scores for the four industrial brands on the different IBP dimensions; means are found significantly different from one another ($p < 0.001$). Similarly, a MANOVA with the three IBP dimensions as dependent variables tests if the means of these variables differ between members of different functional areas, that is, management (19.4% of responses) and production (16.9% of responses); significant differences are found between the functional areas with respect to two IBP dimensions (*sensation* and *credibility*, $ps < 0.05$).

Study 5 confirms the structure of the IBP scale using new samples of respondents and brands. The selection of brands is guided by Backhaus, Plinke and Rese's (2003) industrial company systematization and is again validated by an expert panel. A confirmatory factor analysis shows a good fit of the three-factor model to the data ($\chi^2 = 1620.5$; $df = 695$; AGFI = 0.92; GFI = 0.93; RMSEA = 0.039).

Additional EFAs with sub-samples (i.e., men, women, younger and older participants) further support the three-factor solution.

Samples

Study 1 is based on in-depth interviews with 24 German practitioners. Study 2 involves two coders. In study 3, 300 practitioners are identified based on the German federation of employers database, and they are invited to participate in an online survey; 117 of them complete the survey (response rate = 38%). In study 4, 513 alumni from two German universities are invited to participate in an online survey; 138 of them complete the survey (response rate = 26.9%). In study 5, 700 practitioners are identified through XING, a professional social network site, and are invited to participate in an online survey; 248 submit the survey; incomplete responses are dropped, leaving 213 questionnaires (response rate = 35.4%).

Reliability and validity

The reliability of the IBP scale is checked in study 4. Coefficients alpha are equal to 0.95 (*performance*), 0.91 (*sensation*) and 0.88 (*credibility*). All personality traits have item-to-total correlations > 0.51. The construct reliability is also checked in study 5. Composite reliabilities are equal to 0.95 (*performance*), 0.95 (*sensation*) and 0.88 (*credibility*). All standardized item estimates exceed 0.50. Evidence of discriminant validity is provided in study 5. The average variance extracted for the three factors (respectively, 0.48 for *performance*, 0.59 for *sensation* and 0.46 for *credibility*) exceeds the square of the correlations between factors (0.008 between *performance* and *sensation*, 0.33 between *performance* and *credibility* and 0.09 between *sensation* and *credibility*).

Managerial applications

The IBP scale represents a positioning tool which takes into account the peculiarities of the B2B sector. Industrial marketers should therefore use this tool instead of Aaker's personality scale to deal with the personality of their industrial brand. Specifically, the IBP scale can be used to differentiate an industrial brand along the dimensions of *performance, sensation* and *credibility*. Industrial marketers could use the scale to assess actual versus desired personality associations and orient their marketing communication based on this assessment. They could also use the scale to track their competitors' IBP to identify unoccupied positions within these dimensions; if matched with clients' desired associations, these positions should be carefully examined. When developing the personality of their brand, industrial marketers should consider the multi-personal structure of the buying centres as perceptions of IBP vary across members. Marketers should be able to develop a unique and clear brand personality for their industrial brand that appeals to all parties involved.

Brand personality 77

3.11 Baromètre de la personnalité de la marque/Brand personality barometer (Ambroise & Valette-Florence, 2010a, 2010b)

Definition of construct

Ambroise and Valette-Florence (2010a, 2010b) embrace the definition of brand personality given by Ferrandi and Valette-Florence (2002; see this chapter, pp. 53–56), according to whom brand personality is the set of human personality traits that are associated with brands. This definition is favoured over Aaker's (1997; see this chapter, pp. 44–48), which is found too vague, as it includes traits which are not relevant to personality such as cognitive aspects of behaviour, gender, age and social class connections. Ambroise and Valette-Florence conceptualize brand personality as consisting of five dimensions, that is, *introversion, agreeableness, conscientiousness, sophistication* and *disingenuousness*.

Scale description

The brand personality barometer developed by Ambroise and Valette-Florence includes five dimensions, nine facets and 23 items. The *introversion* and *conscientiousness* dimensions include one facet each (two items the former, three items the latter). The *agreeableness* dimension includes the facets "congeniality" (three items), "seduction" (two items) and "creativity" (three items). The *sophistication* dimension includes the facets "originality" (two items) and "preciousness" (two items). The *disingenuousness* dimension includes the facets "deceitfulness" (three items) and "dominance" (three items). Items are evaluated on 6-point Likert scales. Items can be averaged either within each facet to obtain a facet score or within each dimension to obtain a dimension score. The barometer is originally developed in French (Ambroise and Valette-Florence 2010a), but an English version is also provided (Ambroise and Valette-Florence 2010b).

TABLE 3.11 *Baromètre de la personnalité de la marque*/Brand personality barometer

Scale dimension French/English	Scale facet French/English	Scale item French/English
Introversion/Introversion	*Introversion*/Introversion	• *Réservée*/Reserved • *Timide*/Shy
Caractère agréable/Agreeableness	*Convivialité*/Congeniality	• *Attachante*/Endearing • *Plaisante*/Pleasant • *Sympathique*/Friendly
	Séduction/Seduction	• *Charmeuse*/Charming • *Séductrice*/Seductive
	Créativité/Creativity	• *Astucieuse*/Resourceful • *Créative*/Creative • *Imaginative*/Imaginative

(*Continued*)

TABLE 3.11 (Continued)

Scale dimension French/English	Scale facet French/English	Scale item French/English
Caractère consciencieux/ Conscientiousness	Consciencieux/ Conscientiousness	• Organisée/Organized • Rigoureuse/Meticulous • Sérieuse/Serious
Sophistication/Sophistication	Originalité/Originality	• Branchée/Trendy • Moderne/Modern
	Préciosité/Preciousness	• Classe/Classy • Qui a du style/Stylish
Caractère fallacieux/ Disingenuousness	Trompeur/Deceitfulness	• Hypocrite/Hypocritical • Menteuse/Lying • Trompeuse/Deceitful
	Ascendant/Dominance	• Arriviste/Parvenu • Arrogante/Arrogant • Prétentieuse/Pretentious

Scale development

To develop their brand personality barometer, Ambroise and Valette-Florence follow a three-stage approach, as recommended by Peabody (1987), and complement it with five studies.

The first stage results in the set of brand personality items. Two interviews with consumers and one interview with brand experts are made. Respondents are asked to generate brand personality items and to specify the semantic content of each item through the use of the nominal group technique. They are also asked to judge the applicability of brand personality items derived from the literature to describe brands. The resulting list of items is then assessed by independent judges. Sixty-six items are produced at the end of this stage.

The second stage examines the composition of brand personality. A content analysis of the interviews collected in the previous step is conducted through the Alceste textual data analysis software. The analysis is conducted for the three interviews both separately and jointly. Results show the presence of three to six principal lexical classes, that is, five classes using experts' interview, three and six classes using consumers' interviews and four using the interviews jointly. Results also show the presence of 11 to 14 facets, that is, 13 facets using experts' interview, 11 and 13 facets using consumers' interviews and 14 facets using the interviews jointly. Overall, the analysis shows similarities across the different interviews.

The third stage is based on several consumer datasets, which are collected with respect to 11 brands. A series of exploratory and confirmatory factor analyses is used to reduce the set of items to 23 and to identify the structure of brand personality as consisting of nine first-order and five second-order factors. In the context of confirmatory factor analyses, overall fit indexes are analysed (RMSEA = 0.081; γ = 0.904; adjusted γ = 0.861). A structural equation model using PLS software is also tested (absolute GoF = 0.571, relative GoF = 0.898, external model GoF = 0.998, internal model GoF = 0.900). Reliability and internal validity tests are conducted.

Five complementary studies are conducted in order to ensure the ecological validity of the scale using a comprehensive dataset of 39 brands from 14 product categories.

Samples

Stage 1 uses 22 consumers, a group of experts and three judges. Stage 3 includes different samples of consumers (students and non-students). In the five complementary studies, 4,815 consumers are involved. All studies are conducted in France.

Reliability and validity

The reliability and validity of the brand personality barometer are tested in the third stage of the scale-development process. Reliability is evaluated through Jöreskog's rho, whereas the heuristic proposed by Fornell and Larcker (1981) is used to test the scale's internal validity and internal discriminant validity.

The scale's ecological validity is tested in five complementary studies with 39 brands from 14 product categories. Using 10 of these categories (for which there are at least two brands per category), the invariance of the scale across product categories is tested. Ten multi-group analyses are performed contrasting, each time, one product category versus all the others (risk threshold = 5%). Results show that only 8 items over 23 vary across the 10 categories; when the factor loading varies, they still have high values greater than 0.609, with the exception of one item in one category.

Another multi-group analysis of variance is conducted at the latent level. Results show that the cumulative influence of the product category on the dimensions of brand personality is weak for the dimensions of *introversion* ($\Sigma R^2 = 8.4\%$), *conscientiousness* ($\Sigma R^2 = 8.6\%$) and *disingenuousness* ($\Sigma R^2 = 15\%$). It is higher but still acceptable for the other two dimensions ($\Sigma R^2 \approx 20\%$).

Complementary analyses of variance are performed in order to dissociate the effect of product categories from that of the brand. Results show a more significant effect for the brand alone compared to the effect previously observed for product categories alone. The dimensions of *sophistication* ($R^2 = 29\%$), *agreeableness* ($R^2 = 29.4\%$) and *disingenuousness* ($R^2 = 25.2\%$) contribute the most to contrasts among brands, followed by *introversion* ($R^2 = 13\%$) and *conscientiousness* ($R^2 = 16.8\%$) to a lesser degree.

Managerial applications

The brand personality barometer developed by Ambroise and Valette-Florence is specific for the French context. It represents a tool that managers can use to better understand how consumers view the personality of their brand. By averaging items within either each of the five dimensions or the nine facets, managers could use the barometer to see how their brand performs on each of these dimensions/facets and compare it with other brands. These other brands can be competitors' brands or other brands in the company's portfolio. In this sense, the application of the barometer

3.12 Brand personality appeal (Freling, Crosno & Henard, 2011)

Definition of construct

Freling, Crosno and Henard (2011, p. 393) define brand personality appeal (BPA) as "a brand's ability to appeal to consumers through the combination of human characteristics associated with it". BPA consists of three interrelated dimensions: *favourability, originality* and *clarity*. The *favourability* dimension refers to the degree to which consumers consider the personality of a given brand in positive terms. The *originality* dimension refers to the degree to which consumers consider the personality of a given brand to be novel and distinct from the personality of other brands in the same product category. The *clarity* dimension refers to the degree to which consumers consider the personality of a given brand to be apparent and recognizable.

Scale description

The BPA scale is composed of the three dimensions of *favourability, originality* and *clarity* for a total of 16 items, of which 5 are reverse coded. The *favourability* dimension includes 7 items, three of which are reverse coded. The *originality* dimension includes 4 items. The *clarity* dimension includes 5 items, two of which are reverse coded. All items are measured on 7-point semantic differential scales. Items can be summed and averaged within each dimension to form dimension scores (i.e., *favourability* score).

TABLE 3.12 Brand personality appeal scale

Scale dimension	Scale item
Favourability	• Satisfactory/Unsatisfactory*
	• Unpleasant/Pleasant
	• Attractive/Unattractive*
	• Positive/Negative*
	• Bad/Good
	• Poor/Excellent
	• Undesirable/Desirable
Originality	• Common/Distinctive
	• Ordinary/Novel
	• Predictable/Surprising
	• Routine/Fresh

(Continued)

TABLE 3.12 (Continued)

Scale dimension	Scale item
Clarity	• Unapparent/Apparent • Distinct/Indistinct* • Obvious/Not Obvious* • Vague/Well-defined • Unclear/Clear

Note: *indicates the item is reverse coded.

Scale development

The scale-development process for the BPA scale consists of a preliminary study and five subsequent studies.

The preliminary study is used to generate items and check their content validity. A set of items is generated through the use of focus groups, in-depth interviews and a literature review. In the focus group, participants are asked to use Aaker's scale (1997; see this chapter, pp. 44–48) to describe their preferred brands and then to discuss the importance of each brand's personality, the difference from other similar brands and the thoughts, feelings and behaviours that it elicits. A similar discussion guide and procedure is used in the interviews. The resulting set of items is assessed using three different panels of expert judges. An initial set of 40 items representing each of the three dimensions of the BPA scale is generated at the end of this preliminary study.

Study 1 purifies the initial set of items. Respondents are asked to use the 40 BPA items to evaluate five brands. These brands are identified through a pre-test using Aaker's (1997) brand personality scale, Zaichkowsky's (1994) personal involvement inventory and Kent and Allen's (1994) brand familiarity scale: they are well known and represent a spectrum of brand personalities and product categories. A principal factor analysis using oblimin rotation is conducted on the aggregate data, and the inter-item correlation for each factor is checked. Items are dropped if their factor loading is < 0.40, their corrected item-to-total subscale correlations is < 0.30, their inter-item correlation is < 0.20 and if they do not have a statistically higher correlation with the hypothesized dimension. The analysis results in a set of 18 BPA items.

Study 2 involves a content validity assessment of the 18-item scale using a panel of experts. Two items are removed, leaving the BPA scale with 16 items: 7 for *favourability*, 4 items for *originality* and 5 items for *clarity*.

In study 3, the latent structure and dimensionality of the scale are assessed, as well as its reliability and validity. Respondents are asked to evaluate one brand using the 16 BPA items as well as three single-item measures corresponding to the three BPA dimensions and four items on purchase intentions (Juster, 1966; Kalwani & Silk, 1982); these measures are included for validity purposes. Confirmatory factor analysis identifies the best model representing the data, that is, the three-factor correlated model ($\chi^2(101)$ = 212.55, GFI = 0.88, CFI = 0.98, TLI = 0.98 and RMSEA = 0.075). The other models that are estimated include the null model, one-factor model, two-factor uncorrelated model, two-factor correlated

82 Brand personality

model and three-factor uncorrelated model. Tests of internal reliability, convergent validity and discriminant validity are also conducted.

Study 4 checks the test-retest reliability of the BPA scale. To accomplish this, a sample of students is asked to evaluate the same brand used in study 3 using the BPA scale on two different occasions separated by about two months.

Finally, study 5 assesses the concurrent validity of the scale. The study examines the ability of the BPA scale to distinguish between respondents for which differences in the scale dimensions are expected to occur. Respondents are divided into two groups based on their actual car ownership (Ford or Chevrolet), and each group is asked to evaluate both brands using scales on BPA, brand personality (Aaker, 1997) and purchase intention.

Samples

The preliminary study uses 10 focus groups, each with 8 to 10 participants (MBA students); in-depth interviews with a convenience sample of 25 adult respondents; and three panels of 78 experts. Study 1 is based on a convenience sample of 53 adult respondents in the pre-test and 241 adult respondents in the study. Study 2 is conducted via a panel with five expert judges. Study 3 uses 196 adult respondents. Study 4 uses 157 undergraduate marketing students. Study 5 uses 171 adult respondents who own a Ford ($N = 87$) or Chevrolet ($N = 84$) vehicle and whose contact details are provided by a local automobile repair shop where these respondents had their vehicle serviced in the preceding six months; the initial mailing was sent to 300 customers (50% Ford, 50% Chevrolet).

Reliability and validity

Reliability and validity checks are reported at different stages of the scale-development process.

The internal scale reliability is first checked in study 2. Only items with an item-to-total correlation ≥ 0.50 on their respective subscale and a Cronbach's alpha level and Guttman's split-half reliability estimate > 0.90 for each of the five brands are retained. The internal scale reliability using the 16-item BPA scale is assessed in study 3. Estimates of internal consistency reliability for each dimension are: $\alpha = 0.948$ and $r_g = 0.936$ (*favourability*), $\alpha = 0.788$ and $r_g = 0.757$ (*originality*) and $\alpha = 0.866$ and $r_g = 0.866$ (*clarity*). Construct reliability estimates are equal to 0.875 (*favourability*), 0.796 (*originality*) and 0.833 (*clarity*). Internal consistency reliabilities are checked again in study 5. The estimates for each dimension are $\alpha = 0.933$ and $r_g = 0.925$ (*favourability*), $\alpha = 0.912$ and $r_g = 0.896$ (*originality*) and $\alpha = 0.925$ and $r_g = 0.903$ (*clarity*).

Finally, a test-retest reliability check is reported in study 4. The test-retest correlation coefficient is equal to 0.852 (*favourability*), 0.694 (*originality*) and 0.740 (*clarity*) and is significant at $p < 0.05$.

Validity is checked by assessing content validity, convergent validity, discriminant validity and concurrent validity. Content validity is checked in the preliminary study through the use of expert judges following a three-stage process. First, the judges are asked to examine the degree to which each pair of items represents opposites of the same continuum. Second, they are asked to assign each item to one of the three dimensions. Third, the judges are asked to rate the degree to which each item is representative of the corresponding dimension using a three-point scale ("clearly representative", "somewhat representative" and "not representative"). This process results in the rewording of some items and elimination of some others. Content validity is checked again in study 2. Experts are asked to indicate whether each item is "essential", "useful but not essential" or "not necessary" to the measurement of the construct of reference. The content validity ratio (CVR) and content validity index (CVI) are computed based on the responses obtained. Two items (with CVR = 0.20) are eliminated.

Evidence of convergent validity is provided in study 3. Pairwise correlations between the three BPA dimensions and the three single-item measures on the three BPA dimensions are computed. All correlations are significant ($p < 0.05$) and equal to, respectively, 0.643 (*favourability*), 0.507 (*originality*) and 0.652 (*clarity*).

Evidence of the discriminant validity of the BPA scale is provided in study 3 as well with respect to purchase intentions. The average correlation between the three BPA dimensions and purchase intentions is equal to 0.521 ($p \leq 0.05$). The AVE for *favourability* (0.729), *originality* (0.501) and *clarity* (0.582) exceed the square of their correlations with purchase intentions. The AVE for purchase intention (0.881) exceed the square of its correlations with the three factors.

Concurrent validity is tested in study 5. The BPA scale proves to be able to distinguish between two different groups of respondents, each associated with a different (competing) brand. Ford owners rate Ford trucks significantly higher on *favourability* ($M = 6.32$, $SD = 0.564$), *originality* ($M = 6.24$, $SD = 0.523$) and *clarity* ($M = 6.37$, $SD = 0.509$) than do Chevrolet owners ($M_{favourability} = 3.67$, $SD = 0.617$, $t(169) = 17.33$, $p \leq 0.05$; $M_{originality} = 3.58$, $SD = 0.561$, $t(169) = 16.12$, $p \leq 0.05$; $M_{clarity} = 3.61$, $SD = 0.617$; $t(169) = 18.01$, $p \leq 0.05$). Similarly, Chevrolet owners rated Chevrolet trucks significantly higher on *favourability* ($M = 6.21$, $SD = 0.591$), *originality* ($M = 6.29$, $SD = 0.614$) and *clarity* ($M = 6.33$, $SD = 0.578$) than did Ford owners ($M_{favourability} = 3.59$, $SD = 0.628$, $t(169) = 18.21$, $p \leq 0.05$; $M_{originality} = 3.53$, $SD = 0.601$, $t(169) = 18.78$, $p \leq 0.05$; $M_{clarity} = 3.71$, $SD = 0.552$; $t(169) = 16.41$, $p \leq 0.05$).

Managerial applications

The BPA scale can be applied by managers for different reasons. First, it can help managers plan advertising and promotional campaigns. Brands with stronger brand personality appeal should linger in consumers' minds longer than those for which no communication is implemented. Second, the BPA scale can help managers define positioning and repositioning strategies for their brands relative to competitors. Third, the BPA scale complements the set of tools that managers can use to study the particular personality of their brands. By providing a quantitative assessment of the three BPA dimensions, this tool could be used together with

84 Brand personality

more qualitative techniques in order to gain a broader and deeper understanding of the effects of marketing strategies on the personality of the brand.

3.13 Brand masculine patterns (Azar, 2013)

Definition of construct

Azar (2013) focuses on one specific component of brand personality, that is, brand masculinity. He defines brand masculinity as "the set of masculine human personality traits associated with masculinity applicable and relevant to brands" (p. 503). Contrary to previous research, which measures masculinity with one single item (Aaker, 1997; see this chapter, pp. 44–48) or treats it as a unidimensional construct (Grohmann, 2009; see this chapter, pp. 62–66), Azar views brand masculinity as a multi-dimensional construct. The researcher identifies two correlated dimensions: the *male chauvinism* dimension, which reflects the notions of force, need for power and need for control; and the *heroic* dimension, which deals with the notion of courage, adventure and high-risk behaviours.

Scale description

The brand masculine dimensions (BMD) scale is formed by two dimensions, *male chauvinism* and *heroic*, which include three and two items respectively. To rate items, respondents are provided with 7-point agree/disagree Likert-type scales.

TABLE 3.13 Brand masculinity dimensions scale

Scale dimension	Scale item
Male chauvinism	• Hard • Macho • Rough
Heroic	• Courageous • Adventurous

Scale development

The BMD scale is developed through a four-step process in accordance with Churchill (1979) and Osgood et al. (1957).

Step 1 generates a pool of items on brand masculinity. To that end, the researcher uses an extensive literature review on gender/brand personality as well as qualitative research. Semi-structured interviews and a paper-and-pencil exercise are conducted, whereby respondents are asked to separately list the personality traits they use to describe brands for men and for women. This results in the generation of 103 items. A check with experts examining the items' face validity reduces the items to 29. A study is then conducted to further reduce the items. Respondents are asked to evaluate the 29 items in terms of their representation of a brand for man and a brand for a woman. Paired sample *t*-tests are conducted on the overall sample as well as for men and women separately. Fourteen items considered masculine by the overall sample, men and women, are retained.

Step 2 explores the dimensionality of brand masculinity. A survey is conducted, and respondents are asked to evaluate four brands on the 14 items using a 7-point Likert-type scale. Sixteen brands in total, covering both symbolic and utilitarian aspects, are used. To identify these brands, a first set is derived from BrandZ and is then assessed by experts and students in terms of brand familiarity and variety of masculinity. Exploratory factor analysis (EFA), performed using principal component analysis with oblique rotation, reveals the presence of two dimensions of brand masculinity (eigenvalues > 1, total variance explained = 55.42% and 14.48%). Six items with the highest loadings are retained.

Step 3 confirms the dimensionality of the BMD scale and identifies the final pool of items. A new survey is conducted using 12 brands deriving from the pre-test. Each respondent is asked to evaluate three brands on the six brand masculinity items. EFA supports the two-factor solution previously identified. A first confirmatory factor analysis (CFA) is run (χ^2/df = 4.654, NFI = 0.961, TLI = 0.942, CFI = 0.969, GFI = 0.972, AGFI = 0.928, SRMR = 0.043 and RMSEA = 0.082). After removing one item, a new CFA is run and a better fit obtained (χ^2/df = 3.153, NFI = 0.983, TLI = 0.971, CFI = 0.988, GFI = 0.989, AGFI = 0.958, SRMR = 0.026 and RMSEA = 0.069). Reliability and validity tests are conducted.

Step 4 demonstrates the generalizability of the BDM scale across product categories associated with different genders and the applicability of the scale to product categories that are not gender specific. A pre-test is conducted to identify the genders of product categories. Respondents are asked to evaluate different product categories using Allison, Golden and Mullet's (1980) scale. After performing *t*-tests and classifying categories based on median splits, four genders of product categories are identified: masculine, feminine, androgynous and undifferentiated. In the study, 33 well known brands representing these categories are used; brands are divided into four groups of nine brands each, with one brand (Chanel) included in all groups. Each respondent is asked to evaluate nine brands on the BMD scale. Tests of structural and metric invariance are conducted.

Data collected in steps 3 and 4 are also used to identify types of brand masculinity. Hierarchical and non-hierarchical cluster analyses reveal four clusters with different scores on the BMD: hegemonic masculinity (low on *heroism*, high on *male chauvinism*), emerging masculinity (high on both BMD), chivalrous masculinity (low on *male chauvinism*, high on *heroism*) and subaltern masculinity (low on both BMD).

Samples

Step 1 is conducted using multiple samples, including 18 respondents for the semi-structured interviews, 50 respondents in the paper-and-pen exercise, four experts to assess the scale's content validity and 157 respondents in the study. These

157 respondents are representative of the national population in terms of age, gender and level of education. Step 2 involves 140 undergraduate students. Step 3 involves 155 undergraduate students. Step 4 uses a sample of 138 undergraduate students in the pre-test and a sample of 140 undergraduate students in the survey. All studies are conducted in France.

Reliability and validity

Step 1 includes content and face validity tests of the initial pool of items. These tests, conducted through experts and consumers, help reduce the number of items to use in the following part.

The reliability of the BMD scale is checked in step 2. The *male chauvinism* dimension reports a Cronbach's alpha of 0.845, and the *heroic* dimension reports an alpha of 0.720.

The scale's reliability and internal validity are checked in step 3. The *male chauvinism* dimension reports an alpha of 0.821 and a Jöreskog's rho of 0.826, whereas the *heroic* dimension reports an alpha of 0.681 and a Jöreskog's rho of .683. The two dimensions are correlated to one another ($r = 0.522$, $p < 0.0001$). A second-order exploratory analysis shows that the two dimensions load on a single factor, which accounts for 71.09% of total variance; together they report an alpha of 0.720 and a Jöreskog's rho of 0.735.

Evidence of convergent and discriminant validities is provided in step 3. The average variance extracted (AVE) for each dimension and for the total BDM is greater than 0.50: specifically, it is equal to 0.613 for the *male chauvinism* dimension, to 0.520 for the *heroic* dimension and to 0.581 for the total BDM. The AVE for each dimension is also greater than the square of the correlation between the two constructs (0.337).

Step 3 also reports the structural and metric invariance of the scale. For the former, a multi-group analysis using a maximum likelihood fitting process is conducted for the aggregate sample and for each of the four product categories' gender datasets. The fit of the model across product categories' gender is as follows: $\chi^2/df =$ 1.579; NFI = 0.984, TLI = 0.997, CFI = 0.994, GFI = 0.991, AGFI = 0.968, SRMR = 0.0174 and RMSEA = 0.022, with all loadings positive and significant. Good fit indexes are obtained for thee datasets, fairly good indexes are obtained for one (androgynous product category, RMSEA = 0.089); all loadings are positive and significant. For metric invariance, an unconstrained model of the BMD scale is compared with four models presenting increasing constraints on the number of invariant parameters (measurement weights, structural weights, structural residuals and measurement residuals). Data analysis shows that structural factors and measurement weights are invariant across the four groups of product categories.

Managerial applications

The BDM scale represents a tool that managers can use to identify and develop masculine gender-based strategies. The BMD scale highlights the necessity of treating brand masculinity not as a single concept but in the light of the different meanings it can be associated with. The BMD scale can also offer managers guidance in masculine gender-based positioning and segmentation strategies, as it allows the distinction among four different types of brand masculinities: hegemonic, emerging, chivalrous and subaltern.

3.14 Academic focus

- The literature suggests that consumers choose, buy and use brands that match their personality (Aaker, 1999; Huang, Mitchell & Rosenaum-Elliot, 2012; Maehle & Shneor, 2010). A dissertation could therefore investigate the personality of a given brand in a given industry and the personality of the consumers who are part of the target market for that brand. How do the two personality profiles compare to each other? How should the brand personality be changed to better match that of their target consumers?
- One recent paper (Malär et al., 2011) shows that, on average, the congruency between brand personality and actual self has the greatest impact on consumers' emotional attachment to the brand compared to the congruency between brand personality and desired self. In a dissertation, one may verify the replicability of this finding into specific product categories, industries or market segments.
- Brand elements are of vital importance for building brands (Keller, 2012). It may be interesting to focus a dissertation on one specific brand element of a given brand. According to Keller (2012), brand elements may include names, URLs, logos and symbols, characters, slogans, jingles and packaging. How does a specific brand element contribute to the personality of the brand?
- A dissertation may want to compare the personality of a brand as the company would like it to be, with the personality of a brand as perceived by consumers. By taking the company perspective first, one could derive the personality that a company would like for its brand. To that purpose, one may want to use all brand's visible activities such as advertising, websites, endorsers and flagship stores and apply a strategic tool such as the brand identity prism (Kapferer, 2012). After that, by taking the consumer perspective, one may investigate the personality of that brand as perceived by consumers. How far are the two brand personalities from one another? If there is a significant mismatch, what could be the causes? What should be done by the brand to reduce such a distance?
- Place branding represents a recent application of brand personality theories (Pereira, Correia & Schutz, 2012). Considering the personality of either a city (Kaplan et al., 2010) or a tourism destination (Ekinci & Hosany, 2006), one may investigate the extent to which such personality contributes to consumers' willingness to explore a new place versus going back to places already visited.

88 Brand personality

3.15 Managerial focus

- **Why is it important to measure brand personality?**
  Brand personality measures allow managers to define consumers' brand perception using exclusively human personality traits. Brand personality can be useful to differentiate brands from competitors on specific personality traits, which is very interesting, as consumers tend to buy brands which are more in coherence with their own personalities (Aaker, 1997; Koebel & Ladwein, 1999). Therefore, managers can target consumers who are sensitive to the personality which is presented by the brand and reinforce the brand relationship with consumers. Therefore, if personality scales are useful to measure the efficiency of a campaign in reinforcing some specific traits of personality, they also become nowadays a strategic tool for consumer relationship management. Personality scales can be integrated in segmentation studies and offer the possibility to create a strong relationship with consumers who are in line with the brand personality.

- **Is your brand personality appealing to new targets?**
  Strong brands have managed to build brand personalities which are relevant and coherent and resonate with consumers. Nevertheless, when managers want to increase sales by attracting other targets, they must evaluate whether the brand personality is able to seduce these consumers and whether the strategy needed to reach this new target doesn't alter the brand personality which is appreciated by the current consumers. Brand personality scales can be used to evaluate the personality among different targets in order to understand which traits of personality can be reinforced in communication to attract new target consumers without risking confusing the loyal consumers.

- **Do you deliver brand personality consistently across all the brand's channels?**
  A brand's personality describes the way the brand expresses and represents itself. The personality of the brand may be impacted by the shopping environment and the experience that the consumer has with the brand. Managers need to check if the personality of their brands is consistent across all the brand's channels in order to avoid confusion in consumers' minds. Brand personality scales can help identify which traits should be enhanced in which channels and develop specific communication actions.

- **Does your global communication allow you to create the same personality across countries?**
  Even if your global marketing strategy has been defined in order to ensure that the brand has a consistent positioning around the world, a

single tone of voice used in a communication may change brand personality and fail in creating a relationship with the brand in some countries due to cultural perceptions. Marketers can use personality scales in order to measure the impact of communication on the brand personality and understand how the cultural context may change the perception of the message and the tone of the communication, resulting in modifying the perception of the brand personality.

- **Have you checked whether changing the colour of you brand logo will modify the personality of your brand?**
Colour is an important driver of brand personality, and when a colour becomes attached to a brand, it is difficult to change it (Labrecque & Milne, 2012). Before changing the colour of a logo or packaging, it is important to evaluate if the new colour will influence the brand personality. For example, the colour red may enhance the excitement trait of personality, whereas blue may increase the perceived competence and black the sophistication (Labrecque & Milne, 2012). The replacement by McDonald's of the red background with the green one in Europe provides a more environmentally friendly image and may enhance the sincerity trait of the brand personality.

References

Aaker, J. (1997). Dimensions of brand personality. *Journal of Marketing Research*, 34 (4), 347–356.
Aaker, J. (1999). The malleable self: the role of self-expression in persuasion. *Journal of Marketing Research*, 36 (1), 45–57.
Aaker, J. L., Benet-Martínez, V., & Garolera, J. (2001). Consumption symbols as carriers of culture: a study of Japanese and Spanish brand personality constructs. *Journal of Personality and Social Psychology*, 81 (3), 492–508.
Allison, N. K., Golden, L. L., & Mullet, G. M. (1980). Sex-typed product images: the effects of sex, sex role self-concept and measurement implications. *North America Advances in Consumer Research*, 7, 604–609.
Ambroise, L., & Valette-Florence, P. (2010a). Métaphore de la personnalité de la marque et stabilité inter-produits d'un baromètre spécifique. *Recherche et Applications en Marketing*, 25 (2), 3–29.
Ambroise, L., & Valette-Florence, P. (2010b). The brand personality metaphor and inter-product stability of a specific barometer. *Recherche et Applications en Marketing* (English Edition), 25 (2), 3–28.
Azar, S. L. (2013). Exploring brand masculine patterns: moving beyond monolithic masculinity. *Journal of Product & Brand Management*, 22 (7), 502–512.
Backhaus, K., Plinke, W., & Rese, M. (2003). *Marketing: an economic perspective*. Berlin: Münster.
Barak, B., & Stern, B. (1986). Sex-linked trait indexes among baby-boomers and pre-boomers: a research note. *Association for Consumer Research*, 13, 204–209.
Bem, S. L. (1974). The measurement of psychological androgyny. *Journal of Consulting and Clinical Psychology*, 42 (2), 155–162.

Bhat, S., & Reddy, S. K. (2001). The impact of parent brand attribute associations and affect on brand extension evaluation. *Journal of Business Research*, 53 (2), 111–122.

Chaudhuri, A., & Holbrook, M. B. (2001). The chain of effects from brand trust and brand affect to brand performance: the role of brand loyalty. *Journal of Marketing*, 65 (April), 81–93.

Churchill, G. A., Jr. (1979). A paradigm for developing better measures of marketing constructs. *Journal of Marketing Research*, 16 (1), 64–73.

Cronin, J. J., & Taylor, S. A. (1992). Measuring service quality: a reexamination and extension. *Journal of Marketing*, 56, 55–68.

Ekinci, Y., & Hosany, S. (2006). Destination personality: an application of brand personality to tourism destinations. *Journal of Travel Research*, 45 (2), 127–139.

Ferrandi, J.-M., & Valette-Florence, P. (2002). Premiers test et validation de la transposition d'une échelle de personnalité humaine aux marques. *Recherche et Applications en Marketing*, 17 (3), 21–40.

Fornell, C., & Larcker, D. F. (1981). Evaluating structural equations models with unobservable variables and measurement error. *Journal of Marketing Research*, 18 (1), 39–50.

Freling, T. H., Crosno, J. L., & Henard, D. H. (2011). Brand personality appeal: conceptualization and empirical validation. *Journal of the Academy of Marketing Science*, 39, 392–406.

Geuens, M., Weijters, B., & De Wulf, K. (2009). A new measure of brand personality. *International Journal of Research in Marketing*, 26 (2), 97–107.

Grohmann, B. (2009). Gender dimensions of brand personality. *Journal of Marketing Research*, 46 (1), 105–119.

Herbst, U., & Merz, M. A. (2011). The industrial brand personality scale: building strong business-to-business brands. *Industrial Marketing Management*, 40 (7), 1072–1081.

Huang, H., Mitchell, V., & Rosenaum-Elliott, R. (2012). Are consumer and brand personalities the same? *Psychology & Marketing*, 29 (5), 334–349.

Hui, C. H., & Triandis, H. C. (1985). Measurement in cross-cultural psychology: a review and comparison of strategies. *Journal of Cross-Cultural Psychology*, 16 (2), 131–152.

Juster, F. T. (1966). Consumer buying intentions and purchase probability: an experiment in survey design. *Journal of the American Statistical Association*, 61, 658–696.

Kalwani, M. U., & Silk, A. J. (1982). On the reliability and predictive validity or purchase intention measures. *Marketing Science*, 1, 243–286.

Kapferer, J.-N. (2012). *The new strategic brand management: advanced insights and strategic thinking (New strategic brand management: Creating and sustaining brand equity)* (5th ed.). London: Kogan Page.

Kaplan, M. D., Yurt, O., Guneri, B., & Kurtulus, K. (2010). Branding places: applying brand personality concept to cities. *European Journal of Marketing*, 44 (9/10), 1286–1304.

Keller, K. L. (1993). Conceptualizing, measuring, and managing customer-based brand equity. *Journal of Marketing Research*, 29, 1–22.

Keller, K. L. (1998). *Strategic brand management: building, measuring, and managing brand equity*. Upper Saddle River, NJ: Prentice Hall.

Keller, K. L. (2012). *Strategic brand management* (4th ed.). Harlow: Pearson.

Kent, R. J., & Allen, C. T. (1994). Competitive interference effects in consumer memory for advertising: the role of brand familiarity. *Journal of Marketing*, 58 (3), 97–105.

Kim, C. K., Han, D., & Park, S.-B. (2001). The effect of brand personality and brand identification on brand loyalty: Applying the theory of social identification. *Japanese Psychological Research*, 43 (4), 195–206.

Koebel, M.-N., & Ladwein, R. (1999). L'échelle de personnalité de la marque de Jennifer Aaker: adaptation au contexte français. *Décisions Marketing*, 16 (January–April), 81–88.

Labrecque, L. I., & Milne, G. R. (2012). Exciting red and competent blue: the importance of color in marketing, *Journal of the Academy of Marketing Science*, 40 (5), 711–727.

Lindeman, M., & Verkasalo, M. (2005). Measuring values with the short Schwartz's value survey. *Journal of Personality Assessment*, 85 (2), 170–178.

Maehle, N., & Shneor, R. (2010). On congruence between brand and human personalities. *Journal of Product & Brand Management*, 19 (1), 44–45.

Malär, L., Krohmer, H., Hoyer, W. D., & Nyffenegger, B. (2011). Emotional brand attachment and brand personality: the relative importance of the actual and the ideal self. *Journal of Marketing*, 75 (4), 35–52.

Marchetti, R., & Usunier, J.-C. (1990). Les problèmes de l'étude de marché dans un contexte interculturel. *Revue Française de Marketing*, 130, 5–17.

Ong, B. S., & Horbunluekit, S. (1997). The impact of a Thai cultural show on Thailand's destination image. *American Business Review*, 15 (2), 97–103.

Osgood, C. E., Suci, G. J., & Tannenbaum, P. H. (1957). *The measurement of meaning*. Chicago: University of Illinois Press.

Peabody, D. (1987). Selecting representative trait adjectives. *Journal of Personality and Social Psychology*, 52 (1), 59–71.

Pereira, R.L.G., Correia, A.L., & Schutz, R.L.A. (2012). Destination branding: a critical overview. *Journal of Quality Assurance in Hospitality & Tourism*, 13 (2), 81–102.

Romaniuk, J., & Ehrenberg, A.S.C. (2012). Do brands lack personality? *Marketing Theory*, 12 (3), 333–339.

Rossiter, J. R. (2002). The C-OAR-SE procedure for scale development in marketing. *International Journal of Research in Marketing*, 19 (4), 305–335.

Russell, J. A. (1980). A circumplex model of affect. *Journal of Personality and Social Psychology*, 39 (6), 1161–1178.

Saucier, G. (1994). Mini-markers: a brief version of Goldberg's unipolar big-five markers. *Journal of Personality Assessment*, 63 (3), 506–516.

Sirgy, M. J., Grewal, D., Mangleburg, T. F., Park, J.-O., Chon, K.-S., & Claiborne, C. B. (1997). Assessing the predictive validity of two methods of measuring self-image congruence. *Journal of the Academy of Marketing Science*, 25 (3), 229–241.

Spence, J. T., Helmreich, R., & Stapp, J. (1974). The personal attributes questionnaire: a measure of sex role stereotypes and masculinity-femininity. *JSAS Catalog of Selected Documents in Psychology*, Vol. 4. New York, NY: Johnson Associates, 43–44.

Venable, B. T., Rose, G. M., Bush, V. D., & Gilbert, F. W. (2005). The role of brand personality in charitable giving: an assessment and validation. *Journal of the Academy of Marketing Science*, 33 (3), 295–312.

Zaichkowsky, J. L. (1994). The personal involvement inventory: reduction, revision, and application to advertising. *Journal of Advertising*, 23 (4), 59–70.

4
BRAND AUTHENTICITY

4.1 Overview

Authenticity in the consumption context represents an important topic in the marketing literature (Beverland & Farrelly, 2010; Brown, Kozinets & Sherry, 2003; Grayson & Martinec, 2004; Leigh, Peters & Shelton, 2006) and an emergent trend in branding (Beverland, 2005; Gilmore & Pine, 2007). Brands can be seen as cues that deliver experiences with varying levels of authenticity. Triggering consumers' perceptions of authenticity through brands seems to be relevant nowadays, as there is evidence that consumers favour authentic over inauthentic brands and that brand authenticity is positively related to important outcomes such as, for example, brand trust, brand credibility, brand attitudes and purchase intention (Ilicic & Webster, 2014; Napoli et al., 2014).

This chapter includes four scales that propose different approaches to brand authenticity. Bruhn, Schoenmüller, Schäfer and Heinrich (2012)'s brand authenticity scale and Napoli, Dickinson, Beverland and Farrelly (2014)'s consumer-based brand authenticity scale view the phenomenon of brand authenticity from a brand image/brand associations perspective. Their scales allow researchers to get a better understanding of consumers' overall perceptions of the level of authenticity that is attached to brands. These two scales differ from one another because of the specific dimensions that are proposed as being part of the brand authenticity concept.

Moreover, in the light of the importance of consumer–brand relationships in the field of brand management (cf. Chapter 10), as well as emotions and bonds comprised in these relationships (cf. Chapters 8–9), Ilicic and Webster (2014) look at brand authenticity from the lenses of consumer–brand relationships. Their consumer–brand relational authenticity scale aims to capture consumers' perceptions of a brand's authenticity in the context of the relationships between consumers and brands.

Finally, Spiggle, Nguyen and Caravella (2012) consider brand authenticity in the context of brand extensions. Their brand extension authenticity scale captures the degree of legitimacy and cultural connectedness that consumers perceive between a brand extension and its parent brand. They argue that a more comprehensive understanding of how consumers evaluate brand extensions can be achieved through their scale.

4.2 Brand authenticity (Bruhn, Schoenmüller, Schäfer & Heinrich, 2012)

Definition of construct

The notion of brand authenticity is developed by the researchers with regard to three aspects. First, brand authenticity deals with authenticity of market offerings (objects and services) in contrast to the authenticity of human beings. Second, brand authenticity is based on the evaluations of individuals rather than inherent attributes of the brand. Third, brand authenticity corresponds to a variety of attributes of the brand. Brand authenticity includes four dimensions: *continuity*, based on which the brand is stable and/or continuous over time; *originality*, according to which the brand is creative, original and/or innovative; *reliability*, which refers to the brand keeping its promises and/or being reliable; and *naturalness*, for which the brand is genuine and/or natural.

Scale description

The scale includes four dimensions for a total of 15 items: the dimensions *continuity*, *originality* and *reliability* contain four items each, whereas the dimension *naturalness* contains three items. Items are measured using 7-point Likert scale anchored at 1 = "strongly disagree" and 7 = "strongly agree". Items within each dimension can be summated to form an overall dimension score (e.g., *continuity* score).

TABLE 4.1 Brand authenticity scale

Scale dimension	Scale item
Continuity	• I think (brand X) is consistent over time
	• I think the brand (brand X) stays true to itself
	• (Brand X) offers continuity
	• The brand (brand X) has a clear concept that it pursues
Originality	• The brand (brand X) is different from all other brands
	• (Brand X) stands out from other brands
	• I think the brand (brand X) is unique
	• The brand (brand X) clearly distinguishes itself from other brands

(Continued)

TABLE 4.1 (Continued)

Scale dimension	Scale item
Reliability	• My experience of the brand (brand X) has shown me that it keeps its promises • The brand (brand X) delivers what it promises • (Brand X)'s promises are credible • The brand (brand X) makes reliable promises
Naturalness	• The brand (brand X) does not seem artificial • The brand (brand X) makes a genuine impression • The brand (brand X) gives the impression of being natural

Scale development

The brand authenticity scale is developed through a five-study process.

Study 1 assesses consumers' notion of brand authenticity. Respondents are asked to think of a highly authentic brand and to write down the reasons they perceive it this way; the task is repeated with hardly authentic or totally inauthentic brands. The descriptions provided by respondents are analysed and grouped in four categories (continuity, originality, reliability and naturalness) by three coders.

Study 2 generates and selects the items for the brand authenticity scale. An initial set of items is generated through a literature review and is assessed in a survey, where respondents are asked to indicate the extent to which each item is descriptive of brand authenticity on a 7-point Likert scale (1 = "not at all", 7 = "very much"). Respondents are also asked to provide additional associations of brand authenticity that are missing from the list. The resulting set of 67 items is administered to a new sample of respondents, who are asked to evaluate an authentic brand of their choice on those items using a 7-point Likert scale (1 = "describes poorly", 7 = "describes very well"). Items that are not rated by 10% of respondents or that present a mean rating < 4.0 are dropped. A set of 24 items is retained. Another sample of respondents completes a comparative rating task for the assessment of substantive validity.

Study 3 further reduces the set of items and establishes the dimensionality of the scale. In a survey, respondents are asked to name one authentic brand within two product categories (durables and soft drinks) frequently mentioned in previous studies. In the main study, respondents are asked to evaluate one of the brands identified on the 24 brand authenticity items. Exploratory factor analysis using varimax rotation and limiting the number of factors to extract to four reveals four factors with eigenvalues > 1.0 and the total variance explained equal to 70.33%. Items with a loading greater than 0.70 are retained, leaving a set of 15 items.

Study 4 validates the dimensions of brand authenticity. A set of 15 of authentic and inauthentic brands in five product categories is identified based on interviews (automobile, sports apparel, beverages and body care) and literature (retailing). The main study uses these brands. Data analysis using structural equation models compares the four-factor model resulting from previous studies and two alternative ones (i.e., one factor-model and a second-order model with four sub-dimensions).

The four-factor model fits the data better than the others ($\chi^2(84) = 457.63$, $p < 0.001$, NFI = 0.97, CFI = 0.98, GFI = 0.93 and RMSEA = 0.07).

Study 5 assesses the discriminant validity of the scale. Respondents are asked to identify a brand in one of three conditions to which they are randomly assigned (strongly authentic, moderately authentic and not authentic) and are asked to evaluate it on the brand authenticity scale and other scales on brand involvement (based on Zaichkowsky, 1985), brand image (based on Laroche et al., 2005), brand satisfaction (based on Brakus, Schmitt & Zarantonello, 2009; Hausman, 2004, Oliver, 1980; Westbrook & Oliver, 1981, cited after Swan & Mercer, 1982). Exploratory factor analyses are performed to test the scale's discriminant validity.

Samples

Study 1 uses a sample of 17 respondents and three coders. Study 2 uses 10 students and marketing experts in the first survey, 20 students in the second survey and 10 test-persons in the assessment of substantive validity. Study 3 uses 60 students in the brand selection and 288 students in the main study. Study 4 uses 27 respondents in the brand selection and 857 participants in the main study. Study 5 involves a sample of 115 respondents.

Reliability and validity

The reliability of the scale is examined in study 3 through Cronbach's alpha. Values are equal to 0.90 for *continuity*, 0.90 for *originality*, 0.96 for *reliability* and 0.95 for *naturalness*.

The face and substantive validities of the scale are tested in study 2. A face validity test is conducted in order to ensure the plausibility of the items. To check substantive validity, respondents are asked to assign each item to one of the four brand authenticity dimensions. The substantive validity coefficient is computed, which confirms the validity of all the items surveyed.

The discriminant validity of the scale is checked in study 5. Exploratory factor analysis with varimax rotation is performed using composite scores of brand authenticity and brand involvement, brand image and brand satisfaction scale items. The analysis shows that brand authenticity dimensions load on a different factor than the other constructs (loading > 0.65 and cross loadings < 0.47).

Managerial applications

The brand authenticity scale helps companies understand and improve the perceptions of authenticity associated with their brand. Managers who want to increase the perceptions of authenticity of their brand should focus on the dimensions of brand authenticity, that is, *continuity*, *originality*, *reliability* and *naturalness*. To stimulate the brand's *continuity*, managers should bring the brand's traditional elements and values into the marketing mix. To stimulate the brand's *originality* and *naturalness*, managers should focus on the values of a specific country and culture, find the symbols that represent these values and use the appropriate channels to deliver them (i.e., packaging, product design, communication, pricing strategy, distribution channel). To stimulate the brand's *reliability*, managers should ensure persistent and consistent communication activities and their implementation over time.

The brand authenticity scale can be used for assessment, planning and tracking purposes. Specifically, managers could use the scale to position or reposition their brand with authenticity as a major component. It can be used to track changes in consumers' perception of the brand over time. Perceptions about competitors' brands could also be tracked.

4.3 Brand extension authenticity (Spiggle, Nguyen & Caravella, 2012)

Definition of construct

Brand extension authenticity (BEA) is defined by Spiggle, Nguyen and Caravella (2012, p. 969) as "a consumer's sense that a brand extension is a legitimate, culturally consistent extension of the parent brand". BEA refers to the cultural link between the extension and the parent brand and is concerned with the essence, aura or DNA of the parent brand and its reflection in the extension. In this sense, BEA differs from the traditional, culturally neutral concept of brand extension fit, typically described as perceived similarity between the extension and the parent brand, as well as relevance of parent brand association. BEA is multi-dimensional and includes four dimensions: *maintaining brand standards and style*, which refers to the consistency in style and aesthetics between the extension and the parent brand; *honouring brand heritage*, which refers to the extension remaining true to the heritage, origins and traditions associated with the parent brand; *preserving brand essence*, which refers to maintaining the soul of the brand and its values; and *avoiding brand exploitation*, which refers to resisting exploiting the brand through opportunities that are only externally driven and profit focused.

Scale description

The BEA scale includes four dimensions and 12 items. The dimension called *maintaining brand standards and style* includes three items. The dimension labelled *honouring brand heritage* contains three items, two of which are reverse coded. The dimension *preserving brand essence* comprises three items, one of which is reverse coded. The dimension *avoiding brand exploitation* consists of another three items, one of which is reverse coded. Items are measured on 7-point Likert scales where 1 = "strongly disagree" and 7 = "strongly agree". Respondents' scores on items within each dimension can be summed to compute a dimension score; all items of the scale can be summated to compute a composite BEA measure.

TABLE 4.2 Brand extension authenticity scale

Scale dimension	Scale item
Maintaining brand standards and style	• The standards of (parent brand X) are apparently contained in this extension
	• The style of this extension seems to reflect that of (parent brand X)
	• This extension appears to reflect the quality I associate with (brand X)
Honouring brand heritage	• This extension appears to connect with what I know about (parent brand X)'s origins
	• There is no link between this extension and what I know about (parent brand X)'s legacy*
	• (Parent brand X) seems to have abandoned its roots with this extension*
Preserving brand essence	• This extension is not consistent with my image of (parent brand X)*
	• This extension preserves what (parent brand X) means to me
	• This extension captures what makes (parent brand X) unique to me
Avoiding brand exploitation	• The extension likely trades off the essence of (parent brand X) strictly for profit*
	• This extension likely sacrifices what I think makes (parent brand X) special in exchange for commercial gain*
	• With this extension, it seems that (parent brand X) was more concerned about preserving the brand rather than growing the market

Note: *indicates the item is reverse coded.

Scale development

The brand extension authenticity scale is developed through a series of three studies.

Study 1 develops and validates the BEA scale. Literature review and exploratory study, where participants describe in an open fashion how they perceive an authentic brand extension, are used to derive four dimensions of BEA and an initial pool of 39 items representing these dimensions. The pool of items is reduced to 25 after a content validity check and is further reduced to 16 items following three focus groups in which respondents are questioned about the understandability and meaning of the items. As stimuli, 12 hypothetical brand extensions are developed ensuring well-known brands, variety in product categories and variance in BEA (i.e., three extensions with high BEA and three with low BEA). A survey is then conducted. Each respondent evaluates one of these brand extensions on the 16 BEA items.

Exploratory factor analysis reveals four factors explaining 66.78% of total variance. After removing four items with item-to-total correlation < 0.7, a principal component analysis is performed. The analysis confirms the four-factor structure of BEA (79.37% of total variance explained). A confirmatory factor analysis (CFA) is used to estimate three models: four-factor oblique model, one-factor model and four-factor orthogonal model. The four-factor oblique model displays a better fit (χ^2 = 65.83, df = 48, p < 0.05, CFI = 0.988, TLI = 0.984, RMSEA = 0.040); it reports standardized factor loadings > 0.50 and significant correlation coefficients from 0.27 to 0.47. Scale reliability and test-retest reliability are checked, the latter following a new data collection after two months.

Study 2 tests the discriminant validity of BEA compared to fit as similarity and relevance. A two-factor scale measuring fit as similarity and relevance is developed in a pre-test. Similarity is measured through three items on global similarity and three items on dimensional similarity, whereas relevance is measured through three items (see box below). Discriminant validity tests are conducted.

Brand extension fit: global similarity

- The extension is a good fit with (parent brand X)'s products
- The extension is inconsistent with (parent brand X)'s products*
- The extension is similar to (parent brand X)'s products
- The extension is not representative of (parent brand X)*

Brand extension fit: dimensional similarity

- It is likely that one would use the extension in the same situation as I connect to (parent brand X)'s products
- The level of similarity or overlap between the target market for the extension and the consumer group you associate with (parent brand X)'s products is high
- (Parent brand X)'s product category and the extension's product category are not similar*

Brand extension fit: relevance

- The benefits I associate with (parent brand X) are not relevant to the extension's product category*
- The characteristics I associate with (parent brand X) are relevant to the extension's product category
- The associations that I have for (parent brand X) are important to the extension's product category

Note: * indicates the item is reverse coded.

Study 3 tests the predictive validity of BEA, compared to fit, for brand extension favourability. The study is designed as 2 (high versus low similarity) × 2 (low versus high relevance) × 2 (low versus high BEA) between-subjects design. The eight hypothetical brand extensions used are the same as in study 2. Each respondent evaluates one extension on BEA as well as on scales of brand extension attitudes (adapted from Broniarcyk & Alba, 1994; McCarthy, Heath & Milberg, 2001; Meyers-Levy, Louie & Curran, 1994), purchase intentions (adapted from Dawar, 1996), willingness to recommend and brand knowledge (adapted from Dawar, 1996). Regression analyses are performed to confirm the predictive validity of the BEA scale.

Samples

Study 1 uses, in the item generation and selection, a sample of 61 undergraduate students in the exploratory study, 9 doctoral students in the content validity check and 16 undergraduate students and 10 staff members in the focus groups. The study uses 132 undergraduate students in the stimuli development and selection; 232 participants, of which about half are non-students in the survey; and 118 undergraduate students in the retest. Study 2 employs a sample of 186 undergraduate students to develop the fit scale and a sample of 80 adults recruited in a high-pedestrian-traffic area at a large northeastern U.S. university. Study 3 is based on a sample of 236 adults recruited in a high-pedestrian-traffic area at a large northeastern U.S. university. All students are from a large northeastern U.S. university.

Reliability and validity

The internal reliability of the BEA scale is assessed in study 1 in various ways. The Cronbach's alpha is equal to 0.85 (*maintaining brand standards and style*), 0.87 (*honouring brand heritage*), 0.88 (*preserving brand essence*), 0.91 (*avoiding brand exploitation*) and 0.89 (entire scale). The BEA four-factor structure is further supported by the results of exploratory and confirmatory factor analyses, which are conducted on two randomly split subsamples. Test-retest reliability is equal to 0.73, with $p < 0.01$.

The predictive validity of the BEA scale is tested in study 3. For each of the dependent variables (brand extension attitude, purchase intention and willingness to recommend), various regression models are estimated: one with BEA only, one with fit only, one with BEA and fit and one with BEA, fit and their interactions. Results show that models with BEA and fit together perform better than models with BEA or fit alone and that the best models are those with interactions ($F(8, 227) > 28$, $p < 0.001$; $R^2 = 0.39$–0.49). In these latter models, there are main effects of similarity, relevance and BEA on the three dependent variables ($t(235) > 2$, $p < 0.05$), and BEA moderates the main effects of fit, according to the significant, positive, two-way interaction effects ($t(235) > 2$, $p < 0.05$). Slope tests also show that respondents' favourable responses to authentic extensions are unchanged regardless of similarity ($t(122) > 1.20$, $p > 0.20$) or relevance ($t(122) < 1$, $p > 0.30$) and that their responses to inauthentic extensions decrease as the extensions move from similar to dissimilar product categories ($t(112) > 3$, $p < 0.01$) and from relevant to irrelevant parent brand-specific associations ($t(112) > 3.5$, $p < 0.001$).

Managerial applications

The BEA scale is intended to complement cognitive scales in the evaluation of brand extension opportunities. Whereas cognitive scales are centred on the perceived similarity between the extension and the parent brand, as well as the relevance of parent brand associations, the BEA scale is concerned with the sociocultural legitimacy of the extension. This sociocultural dimension incorporated in the BEA construct and scale proves to be relevant as capable of shaping consumers' reactions to extension. Using a wider approach to evaluating brand extensions, managers can therefore better understand consumer responses to extensions and, finally, the enhancement or dilution of the parent brand.

4.4 Consumer-based brand authenticity (Napoli, Dickinson, Beverland & Farrelly, 2014)

Definition of construct

Consumer-based brand authenticity (CBBA) is defined by Napoli, Dickinson, Beverland and Farrelly (2014, p. 1091) as a "subjective evaluation of genuineness ascribed to a brand by consumers". CBBA is conceptualized as a multifaceted construct, as consumers may use a variety of cues to make inferences and evaluations about the authenticity of a brand. In their view, CBBA is built around consumers' perceptions of the heritage of a brand, feelings of nostalgia conveyed by a brand, the level of sincerity of the brand, the craftsmanship of the brand's products, the brand's and firm's commitment to quality and the consistency of the design across the brand's products. These aspects are captured by the three dimensions of brand authenticity, that is, *quality commitment, heritage* and *sincerity*.

Scale description

The CBBA scale includes three dimensions for a total of 14 items. The *quality commitment* dimension includes seven items, of which five focus on brand quality and two on craftsmanship. The *heritage* dimension includes five items, of which two focus on the brand heritage, two on feelings of nostalgia and one on design consistency. The *sincerity* dimension includes two items focusing on sincerity. Respondents are asked to indicate how strongly they feel each item reflects the brand they are asked to think of. Responses are provided on a 7-point Likert scale anchored at 1 = "strongly disagree" and 7 = "strongly agree". Scores for brand authenticity dimensions can be obtained by summating the individual items included in each dimension.

TABLE 4.3 Consumer-based brand authenticity scale

Scale dimension	Scale item
Quality commitment	• Quality is central to the brand[a]
	• Only the finest ingredients/materials are used in the manufacture of this brand[b]
	• The brand is made to the most exacting standards, where everything the firm does is aimed at improving quality[a]
	• The brand is manufactured to the most stringent quality standards[a]
	• The brand is a potent symbol of continued quality[a]
	• The brand is made by a master craftsman who pays attention to detail and is involved throughout the production process[b]
	• The firm is committed to retaining long-held quality standards for the brand[a]
Heritage	• The brand has a strong connection to an historical period in time, culture and/or specific region[c]
	• The brand has a strong link to the past, which is still perpetuated and celebrated to this day[d]
	• The brand reminds me of a golden age[d]
	• The brand exudes a sense of tradition[c]
	• The brand reflects a timeless design[e]
Sincerity	• The brand refuses to compromise the values upon which it was founded
	• The brand has stuck to its principles

Note: [a] indicates that the item describes brand quality, whereas [b] indicates the item describes craftsmanship; [c] indicates the item describes brand heritage, whereas [d] indicates an item that describes the feeling of nostalgia; and [e] indicates that the item describes design consistency.

Scale development

The CBBA scale is developed following a four-study process.

Study 1 generates and refines CBBA scale items. Based on the literature, an initial set of 157 items is generated covering seven dimensions of brand authenticity (brand heritage, quality commitment, craftsmanship, sincerity, nostalgia, cultural symbolism and design consistency). Two assessments with judges are performed to test the content validity of the scale, which result in a set of 33 items. These items are pilot tested; respondents are asked to think of a brand they consider truly authentic and record how strongly they feel each item reflects their nominated brand using a 7-point Likert scale from 1 = "strongly disagree" to 7 = "strongly agree". All items are retained for the next study.

Study 2 further reduces the items and tests the scale reliability. Respondents are provided with the same instructions as in the pilot study. To purify the scale, the researchers first remove four items with a corrected item-to-total correlation < 0.4. The remaining items are subjected to a principal component analysis with an oblique rotation; 10 items are removed because they do not exhibit a simple factor structure on any one factor, leaving a final solution with 19 items and accounting for 60% of total variance explained. Reliability tests for the 19-item scale are conducted.

Study 3 confirms the underlying factor structure of the scale. Respondents are asked to think of a brand they consider somewhat authentic and record how strongly they feel each item reflects their nominated brand using a 7-point Likert scale from 1 = "strongly disagree" to 7 = "strongly agree". A series of confirmatory factor models is examined, including the null model, a one-factor model, several two-factor models, a three-factor uncorrelated model and a three-factor correlated one. Five additional items are deleted, based on modification indexes and standardized residual covariances, leaving a set of 14 items. New confirmatory factor analyses reveal that the three-factor correlated model provides the best fit of the data (χ^2 = 100.84, df = 74, p = 0.021, CFI = 0.976, TLI = 0.971, NFI = 0.917, RMSEA = 0.042). Reliability, convergent validity and discriminant validity tests are conducted on the final set of 14 items.

Study 4 tests the CBBA scale's construct and predictive validities. Respondents are asked to evaluate either a brand they view as authentic or a brand they judge as inauthentic on the CBBA scale as well as on brand trust (adapted from Delgado-Ballester, 2004), brand credibility (adapted from Kirmani, 1997) and purchase intention (adapted from Putrevu & Lord, 1994) scales. Construct validity tests are conducted comparing respondents who score high versus low on the CBBA scale within each of the two samples of authentic versus inauthentic brands.

Samples

Study 1 uses a sample of five marketing academics and a sample of four marketing academics in the content validity assessments, as well as a sample of 40 undergraduate students in the pilot test. Study 2 is based on 247 usable responses from undergraduate students at a large inner-city university. Study 3 employs a sample of 203 university students. Study 4 uses a sample of 312 adult consumers recruited through an organization that specializes in administering surveys online; the sample that evaluates an authentic brand includes 206 respondents, whereas the sample that evaluates an inauthentic brand comprises 106 respondents.

Reliability and validity

The content validity of CBBA scale items is tested in two assessments in study 1. In the first assessment, judges are asked to assign each of the items to the provided definitions of brand authenticity dimensions. Items that are not correctly classified by four out of five judges are removed. In the second assessment, judges are asked to evaluate each item as being "not at all representative", "somewhat representative" or "clearly representative" of the provided dimensions of brand authenticity. Items that are evaluated as "clearly representative" by at least three of the four judges but not worse than "somewhat representative" by the fourth judge are retained.

Reliability tests are conducted throughout the scale-development process. However, the reliability of the final set of items which constitute the CBBA scale is tested in studies 3 and 4. Cronbach's alpha is equal to 0.879 (*quality commitment*), 0.783 (*heritage*) and 0.605 (*sincerity*). Composite reliability is equal to 0.892 (*quality commitment*), 0.792 (*heritage*) and 0.608 (*sincerity*). For the two-item *sincerity* dimension, the Spearman-Brown coefficient is also computed and is equal to 0.637.

Convergent and discriminant validities are tested in study 3. To establish convergent validity, AVE proves to be greater or close to the cut-off point of 0.5 (*quality commitment* = 0.546, *heritage* = 0.442 and *sincerity* = 0.437). To show discriminant validity, it is verified that AVE is greater than the squared correlation between a construct and any other construct in the model (correlation between *quality commitment* and *heritage* = 0.217, correlation between *quality commitment* and *sincerity* = 0.376 and correlation between *sincerity* and *heritage* = 0.287).

Construct validity is established in study 4 by comparing respondents with low versus high scores on the CBBA scale within each sample group (authentic versus inauthentic brands). All *t*-tests show significant differences between high versus low authenticity evaluations on brand trust and brand credibility ($p < 0.001$), such that higher levels of brand authenticity are associated with higher levels of brand trust and brand credibility. This type of validity is also demonstrated by showing that CBBA is correlated but distinct from brand trust and brand credibility. Correlations between CBBA and, respectively, brand trust dimensions (reliability and intention) and brand credibility are included between 0.523 and 0.788 (all $ps < 0.001$). To show that the CBBA scale is discriminated from brand trust and brand credibility, relevant models are estimated including one-factor and two-factor correlated models. The analysis shows that two-factor models fit the data significantly better than the one-factor models. For brand trust, the chi-square difference between the two-factor and one-factor models is equal to 7.684 and is significant at $p < 0.01$. For brand credibility, the chi-square difference between the two-factor and one-factor models is equal to 50.185 and is significant at $p < 0.01$. Finally, as a further support to the scale's convergent validity, the CBBA dimensions of *quality commitment*, *heritage* and *sincerity* report an AVE > 0.50 (respectively, 0.659, 0.541 and 0.524).

The predictive validity of the CBBA scale is tested in study 4, with respect to purchase intention. Composite measures of the three brand authenticity dimensions are regressed against purchase intention. All three factors emerge as predictors at different significance levels (beta for *quality commitment* = 0.646 with $p < 0.001$, beta for *sincerity* = 0.162 with $p < 0.05$ and beta for *heritage* = 0.112 with $p < 0.1$). The predictive validity of the CBBA scale is also examined through structural equation modelling, where the three interrelated first-order factors of *quality commitment*, *heritage* and *sincerity* load into a second-order factor of global CBBA which, in turn, predicts purchase intention. The model reports chi-square = 259.92

104 Brand authenticity

with $df = 87$ and $p < 0.001$, CFI = 0.917, TLI = 0.899, NFI = 0.881 and RMSEA = 0.098 and shows that global CBBA is a significant predictor of purchase intention ($\gamma = 0.697$, $p < 0.001$).

Managerial applications

The scale allows managers to measure and examine the level of authenticity as perceived by consumers in a given time, as well as to track brand authenticity over time and in relation to competing brands. The knowledge resulting from these assessments may assist managers in identifying new opportunities in terms of brand positioning and value creation, defining the direction of future advertising and communication strategies and making decisions about future brand extensions, sponsorship choices and co-branding partnerships.

4.5 Consumer–brand relational authenticity (Ilicic & Webster, 2014)

Definition of construct

Ilicic and Webster (2014) consider authenticity in the context of consumer–brand relationships. They take a different approach from previous literature, where authenticity is typically examined in terms of quality, heritage and values (Napoli et al., 2014, see this chapter, pp. 100–104; Spiggle, Nguyen & Caravella, 2012, see this chapter, pp. 96–100). They view consumer–brand relational authenticity as a unidimensional construct, which refers to brands being true, or genuine, in their relationship with consumers. Their notion of consumer–brand relational authenticity is based on the authenticity inventory advanced by Kernis and Goldman (2006).

Scale description

The consumer–brand relational authenticity includes four items which must be evaluated using a 5-point Likert scale anchored at 1 = "strongly disagree" and 5 = "strongly agree".

TABLE 4.4 Consumer–brand relational authenticity scale

Scale item
• (Brand X) cares about openness and honesty in close relationships with consumers
• In general, (brand X) places a good deal of importance on consumers understanding who they truly are
• (Brand X) wants consumers to understand the real them rather than just their public "image"
• Consumers can count on (brand X) being who they are regardless of the situation

Scale development

The process to develop the consumer–brand relational authenticity scale follows Churchill's approach (1979). An initial set of 21 items is derived from the sections on behaviour and relational authenticity of Kernis and Goldman's (2006) authenticity inventory. Two scale purification stages are taken next.

The first purification stage identifies the dimensions of consumer–brand relational authenticity. Respondents are shown a corporate brand and, if familiar with it, are asked to rate the brand on the 21 relational authenticity items. Based on Cronbach's alpha scores, four behaviour items are removed. An exploratory factor analysis using maximum likelihood with varimax rotation is performed using the remaining items. Based on factor loadings, their sign and cross-loadings, one factor and four items are retained. These items are subjected to a confirmatory factor analysis next. Results support the solution previously identified ($\chi^2 = .325$, $df = 2$, $p < 0.05$, GFI = 0.99, CFI = 1.00, RMSEA = 0.00).

The second purification stage assesses the convergent and discriminant validities of the scale with respect to brand attachment. Respondents are asked to evaluate one of two brands using the four-item consumer–brand relational authenticity scale and three items on separation distress, which represents a measure of the strength on an attachment bond (Bernam & Sperling, 1994; Thomson, 2006). Validity tests are performed.

The last stage of the scale-development process examines the predictive validity of the scale and includes two studies. The first study compares consumer–brand relational authenticity with brand attachment and verifies their predictive power with respect to brand attitudes and purchase intentions. Respondents are shown one of two brands and are asked to rate it in terms of their familiarity (one item generated by the authors), brand attachment (Thomson, 2006), brand attitudes and purchase intentions (Mitchell & Olson, 1981), in addition to relational authenticity. Various regression models are estimated.

The second study compares consumer–brand relational authenticity with indicators of brand relationship quality (trust, satisfaction and commitment) and examines their predictive power with respect to brand attitudes and purchase intentions. Respondents are asked to evaluate one brand in terms of relational authenticity, brand familiarity (one item generated by the authors), attitudes and purchase intentions (Mitchell & Olson, 1981), as well as trust, satisfaction and commitment (Thomson, 2006). Exploratory factor analysis and regression analyses are performed.

Samples

For the first purification stage, 343 potential respondents are randomly selected from a research company panel; 147 provide complete and valid responses. The second purification stage is based on a sample of 353 respondents randomly selected from a research panel from metropolitan areas of Australia. The first predictive validity stage uses a sample of 342 respondents randomly recruited from a panel. The second predictive validity stage is based on a sample of 309 respondents randomly selected from a research panel from metropolitan areas of Australia.

Reliability and validity

The reliability of the consumer–brand relational authenticity scale is checked throughout the scale-development process. In the second purification stage, the scale's Cronbach's alpha is 0.93, in the first predictive validity study the coefficient is 0.95, and in the second predictive validity study, the coefficient is 0.90.

The scale's convergent validity is demonstrated in the second purification stage through CFA results: standardised regression estimates range between 0.83 and 0.93, the average variance extracted is equal to 0.77, and the composite reliability is equal to 0.99. The scale's discriminant validity is also shown in this stage through an exploratory factor analysis, which reveals that relational authenticity and brand attachment items load on distinct factors.

The predictive validity of the scale is tested in the last two studies. Using regression analyses, the first study shows that relational authenticity is a stronger predictor of brand attitudes and purchase intentions than brand attachment, but when both relational authenticity and brand attachment are considered, the models are stronger. Using simple slope analysis, the study also reveals that when consumers have strong brand attachment, relational authenticity has no effect on brand attitudes ($p > 0.05$), whereas when consumers have weak attachment, relational authenticity increases brand attitudes (unstandardized $\beta = -0.23$, $t = 4.271$, $p < 0.001$). For purchase intention, when consumers have strong attachment, relational authenticity has an effect (unstandardized $\beta = 0.94$, $t = 8.338$, $p < 0.001$), but when consumers have weak brand attachment, this effect is greater (unstandardized $\beta = 1.03$, $t = 9.161$, $p < 0.001$).

In the second study, regression analyses indicate that relational authenticity, trust, satisfaction and commitment are all significant predictors of brand attitudes and purchase intentions. However, for brand attitudes, trust is the strongest predictor, and relational authenticity is stronger than commitment; for purchase intention, commitment is the strongest predictor, and relational authenticity is stronger than trust. Using simple slope analysis, the study also shows that relational authenticity has a stronger influence on brand attitudes and purchase intentions for consumers with low trust in the brand but high commitment (brand attitudes: unstandardized $\beta = 0.54$, $t = 4.34$, $p \leq 0.001$; purchase intention: unstandardized $\beta = 0.73$, $t = 2.483$, $p < 0.05$) and for consumers with high trust in the brand but low commitment (brand attitudes: unstandardized $\beta = 0.42$, $t = 3.322$, $p \leq 0.001$; purchase intention: unstandardized $\beta = 0.42$, $t = 3.322$, $p \leq 0.001$).

Managerial applications

The consumer–brand relational authenticity scale can be used by managers to measure and assess the degree to which their brands are perceived as genuine and true in their relationships with consumers. This information can then be used to develop marketing strategies aimed at building the relational authenticity of the brands, as well as to position or reposition them. The scale also offers managers guidelines about how to facilitate perceptions of relational authenticity of their brand: communicate interest in connecting with consumers on a genuine level, ensure transparency about what they are and stand for and convey honesty in their interactions with consumers.

4.6 Academic focus

- Consumers' perceptions of brand authenticity may be industry specific and vary across different industries (see, for example, Beverland, 2005). Focusing on a selection of brands in a product category, one dissertation may investigate the extent to which these brands are perceived as authentic by consumers and the dimensions of brand authenticity that are triggered the most in that particular context.
- One dissertation may focus on one brand that is usually considered as authentic by consumers (several rankings are available such as the "brand authenticity index", www.authenticbrandindex.com/results1.htm). This dissertation may take into account the various different communication messages of this brand and examine how the brand generates perceptions of authenticity. Using the frameworks of brand authenticity advanced by Bruhn, Schoenmüller, Schäfer and Heinrich (2012) and/or Napoli, Dickinson, Beverland and Farrelly (2014), the dissertation may understand which of these dimensions are reflected in the communication strategies of the company's brand.
- Brand authenticity scales have been developed using different types of consumer brands. A dissertation may be concerned with the application of the brand authenticity scales to other types of brands, for example place brands, sports brands or political brands. More specifically, the dissertation may investigate if, in one such context, the conceptualizations advanced by brand authenticity researchers still hold and if the scales still represent a reliable and valid measurement tool that could be used. It may also be interesting to investigate the outcomes of brand authenticity in such contexts: for example, willingness to come back (place brands), fan behaviour (sports brands) and intention to vote (political brands).
- A dissertation could concentrate on the topic of brand extension authenticity. In their findings, Spiggle, Nguyen and Caravella (2012) show that brand extension authenticity has a different influence on consumers' evaluations of the brand extension depending on the nature of products (functional versus experiential) and the degree of self–brand connections (low versus high). In a dissertation, one might examine whether the impact of brand extension authenticity is altered by other types of products (e.g., mass market/luxury, tangible/intangible) or other consumer-related and brand-related variables, such as

consumers' emotions toward the parent brand (cf. Chapter 8), consumers' attachment to the parent brand (cf. Chapter 9) and consumer–brand relationship components (cf. Chapter 10).
- A dissertation may approach the topic of brand authenticity in the context of brand portfolios and architectures (Aaker, 2004). It may be worth investigating how consumers' perceptions of authenticity versus inauthenticity with respect to a given brand affect the attitudes toward other brands in a company's portfolio as well as the attitudes toward the corporate brand. Different types of brand architectures may be considered (Aaker & Joachimsthaler, 2000).

4.7 Managerial focus

- **Why is it interesting to measure the perception of brand authenticity among your attached/passionate consumers?**
  Consumers are attached and loyal to brands which they perceive as trustworthy and with whom they share common values. Attached consumers can be really passionate about the brand; they want to know the history and the origin of the brand, they want to interact with the brand and share information with other peers. Passionate consumers appreciate the authenticity of the brand and become real advocates of the brand. Therefore, it is important to evaluate the perception of brand authenticity among the attached/loyal consumers, to make sure that the brand always meets their expectations to avoid deceiving them and to make them real ambassadors for brand.
- **Are you sure that the authenticity of the brands remains consistent across channels?**
  Brands have nowadays the opportunity to have many touchpoints with consumers. Nevertheless, it is important that brands remain consistent not only over time but also across channels. Being authentic means that brands need to stay true to who they are over all touchpoints and should act in offline and online environments in the same way. The brand authenticity scales (Bruhn *et al.*, 2012; Ilicic & Webster, 2014; Napoli *et al.*, 2014) included in this chapter can help brand managers measure the perceptions of brand authenticity across channels. By assessing the perceptions of brand authenticity associated with different touchpoints, brand managers can identify which actions they can implement in order to enhance the different dimensions of brand authenticity and ensure consistency across channels.

- **Have you thought about revitalizing your brand through authentic brand associations from the past?**
  There are some brand associations which were at the core of the brand in past times but which have been left dormant over time because communications were focusing on some other strategic messages. In order to revitalize your brand, it can be interesting for brand managers to enhance these important values which were present at the origin of their brand but may have disappeared from consumers' minds. By reactivating theses authentic values which are appealing for consumers through communications, packaging and products, brand managers will reinforce the brand equity and will clarify the meaning of the brand. Tracking the perception of brand authenticity can be useful in order to check if the repositioning of the brand on its core historical values is successful.
- **Are you sure that your new brand extension will be evaluated positively by your consumers?**
  When deciding on a brand extension, it is important that brand managers check the fit between the parent brand and the extension. If there is a physical fit and a conceptual fit among the parent brand, the brand extension and the original product, the brand extension will be positively evaluated (Boush & Loken, 1991; Cegarra & Merunka, 1993). But the traditional assessment of the fit does not include an examination of the extensions from a cultural and relational point of view. Spiggle, Nguyen and Caravella (2012)'s scale can be used to evaluate if the brand extension is perceived as authentic by consumers, that is, if it is legitimate, coherent with the heritage, origins and traditions associated with the brand. By evaluating the brand extension authenticity, managers can achieve a broader understanding of its acceptance in the marketplace.
- **Does your communication on social media enhance your brand authenticity?**
  On social media, brands can use different means to present themselves and interact with consumers (e.g., words, video, advertising, games). Social media language is often a bit more informal, like a conversation, than other channels. Nevertheless, the way the brand communicates should remain true and coherent with the brand's DNA. Being authentic for brands means also staying true, engaging in real talk and encouraging real consumers to share real information. The brand should be transparent and honest with its consumers. Therefore, it is important to make sure that the brand is posting true information. Then it can be useful to measure the brand authenticity in order to check if the communication on social media and online environments enhances the authenticity perception.

References

Aaker, D. A. (2004). *Brand portfolio strategy: creating relevance, differentiation, energy, leverage, and clarity.* New York, NY: Free Press.

Aaker, D. A., & Joachimsthaler, E. (2000). The brand relationship spectrum: the key to the brand architecture challenge. *California Management Review*, 42 (4), 8–23.

Berman, W. H., & Sperling, M. B. (1994). The structure and function of adult attachment, in M. B. Sperling and W. H. Berman (eds.). *Attachment in Adults: Clinical and Developmental Perspectives.* New York: Guilford Press, 3–28.

Beverland, M. (2005). Brand management and the challenge of authenticity. *Journal of Product & Brand Management*, 14 (7), 460–461.

Beverland, M. B., & Farrelly, F. J. (2010). The quest for authenticity in consumption: consumers' purposive choice of authentic cues to shape experienced outcomes. *Journal of Consumer Research*, 36 (5), 838–856.

Boush, D. M., & Loken, B. (1991). A process-tracing study of brand extension evaluation. *Journal of Marketing Research*, 28, 16–28.

Brakus, J. J., Schmitt, B. H., & Zarantonello, L. (2009). Brand experience: What is it? How is it measured? Does it affect loyalty? *Journal of Marketing*, 73 (May), 52–68.

Broniarcyk, S. M., & Alba, J. W. (1994). The importance of the brand in brand extension. *Journal of Marketing Research*, 31 (May), 214–228.

Brown, S., Sherry, J., Jr., & Kozinets, R. (2003). Teaching old brands new tricks: retro branding and the revival of brand meaning. *Journal of Marketing*, 67 (3), 19–33.

Bruhn, M., Schoenmüller, V., Schäfer, D., & Heinrich, D. (2012). Brand authenticity: towards a deeper understanding of its conceptualization and measurement. *Advances in Consumer Research*, 40, 567–576.

Cegarra, J. J., & Merunka, D. (1993). Les extensions de marque: concepts et modèles. *Recherche et Applications en Marketing*, 8 (1), 53–76.

Churchill, G. A., Jr. (1979). A paradigm for developing better measures of marketing constructs. *Journal of Marketing Research*, 16 (1), 64–73.

Dawar, N. (1996). Extensions of broad brands: the role of retrieval in evaluations of fit. *Journal of Consumer Psychology*, 5 (2), 189–207.

Delgado-Ballester, E. (2004). Applicability of a brand trust scale across product categories. *European Journal of Marketing*, 38 (5/6), 573–592.

Gilmore, J. H., & Pine, B. J., Jr. (2007). *Authenticity: What consumers really want.* Boston, MA: Harvard Business School Press.

Grayson, K., & Martinec, R. (2004). Consumer perceptions of iconicity and indexicality and their influence on assessments of authentic market offerings. *Journal of Consumer Research*, 31 (2), 296–312.

Hausman, A. (2004). Modeling the patient-physician service encounter: improving patient outcomes. *Journal of the Academy of Marketing Science*, 32 (4), 403–417.

Ilicic, J., & Webster, C. M. (2014). Investigating consumer-brand relational authenticity. *Journal of Brand Management*, 21 (4), 342–363.

Kernis, M. H., & Goldman, B. M. (2006). A multicomponent conceptualization of authenticity: theory and research. *Advances in Experimental Social Psychology*, 38 (1), 283–357.

Kirmani, A. (1997). Advertising repetition as a signal of quality: if it's advertised so much, something must be wrong. *Journal of Advertising*, 26 (3), 77–87.

Laroche, M., Zhiyong, Y., McDougall, G.H.G., & Bergeron, J. (2005). Internet versus brick and mortar retailers: an investigation into intangibility and its consequences. *Journal of Retailing*, 81 (4), 251–267.

Leigh, T., Peters, C., & Shelton, J. (2006). The consumer quest for authenticity: the multiplicity of meanings within the MG subculture of consumption. *Journal of the Academy of Marketing Science*, 34 (4), 481–493.

McCarthy, M. S., Heath, T. B., & Milberg, S. J. (2001). New brands versus brand extensions, attitudes versus choice: experimental evidence for theory and practice. *Marketing Letters*, 12 (1), 75–90.

Meyers-Levy, J., Louie, T. A., & Curran, M. T. (1994). How does the congruity of brand names affect the evaluation of brand name extension? *Journal of Applied Psychology*, 79 (1), 46–53.

Mitchell, A. A., & Olson J. C. (1981). Are product attribute beliefs the only mediator of advertising effects on brand attitude? *Journal of Marketing Research*, 18, 318–332.

Napoli, J., Dickinson, S. J., Beverland, M. B., & Farrelly, F. (2014). Measuring consumer-based brand authenticity. *Journal of Business Research*, 67 (6), 1090–1098.

Oliver, R. L. (1980). A cognitive model of the antecedents and consequences of satisfaction decisions. *Journal of Marketing Research*, 17 (4), 460–469.

Putrevu, S., & Lord, K. R. (1994). Comparative and noncomparative advertising: attitudinal effects under cognitive and affective involvement conditions. *Journal of Advertising*, 23 (2), 77–91.

Spiggle, S., Nguyen, H. T., & Caravella, M. (2012). More than fit: brand extension authenticity. *Journal of Marketing Research*, 49 (6), 967–983.

Swan, J. E., & Mercer, A. A. (1982). Consumer satisfaction as a function of equity and disconfirmation. In H. K. Hunt & R. L. Day (eds.), *Proceedings of the 1981 CS/D&CB conference. Conceptual and empirical contributions to consumer satisfaction and complaining behavior*. Bloomington: Indiana University Press, 2–8.

Thomson, M. (2006). Human brands: Investigating antecedents to consumers' strong attachments to celebrities. *Journal of Marketing*, 70 (3), 104–119.

Westbrook, R. A., & Oliver, R. L. (1981). Developing better measures of consumer satisfaction: Some preliminary results. In K. B. Monroe (ed.), *Advances in consumer research*, Vol. 8. Ann Arbor, MI: Association for Consumer Research, 94–99.

Zaichkowsky, J. L. (1985). Measuring the involvement construct. *Journal of Consumer Research*, 12 (3), 341–352.

5
PERCEIVED BRAND DIFFERENTIATION

5.1 Overview

This chapter regroups different scales which aim at measuring the perceived brand differentiation under different angles. Indeed, differentiation strategy is key to occupying a unique and favourite place in the minds of consumers and, therefore, improving perceptions of product performance and quality, reducing the vulnerability to competitive marketing actions and enhancing brand loyalty (Keller, 1993). Brand differentiation can be achieved by companies in different ways. One way, for global brands, is related to leveraging consumers' perceptions about the degree of globalness conveyed by a brand. Consumers usually attribute more value to global brands than to local ones (Kapferer, 1997; Shocker et al., 1994). The perceived brand globalness scale developed by Steenkamp, Batra and Alden (2003) measures the degree to which consumers believe a brand is global, that is, the degree to which they think the same brand is marketed in other countries and is recognized as a global brand.

In the case of luxury brands, the challenge that companies may have to face is related to maintaining strong perceptions of luxuriousness, especially in a time when luxury is accessible to a higher number of consumers. Luxury brands are characterised in the minds of consumers by higher levels of prices, quality, aesthetics, rarity, extraordinariness and other types of symbolic associations (Kapferer & Bastien, 2012). The brand luxury index scale proposed by Vigneron and Johnson (2004) allows researchers to identify the amount of luxury that is perceived as contained in a brand. To do that, the scale evaluates the non–personal-oriented perceptions of luxury brands which are linked to functional aspects of brand management, as well as the personal-oriented perceptions of luxury brands which are consumer driven.

Other brands, in general, can achieve differentiation by, for example, forging perceptions of higher perceived quality, perceived value, perceived innovativeness and perceived popularity, which, according to Chang and Jae Ko (2014), determine the leadership of a brand. Their brand leadership scale evaluates consumer perceptions about the distinctive ability of the brand to achieve good performance and superiority and allows researchers to have a better understanding of competitive relationships among leading and trailing brands from a strategic perspective based on consumers' perceptions.

Nevertheless, in some cases, consumers believe that there are few distinctions between competing brands. Perceived brand parity can be defined as consumers' belief that major offerings in a product category are similar (Iyer & Muncy, 2005). The brand parity scale proposed by Muncy (1996) enables researchers to capture this belief, whose centrality relates to the fact that, as demonstrated, high parity perceptions inhibit a company's ability to develop loyal consumers. Indeed, if consumers perceive few differences between brands within a category, they will be more sensitive to price and competitive brand actions. Thus, a starting point of brand positioning is a clear understanding of both the level of parity with other brands and the degree of brand differentiation.

5.2 Brand parity (Muncy, 1996)

Definition of construct

Brand parity is defined as "the overall perception held by the consumer that the differences between the major brand alternatives in a product category are small" (Muncy, 1996, p. 411). Being defined as a perception, brand parity is not necessarily an intrinsic characteristic of a product class. Actual product similarity may influence the degree of perceived brand similarity as well as other marketplace factors (such as advertising) and consumer characteristics (such as product experience). Moreover, brand parity is conceptualized as the opposite of brand differentiation: when a company can differentiate itself in consumers' minds, then it is diminishing brand parity. However, whereas brand differentiation usually refers to a brand, brand parity relates to an entire product category, or at least to the major alternatives in the product category.

Scale description

The brand parity scale is composed of five items. Items are evaluated by respondents using 5-point Likert scales from "strongly agree" to "strongly disagree".

TABLE 5.1 Brand parity scale

Scale item
• I can't think of many differences between the major brands of (product category Y)
• To me, there are big differences between the various brands of (product category Y)*
• The only difference between the major brands of (product category Y) is the price
• (Product category Y) is (product category Y); most brands are basically the same
• All major brands of (product category Y) are basically alike

Note: *indicates the item is reverse scored.

Scale development

The brand parity scale is developed in accordance with Churchill (1979). A first sample of respondents is asked to give statements that describe products based on their similarity to other brands. These responses, together with previous research, are used to generate a set of eight items on brand parity. These items are evaluated by a second sample of respondents. This study also serves to develop other brand-related measures on cognitive loyalty, price sensitivity and perceived usefulness of market information, which are employed next. After an iterative process of pre-testing and refinement, five items on brand parity are retained.

A study is then conducted applying the brand parity scale to three non-durable product categories (i.e., laundry detergent, shampoo and toothpaste). Each respondent receives a questionnaire about one of the three product categories and is asked to rate the items on brand parity, cognitive brand loyalty, price sensitivity to the brand and perceived usefulness of market information about brands (see boxes below). Reliability and validity analyses are conducted.

Cognitive brand loyalty

- If I went to the store and they were out of my favourite brand of (product category Y), I would simply purchase another brand*
- Only under extreme circumstances would I consider purchasing a brand of (product category Y) different from the one I usually buy
- There are other brands of (product category Y) which are just as good as the one I usually purchase*
- To me, the brand of (product category Y) I usually purchase is clearly the best brand on the market
- If the store was out of my favourite brand of (product category Y), I would go somewhere else or wait until later to buy some

Note: *indicates the item is reverse coded.

Price sensitivity

- I would be willing to pay more to buy my regular brand of (product category Y) rather than buy another brand*
- If I had a coupon for a brand of (product category Y) other than the one I usually purchase, I would probably use it
- I generally buy the least expensive brand of (product category Y) I can find
- If a brand of (product category Y) other than the one I usually purchase was on sale, I would probably buy it

Note: *indicates the item is reverse coded.

Perceived usefulness of market information

- It can be helpful to read the information on a box of (product category Y)
- I cannot get any useful information from watching a television advertisement about (product category Y)*
- Magazine advertisements for (product category Y) contain useful information which can be helpful in identifying the best brand
- Information about the various brands of (product category Y) is both available and useful

Note: *indicates the item is reverse coded.

Samples

The instrument development involves 29 students enrolled in an undergraduate consumer behaviour class at a major southeast university in the United States, as well as 93 students enrolled in an introductory marketing class. The applied study is based on a sample of 1,200 heads of household obtained from a large mailing-list company from New York; the response rate for this study is 82%.

Reliability and validity

Reliability and validity tests are conducted in the applied study. Cronbach's alpha is equal to 0.905 (laundry detergent), 0.909 (shampoo) and 0.885 (toothpaste). Correlations between brand parity and the other constructs (i.e., cognitive loyalty, price sensitivity and perceived usefulness of market information) are examined using LISREL 7. A structural equations model is estimated for each product category (laundry detergent: GFI = 0.890, AGFI = 0.857, RMSR = 0.072; shampoo: GFI = 0.874, AGFI = 0.836, RMSR = 0.074; toothpaste: GFI = 0.900, AGFI = 0.869, RMSR = 0.068). Across the different product categories, brand parity is negatively related to cognitive loyalty (absolute value > 0.7) and perceived usefulness of market information (between −0.289 and −0.481), whereas it is positively related to price sensitivity (between 0.11 and 0.21).

Managerial applications

The brand parity scale enables marketing practitioners to evaluate if and to what extent consumers perceive brands as similar to each other within a same product category. If high parity perceptions are found, marketing managers should focus on differentiating their product and brand from major alternatives in the category. As consumers with high parity are less loyal, more sensitive to price and less receptive to brand-related information, it is therefore crucial to identify them in order to retain them by enhancing brand differentiation.

5.3 Perceived brand globalness (Steenkamp, Batra & Alden, 2003)

Definition of construct

Perceived brand globalness (PBG) corresponds to the consumers' belief that the brand is marketed in multiple countries and is recognized as global in these countries. This perception can be formed through media coverage, word of mouth, consumers' own travel and/or global associations stressed through marketing communications that use brand names, endorsers, advertising themes, packaging and other symbols that recall modern, urban lifestyles.

Scale description

The PBG scale consists of three items which measure the degree to which consumers think the same brand is marketed in other countries beyond their own. Items are scored on 7-point bipolar scales.

TABLE 5.2 Perceived brand globalness scale

Scale item
• To me, this is a global brand/To me, this is a local brand
• I don't think consumers overseas buy this brand/I do think consumers overseas buy this brand
• This brand is sold only in (specific country name)/This brand is sold all over the world

Scale development

The PBG scale takes its root from Batra et al.'s scale (2000) and is developed through a focus group and a survey in the United States and Korea. These two countries are selected because they are the opposite of one another from a cultural viewpoint (Hofstede, 1991).

The focus groups in both countries identify the product categories and the brands to be used in the survey. Four categories including durables and non-durables are chosen (cola drinks, facial cream, colour TV sets and wristwatches in the United States; facial cream and wristwatches are replaced by toothpaste and refrigerators in Korea), involving eight brands per country (global and well-known local brands).

The survey is conducted via mail questionnaire in the United States and personal interview in Korea. The English version of the questionnaire is double back-translated into Korean. The four identified product categories are divided into two sets of two, and respondents answer questions for two brands in each of the two product categories. The questionnaire contains the PBG scale; brand-related scales, that is, perceived brand quality (Keller & Aaker, 1992), perceived brand prestige (Han & Terpstra, 1988), brand as icon of local culture (new measure; see box below), brand familiarity (new measure; see box below) and likelihood of purchasing the brand (Dodds, Monroe & Grewal, 1991); and other non–brand-related measures, that is, country-of-origin perception (Hunter & Nebenzahl, 1984) and consumer ethnocentrism (Shimp & Sharma, 1987). Tests of the PBG scale's reliability, cross-national invariance and validity are conducted.

Brand as icon of local culture

- I associate this brand with things that are (specific nationality)/I do not associate this brand with things that are (specific nationality)
- To me, this brand represents what (specific country name) is all about/To me, this brand does not represent what (specific country name) is all about
- To me, this brand is a very good symbol of (specific country name)/To me, this brand is not a very good symbol of (specific country name)

Brand familiarity

- This brand is very familiar to me/This brand is very unfamiliar to me
- Everybody here has heard of this brand/Almost nobody here has heard of this brand
- I'm not at all knowledgeable about this brand/I'm very knowledgeable about this brand
- I have never seen advertisements for it in (specific nationality) magazines, radio, or TV/I have seen many advertisements for it in (specific nationality) magazines, radio, or TV

Samples

The samples used in both countries are constituted of resident women responsible for at least half of the shopping in the household. The U.S. sample is obtained from a leading sampling firm's list and is composed of 2,093 respondents, of which 247 return the questionnaire (12% response rate). The Korean sample is obtained using randomized cluster sampling and includes 2,000 households in Seoul, of which 370 agree to participate (18.5% response rate).

Reliability and validity

The reliability of the PBG scale is tested through the alpha coefficient ($\alpha_{U.S.}$ = 0.799 and α_{Korea} = 0.785).

For the cross-national measurement validation, the configural and metric invariance of the PBG scale are tested simultaneously with the other brand-related measures (perceived brand quality, perceived brand prestige, brand as icon of local culture, brand familiarity, likelihood of purchasing the brand) using multi-group confirmatory factor analysis. The configural invariance of the PBG scale and the other five brand constructs is supported, as the six-factor CFA model fit is good: $\chi^2(152) = 1218.69$ ($p < 0.001$), CFI = 0.933, TLI = 0.907, CAIC = 1990.10. All factor loadings are significant at $p < 0.001$, and the factor loadings are above 0.5. All factor correlations are significantly below unity ($p < 0.0001$), which supports discriminant validity between constructs. Equality of factor loadings is also supported by an overall improved fit: $\chi^2(161) = 1266.20$ ($p < 0.001$), CFI = 0.931, TLI = 0.909, CAIC = 1958.71, thus providing evidence of metric invariance.

The impact of PBG on brand prestige, perceived quality and purchase likelihood is examined in the next part of the analysis. A multi-group model with the United States and Korea as two groups is estimated through structural equation analysis. The model also includes similar paths related to brand as icon of local culture, and the other variables measured are included as covariates. The model reports a good fit: $\chi^2(21) = 48.187$ ($p < 0.001$), CFI = 0.997, TLI = 0.976, CAIC = 1704.80, and it reveals that PBG is positively associated with brand prestige (U.S.: $b = 0.361$, $p < 0.001$; Korea: $b = 0.434$, $p < 0.001$) and perceived quality (U.S.: $b = 0.152$, $p < 0.05$; Korea: $b = 0.573$, $p < 0.001$). The lack of a direct effect from PBG to purchase likelihood is detected, as this effect is mediated by brand prestige and perceived quality (U.S.: direct effect = 0.317, $p < 0.001$, indirect effect = 0.205; Korea: direct effect = 0.367, $p < 0.001$, indirect effect = 0.399). The analysis also shows that the total effect of PBG on purchase likelihood is greater than the effect of brand as icon of local culture. Two rival models are also tested, including reverse causal direction between prestige/quality and PBG as well as bidirectional relations between prestige/quality and PBG, but they both perform worse than the hypothesized model.

Managerial applications

The PBG scale represents a tool that international managers can use to measure the globalness perception of the brand in different countries. Indeed, companies want to take advantage of perceived brand globalness because it may create consumer perceptions of brand superiority. As the researchers demonstrate, PBG may provide a significant source of competitive strength as it impacts purchase likelihood. This scale can also be used by international managers to evaluate the performance of their brands in order to increase the profitability of their portfolio by replacing some weaker brands by stronger and more global brands.

5.4 Perceptions of brand luxury (Vigneron & Johnson, 2004)

Definition of construct

Vigneron and Johnson (2004) focus on consumers' perceptions of brand luxury, that is, the perceived luxuriousness of a brand, or, in other terms, the amount of luxury contained in a brand. They define perceptions of brand luxury as a multi-dimensional concept consisting of five dimensions: *perceived conspicuousness*, which refers to social representation, social position and social status associations that consumers make with respect to a luxury brand; *perceived uniqueness*, which refers to perceptions of exclusivity and rarity connected with a luxury brand; *perceived quality*, which refers to the perception that a luxury brand offers superior product qualities and performance compared to non-luxury brands; *perceived hedonism*, which reflects consumers' tendency to use a luxury brand for achieving personal rewards and fulfilment, subjective emotional benefits and intrinsically pleasing properties, rather than functional benefits; and *perceived extended self*, which reflects consumers' use of a luxury brand to classify or distinguish themselves, as well as to build their own identity. *Perceived conspicuousness, perceived uniqueness* and *perceived quality* are described as non–personal-oriented constructs, whereas *perceived extended self* and *perceived hedonism* are defined as personal-oriented constructs. The five dimensions of brand luxury are correlated to one another, although they refer to different concepts.

Scale description

The brand luxury index (BLI) scale measures consumers' perceptions of brand luxury; it is intended to measure and compare the brand luxury differential among brands which are deemed already luxurious. The BLI scale includes five dimensions and 20 items: 4 items are on *perceived conspicuousness*, 4 items on *perceived uniqueness*, 5 items on *perceived quality*, 3 items on *perceived hedonism* and 4 items on *perceived extended self*. All items consist of pairs of bipolar adjectives (semantic differential scale), where one adjective describes the maximum level of luxury and the other adjective describes the minimum level. Respondents are asked to evaluate where, along this continuum, a luxury brand is placed on each item. Items within each dimension can be averaged to form a dimension score. All items of the scale can also be averaged to form a total BLI score.

TABLE 5.3 Brand luxury index scale

Scale dimension	Scale item
Perceived conspicuousness[a]	• Conspicuous/Noticeable
	• Popular/Elitist*
	• Affordable/Extremely expensive*
	• For wealthy/For well-off
Perceived uniqueness[a]	• Fairly exclusive/Very exclusive*
	• Precious/Valuable
	• Rare/Uncommon
	• Unique/Unusual

(*Continued*)

TABLE 5.3 (Continued)

Scale dimension	Scale item
Perceived quality[a]	• Crafted/Manufactured
	• Upmarket/Luxurious*
	• Best quality/Good quality
	• Sophisticated/Original
	• Superior/Better
Perceived hedonism[b]	• Exquisite/Tasteful
	• Attractive/Glamorous*
	• Stunning/Memorable
Perceived extended self[b]	• Leading/Influential
	• Very powerful/Fairly powerful
	• Rewarding/Pleasing
	• Successful/Well regarded

Note: *indicates that the item is reverse scored; [a]indicates a non–personal-oriented construct, whereas [b]indicates a personal-oriented construct.

Scale development

The process for developing the BLI scale consists of three stages, which are labelled by the authors as "item generation", "reliability" and "validity".

In the item-generation stage, an initial pool of items is generated based on academic and commercial literature on luxury brands, qualitative interviews with managers from luxury companies and focus groups with postgraduate business students. The resulting 157 items are reduced to 30 following a content validity check by a panel of reviewers.

The reliability stage includes two studies. The first study is used to check the reliability of the scale and its dimensions. Respondents are asked to evaluate four luxury brands, identified through a pre-test, on the 30 BLI items. Exploratory factor analysis using principal component analysis and varimax rotation is conducted: all items displayed a loading of at least 0.60 on one of the five dimensions. Confirmatory factor analysis (CFA) performed using the 30 items reveals a moderate fit to the data (χ^2 = 1428.21, df = 395, p = 0.000, GFI = 0.78, AGFI = 0.74, NFI = 0.85, TLI = 0.87, RMSEA = 0.07). After removing eight items, a new CFA is performed and reveals an improved fit (χ^2 = 255.30, df = 160, p = 0.000, GFI = 0.94, AGFI = 0.93, NFI = 0.96, TLI = 0.98, RMSEA = 0.04). All analyses are conducted for each brand separately as well as on the aggregate sample.

The second study is aimed to check the test-retest reliability of the scale. Two data collections are conducted using the same sample of respondents and separated by two weeks from each other. Respondents are asked to evaluate three new luxury brands. Data analysis (correlation between time 1 and 2, internal scale reliability and new CFA) leads to removing two more items, leaving the BLI scale with 20 items. The 20-item model reports the following fit: χ^2 = 240.74, df = 160, p = 0.000, GFI = 0.96, AGFI = 0.95, NFI = 0.97, TLI = 0.99, RMSEA = 0.02.

The third and last stage, validity, includes four studies directed at demonstrating various types of validities of the BLI scale, that is, content validity, predictive validity, nomological validity, and construct validity. In the first of these studies, respondents are asked to rate three brands on the BLI scale and to provide an explanation of the reasons of their evaluation. In the second study, one sample of respondents is asked to rate three new brands on the BLI scale, and another sample of respondents is instructed to classify the three brands in two distinct categories (i.e., high and low luxury). In the third study, respondents are asked to evaluate the same three brands used previously on the BLI scale as well as on scales on materialistic attitudes (Moschis & Churchill, 1978), fashion involvement (Tigert, Ring & King, 1976), enduring involvement (Higie & Feick, 1988), money-prestige (Yamauchi & Templer, 1982) and price-based prestige sensitivity (Lichtenstein, Ridgway & Netemeyer, 1993). In the last study, respondents are asked to express their evaluations on the BLI scale items, which are expressed in various forms (Likert and Staple scales, in addition to semantic differential).

Samples

The item-generation stage involves 12 managers, 25 students, and 77 reviewers. The reliability stage uses a sample of 418 business students in the first study and a sample of 176 business students in the second study. The validity stage uses a sample of 186 university students in the study on content validity, 132 university students in the study on predictive validity, 331 university students in the study on nomological validity and 342 university students in the study on construct validity. All studies are conducted in Australia.

Reliability and validity

Several tests of reliability and validity are conducted for the BLI scale.

With regard to reliability, Cronbach's alpha is first computed for the 30-item scale for both individual dimensions and overall BLI scale. All values are included between 0.69 and 0.95 (analyses performed for both each brand separately and the aggregate sample). Item-to-total correlations within all samples range from 0.30 to 0.80. Evidence of the scale reliability is also provided for the final 20-item scale. In the second stage, the correlation between time 1 and 2 on the total BLI score is equal to 0.84 (0.83, 0.86 and 0.82 for the three brands surveyed), the Cronbach's alpha for the three brands ranges from 0.89 to 0.91 and the item-to-total correlations are from 0.35 to 0.65. In the third stage, the Cronbach's alpha is equal to 0.82, with values ranging from 0.71 to 0.90 for the different brands.

The validity of the BLI scale is tested with respect to content validity, predictive validity, nomological validity and construct validity.

Content validity is verified twice, once at the beginning of the scale development process and once the final set of items is retained. Initially, the content validity check allows the authors to reduce the set of items to 30. Once the final 20-item scale is identified, further evidence of content validity is provided by calculating the association between judges' classification of respondents' open-ended answers (as "low", "medium" or "high" perceptions of luxury toward the brand) and respondents' total BLI score. Associations are equal to 78%, 81%, and 72% for the three brands.

The predictive validity of the BLI scale is demonstrated by examining the presence of correlation between respondents' classification of three brands into high/low luxury categories and other respondents' ratings of these brands on the BLI scale. Correlations are equal to 0.32, 0.34 and 0.42 for the three brands.

The nomological validity of the BLI scale is proved by showing the presence of correlation ($ps < 0.01$) between BLI and five related constructs (i.e., materialistic attitudes, fashion involvement, enduring involvement, money-prestige and price-based prestige sensitivity). Correlations range from 0.47 to 0.69.

Finally, the construct validity is demonstrated using the multi-trait–multi-method (MTMM) matrix. Likert and Staple scales, obtained by adapting the BLI scale semantic differential items, are used for the two other measurement procedures. All Campbell and Fiske's (1959) requirements are satisfied. Validity coefficients of the five traits range from 0.48 to 0.81 ($ps < 0.001$).

Managerial applications

The BLI scale represents a managerial instrument which allows managers to measure the amount of luxury contained in a luxury brand. The scale highlights the dimensions that must be considered to create, maintain and evaluate luxury brands, that is, *perceived conspicuousness, perceived uniqueness, perceived quality, perceived hedonism* and *perceived extended self*. Managers could use these dimensions as guidelines to develop their luxury brands and to upgrade a brand already perceived as upscale or premium to the luxury level. Managers could also use the BLI scale to assess the strengths and weaknesses of their luxury brand, in relation to their competitors. This assessment could be done using either the 20 items or the dimension scores or the total BLI score.

5.5 Brand leadership (Chang & Ko, 2014)

Definition of construct

Brand leadership refers to a firm's competitive advantage over other brands. Brand leadership is defined as consumers' perception about the relatively distinctive ability of a brand to continually achieve excellence through sufficient combinations of trendsetting and brand positioning with an industry segment. Consistently with literature, brand leadership is conceptualized with four dimensions: *perceived quality*, defined as consumers' judgment about a product's relative superiority; *perceived value*, which refers to consumers' evaluation of a product's relative financial value based on what they give and receive; *perceived innovativeness*, which corresponds to consumers' perception about a brand's relative capability to be open to innovative ideas and work on new solutions; and *perceived popularity*, which refers to consumers' perception about a brand's relative popularity reflected by brand awareness and consumption.

Scale description

The measurement tool assessing perceived brand leadership (i.e., brand leadership scale, BLS) contains four dimensions, namely *perceived quality, perceived value, perceived innovativeness* and *perceived popularity*. Each dimension contains three items. Items are evaluated using a 7-point Likert scale, where 1 = "strongly disagree" and 7 = "strongly agree".

TABLE 5.4 Brand leadership scale

Scale dimension	Scale item
When compared with other competing brands of (product/service Y), this brand:	
Perceived quality	• Is higher in quality standards
	• Is superior in quality standards
	• Offers higher quality (product/service Y) features
Perceived value	• Is reasonably priced
	• Has better (product/service Y) features for the price
	• Offers more benefits for the price
Perceived innovativeness	• Is more dynamic in improvements
	• Is more creative in products and services
	• Is more of a trendsetter
Perceived popularity	• Is more preferred by customers of (product/service Y)
	• Is more recognized by customers of (product/service Y)
	• Is better known among customers of (product/service Y)

Scale development

The BLS is developed through a series of steps in accordance with Netemeyer, Bearden and Sharma (2003).

Study 1 consists of an item-generation phase, an item-purification phase and an assessment of nomological validity. The initial pool of BLS items (more than 100 items) is generated based on a literature review and exploratory in-depth interviews. In the interview, respondents are asked to think of brand leaders in six product categories and describe why these brands are leaders. The results of the interviews are analysed and converted into items, and then these items are compared with the results of the literature review. This process reduces the initial pool of items to 61 statements. An expert jury then judges the relevance, clarity and representativeness of these items according to the four dimensions of brand leadership, which results in a selection of 20 items.

A data survey is then conducted in order to purify the measurement scale on the basis of its psychometric properties. The respondents are asked to evaluate a dominant brand in the electronic body protector category in terms of brand leadership, as well as their attitude and loyalty toward the brand. Data are analysed using a confirmatory factor analysis (CFA). After dropping 6 items, the results of the CFA shows that the measurement model with 14 items achieves a good fit to the data for the first-order (χ^2/df = 214.944/71 = 3.027, RMSEA = 0.073, CFI = 0.96, SRMR = 0.0366) and the second-order analysis (χ^2/df = 222.671/73 = 3.050, RMSEA = 0.073, CFI = 0.96, SRMR = 0.0405). The scale's reliability and construct validity are then assessed. The nomological validity is checked by testing if the four dimensions of brand leadership influence consumers' attitude and loyalty toward the brand.

Study 2 revalidates the BLS by using an additional data set. Data are collected in five golf courses, where respondents are asked to evaluate the brand leadership perception of the golf courses. The measurement model specifying four latent factors to be correlated with each other is tested. Based on the results of the initial CFA, two more items are dropped. The model with 12 items (3 items for each dimension) shows good fit for the first-order (χ^2/df = 146.388/48 = 3.050; RMSEA = 0.080; CFI = 0.961, SRMR = 0.043) and the second-order measurement model (χ^2/df = 146.802/50 = 2.936; RMSEA = 0.076; CFI = 0.961, SRMR = 0.043). Tests of the scale's reliability, validity and measurement invariance are finally conducted.

Samples

Study 1 uses a sample of 20 graduate students for the exploratory phase. The expert jury is composed of five faculties and seven graduate students in the fields of marketing and management. The sample of the survey is obtained by distributing the questionnaire to 800 participants of the 2010 US Open Taekwondo Championship in Florida and results in 351 completed forms. The sample used in study 2 is composed of 370 golfers from five golf courses in North Florida, resulting in 333 usable questionnaires. For the measurement invariance test, this sample is divided into two groups: participants of private golf clubs (n = 161) and participants of public golf clubs (n = 172).

Reliability and validity

The scale's reliability and validity are tested through study 1 and are revalidated in study 2, when the final brand leadership scale is developed. With respect to reliability, study 1 reports that construct reliability ranges from 0.85 (*popularity*) to 0.90 (*quality*) and that all AVE measures are greater than the 0.5 standard, ranging from 0.59 (*popularity*) to 0.72 (*perceived value*). In study 2, reliability is tested through the Cronbach's alpha (equal to 0.75; 0.90; 0.81; 0.91, respectively, for *quality*, *value*, *innovativeness* and *popularity*) and composite reliability, which ranges from 0.70 (*quality*) to 0.83 (*value*). All AVE measures are greater than 0.5 except two factors (0.44 for *quality* and 0.45 for *innovativeness*).

With respect to validity, evidence of face and content validities is also assured with the use of in-depth interviews and experts' judgments in the item-generation phase in study 1.

Convergent and discriminant validities are shown in both studies 1 and 2. Convergent validity is demonstrated with acceptable CFA model fits and high factor loadings ranging from 0.71 to 0.90 (study 1) and from 0.65 to 0.95 (study 2). Significant relationships among the four dimensions and the second-order construct of brand leadership further support the scale's convergent validity (loadings range from 0.70 to 0.92 in study 1 and from 0.51 to 0.74 in study 2). Discriminant validity is also established through reasonably high levels of factor correlations among brand leadership factors (0.53 between *perceived value* and *popularity* and 0.81 between *quality* and *innovativeness* in study 1; 0.30 between *value* and *popularity* and 0.50 between *value* and *innovativeness* in study 2) and the comparison between the squared correlations among the constructs and AVE values. The nomological validity tested in study 1 confirms that the four dimensions of brand leadership influence positively and significantly attitude and loyalty toward the brand. The global fit indices indicate that the hypothesized model is strongly supported by the data (χ^2/df = 467.411/209 = 2.24, RMSEA = 0.057, CFI = 0.97, SRMR = 0.03, TLI = 0.97).

Furthermore, measurement invariance is tested across two groups in study 2 (consumers for private golf clubs versus for public golf clubs) using a series of hierarchically nested models. The hierarchy starts with the unconstrained model, which is used as a baseline to compare five nested models with an increasing number of constraints. The chi-square difference among the baseline and three nested models with constraints of invariance of first-order factor loadings, invariance of second-order factor loadings and invariance of factor variance is not significant, whereas the difference between the baseline and two nested models with increased constraints (invariance of disturbances of first-order factors and invariance of error variance) is significant ($p < 0.05$). However, similar CFI values (0.96, for the baseline model and 0.95 for the two models) lead the researchers to believe that these two models do not present an appreciable difference. Overall, the results show that the second-order factor structure is statistically equivalent across the two groups, which indicate a stability of the measurement model of brand leadership across various market segments.

Managerial applications

Market dynamics are getting intensive and complex due to the competitive relationship between leading and following brands. In this respect, the BLS represents a useful tool for managers to evaluate their brands about their relative strengths and weaknesses on a regular basis and in a simpler manner. This scale can also help managers to optimize their marketing actions by reinforcing a certain brand leadership dimension such as innovativeness or quality in order to differentiate their brands from competitors. All in all, it is strongly recommended that by adapting a brand leadership framework and the BLS outlined herein, firms distinguish their brand from other competing brands and stay competitive within a saturated market environment.

5.6 Academic focus

- A dissertation may focus on the brand parity construct (Muncy, 1996) and relate it to brand personality (see Chapter 3). There is evidence in literature that consumers' perceptions about the personality of a brand do not change much within a given product category (Romaniuk & Ehrenberg, 2012). One may therefore investigate if consumers' perceptions of brand personalities in a given product category are influenced by perceptions of brand parity.
- In a dissertation, one may want to relate consumers' perceptions of brand globalness to brand equity (see, for example, the framework developed by Buil, de Chernatony & Martínez, 2008, Chapter 11, pp. 248–252) in a multicultural context. How do these perceptions contribute to brand equity in different cultures? Frameworks that could be employed in a cross-cultural analysis include GLOBE's and Hofstede's (for a review, see Javidan *et al.*, 2006).
- A dissertation may want to understand how, in a given culture or in a multicultural context, marketers could stimulate consumers' perceptions of brand globalness through advertising. For example, what advertising creative and executional elements could be employed to that end? The dissertation may build on findings from Alden, Steenkamp and Batra (1999).
- A dissertation may investigate the extent to which consumers' perceptions of a brand's luxuriousness vary across cultures. In fact, a recent paper (Christodoulides, Michaelidou & Ching Hsing, 2009) has examined the extendibility of Vigneron and Johnson's (2004) brand luxury index scale, originally developed in Australia, to another country (Taiwan) and has found several issues in relation to the psychometric properties of the scale. Frameworks that could be used to investigate consumers' perceptions of a brand luxuriousness across cultures include GLOBE's and Hofstede's (for a review, see Javidan *et al.*, 2006).
- In a dissertation, one may investigate possible sources of brand leadership. One could, for example, take into account the country-of-origin construct and examine to what extent it influences consumers' perceptions of overall brand leadership as well as its dimensions (Chang & Jae Ko, 2014).

5.7 Managerial focus

- **For a few years now, your brand has been losing its performance. Have you checked your perceived brand globalness?**
  Your brand may lose its performance in some countries because its perceived brand globalness is weaker. Indeed, in general, consumers

tend to prefer brands with a global image because they associate it with a perception of brand superiority (Kapferer, 1997; Shocker *et al.*, 1994). Just think about brands such as Nike and Coca-Cola: consumers love them because they think everyone around the world enjoys them. Steenkamp, Batra and Alden (2003) suggest that the perceived brand globalness may provide a significant source of competitive strength, as it impacts purchase likelihood. Therefore, the scale developed by these authors can be helpful for checking the perceived globalness of your brand in order to develop offline or online communication which can reinforce the global image when needed and enhance the performance of the brand locally.

- **You are losing market share; have you checked your brand leadership?**
It is sometimes difficult to understand why the brand is losing market share. Is it due to a lack of a differentiation toward competitors or a lack of perceived value or perceived quality because competitors or private labels have improved their offers? The brand leadership scale (Chang & Jae Ko, 2014) represents a useful tool for managers to benchmark brand performance by measuring consumer perceptions of their brand competitiveness toward other brands. The analysis of the measures can help managers optimize their marketing actions by reinforcing certain brand leadership dimensions, such as innovation or perceived product quality or value, in order to regain market share toward competitors.

- **Before launching your brand extension in a new category, have you checked the brand parity of the new category?**
Before deciding to extend the brand in another category of products, it could be interesting to evaluate the brand parity in order to identify if competitors in this category are perceived quite similarly or if some of them have a unique positioning for consumers. The fact that products are perceived as quite similar to each other can offer opportunities for brand extensions. Indeed, a brand coming from another category may bring new expertise and specific know-how and gain a competitive edge by offering real differences compared to the major brand alternatives.

- **Have you checked that your brand is still perceived as a luxury brand?**
In recent years, luxury brands have developed many brand extensions in order to offer more accessible products such as accessories and sunglasses, making them more democratic. Nevertheless, it is important to check that these brand extensions are not altering the luxury brand image. The brand luxury index scale developed by Vigneron and Johnson (2004) represents a useful tool to evaluate the luxury perception of the brand through different dimensions, which allows managers to identify which aspects to reinforce in order to protect the luxury image.

> - **Have you checked that your brand is still perceived as luxurious across channels?**
>   Luxury brands have been associated with selective distribution for many years. Nowadays, many luxury brands are sold online via different marketplaces, which may impact the perception of brand luxuriousness. Furthermore, it is also important that throughout the different touchpoints, consumer have the same luxurious perception. The brand luxury index scale developed by Vigneron and Johnson (2004) can be used to evaluate if the luxurious image remains consistent across channels and if the development of the different means of distribution has not altered this perception.

References

Alden, D. L., Steenkamp, J.-B.E.M., & Batra, R. (1999). Brand positioning through advertising in Asia, North America, and Europe: the role of global consumer culture. *Journal of Marketing*, 63, 75–87.

Batra, R., Ramaswamy, V., Alden, D. L., Steenkamp, J.-B.E.M., & Ramachander, S. (2000). Effects of brand local/nonlocal origin on consumer attitudes in developing countries. *Journal of Consumer Psychology*, 9, 83–95.

Buil, I., de Chernatony, L., & Martinez, E. (2008). A cross-national validation of the consumer-based brand equity scale. *Journal of Product and Brand Management*, 17 (6), 384–392.

Campbell, D. T., & Fiske, D. W. (1959). Convergent and discriminant validation by the multitrait-multimethod matrix. *Psychological Bulletin*, 56, 81–105.

Chang, Y., & Ko, Y. J. (2014). The brand leadership: scale development and validation. *Journal of Brand Management*, 21 (1), 63–80.

Christodoulides, G., Michaelidou, N., & Ching Hsing, L. (2009). Measuring perceived brand luxury: an evaluation of the BLI scale. *Journal of Brand Management*, 16 (5/6), 395–405.

Churchill, G. A., Jr. (1979). A paradigm for developing better measures of marketing constructs. *Journal of Marketing Research*, 16 (1), 64–73.

Dodds, W. B., Monroe, K. B., & Grewal, D. (1991). Effects of price, brand, and store information on buyers' product evaluations. *Journal of Marketing Research*, 28, 307–319.

Han, C. M., & Terpstra, V. (1988). Country of origin effects for uni-national and bi-national products. *Journal of International Business Studies*, 19 (2), 235–256.

Higie, R. A., & Feick, L. (1989). Enduring involvement: conceptual and measurement issues. In T. K. Sroll (ed.), *Advances in consumer research*. Provo, UT: Association for Consumer Research, 690–696.

Hofstede, G. (1991). *Cultures and organizations: software of the mind*. London: McGraw-Hill.

Hunter, E. D., & Nebenzahl, I. D. (1984). Alternative questionnaire formats for country image studies. *Journal of Marketing Research*, 21, 463–471.

Iyer, R., & Muncy, J. A. (2005). The role of brand parity in developing loyal customers. *Journal of Advertising Research*, 45 (2), 222–228.

Javidan, M., House, R., Dorfman, P., Hanges, P., & De Luquet, M. (2006). Conceptualizing and measuring cultures and their consequences: a comparative review of GLOBE's and Hofstede's approaches. *Journal of International Business Studies*, 37 (6), 897–914.

Kapferer, J.-N. (1997). *Strategic brand management* (2nd ed.). Dover, NH: Kogan Page.
Kapferer, J.-N., & Bastien, V. (2012). *The luxury strategy: break the rules of marketing to build luxury brands* (2nd ed.). London: Kogan Page.
Keller, K. L. (1993). Conceptualizing, measuring and managing customer-based brand equity. *Journal of Marketing*, 1, 1–22.
Keller, K. L., & Aaker, D. A. (1992). The effects of sequential introduction of brand extensions. *Journal of Marketing Research*, 29, 35–50.
Lichtenstein, D. R., Ridgway, N., & Netemeyer, R. G. (1993). Price perceptions and consumer shopping behavior: a field study. *Journal of Marketing Research*, 30 (May), 234–245.
Moschis, G. P., & Churchill, G. A., Jr. (1978). Consumer socialization: a theoretical and empirical analysis. *Journal of Marketing Research*, 15 (4), 599–609.
Muncy, J. A. (1996). Measuring perceived brand parity. *Advances in Consumer Research*, 23, 411–417.
Netemeyer, R. G., Bearden, W. O., & Sharma, S. (2003). *Scaling procedures: issues and applications*. London: SAGE.
Romaniuk, J., & Ehrenberg, A.S.C. (2012). Do brands lack personality? *Marketing Theory*, 12 (3), 333–339.
Shimp, T. A., & Sharma, S. (1987). Consumer ethnocentrism: construction and validation of the CETSCALE. *Journal of Marketing Research*, 24, 280–289.
Shocker, A. D., Srivastava, R. K., & Ruekert, R. W. (1994). Challenges and opportunities facing brand management: an introduction to the special issue. *Journal of Marketing Research* 31, 19–158.
Steenkamp, J.-B.E.M., Batra, R., & Alden, D. L. (2003). How perceived brand globalness creates brand value. *Journal of International Business Studies*, 34 (1), 53–65.
Tigert, D. J., Ring, L. J., & King, C. W. (1976). Fashion involvement and buying behavior: a methodological study. *North America Advances in Consumer Research*, 3, 46–52.
Vigneron, F., & Johnson, L. W. (2004). Measuring perceptions of brand luxury. *Journal of Brand Management*, 11 (6), 484–506.
Yamauchi, K. T., & Templer, D. I. (1982). The development of a money attitude scale. *Journal of Personality Assessment*, 46, 522–528.

6

ATTITUDES TOWARD THE BRAND

6.1 Overview

Consumers' attitudes represent a cornerstone of the marketing and consumer research literature (Solomon, Bamossy, Askegaard & Hogg, 2006). Attitudes are defined as individual internal evaluations of an object: they refer to a state that is internal to the individual, and they are always directed toward an object. They are lasting, as they endure over time, and they typically include affective, behavioral and cognitive components (Olson & Zanna, 1993). The importance of consumers' attitudes for marketing researchers is related to the fact that it has been shown that attitudes can guide future behaviour (Glasman & Albarracín, 2006) and, in a marketing context, that they can predict behavioral intentions (Bagozzi, 1981).

Because of the centrality of consumer attitudes for understanding consumer behaviour, marketing researchers have been traditionally concerned with the measurement of attitudes toward a multitude of objects, including brands (Spears & Singh, 2004). Various measures of brand attitudes are available in literature (Bruner, Hensel & James, 2001; see also pp. 64, 149, 230 in this book). Nevertheless, only a few scales on attitudes have been developed following a rigorous approach.

This chapter includes three such scales on brand attitudes, which refer to specific contexts of applications. In light of the importance, especially in times of crisis, of private-label brands, Burton, Lichtenstein, Netemeyer and Garretson (1998) advance a scale about attitude toward private-label brands. This scale represents a measurement tool that marketing researchers can use to assess consumers' attitudes toward private-label brands. The other two scales refer to specific targets of consumers, that is, children and adolescents, who are selected given their increasingly important roles in consumption processes (McNeal, 2007). The scale developed by Pecheux and Derbaix (1999) measures the attitudes toward brands of 8- to 12-year-olds. The scale proposed by Derbaix and Leheut (2008a; 2008b) captures the attitudes toward brands of consumers between 12 and 18 years of age.

6.2 Attitude toward private-label brands (Burton, Lichtenstein, Netemeyer & Garretson, 1998)

Definition of construct

Private-label brands are those sold under retailers' own labels and across various categories of products and have become real competitors of national brands. Attitude toward private-label brands is defined by the authors as "a predisposition to respond in a favourable or unfavourable manner due to product evaluations, purchase evaluations, and/or self-evaluations associated with private label grocery products" (Burton, Lichtenstein, Netemeyer & Garretson, 1998, p. 298). This definition is sufficiently broad to be of use in a general sense across grocery product categories and to encompass a single-dimension attitude that reflects a favourable or unfavourable predisposition toward private labels based on both economic (e.g., quality, price) and noneconomic (e.g., joy associated with getting a good deal) factors.

Scale description

The attitude toward private-label brands scale consists of one dimension and six items. Items are evaluated using a 7-point Likert scale, where 1 = "strongly disagree" and 7 = "strongly agree".

TABLE 6.1 Attitude toward private-label brands scale

Scale item
• Buying private-label brands makes me feel good
• I love it when private-label brands are available for the product categories I purchase
• For most product categories, the best buy is usually the private-label brand
• In general, private-label brands are poor-quality products*
• Considering value for the money, I prefer private-label brands to national brands
• When I buy a private-label brand, I always feel that I am getting a good deal

Note: *indicates the item is negatively phrased and reverse coded.

Scale development

The attitude toward private-label brands scale is developed through a pre-test and a main study.

The pre-test examines an initial pool of 12 items, which is generated by the researchers based on the literature review. Completed questionnaires are subjected to a series of principal components analyses, without any restrictions on the number of factors to extract. The first analysis reveals two factors with eigenvalue > 1.0, but only one is strong based on scree-plot; items with loadings < 0.60 are deleted. The second analysis shows one factor with eigenvalue > 1.0;

items with loadings below 0.7 or above 0.85 are deleted. The third analysis is made on the remaining six items and allows the authors to extract one principal component, which explains 65% of the total variance. A confirmatory factor analysis is then performed using LISREL VIII, which supports the one one-factor model with the six items (χ^2 = 22.1, df = 9, p < 0.01, GFI = 0.95, AGFI = 0.88, CFI = 0.97, TLI = 0.95).

The main study further confirms the six-item unidimensional structure of the private-label attitude scale. Shoppers are asked to answer a few questions relative to their purchase in the store and then to complete the questionnaire at home. In addition to private-label attitude, the questionnaire contains measures on price consciousness, value consciousness and price-quality perception (Lichtenstein, Ridgway & Netemeyer, 1993), general and deal-specific deal proneness (Lichtenstein, Netemeyer & Burton, 1995), impulsiveness (adapted from Martin, Weun & Beatty, 1994), brand loyalty (Lichtenstein, Netemeyer & Burton, 1990), and others on smart-shopper self-perception, risk averseness and reliance on internal reference price developed by the authors. The six-item measure of private-label attitude is subjected to a confirmatory analysis using LISREL VIII to assess the psychometric properties of the scale. The results confirm the solution previously identified with acceptable indexes (χ^2 = 65.4, df = 9, p < 0.01, GFI = 0.94, AGFI = 0.86, CFI = 0.94, TLI = 0.91). Validity tests are conducted using the other constructs measured.

Samples

The pre-test includes a convenience sample of 140 non-student respondents who are primary shoppers for their households. The main study is based on a convenience sample composed of 333 shoppers who are contacted in store and who return the completed survey (survey distributed to 896 shoppers in store; response rate = 37%).

Reliability and validity

The reliability of the attitude toward private-label brands scale is tested through coefficient alpha, which is equal to 0.89 in the pre-test and 0.873 in the main study.

The scale's validities are tested in the main study. Convergent validity is checked through the average variance extracted estimate, which is equal to 0.56, and through item loadings, which are all highly significant (t-values associated with the loadings ranging from 10.8 to 18.2).

Discriminant validity is demonstrated with respect to coupon proneness and value consciousness. Confirmatory models are estimated including a correlated three-factor model, a one-factor model and three different two-factor models. The analysis shows that the correlated three-factor model (χ^2 = 324.5, df = 132,

GFI = 0.90, AGFI = 0.87) performs better than the one-factor (delta χ^2 = 1,433.5, df = 3, p < 0.01) and two-factor models (delta χ^2 between 595.7 and 780.5, df = 2, p < 0.01). In addition, in the correlated three-factor model, the correlations among the three constructs are significantly less than 1.0 (completely standardized phi estimates range from 0.19 to 0.32). Finally, it is shown that the squares of the phi estimate (ranging from 0.04 to 0.10) are less than the average variance extracted for private-label attitude, coupon proneness and value consciousness (equal to, respectively, 0.56, 0.47 and 0.56).

To support the nomological validity of the scale, bivariate correlations between private-label attitude and, respectively, price perception, general consumer marketplace and deal proneness–related constructs are tested. The results support the predicted relationships between private-label attitude and price perception variables (r = 0.29 for value consciousness, r = 0.26 for price consciousness and r = −0.25 for price-quality perceptions; all ps < 0.01). Three of the four correlations between private-label attitude and general consumer marketplace constructs are significant and in the postulated direction (r = −0.27 for brand loyalty, r = −0.20 for impulsiveness and r = 0.27 for smart shopping, all ps < 0.01), while no significant correlation with risk averseness is found. Private-label attitude is also positively related to consumer general deal proneness (r = 0.18, p < 0.01) and reliance on internal reference price (r = 0.14, p < 0.05) and is more strongly related to price-related deals (r = 0.30, p < 0.01) than nonprice deals (r = 0.15, p < 0.05; difference between the two is significant with t = 2.63, p < 0.01).

The scale's predictive validity is finally tested. Hierarchical stepwise regression is conducted, where the percentage of private-label purchases is the dependent variable. In stage 1, impulsiveness and price-quality perceptions enter the equation as significant predictors, whereas in stage 2, private-label attitude is entered as significant predictor (F change = 14.1, p < 0.01), increasing the model's adjusted R^2 from 0.06 to 0.12. The predictive validity of the attitude scale is also demonstrated by the percentages of private-label brands purchased by consumer segments higher (24.8%) and lower (15.1%) on the attitude scale.

Managerial applications

Considering the important role of private-label brands for retailers and the increasing competition that they represent for national brand manufacturers, this scale represents a tool to understand the consumer attitude toward private labels. The private-label attitude scale allows managers to track the change in consumer attitude toward private labels and can enrich the analysis of private-label sales information. This scale can be used to identify consumers who constitute a primary target market for private-label brands in order to develop specific marketing actions dedicated to them. This measure also provides interesting insights for national brand manufacturers concerned about competition provided by private-label products.

6.3 Children's attitude toward the brand (Pecheux & Derbaix, 1999)

Definition of construct

Children's attitude toward the brand is defined by Pecheux and Derbaix (1999) by referring to a classic definition of brand attitude as "a psychological tendency that is expressed by evaluating a brand with some degree of favour or disfavour" (Eagly & Chaiken, 1993 as reported in Pecheux and Derbaix, 1999, p. 21). Children's attitude toward the brand includes a *hedonic* component, which refers to more affective aspects, and a *utilitarian* component, which refers to more cognitive aspects. The focus of the two researchers is on children in the 8- to 12-year-old range due to their relevance for marketers. Children in this age range, in fact, are both actual buyers (they have their own money) and prescriptors of the purchase of many household items.

Scale description

The scale on children's attitude toward the brand includes two dimensions and seven items: the *hedonic* dimension, which is measured using four items, and the *utilitarian* dimension, which is measured through three items. Both an English and a French version of the items are provided. Respondents can rate these items using a 4-point scale anchored at 1 = "definitely disagree" and 4 = "definitely agree".

TABLE 6.2 Children's attitude toward the brand scale

Scale dimension	Scale item (English)	Scale item (French)
Hedonic	• I like it	• J'aime ça
	• It is cheerful/fun	• C'est gai
	• It is great/brilliant	• C'est génial
	• I like it very much	• J'aime beaucoup
Utilitarian	• It is useful	• C'est utile
	• It practical/handy	• C'est pratique
	• It is useless*	• Ça ne sert à rien*

Note: *indicates the item is reverse coded.

Scale development

The scale development process follows Churchill (1979) and includes an exploratory study, four (quantitative) data collections and a follow-up data collection.

The exploratory study clarifies the construct studied, that is, children's attitude toward the brand. The study identifies the vocabulary used by children and the associations they make when talking about brands; it also identifies a set of brands well known by children and the prototypical products of these brands. To that end, the following is conducted: four focus groups with mothers and teachers; one interpretative study, where children are interviewed twice at home and are observed while shopping over a period of six months; and a series of in-depth interviews with two children at a time. This exploratory study results in the generation of 18 items.

In the first data collection, children are asked to evaluate two out of four brands on the 18 items using a 4-point Likert scale (1 = "definitely disagree" and 4 = "definitely agree"). An exploratory factor analysis with oblique rotation is conducted on the pooled data and for each brand individually. The analysis leads to the suppression of five items not properly understood or with poor loading (< 0.50). A hierarchical cluster analysis using two methods (complete linkage or furthest neighbour and single linkage or nearest neighbour) is also implemented and further supports previous findings. This new analysis shows that items are divided into two groups and that the five eliminated items do not constitute a separate cluster, as they are included in the biggest one. A set of 13 items is therefore left from the first data collection.

In the second data collection, children are asked to evaluate the same set of brands (two out of four) on the 13 items using a 4-point Likert scale. Data analysis is conducted on the pooled data and on each brand individually. A new exploratory factor analysis using oblique rotation leads to the suppression of four additional items either because absent from the pooled solution, because of poor loadings or because redundant. A set of nine items results from the study.

The third and fourth data collections are performed as a test-retest survey and are separated one another by two weeks. A new set of three brands (one per child) is employed in these two data collections. For validity purposes, children are asked to evaluate the brands not only on the nine attitude items but also on an eight-item involvement scale (Derbaix & Pecheux, 1997). To do that, they are asked to use two scale formats (Likert and semantic differential). Data analysis is conducted separately for both formats and data collections. The results of the exploratory factor analysis with oblique rotation support the two-factor solution previously identified. Confirmatory factor analysis, using LISREL 8, leads to a satisfying solution after removing two additional items (third collection: χ^2 = 16.750, df = 9, p = 0.0559, RMSEA = 0.0653, GFI = 0.977, NNFI = 0.971, CFI = 0.988 for the Likert scale and χ^2 = 19.686, df = 10, p = 0.0324, RMSEA = 0.0701, GFI = .973, NNFI = 0.980, CFI = .990 for the semantic differential scale; fourth collection: χ^2 = 15.860, df = 9, p = 0.0699, RMSEA = 0.0622, GFI = 0.978, NNFI = 0.983, CFI = 0.993 for the Likert scale and χ^2 = 15.861, df = 10, p = 0.104, RMSEA = 0.0545, GFI = 0.977, NNFI = 0.989, CFI = 0.995 for the semantic differential scale). Validity tests are conducted on the seven-item scale.

To further test the scale validity, a follow-up data collection is conducted on two different days. Each child is asked to evaluate 11 brands from three product categories. On the first day, children are questioned about their attitude toward the brand, whereas on the second day, they are asked about their purchase intention. The measure for purchase intention is formulated on the basis of a pre-test. Validity tests are performed.

Samples

The exploratory study employs 13 children in the interpretative study and 49 children in in-depth interviews. The first data collection is based on a sample of 155 children. The second data collection is based on a sample of 149 children. The third and fourth data collections use 198 matched questionnaires. The follow-up study utilizes a sample of 53 children. All children are Belgian, aged 8 to 12 years.

Reliability and validity

Reliability tests are conducted in each data collection. With regard to the final scale, the Cronbach's alpha coefficients are computed in the third and fourth data collections for each dimension (*hedonic* and *utilitarian*) and scale format (Likert and semantic differential) separately. The third data collection reports a Cronbach's alpha of 0.828 (Likert) and 0.864 (semantic differential) for the *hedonic* dimension and one of 0.635 (Likert) and 0.804 (semantic differential) for the *utilitarian* dimension. The fourth data collection reports a Cronbach's alpha of 0.855 (Likert) and 0.883 (semantic differential) for the *hedonic* dimension and one of 0.765 (Likert) and 0.811 (semantic differential) for the *utilitarian* dimension.

Using a multi-trait multi-method matrix (MTMM), evidence of test-retest reliability is provided. Test-retest reliability diagonal is obtained by correlating the scores of each child on both occasions for each dimension. Values displayed are acceptable. The MTMM is also used to check the convergent validity of the scale, as well as its discriminant validity with respect to involvement, which is chosen as alternative construct. For discriminant validity, it is also shown that, in 22 out of 24 cases, the average variance extracted for each of the two factors is greater than the squared correlation of the two factors and that factor correlation is significantly different from unity.

The scale criterion validity is examined in the follow-up study with regard to purchase intention. Evidence that attitude impacts behaviour is provided by regression intention on the attitude ($R^2 = 0.198$, t-test for the attitude variable = 11.438).

Managerial applications

The scale on children's attitude toward the brand consists of a small number of items and thus can be implemented easily in different contexts. The researchers suggest using the scale in a variety of children-focused studies; for example, in studies dealing with brand loyalty, brand extensions, brand image, brand equity and impact of advertising.

6.4 Adolescents' attitude toward the brand (Derbaix & Leheut, 2008a, 2008b)

Definition of construct

To conceptualize adolescents' attitude toward the brand, Derbaix and Leheut (2008a; 2008b) build on a classic definition of general attitude as "a psychological tendency that is expressed by evaluating a particular entity with a certain degree of favour or disfavour, generally expressed in cognitive, affective and behavioural responses" (Eagly & Chaiken, 1993 as reported in Derbaix & Leheut 2008b, p. 47). They also conceptualize adolescents' attitude toward the brand as a multidimensional construct, as it includes three dimensions which cover *affective, functional* and *social* aspects of attitude. The *social* dimension is of particular importance for adolescents and is specific to this type of consumer.

Scale description

The scale assesses adolescents' attitude toward the brand with respect to three aspects: *affective, functional* and *social*. The scale includes 10 items, three for both the *affective* and *social* dimension and four for the *functional* dimension. Items are evaluated on Likert scales. The scale is originally developed in French, but an English version is also provided.

TABLE 6.3 Adolescents' attitude toward the brand scale

Scale dimension	Scale item (English)	Scale item (French)
Affective	• I like it very much • I appreciate it • It's cool	• J'aime beaucoup • J'apprécie • C'est cool
Functional	• It's useful • It's necessary • It's practical • It's efficient	• C'est utile • C'est nécessaire • C'est pratique • C'est efficace
Social	• It helps you become part of a group • It allows you not to go unnoticed • It allows you to get more respect	• Ça aide à s'intégrer dans un groupe • Ça permet de ne pas passer inaperçu(e) • Ça permet d'être plus estimé(e)

Scale development

The adolescents' attitude toward the brand scale is developed through a 10-stage process, in accordance with Churchill (1979).

In stage 1, the domain of the construct is specified following the guidelines provided by Rossiter (2002). Adolescents' attitude toward the brand is defined with respect to its object (the brand), attributes (attitude) and raters (adolescents).

In stage 2, a set of 49 items is generated based on literature review and a pre-survey conducted on adolescents who are interviewed individually. The pre-survey has also the purpose of identifying the brands to use in the next stages.

Stage 3 includes the first data collection. Respondents are asked to evaluate two brands on the attitude items; three brands are used in total, and different combinations are proposed in the survey. In stage 4, these data are analysed using exploratory factor analysis with oblique rotation. Data analysis is performed both at aggregate level and for each of the brands separately. Based on different criteria including loadings < 0.40, high cross-loadings, items not behaving consistently in the different solutions, Cronbach's alpha and redundancy of similar items, 13 items are eliminated and 31 are retained. Data analysis reveals five dimensions accounting for 53.6% of total variance.

Stage 5 includes the second data collection, which is conducted in a similar way as the first data collection. Stage 6 consists of the analysis of these data. Data analysis reveals three dimensions accounting for 68.93% of total variance and results in the elimination of 19 items and the retention of 12 items.

Stage 7 consists of two data collections, that is, test and retest studies. In the test study, respondents evaluate items about attitude toward the brand and involvement (Strazzieri, 1994) using the Likert format. In the retest, respondents evaluate the same items using the semantic differential format. Two brands and two product categories (clothing, cell phone) are used. Data are analysed through factor analysis (principal component analysis with oblique rotation). An MTMM matrix is developed, and the three-dimension solution is confirmed irrespective of scale format.

Stage 8 consists of two additional data collections (test and retest studies). Instead of the involvement construct used previously, the researchers now use a scale on adolescents' involvement in product categories that they develop. Confirmatory factor analysis is carried out using AMOS 7.0, and results support the three-dimensional structure with 10 items; for the Likert format: Likert: χ^2 = 40.233, df = 32, p = 0.151, χ^2/df = 1.257, RMSEA = 0.036, RMR = 0.057, GFI = 0.962, CFI = 0.992, TLI = 0.989. For semantic differential format: χ^2 = 61.794, df = 32, p = 0.001, χ^2/df = 1.931, RMSEA = 0.069, RMR = 0.090, GFI = 0.943, CFI = 0.971, TLI = 0.959. In stage 9, these data are used to build a new MTMM matrix, which uses semantic differential format as alternative method and adolescents' involvement in product categories as alternative traits; the MTMM is used to test trait reliability and validity.

Stage 10 is based on a new data collection. Respondents are asked to evaluate two out of three brands in terms of brand attitude, involvement in product category (measured as in the previous stage) and purchase intention (measured as purchase probability scale ranging from 1 to 10). Regression analyses are performed to check the scales' predictive validity.

Samples

Stage 2 involves 18 adolescents in the interviews. Stage 3 is based on a sample of 225 respondents. Stage 5 is based on a sample of 180 respondents. Stage 7 uses 120 respondents in the test and 108 respondents in the retest. Stage 8 uses 200 respondents in the test and 158 respondents in the retest. Stage 10 is based on a sample of 122 respondents. All respondents are adolescents aged in the 12- to 18-year-old age range.

Reliability and validity

The overall reliability of the scale about adolescents' attitude toward the brand is demonstrated in stage 7, through the first MTMM. The scale's reliability is also tested in stage 8 through the Cronbach's alpha: scores are equal to 0.877 for the *affective* dimension, 0.907 for the *functional* dimension and 0.722 for the *social* dimension. The scale's temporal stability is demonstrated in stage 9, through the new MTMM (for Likert scale: reliability diagonal coefficients range from 0.644 to 0.77; for semantic differential, reliability diagonal coefficient range from 0.517 to 0.723).

The scale convergent validity is first assessed in stage 7, through the first MTMM, and then fully assessed in stage 9, along with discriminant validity. Convergent validity is assessed by checking the correlation between the same traits measured by different methods. Correlation scores between 0.63 and 0.749 indicate convergence of methods. Discriminant validity is proven by showing that the correlation of a trait with itself, measured by different methods, is higher than the correlation between different traits measured by either the same or different methods.

Finally, the predictive validity of the adolescents' attitude toward the brand scale is demonstrated in stage 10. Regression analyses show that adolescents' attitude is predictive of their intention to buy for all three brands surveyed: the regression coefficient is equal to 0.159, 0.221 and 0.173, respectively (all $ps < 0.000$).

Managerial applications

From a practical viewpoint, the scale about adolescents' attitude toward the brand can be used to measure the different aspects of attitude (i.e., *affective, functional* and *social*). The measurement of the facets will allow marketers to better understand and attribute the origin of the observed variance in adolescents' behaviour regarding a brand. It also allows advertisers to test the effectiveness of advertising campaigns emphasizing a specific positioning strategy (for example, social, utilitarian, etc.). The scale can finally serve as a basis for segmenting markets.

6.5 Academic focus

- By focusing on one product category such as food, where private-label brands seem to be quite popular (Olbrich & Grewe, 2013), a dissertation may examine the role that store-related aspects have on attitudes toward private-label brands. One could consider, for example, store atmospherics, store image, and/or in-store experience associated with the store where private-label brands are sold and examine how each of these aspects impacts attitudes toward private-label brands.
- A dissertation may focus on one new type of marketing communication (e.g., advergames, online advertising, branded viral campaigns in social network sites; see de Pelsmacker & Neijens, 2012) and understand how brand attitudes that are formed after being exposed to this new type of marketing communication influence children's (Pecheux & Derbaix, 1999) or adolescents' (Derbaix & Leheut, 2008a; 2008b) behavioral intentions and actual behaviours. Examples of possible outcomes include purchase intentions, brand loyalty and word of mouth.
- Recent papers (Decoopman, Gentina & Fosse-Gomez, 2010; Hsieh, Chiu & Lin, 2006) show the influence exerted by family and parents on the formation of brand attitudes in children or adolescents. One dissertation may investigate the influence exerted by peers, in addition to family and parents, that is, other children of similar age, such as classmates or playmates.
- General concern is present around the topic of child obesity and marketing practices promoting unhealthy lifestyles. A dissertation may be concerned with the ability of brands to instigate healthy behaviours in young consumers, for example, through the use of product placement (Charry, 2014). Brands toward which consumers have varying attitudes (see frameworks of Derbaix & Leheut, 2008a; 2008b; Pecheux & Derbaix, 1999) may be considered to that purpose.
- Recent research (Hota, Chumpitaz Cáceres & Cousin, 2010) analyses the impact of public-service advertising on children's nutrition habits. Building on it, a dissertation may investigate the effectiveness of a communication campaign developed by a brand to promote branded healthy products on children's attitude toward the brand (Pecheux & Derbaix, 1999) and the branded healthy product.

6.6 Managerial focus

- **Have you checked the attitude of your consumers toward private labels?**
  Private labels have been part of the fast-moving consumer goods (FMCG) industry for at least the last 30 to 35 years, but they have

reinforced their position during the recession. Indeed, private labels no longer offer only copycat products but have improved the quality of their products and have developed more premium products. Private labels today carry significant value in consumers' minds and have become, more than ever, legitimate and strong competitors of national brands. Therefore, to protect market share, national brands should reinforce their core values and uniqueness in order to compete against private labels. Managers should track the attitude of their consumers toward private labels in order to compete effectively against private labels and keep consumers' loyalty.

- **Have you checked the influence of promotion using a cartoon character on children's attitude toward your brand?**
Promotions such as cross-selling and premiums are commonly used marketing tools for reaching children and adolescents. Food marketers are especially interested in youth from the 8- to 12-year-old age group because of their influence on many households' consumption decisions and their pocket money used for food products (Boland et al., 2012). Brands such as Coca-Cola, McDonald's and Kellogg's commonly give premiums in the form of toys, cards or games. Premiums can increase short-term sales since children may desire the item over the food, but they can also help elevate the image of that brand in children's minds. Therefore, it is interesting for marketers to evaluate the influence of using a cartoon character in promotion on children's attitude toward the brand using Pecheux and Derbaix' scale (1999). Indeed, at the stage of children's construction, relationship to brands evolves significantly, and preadolescents are deciders of consumption both today and tomorrow as future adult consumers.

- **Is brand extension a solution to keep on growing with your consumers?**
There are some strong brands such as Oasis, Kinder, Kellogg's and Nutella which specifically target children but which also remain present in the minds of consumers when they become adolescent. These brands try to enlarge their portfolio with brand extensions in order to reach adolescents with products more aligned with their needs. Nevertheless, developing specific products may not be enough to attract this target. Even though brand extensions can be positively perceived for their functional attributes, they may not have the capacity to answer adolescents' important affective and social needs. The measurement of the adolescents' attitude toward brands through affective, functional and social dimensions (Derbaix & Leheut, 2008a; 2008b) can provide a better understanding of the perception and reaction of adolescents toward these brand extensions. On the other hand, it is also important to check that these brand extensions are not altering the parent brand image for children. Therefore, it could be interesting to track the children's attitude toward the brand using the scale developed by Pecheux and Derbaix (1999).

- **Does your brand really answer adolescents' social needs?**
  Even though the adolescents' segment represents an interesting target for brands and retailers, it is difficult to attract them. They have a volatile attitude toward brands and like to have shopping experiences with friends rather than with family (Breazaele & Lueg, 2011). Managers aiming at targeting adolescents should try to better understand adolescents' attitude in order to define strategies allowing them to answer their individualism needs but also their needs of socialization (Gentina & Chandon, 2014). Therefore, brand managers should consider them more as young adults rather than older children and should also evaluate if the promotion or the shopping experience is able to satisfy the social assimilation among their group of friends.
- **Do you monitor adolescents' attitude toward your brand after being exposed to online communication?**
  Even though adolescents enjoy shopping with friends, they also like chatting online or sharing information with other members of their online community. Adolescents have in general a good understanding of sales promotion mechanisms (Fosse-Gomez, 2011). They like to win goodies and they are more sensitive to advergames and storytelling. They like to share video and music with others. Therefore, the adolescents' attitude toward brand scale (Derbaix & Leheut, 2008a; 2008b) can be very useful to evaluate the brand attitude formed after being exposed to different forms of online communication and measure how it influences their online participation and positive word of mouth.

References

Bagozzi, R. P. (1981). Attitudes, intentions, and behavior: a test of some key hypotheses. *Journal of Personality and Social Psychology*, 41 (4), 607–627.

Boland, W. A., Connell, P. M., & Erickson, L. M. (2012). Children's response to sales promotions and their impact on purchase behaviour. *Journal of Consumer Psychology*, 22 (2), 272–279.

Breazaele, M., & Lueg, E. (2011). Retail shopping typology of American teens. *Journal of Business Research*, 64 (6), 565–571.

Bruner, G. C., II, Hensel, P. J., & James, K. E. (2001). *Marketing scales handbook: a compilation of multi-item measures for consumer behavior & advertising*, Vol. IV. Mason, OH: Thomson.

Burton, S., Lichtenstein, D. R., Netemeyer, R. G., & Garretson, J. A. (1998). A scale for measuring attitude toward private label products and an examination of its psychological and behavioral correlates. *Journal of the Academy of Marketing Science*, 26 (4), 293–306.

Charry, K. (2014). Product placement and the promotion of healthy food to pre-adolescents: When popular TV series make carrots look cool. *International Journal of Advertising*, 33 (3), 599–616.

Churchill, G. A., Jr. (1979). A paradigm for developing better measures of marketing constructs. *Journal of Marketing Research*, 16 (February), 64–73.

Decoopman, I., Gentina, E., & Fosse-Gomez, M. H. (2010). La confusion des générations? Les enjeux identitaires des échanges vestimentaires entre les mères et leur fille adolescente. *Recherche et Applications en Marketing*, 25 (3), 7–27.

Derbaix, C., & Leheut, É. (2008a). Adolescents: implication envers les produits et attitude envers les marques (French). *Recherche et Applications en Marketing*, 23 (2), 37–66.

Derbaix, C., & Leheut, É. (2008b). Adolescents: involvement in product categories and attitude toward brands. *Recherche et Applications en Marketing* (English edition), 23 (2), 37–64.

Derbaix, C., & Pecheux, C. (1997). L'implication et l'enfant: proposition d'une échelle de mesure. *Recherche et Applications en Marketing*, 12 (1), 45–68.

Eagly, A., & Chaiken, S. (1993). *The psychology of attitudes*. Fort Worth, TX: Harcourt Brace Jovanovitch College.

Fosse-Gomez, M. H. (2011). De la boum à lol. In M. H. Fosse-Gomez (ed.), *Les paradoxes du marketing*. Paris: Eyrolles, 47–60.

Gentina, E., & Chandon, J. L. (2014). Le rôle du genre sur la fréquence de shopping en groupe des adolescents: entre besoin d'individualisation et besoin d'assimilation. *Recherche et Applications en Marketing*, 29 (4), 35–64.

Glasman, L. R. & Albarracín, D. (2006). Forming attitudes that predict future behavior: a meta-analysis of the attitude–behavior relation. *Psychological Bulletin*, 132 (5), 778–822.

Hota, M., Chumpitaz Cáceres, R., & Cousin, A. (2010). Can public-service advertising change children's nutrition habits? *Journal of Advertising Research*, 50 (4), 460–477.

Hsieh, Y.-C., Chiu, H.-C., & Lin, C.-C. (2006). Family communication and parental influence on children's brand attitudes. *Journal of Business Research*, 59 (10–11), 1079–1086.

Lichtenstein, D. R., Netemeyer, R. G., & Burton, S. (1995). Assessing the domain specificity of deal proneness: a field study. *Journal of Consumer Research*, 22 (3), 314–326.

Lichtenstein, D. R., Netemeyer, R. G., & Burton, S. (1990). Distinguishing coupon proneness from value consciousness: An acquisition transaction utility theory perspective. *Journal of Marketing*, 54 (July), 54–67.

Lichtenstein, D. R., Ridgway, N., & Netemeyer, R. G. (1993). Price perceptions and consumer shopping behavior: a field study. *Journal of Marketing Research*, 30 (2), 234–245.

Martin, W., Weun, S., & Beatty, S. (1994). *Validation of an impulse buying tendency scale*. Working paper, University of Alabama, Tuscaloosa.

McNeal, J. U. (2007). *On becoming a consumer. Development of consumer behavior patterns in childhood*. Oxford: Elsevier.

Olbrich, R., & Grewe, G. (2013). Proliferation of private labels in the groceries sector: The impact on category performance. *Journal of Retailing & Consumer Services*, 20 (2), 147–153.

Olson, J. M., & Zanna, M. P. (1993). Attitudes and attitude change. *Annual Review of Psychology*, 44, 117–154.

Pecheux, C., & Derbaix, C. (1999). Children attitude toward the brand: a new measurement scale. *Journal of Advertising Research*, 39 (4), 19–27.

de Pelsmacker, P., & Neijens, P. (2012). New advertising formats: how persuasion knowledge affects consumer responses. *Journal of Marketing Communications*, 18 (1), 1–4.

Rossiter, J. R. (2002). The C-OAR-SE procedure for scale development in marketing, *International Journal of Research in Marketing*, 19 (4), 305–335.

Solomon, M., Bamossy, G., Askegaard, S., & Hogg, M. (2006). *Consumer behavior: a European perspective* (3rd ed.). Harlow: FT Prentice Hall.

Spears, N., & Singh, S. N. (2004). Measuring attitude toward the brand and purchase intentions. *Journal of Current Issues & Research in Advertising*, 26 (2), 53–66.

Strazzieri, A. (1994). Mesurer l'implication durable vis-à-vis d'un produit indépendamment du risque perçu. *Recherche et Applications en Marketing*, 9 (1), 73–91.

7
EXPERIENTIAL CONSUMPTION WITH BRANDS

7.1 Overview

The concept of experience has entered the marketing and consumer research literature in the 1980s, thanks to Holbrook and Hirschman's (1982) pioneer paper on the topic. These two authors advanced an alternative, broader view of consumer behaviour, called "experiential", to contrast the view that was dominant at the time. If the dominant view considers consumers as logic thinkers who solve problems to make purchasing decisions, the experiential view is based on the assumptions that consumers search for fantasies, feelings and fun in their consumption activities. The symbolic, hedonic and aesthetic aspects in consumption are at the centre of this experiential view. Holbrook and Hirschman's view, which stresses the importance of consumption experiences as opposed to buying processes, has drastically marked the study of consumers in the following years and has resulted in several contributions focusing on various aspects of these consumption activities (for a review, see Schmitt & Zarantonello, 2013).

In brand management, a number of scales have been developed building upon this experiential view and taking into account sensory, affective, intellectual, behavioural and relational aspects of experiences with brands. This chapter includes four of these scales (for scales that are specifically focused on the affective dimension, see Chapter 8). Brakus, Schmitt and Zarantonello (2009)'s brand experience scale assesses the intensity by which different types of experiences are stimulated by a brand and its brand-related stimuli such as the brand's design and identity, packaging, marketing communications and environments where the brand is marketed or sold. Their scale captures the overall experience with brands as lived by the individual.

However, brands do not only generate experiences for the consumer as individuals but also for consumers among themselves. Some other existing scales highlight the social, relational nature of experiences with brands. For example, building on the work of Brakus, Schmitt and Zarantonello (2009), Nysveen, Pedersen and Skard (2013) propose a service brand experience scale, which takes into account the relational side of experiences, which proves to be relevant in the context of service brands compared to product brands.

An even stronger focus on social experiences triggered by brands is present in the other two scales included in the chapter. McAlexander, Schouten and Koenig (2002)'s integration in brand community scale is based on the assumption that the value of brand communities lies in the experience of its members and takes into account all the relationships that characterize such experiences within these communities – relationships not only between brand and consumers but also among consumers themselves.

Moving from brand communities to brand tribes, which, according to some authors (Cova & Cova, 2002), are characterized by being less commercial and not interested in the relationship with the brand, Taute and Sierra (2014) propose a brand tribalism scale. This scale, which is centred on the relational experience of members belonging to brand tribes, allows researchers to get a better understanding of the experience of consumers in these tribes based on the interactions and relationships they establish with one another thanks to the brand.

7.2 Brand community (McAlexander, Schouten & Koenig, 2002)

Definition of construct

McAlexander, Schouten and Koenig (2002) look at brand communities from a customer-experiential perspective, as they believe that the existence and meaningfulness of these communities reside in the customer experience rather than in the brand on which that experience is based. They advance the concept of integration in brand community (IBC) as a "comprehensive concept grounded in customer's total life experience with a brand most broadly construed" (McAlexander, Schouten & Koenig, 2002, p. 44). IBC captures relationships with different entities in a brand community: *customer–product relationships*, which refer to customers' feelings toward the product they own; *customer–brand relationships*, which are focused on the bond between customers and the brand; *customer–company relationships*, which concern customers' feelings toward the organization owning the brand; and *customer–customer relationships*, which concern the relationships between the customer and other owners of the product.

Scale description

The IBC scale is composed of four dimensions and 11 revealed items. The *product* dimension consists of three items, the *brand* dimension includes three items, the *company* dimension is made of two items, and the *other owners* dimension contains three items. Two additional items are included in the *brand* dimension, but these items are not disclosed, as they are property of the company that supported the research. It is also worth noting that some of the items in the IBC scale are specific to the product category examined in the study (e.g., "(Brand X) is the ultimate sport-utility vehicle", "My (brand X) vehicle is fun to drive") and could benefit from adaptation for examining other product categories. All items are measured using a 5-point Likert-type scale anchored by 1 = "strongly disagree" to 5 = "strongly agree". Items can be summed and averaged within each dimension to form dimension scores or can be summed and averaged over all the 11 items to form an overall IBC score.

TABLE 7.1 Integration in brand community scale

Scale dimension	Scale item
Product	• I love my (brand X) vehicle • My (brand X) vehicle is one of my favourite possessions • My (brand X) vehicle is fun to drive
Brand*	• If I were to replace my (brand X) vehicle, I would buy another (brand X) • (Brand X) is of the highest quality • (Brand X) is the ultimate sport-utility vehicle
Company	• The (brand X) division understands my needs • The (brand X) cares about my opinions
Other owners	• I have met wonderful people because of my (brand X) • I feel a sense of kinship with other (brand X) owners • I have an interest in a club for (brand X) owners

Note: *indicates that this dimension includes two additional items which are property of the company that supported the research.

Scale development

The development of the BCI scale originates from the model elaborated by the researchers on the basis of their ethnographic fieldwork. This fieldwork is focused on two brands (Jeep and Harley-Davidson) and is conducted in the context of brandfests and other brand-related sites. The data collected on these occasions consist mainly of observations supported by photography, videotaping and informal and formal interviews. Complementary sources are used, including interviews of informants who do not attend events, ongoing involvement with Harley-Davidson owners established eight years earlier and interviews with marketing managers and consumers of two other brands in different industries. The ethnographic analysis results in the conceptualization of IBC and its dimensionality, that is, the customer-centred relationships that are comprised in it.

It follows a quantitative part with two studies that are conducted at two consecutive national Camp Jeep events. The first study is designed as a post-event survey of participants and is used as a pre-test for the design and execution of the survey at the second event. This pre-test, together with the ethnographic fieldwork and literature review, is also used to derive an initial set of IBC scale items.

The second study is structured as one-group pre-test/post-test quasi-experimental design (Cook & Campbell, 1979), where the experimental treatment is the participation in the event. The IBC scale items are included in both pre-event and post-event questionnaires, which are separated by about eight weeks in time. In data analysis, a CFA is used to test the hypothesized four-factor model of IBC. After dropping three items based on the approach suggested by Gerbing and Anderson (1988), an acceptable fit is obtained ($\chi^2(59) = 197.485$, RMSR = 0.0503, CFI = 0.917). Reliability and validity tests are conducted, and the CFA model is compared to a second-order model ($\chi^2(61) = 223.61$). This higher-order model presents a significantly better fit than the CFA model (delta $\chi^2 = 26$, 2 df), despite a slight decrease in the CFI (from 0.917 to 0.903).

The last part of the analysis is centred on the connection between pre-event and post-event IBC scores. An assessment of two models is first carried out: one where the parameter between pre- and post-event IBC is left free and one where this parameter is constrained to zero. When the parameter is estimated, the coefficient is positive and significant (standardized beta = 0.634), and the fit of the model is significantly better (delta $\chi^2 = 67.089$, 1 df). Finally, repeated measures analysis compares respondents with low versus high pre-event scores on both IBC dimensions and overall IBC. Results show that for respondents who are less positive before the event, there are significant changes between pre-event and post-event scores ($ps < 0.001$); for respondents who already report high scores before the event, significant changes occur at the overall IBC, product and brand level ($ps < 0.05$).

Samples

The second study in the quantitative part is based on samples of 453 (pre-test) and 259 (post-test) event participants, for a total of 259 matched questionnaires.

Reliability and validity

The face validity of the IBC scale items is ensured thanks to the ethnographic fieldwork, on the basis of informant interaction. Evidence of the scale's reliability and validity is provided in the second quantitative study. The reliability of the IBC dimensions is equal to 0.90 (*product*), 0.88 (*brand*), 0.88 (*company*) and 0.70 (*other owners*). The AVE of the dimensions is equal to 0.74 (*product*), 0.58 (*brand*), 0.79 (*company*) and 0.61 (*other owners*). With respect to the overall IBC, its reliability is equal to 0.89 and its AVE is equal to 0.68.

Managerial applications

The IBC scale represents a tool that companies can use to evaluate the impact of marketing programs focused on consumers' ownership experience and consumption, such as brand gatherings, on the full range of customer-centred relationships. The IBC offers an understanding about the relationships that marketers can develop to cultivate communities and ultimately to enhance consumer loyalty – not only customer–brand relationships but also relationships between the customer and the product, the company and other customers.

7.3 Brand experience (Brakus, Schmitt & Zarantonello, 2009)

Definition of construct

Brand experience is defined as "subjective, internal consumer responses (sensations, feelings, and cognitions) and behavioural responses evoked by brand-related stimuli that are part of a brand's design and identity, packaging, communications, and environments" (Brakus, Schmitt & Zarantonello, 2009, p. 53). Brand experience is also conceptualized as a multi-dimensional construct. It includes a *sensory* dimension, which refers to the visual, auditory, tactile, gustative and olfactory stimulations provided by a brand; an *affective* dimension, which includes feelings generated by the brand and its emotional bond with the consumer; an *intellectual* dimension, which refers to the ability of the brand to engage consumers' convergent and divergent thinking; and a *behavioural* dimension, which includes bodily experiences, lifestyles and interactions with the brand.

Scale description

The scale consists of four dimensions and 12 items. Each dimension includes three items, of which two are positively worded and one is negatively worded. Items are measured through 7-point Likert scales ranging from 1 = "strongly disagree" to 7 = "strongly agree". Items can be summed and averaged within each dimension to form dimension scores (e.g., *sensory* experience score) or can be summed and averaged over all the 12 items to from an overall brand experience score.

TABLE 7.2 Brand experience scale

Scale dimension	Scale item
Sensory	• This brand makes a strong impression on my visual sense or other senses • I find this brand interesting in a sensory way • This brand does not appeal to my senses*
Affective	• This brand induces feelings and sentiments • I do not have strong emotions for this brand* • This brand is an emotional brand
Intellectual	• I engage in a lot of thinking when I encounter this brand • This brand does not make me think* • This brand stimulates my curiosity and problem solving
Behavioural	• I engage in physical actions and behaviours when I use this brand • This brand results in bodily experiences • This brand is not action oriented*

Note: *indicates the item is negatively phrased and reverse coded.

Scale development

After a qualitative study that ensures that consumers' conceptions of brand experience are aligned with the researchers' conceptions, the brand experience scale is developed through a series of six studies.

Study 1 generates the initial set of items for each brand experience dimension. Items are derived from the literature review, screened and checked for face validity, then tested in a study. Here, respondents are asked to evaluate the extent to which each item describes their experiences with brands using a 7-point Likert scale anchored at 1 = "not at all descriptive" and 7 "extremely descriptive". Items with a mean value > 4.0 and a standard deviation < 2.0 are retained, for a total of 83 items.

Study 2 identifies the dimensions of brand experience and reduces the number of items. Brands are identified in a pre-test, where respondents are asked to think of three product categories and pick one brand in each category that they believe is marketed in an experiential way and one that is not marketed in such a way. The resulting 21 brands (16 experiential and 5 non-experiential) are divided into four groups of 5 each, including 4 experiential and 1 non-experiential; one brand (Apple) is included in all the groups. In the main study, respondents evaluate one group of brands on the 83 items. After removing the items not rated by more than 10% of participants, a series of exploratory factor analysis using varimax rotation is conducted. The results show a four-factor solution explaining 62% of total variance. Only items with a loading > 0.70 are retained, for a total of 20 items. Criterion validity tests are conducted.

Study 3 further reduces the number of items and confirms the dimensionality of the scale. An examination of the items' semantic similarity by independent judges results in 12 revised items. Judges also identify a new set of 30 brands, which are divided into six groups of five brands each. In the study, respondents are asked to rate one group of brands on the 12 items using a 7-point Likert scale (1 = "strongly agree" and 7 = "strongly disagree"). After a series of exploratory factor analyses, various models are tested in the confirmatory factor analysis including three-factor model, four-factor model, nested model, one-factor second-order model with four sub-dimensions and one-factor second order model with three sub-dimensions. The analysis reveals that the best model is the four-factor model with correlated factors ($\chi^2(48)$ = 278.61, p < 0.001, GFI = 0.92, CFI = 0.91, and RMSEA = 0.08). Pairwise comparisons among the 30 brands are conducted on each brand experience dimension, and the criterion validity of the scale is checked.

Study 4 further validates the scale. Respondents are asked to rate one brand (Nokia) on the brand experience scale and three items on brand attitude (see box below). Two weeks after the first data collection, a second data collection takes

---

Brand attitude

- Good/Bad
- Do not like/Like very much
- Not attractive/Very attractive

150 Experiential consumption with brands

place, and respondents are asked to fill out the brand experience scale. A new confirmatory factor analysis confirms the best-fitting model is the four-factor correlated model ($\chi^2(48) = 102.85$, $p < 0.00001$, RMSEA = 0.088); each item loaded on the predicted factor and standardized coefficients are included between 0.77 and 0.90. Test-retest reliability is computed, and exploratory factor analyses are conducted for discriminant validity purposes.

Study 5 provides additional evidence of the scale's discriminant validity. Respondents are asked to think of a brand providing a strong, moderate or weak experience and then to rate it on the scales of brand experience, general brand evaluation, brand involvement (Zaichkowsky, 1985), brand attachment (Thomson, MacInnis & Park, 2005; see Chapter 9, pp. 192–195) and customer delight (Oliver, Rust & Varki, 1997). Discriminant validity is tested through exploratory factor analysis.

Finally, study 6 tests the discriminant and predictive validities of the brand experience scale. Respondents are asked to rate two brands from the same product category on scales of customer satisfaction (Oliver, 1980), brand loyalty (derived from Yoo & Donthu, 2001; see Chapter 10, pp. 228–233) and brand personality (Aaker, 1997; see Chapter 3, pp. 44–48), in addition to brand experience. Twelve brands are surveyed in total for six product categories. Exploratory factor analysis is used to test the discriminant validity of the brand experience scale, whereas structural equation models are used to test its predictive validity.

Samples

Study 1 uses 30 university students. Study 2 is based on samples of 68 university students in the pre-test and 267 university students in the main study. Study 3 employs two independent judges, 193 university students and two experts. Study 4 employs a nonstudent population, 150 consumers in the test and 72 in the retest; consumers in the test are intercepted in the shopping streets of two medium-sized cities. Study 5 is based on a sample of 144 participants. Study 6 is based on a sample of 209 university students.

Reliability and validity

The reliability of the final brand experience scale is tested in studies 3, 4 and 6. Study 3 reports a Cronbach's alpha equal to 0.83 (*sensory*), 0.81 (*affective*), 0.76 (*behavioural*) and 0.79 (*intellectual*); all individual items within each dimension average item-to-total correlations of 0.68, and all exceed 0.52. Study 6 reports a Cronbach's alpha equal to 0.77 (*sensory*), 0.74 (*affective*), 0.79 (*behavioural*) and 0.72 (*intellectual*). Study 4 shows that test-retest reliability for the overall scale is $r = 0.77$, ranging from $r = 0.69$ to $r = 0.73$ for the dimensions.

Validity tests of the brand experience scale are conducted throughout the scale-development process. The face validity of the items is ensured in study 1, where only items that describe relevant brand experiences are retained.

The criterion validity of the final scale is checked in study 3. The brands used in the study are categorized by experts as being either highly or moderately experiential (inter-rater agreement = 85%). Using agreed-on brands, mean values of overall brand experience and specific dimensions are compared, and significant differences are found between the two (M = 4.81 versus M = 3.65) and on each of the experience dimensions (*sensory*: M = 5.13 versus M = 3.89; *affective*: M = 4.92 versus 3.64; *intellectual*: M = 3.88 versus 3.21; *behavioural*: M = 5.03 versus 3.60; all ps < 0.01).

The scale's discriminant validity is tested in studies 4, 5 and 6 using exploratory factor analysis with respect to different constructs. In study 4, unconstrained and constrained exploratory factor analyses with varimax rotation show that brand experience items load on different factors than do overall brand evaluations. In study 5, exploratory factor analysis with promax rotation reveals that brand experience dimensions load different factors: brand evaluation, brand involvement, brand attachment and customer delight. In study 6, exploratory factor analysis with varimax rotation shows that most brand experience dimensions load on factors different from brand personality, but there is an overlap between *behavioural* experience and *ruggedness* personality.

The predictive validity of the scale is tested in study 6. A structural equation analysis ($\chi^2(146)$ = 793.9, p < 0.001, GFI = 0.86, CFI = 0.91, and RMSEA = 0.08) shows that brand experience predicts customer satisfaction and brand loyalty both directly and indirectly via brand personality. The analysis also shows that brand experience is a stronger predictor of brand loyalty than is brand personality, which in turn is a better predictor of satisfaction: the direct effect of experience on loyalty (0.24) is higher than the direct effect of experience on satisfaction (0.15); however, the direct effect of brand personality on loyalty (0.13) is lower than the direct effect of brand personality on satisfaction (0.67).

Managerial applications

The brand experience scale represents an instrument that companies can use to understand and improve the experience that their brands provide for their customers. Through this scale, managers can understand the nature of the experience that is lived by their customers and the intensity with which they live such experience. Once the current experience lived by customers is assessed, managers could plan and implement marketing programs in specific directions. The scale could also be used to track the evolution of brand experiences over time.

7.4 Brand experience in service organizations (Nysveen, Pedersen & Skard, 2013)

Definition of construct

Nysveen, Pedersen and Skard build on the work of Brakus, Schmitt and Zarantonello (2009; see this chapter, pp. 148–151) by extending their conceptualization of brand experience to the context of service brands. They propose the multidimensional concept of "service brand experience". As brand experiences, service brand experiences consist of *sensory, affective, intellectual* and *behavioural* dimensions;

in addition, they include a *social* or *relational* dimension, which takes into account the true, relational nature of services compared to products.

Scale description

The service brand experience scale includes 15 items, 3 for each of its five dimensions: *sensory, affective, intellectual, behavioural* and *relational*. Items are rated by respondents using Likert scales.

TABLE 7.3 Service brand experience scale

Scale dimension	Scale item
Sensory	• (Brand X) makes a strong impression on my senses • Being a customer of (brand X) gives me interesting sensory experiences • (Brand X) appeals to my senses
Affective	• (Brand X) induces my feelings • I have strong emotions for (brand X) • (Brand X) often engages me emotionally
Intellectual	• I engage in a lot of thinking as a customer of (brand X) • Being a customer of (brand X) stimulates my thinking and problem solving • (Brand X) often challenges my way of thinking
Behavioural	• I often engage in action and behaviour when I use (brand X)'s services • As a customer of (brand X) I am rarely passive • (Brand X) engages me physically
Relational	• As customer of (brand X) I feel like I am part of a community • I feel like I am part of the (brand X) family • When I use (brand X) I do not feel left alone

Scale development

The items on *sensory, affective, intellectual* and *behavioural* dimensions are adapted from Brakus, Schmitt and Zarantonello (2009). Items on the *relational* dimension are generated by the researchers based on marketing literature.

A data collection is performed afterwards in order to validate the five-dimension service brand experience scale. Respondents are asked to provide answers on all telecom brands they have a relationship with among a list of 10. Measures in the questionnaire cover, in addition to service brand experience, brand personality (Aaker 1997; see Chapter 3, pp. 44–48), brand satisfaction (derived from Fornell, 1992; Oliver, 1980) and brand loyalty (derived from Brakus, Schmitt & Zarantonello, 2009; Pedersen & Nysveen, 2001). Exploratory factor analyses using principal component analysis and varimax method are run. With no constraints, three factors emerge. After fixing the number of factors to extract to five, the analysis reveals the four established dimensions plus the *relational* one. The variance explained accounts for 61.32% (*sensory*), 9.75% (*relational*), 7.06% (*intellectual*), 4.22% (*behavioural*) and 3.48% (*affective*). Two factors (*behavioural* and *affective*) have eigenvalues < 1.0. Various structural equation models are estimated to examine the nomological validity of service brand experience with respect to brand personality, brand satisfaction and brand loyalty.

Samples

For the data collection, 4,556 adults are invited to participate in the study. Among them, 1,090 complete the survey. The number of usable surveys is 1,000. Respondents are representative of Norwegian online consumers aged 15 or older with respect to age, gender, education, income and other non-disclosed consumer variables.

Reliability and validity

The reliability of the service brand experience scale is examined through Cronbach's alpha. Scores are equal to 0.965 for *sensory*, 0.919 for *relational*, 0.861 for *intellectual*, 0.859 for *behavioural* and 0.921 for *affective*.

To establish the nomological validity of the scale, three structural equation models are estimated. The first model correspond to the one tested by Brakus, Schmitt and Zarantonello (2009): overall service brand experience predicts brand satisfaction and brand loyalty, and brand personality mediates these relationships (χ^2 = 985.8, χ^2/df = 11.7, CFI = 0.94, GFI = 0.86, RMSEA = 0.098). The second model introduces the *relational* dimension of service brand experience; in the model, the five service brand experience dimensions predict brand satisfaction and brand loyalty (χ^2 = 836.4, χ^2/df = 4.97, CFI = 0.97, GFI = 0.92, RMSEA = 0.063). In the third model, the five dimensions of service brand experience predict brand satisfaction and brand loyalty, and brand personality mediates these relationships (χ^2 = 1685.9, χ^2/df = 6.22, CFI = 0.95, GFI = 0.87, RMSEA = 0.072). Overall, the analysis indicates that service brand experience affects brand satisfaction either positively or negatively; that brand personality mediates the effects of experience on brand satisfaction and brand loyalty; and that the *relational* experience dimension is the most important predictor of brand satisfaction, brand loyalty and brand personality.

Managerial applications

The service brand experience scale represents a measurement instrument that can be applied in the specific context of service brands. Because of the dimensions it includes and their mixed effects on consumer behaviour, the scale offers managers guidelines about possible actions. For instance, to increase brand satisfaction, managers could stimulate *sensory* experiences by developing visually interesting and appealing brand elements. At the same time, they should avoid too complex and challenging thinking and should not induce too strong feelings or emotions. To increase brand satisfaction but also brand loyalty, managers could encourage *relational* experiences by, for example, cultivating communities and fostering social networking practices.

7.5 Brand tribalism (Taute & Sierra, 2014)

Definition of construct

Taute and Sierra (2014) focus on brand tribes, which are defined in literature as social networks of heterogeneous individuals linked by a shared passion or emotion (Dionísio, Leal & Moutinho, 2008). Building mainly on Sahlins's (1961) anthropological theory of tribal behaviour, they conceptualize brand tribalism as a multi-dimensional concept captured by four dimensions: *segmentary lineage*, which refers to the common bond that brand tribe members feel beyond the use of the product; *social structure*, which refers to the oneness that brand tribe members share; *sense of community*, which reflects the ability of brand tribe members to coexists in harmony; and *defense of the tribe*, which relates to the brand tribe members' emotional opposition to other brands.

Scale description

The brand tribalism scale includes four dimensions and 16 items: *segmentary lineage* and *social structure* have three items each, whereas *sense of community* and *defense of the tribe* comprise five items each. Three *sense of community* items are borrowed from Algesheimer, Dholakia and Herrmann (2005). All items are rated on 7-point scales ranging from 1 = "strongly disagree" to 7 = "strongly agree".

TABLE 7.4 Brand tribalism scale

Scale dimension	Scale item
Segmentary lineage	• Compared with other brands, people who own or use (brand X) share more than just the product or service use • Owners or users of (brand X) have a bond • (Brand X) owners or users are bound together
Social structure	• People who own or use (brand X) are unique from those owning or using other brands in the same market • I identify uniquely with others who own or use (brand X) • People who own or use (brand X) differentiate themselves from non-owners or non-users of (brand X)

(Continued)

TABLE 7.4 (Continued)

Scale dimension	Scale item
Defense of tribe	• Whenever (brand X) is put down, I react strongly • I often disagree whenever someone prefers a competitive brand to (brand X) • I won't own or use any competitor of (brand X) • (Brand X) fits me personally in a way no other brand will • Owners or users of (brand X) "get it"; non-owners or non-users not so much
Sense of community	• The friendships I have with other (brand X) owners or users mean a lot to me* • If other (brand X) owners or users planned something, I'd think of it as something "we" would do, rather than something "they" would do* • I see myself as part of the (brand X) community* • When the opportunity presents itself, I refer to other owners or users of (brand X) as "us" or "we" • I feel a sense of co-ownership with (brand X)

Note: *indicates items are borrowed from Algesheimer, Dholakia and Herrmann (2005).

Scale development

The brand tribalism scale is developed and validated through a series of three studies.

Study 1 generates a set of 35 items based on marketing literature. Respondents are asked to indicate their favourite brand and evaluate it on the brand tribalism items. Exploratory factor analyses using both maximum likelihood estimation (MLE) and principal component analysis (PCA) result in a set of 16 items for the four theorized dimensions. Items with high cross-loadings are removed. The final solution explains 70.55% of the variance and exhibits high factor loadings for both MLE (0.615 – 0.887) and PCA (0.505 – 0.847) procedures. A confirmatory factor analysis supports the solution ($\chi^2(98) = 431.14$, $p = 0.00$, CFI = 0.97, NNFI = 0.97, GFI = 0.89, RMSEA = 0.088, SRMR = 0.048). The scale's reliability, convergent validity and discriminant validity are tested.

Study 2 validates the scale with respect to brand attitude and repurchase intention and examines response differences for these attitudinal variables and brand tribalism. Respondents are asked to indicate their favourite computer operating system and then to complete scales on brand tribalism, brand attitude (derived from Grossbart, Muehling & Kangun, 1986) and repurchase intention (derived from Holmes & Crocker, 1987; MacKenzie, Lutz & Belch, 1986). Using all these scales, exploratory factor analyses with both PCA and MLE are conducted and reveal loadings between 0.477 and 0.914 for the PCA solution and between 0.641 and 0.944 for the MLE solution, with no meaningful cross-loadings. As respondents' answers include Apple or Windows, a MANOVA is used to check response differences between these two groups. An overall positive effect is exhibited by the analysis (Hotelling's T^2 = 0.606, $F(7, 166)$ = 14.37, $p < 0.01$, Wilk's λ = 0.623, η^2 = 0.377, Power = 1.0), and more positive responses are found in the Apple group on brand tribalism dimensions, brand attitude and repurchase intention.

Study 3 further validates the brand tribalism scale using a different sample of respondents and a different product category and examines the explanatory power of brand tribalism dimensions in predicting brand attitude and repurchase intentions. Respondents are asked to indicate their smartphone (iPhone and Android are most noted) and then to complete the same scales as in the previous study. MANOVA exhibits an overall positive effect (Hotelling's T^2 = .131, $F(4, 455)$ = 14.89, $p < 0.01$, Wilk's λ = 0.884, η^2 = 0.116, Power = 1.0) and reveals significantly higher means associated with iPhone on the four brand tribalism dimensions. Next, CFA measurement models are estimated for iPhone ($\chi^2(237)$ = 1,016.02, p = 0.00, CFI = 0.93, NNFI = 0.92, GFI = 0.75, RMSEA = 0.11, SRMR = 0.054) and Android ($\chi^2(237)$ = 905.42, p = 0.00, CFI = 0.95, NNFI = 0.94, GFI = 0.74, RMSEA = 0.11, SRMR = 0.045). By including brand attitude and repurchase intentions, structural equation models are also estimated for iPhone $\chi^2(237)$ = 1,016.12, p = 0.00, CFI = 0.93, NNFI = 0.92, GFI = 0.75, RMSEA = 0.11, SRMR = 0.05) and Android $\chi^2(237)$ = 905.42, p = 0.00, CFI = 0.95, NNFI = 0.94, GFI = 0.74, RMSEA = 0.11, SRMR = 0.04). These models serve for testing the predictive validity of the brand tribalism dimensions.

Samples

Study 1 is based on a sample of 442 undergraduate students at a business school in the southwest United States. Study 2 is based on a sample of 174 students at a business school located in the mountain West United States; of them, 77 evaluate Windows, whereas 97 evaluate Apple. Study 3 uses 481 smartphone users at a business school the mountain West United States; of them, 261 rate iPhone, whereas 220 rate Android.

Reliability and validity

The reliability and validity of the brand tribalism scale are verified across the three studies. With respect to reliability, study 1 reports item reliabilities > 0.504 and study 2 shows reliability coefficients range from 0.853 to 0.949.

Regarding convergent and discriminant validities, evidence is given in both studies 1 and 3. In study 1, the average variance extracted (AVE) is equal to 62.23% (*segmentary lineage*), 64.18% (*social structure*), 59.42% (*defense of the tribe*) and 65.11% (*sense of community*). These scores are higher than the squared correlations between any two constructs. Study 3 reports results separately for the two brands investigated. For iPhone, the AVE is equal to 72.91% (*segmentary lineage*), 71.20% (*social structure*), 60.35% (*defense of the tribe*) and 70.74% (*sense of community*). For Android, the AVE is equal to 73.09% (*segmentary lineage*), 70.21% (*social structure*), 65.65 (*defense of the tribe*) and 78.16% (*sense of community*). In most cases, AVE scores are greater than the squared correlation between any two constructs.

Evidence of predictive validity is given in study 3 separately for the two brands surveyed. Brand attitude is positively predicted by *segmentary lineage* in the case of iPhone (path coefficient = 0.23, $p < 0.05$) and is positively predicted by *defense of the tribe* in the case of both iPhone and Android (iPhone: path coefficient = 0.48, $p < 0.01$; Android: path coefficient = 0.64, $p < 0.01$); it is also negatively predicted by *sense of community* in the case of both brands (iPhone: path coefficient = −0.25, $p < 0.05$; Android: path coefficient = −0.31, $p < 0.05$). Repurchase intention is positively predicted by *defense of the tribe* for both brands (iPhone: path coefficient = 0.52, $p < 0.01$; Android: path coefficient = 0.53, $p < 0.01$) and negatively predicted by *sense of community* only in the case of iPhone (path coefficient = −0.29, $p < 0.01$).

Managerial applications

The brand tribalism scale can be employed by managers to assess the tribal tendencies of targeted and existing customers. By understanding what keeps consumers together (*segmentary lineage*), their perceived sense of unity (*social structure*), their ability to coexist in harmony (*sense of community*) and their emotionally charged perceived opposition of competing brands (*defense of the tribe*), marketers could reach, appeal to and develop long-term robust relationships with consumers, fans and followers.

7.6 Academic focus

- Past research has shown that brand experience builds brand loyalty through mediators such as brand personality and customer satisfaction (Brakus, Schmitt & Zarantonello, 2009), as well as brand relationship quality (Francisco-Maffezzolli, Semprebon & Muller Prado, 2014). A dissertation may hypothesize and examine other possible mediators of this relationship.
- A dissertation may investigate brand experiences in relation to classic topics in brand management, such as brand hierarchy or brand extensions (see Keller, 1998, for an overview on the topics). This dissertation may try to understand how brand experiences with sub-brands relate to brand experiences with parent brands. Or it may try to understand if there must be an "experience fit" between a brand and its extension in order to be successful.
- Nysveen, Pedersen and Skard (2013) propose a new dimension to the conceptualization and measurement of brand experience advanced by Brakus, Schmitt and Zarantonello (2009), which is relevant for service brands. A dissertation may further examine service brand experiences in specific service contexts, such as higher education or the hospitality

industry. This dissertation may develop an *ad hoc* understanding of service brand experiences within these contexts.
- A dissertation may investigate the relationship between brand community (McAlexander, Schouten & Koenig, 2002) or brand tribalism (Taute & Sierra, 2014) and brand equity (see Chapter 11). How do the different dimensions of brand community integration, or brand tribalism, contribute to building brand equity? A specific area of application (e.g., product category, country) could be considered in the dissertation.
- The marketing literature has acknowledged that brand communities can either be market created or consumer created (e.g., Lee, Kim & Kim, 2011). A dissertation may build on this idea and focus on the differences in terms of consumer experience in these types of brand communities. By adopting McAlexander, Schouten and Koenig's (2002) view, for example, a dissertation may investigate how members' experiences and relationships with the brand, the product, the company and other members change across different types of brand communities.

7.7 Managerial focus

- **Have you thought about using the experiential framework to evaluate the impact of marketing events?**
  Many companies are still unsure whether marketing events can influence outcomes effectively and do not really know how to measure the impact of events on their brand. Marketing events allow consumers to have a direct contact with the brand; they increase consumers' interactions with the brands and may result in memorable brand experiences. Events can create stronger connection with the brand and enhance brand equity through brand attitude and especially brand experiences (Zarantonello & Schmitt, 2013). Therefore, in addition to traditional attitude measures, managers could evaluate the impact of marketing events on their brand using the brand experience scale (Brakus, Schmitt & Zarantonello, 2009).
- **Which kind of experience can a service brand offer in order to increase brand satisfaction?**
  Brakus, Schmitt and Zarantonello (2009) reveal positive effects of brand experience on brand personality, brand satisfaction and brand loyalty. Nevertheless, among the different dimensions of service brand experience measured by Nysveen, Pedersen and Skard (2013), the sensory dimension seems to impact more on brand satisfaction than the affective dimension. Managers can therefore evaluate the performance of

their brand on the different dimensions of the brand experience and develop specific actions which stimulate the appeal of a service brand with, for instance, sensory advertising with attractive music, sensory visuals and design. This sensory strategy is followed, for instance, by brands such as Nespresso, with its strong visuals and colourful capsules associated with different coffee aromas and its experiential boutiques.

- **How can managers enhance their brand community?**
Brand communities are nowadays strategic for companies because they form a club of engaged consumers and ambassadors for the brand. Before purchasing a product, consumers may check the opinion of other community members. Therefore, a key issue for managers is to build a brand community and encourage members in sharing brand content and talking about their experiences in order to post positive customer reviews. Using the integration in the brand community scale developed by McAlexander, Schouten and Koenig (2002), managers can evaluate how the consumer experience relates to the product, the brand, the company and other members of the community. They could then decide on which dimension the next product storytelling should be focused, in order to enhance the relationship between the consumer and this dimension. By enhancing the relationships with consumers, managers will be able to enhance consumers' integration in the community, their satisfaction and their participation.

- **Does your adolescent target behave as a brand tribe?**
Adolescents represents a target that needs social recognition and likes to share experience in groups. In order to reach and reinforce the relationship with this particular target, it can be interesting for managers to understand if adolescents have formed a brand tribe with a tribe identity, feeling and belief about the brand. The brand tribalism scale (Taute & Sierra, 2014) can be useful to evaluate the tribals tendencies of the adolescent target. By understanding what the drivers of the tribe are, their behaviour, their identity, their beliefs, managers can develop social media campaigns to target these tribes in order to reach them, increase the number of followers and develop a strong relationship with them.

- **Can your brand community enhance brand extension success?**
Brand extension strategies are often used by managers for strong brands in order to launch a new product in a new category, reducing the cost of introduction. Indeed, as the parent brand already benefits from strong brand equity among its current consumers, the budget needed to create awareness and promote the product can be reduced. Nevertheless, brand extensions are not always enhancing brand equity and may fail due to incoherence with the core value of

the parent brand (Michel & Donthu, 2014). Managers can check the associations linked with the brand and the new brand extension among the brand community. By identifying the consumers who have a high level of integration among the community using the brand community scale (McAlexander, Schouten & Koenig, 2002), managers can ask them to test the product and provide feedback. This experience with the brand extension may create positive word of mouth and facilitate the introduction of the new product, as they can become missionaries for the brand.

References

Aaker, J. L. (1997). Dimensions of brand personality. *Journal of Marketing Research*, 34 (3), 347–356.
Algesheimer, R., Dholakia, U. M., & Herrmann, A. (2005). The social influence of brand community: evidence from European car clubs. *Journal of Marketing*, 69 (3), 19–34.
Brakus, J. J., Schmitt, B. H., & Zarantonello, L. (2009). Brand experience: What is it? How is it measured? Does it affect loyalty? *Journal of Marketing*, 73 (May), 52–68.
Cook, T. D., & Campbell, D. T. (1979). *Quasi-experimentation: design and analysis issues for field settings*. Boston, MA: Houghton Mifflin.
Cova, B., & Cova, V. (2002). Tribal marketing: the tribalisation of society and its impact on the conduct of marketing. *European Journal of Marketing*, 36 (5/6), 595–620.
Dionísio, P., Leal, C. & Moutinho, L. (2008). Fandom affiliation and tribal behaviour: a sports marketing application. *Qualitative Market Research: An International Journal*, 11 (1), 17–39.
Fornell, C. (1992). A national customer satisfaction barometer: the Swedish experience. *Journal of Marketing*, 56 (1), 6–21.
Francisco-Maffezzolli, E., Semprebon, E., & Muller Prado, P. (2014). Construing loyalty through brand experience: the mediating role of brand relationship quality. *Journal of Brand Management*, 21 (5), 446–458.
Gerbing, D. W., & Anderson, J. C. (1998). An updated paradigm for scale development incorporating unidimensionality and its assessment. *Journal of Marketing Research*, 25 (2), 186–192.
Grossbart, S., Muehling, D. D., & Kangun, N. (1986). Verbal and visual references to competition in comparative advertising. *Journal of Advertising*, 15 (1), 10–23.
Holbrook, M. B., & Hirschman, E. C. (1982). The experiential aspects of consumption: consumer fantasies, feelings, and fun. *Journal of Consumer Research*, 9 (September), 132–140.
Holmes, J. H., & Crocker, K. E. (1987). Predispositions and the comparative effectiveness of rational, emotional, and discrepant appeals for both high involvement and low involvement products. *Journal of the Academy of Marketing Science*, 15 (1), 27–35.
Keller, K. L. (1998). *Strategic brand management: building, measuring and managing brand equity*. Upper Saddle River, NJ: Prentice-Hall.
Lee, D., Kim, H. S., & Kim, J. K. (2011). The impact of online brand community type on consumer's community engagement behaviors: consumer-created vs. marketer-created

online brand community in online social-networking web sites. *CyberPsychology, Behavior & Social Networking*, 14 (1/2), 59–64.

MacKenzie, S. B., Lutz, R. J., & Belch, G. E. (1986). The role of attitude toward the ad as a mediator of advertising effectiveness: a test of competing explanations. *Journal of Marketing Research*, 23 (2), 130–143.

McAlexander, J. H., Schouten, J. W., & Koenig, H. F. (2002). Building brand community. *Journal of Marketing*, 66 (1), 38–54.

Michel, G., & Donthu, N. (2014). Why negative brand extension evaluations do not always negatively affect the brand: the role of central and peripheral brand associations. *Journal of Business Research*, 67 (12), 2611–2619.

Nysveen, H., Pedersen, P. E., & Skard, S. (2013). Brand experiences in service organizations: exploring the individual effects of brand experience dimensions. *Journal of Brand Management*, 20, 404–423.

Oliver, R. L. (1980). A cognitive model of the antecedents and consequences of satisfaction decision. *Journal of Marketing Research*, 17 (4), 460–469.

Oliver, R. L., Rust, R. T., & Varki, S. (1997). Customer delight: foundations, findings, and managerial insight. *Journal of Retailing*, 73 (3), 311–336.

Pedersen, P. E., & Nysveen, H. (2001). Shopbot banking: an exploratory study of customer loyalty effects. *International Journal of Bank Marketing*, 19 (4), 146–155.

Sahlins, M. D. (1961). The segmentary lineage: an organization of predatory expansion. *American Anthropologist*, 63 (2), 332–345.

Schmitt, B., & Zarantonello, L. (2013). Consumer experience and experiential marketing: a critical review. In N. K. Malhotra (ed.), *Review of Marketing Research*, Vol. 10. Bingley: Emerald Group, 25–61.

Taute, H. A., & Sierra, J. J. (2014). Brand tribalism: an anthropological perspective. *Journal of Product & Brand Management*, 23 (1), 2–15.

Thomson, M., MacInnis, D. J., & Park, C. W. (2005). The ties that bind: measuring the strength of consumers' emotional attachments to brands. *Journal of Consumer Psychology*, 15 (1), 77–91.

Yoo, B., & Donthu, N. (2001). Developing and validating a multidimensional consumer-based brand equity scale. *Journal of Business Research*, 52, 1–14.

Zaichkowsky, J. L. (1985). Measuring the involvement construct. *Journal of Consumer Research*, 12, 3441–3352.

8
CONSUMERS' EMOTIONS TOWARD THE BRAND

8.1 Overview

After being neglected for a long time, the study of consumer emotions in marketing is well established now (Bagozzi, Gopinath & Nyer, 1999; Laros & Steenkamp, 2005). Various different measurement scales have been developed with respect to, for example, advertising (Edell & Burke, 1987; Holbrook & Batra, 1987), physical environments (Donovan & Rossiter, 1982) and consumption situations (Richins, 1997). It is more recently that marketing scholars have started investigating consumer emotions with respect to brands.

To date, the majority of scholars has concentrated on specific, extremely positive emotions that consumers may feel toward a brand. The interest of both academics and practitioners in these extremely positive emotions may be related to the possible positive benefits for companies, as passionate consumers are, among others, more loyal, more willing to engage in positive word of mouth and more resistant to negative information (Batra, Ahuvia & Bagozzi, 2012; Carroll & Ahuvia, 2006). Researchers have therefore developed a variety of measurement scales on extremely positive emotions toward the brand, although usefulness of such scales has been questioned (e.g., Romaniuk, 2013). Both Albert, Merunka and Valette-Florence (2009) and Batra, Ahuvia and Bagozzi (2012) propose a brand love scale. Batra, Ahuvia and Bagozzi's brand love scale differs from the Albert, Merunka and Valette-Florence's, as it is developed in the United States (versus France) and is based on a more articulated view of the phenomenon of brand love including its antecedent and consequences. Other researchers talk about brand romance instead of brand love. Patwardhan and Balasubramanian (2011) advance a brand romance scale. Rossiter (2012) focuses on quasi-romantic brand love and develops a contrastive measure of brand love which allows researchers to distinguish this emotion from simple brand liking.

Connected with brand love and brand romance is the love-jealousy framework built by Sarkar and Sreejesh (2014). Their romantic brand jealousy scale is intended to complement brand love measures, as it can serve as a tool to stimulate active engagement behaviours from consumers.

Despite the fact that the majority of brand-related emotion scales has focused on positive emotions toward the brand, the literature offers one scale that is concerned with the negative emotions consumers may feel toward a brand. That is the case of Romani, Grappi and Dalli's (2012) negative emotions toward brands scale, which includes all possible negative emotions consumers may feel toward a brand: dislike, anger, sadness, worry, embarrassment and discontent.

8.2 The feeling of love toward a brand (Albert, Merunka & Valette-Florence, 2009)

Definition of construct

Brand love is conceptualized as a multi-dimensional construct. It consists of two macro-dimensions, "affection" and "passion", which, in turn, include several dimensions. "Affection" for the brand is expressed as *uniqueness*, according to which the consumer views the brand as unique and/or special; *intimacy*, that is, the consumer feels close to the brand; *duration*, which reflects the long-term relationship between the consumer and the brand; *memories*, based on which the consumer associates the brand to his/her past life; and *dream*, which regards the presence of the brand in the consumers' mind. "Passion" for the brand is expressed as *pleasure*, which indicates the pleasure given by the brand to the consumer, and *idealization*, which reflects the magical nature of the relationship between the consumer and the brand.

Scale description

The scale includes 22 items, which are organized in seven first-order dimensions and two second-order dimensions. The "affection" second-order dimension consists of the first-order dimensions of *duration* (three items), *dream* (four items), *memories* (three items), *intimacy* (three items) and *uniqueness* (two items). The "passion" second-order dimension contains the first-order dimensions of *idealization* (three items) and *pleasure* (four items). All items are evaluated on a 10-point scale ranging from 1 = "does not apply at all" to 10 = "totally applies".

TABLE 8.1 Brand love feeling scale

Scale second-order dimension	Scale first-order dimension	Scale item
Affection	Duration	• I feel that this brand has accompanied me for many years
		• I have been using this brand for a long time
		• I have not changed this brand since long

(Continued)

TABLE 8.1 (Continued)

Scale second-order dimension	Scale first-order dimension	Scale item
Passion	Dream	• This brand corresponds to an ideal for me • I dream about this brand since long • This brand is a childhood dream • I dream (or have dreamt) to possess this brand
	Memories	• This brand reminds me someone important to me • This brand reminds me memories, moments of my past (childhood, adolescence, a meeting, . . .) • I associate this brand with some important events of my life
	Intimacy	• I have a warm and comfortable relationship with this brand • I feel emotionally close to this brand • I value this brand greatly in my life
	Uniqueness	• This brand is special • This brand is unique
	Idealization	• There is something almost "magical" about my relationship with this brand • There is nothing more important to me than my relationship with this brand • I idealize this brand
	Pleasure	• By buying this brand, I take pleasure • Discovering new products from this brand is a pure pleasure • I take a real pleasure in using this brand • I am always happy to use this brand

Scale development

The process to construct the brand love feeling scale follows the procedures recommended by Churchill (1979). The process starts with item generation, which is conducted thanks to two exploratory studies: structured interviews and Internet survey. Whereas the structured interviews are conducted mentioning explicitly the word "love" in relation to brands, the Internet survey uses projective technique and does not mention that word. The items resulting from these two studies are combined with existing scales on interpersonal love. By so doing, an initial set of 248 items is generated: of these items, 107 are about the love concept, whereas the remaining ones are about the antecedents and outcomes of brand love.

A new Internet survey and paper-and-pencil questionnaires are used next to develop the scale. Respondents are asked to evaluate a brand they love on the 107 items identified in the previous part, as well as on items related to the outcomes of brand love, which are used for validity purposes. The items on brand love are subjected to an exploratory factor analysis. Items with low loadings or with cross-loadings on two or more factors are dropped. The final solution that is obtained includes seven factors and 22 items. This solution is supported by a confirmatory factor analysis (RMSEA = 0.08, GFI = 0.91, GFI = 0.89), which also shows the presence of two correlated second-order factors. Reliability and validity tests are finally conducted.

Samples

The item generation uses 17 adult respondents in the structured interviews. The scale development is based on a sample of 825 questionnaires.

Reliability and validity

The reliability is computed for each first-order dimension of the brand love scale through the Jöreskog coefficient. The coefficient is equal to 0.703 for *uniqueness*, 0.822 for *pleasure*, 0.771 for *intimacy*, 0.707 for *idealization*, 0.707 for *duration*, 0.856 for *memories* and 0.812 for *dream*.

The scale's convergent validity is verified by computing the variance shared between each first-order dimension and its indicators using bootstrapping analysis. The variance is close to or above 0.50 in all cases, being equal to 0.506 for *uniqueness*, 0.538 for *pleasure*, 0.530 for *intimacy*, 0.447 for *idealization*, 0.446 for *duration*, 0.666 for *memories* and 0.521 for *dream*. All t-values are superior to 2.

The discriminant validity of the scale is verified by comparing the chi-square of a constrained model, where factors' correlation is constrained to 1, with the chi-square of a non-constrained model, where the correlation is let free. All the latter models perform significantly better than the former.

For the nomological validity of the scale, the brand love concept is related to its outcomes of brand trust, brand loyalty and word of mouth, which are measured using items derived from the exploratory studies (see boxes below). Data analysis using structural equation models shows that *passion* is positively related to word of mouth ($\gamma = 0.908$) and that *affection* is positively related to brand trust ($\gamma = 0.707$) and brand loyalty ($\gamma = 0.705$).

Brand trust

- This brand does not disappoint
- In the event of failure from the brand, I think I will forgive. Everyone can make mistakes
- I have never been disappointed by this brand

Word-of-mouth

- I defend this brand at any cost
- Sometimes I talk a lot about this brand
- I think it is a good brand, I will recommend it to friends and family
- I often speak about this brand

Brand loyalty

- I am loyal to this brand and I think I will be for a long time
- I am very loyal to the brand
- I do not intend to switch to another brand

Managerial applications

The brand love feeling scale can help managers identify consumers who love their brand and quantify their love toward the brand with respect to different aspects. The scale can also help managers propose adapted communications, loyalty programs, or novel consumer segmentation schemes.

8.3 Brand romance (Patwardhan & Balasubramanian, 2011)

Definition of construct

Brand romance is a subject-specific construct and is defined as "a state of emotional attachment . . . that is characterized by strong positive affect toward the brand, high arousal caused by the brand, and a tendency of the brand to dominate the consumer's cognition" (Patwardhan & Balasubramanian, 2011, p. 299). It includes three dimensions – *pleasure, arousal* and *dominance* – which come one after the other. The first dimension is *pleasure*, which indicates the extent to which a brand can stimulate positive feelings such as love, attraction, desire, pleasure, fun and excitement. The second dimension is *arousal*, which refers to the intensity of stimulation of these feelings; in order to arouse the consumer, positive feelings must be intense. The third dimension is *dominance*, which refers to the brand's tendency to engage the consumer's cognition.

Scale description

The brand romance scale is a three-dimension, 12-item measure, with each dimension (*pleasure, arousal* and *dominance*) including four items. Items are evaluated on Likert scales.

TABLE 8.2 Brand romance scale

Scale dimension	Scale item
Pleasure	• I love this brand • Using this brand gives me great pleasure • I am really happy that this brand is available • This brand rarely disappoints me
Arousal	• I am attracted to this brand • I desire this brand • I want this brand • I look forward to using this brand
Dominance	• My day dreams often include this brand • This brand often dominates my thoughts • Sometimes I feel I can't control my thoughts as they are obsessively on this brand • This brand always seems to be on my mind

Scale development

The brand romance scale is developed through a process of four studies.

Study 1 generates a pool of items. To that aim, a review of the relevant literature in marketing and psychology and an "experience survey" are conducted. In the survey, respondents are asked to recall a brand in the context of the three hypothesized dimensions of brand romance and to provide statements that describe their feelings toward the recalled brand. An initial pool of 70 items results from the first study.

Study 2 purifies the initial pool of items and explores the factor structure of brand romance. A survey is conducted, with each participant evaluating three brands (i.e., a brand they love, a brand they like and a brand they dislike) on the 70 items. Data are analysed through an exploratory factor analysis using principal component analysis with varimax rotation. Forty-four items are removed for loading on multiple factors. A two-factor solution is identified, with pleasure and arousal items loading on the first factor and dominance items loading on the second one. Twelve items with maximal loadings are retained. Using the robust maximum likelihood estimation approach, a confirmatory factor analysis is then performed to test the hypothesized three-factor structure. The analysis supports the three-factor model, showing acceptable fit indexes (S-B scaled χ^2 = 113.39, $p <$ 0.05, NFI = 0.978, NNFI = 0.984, CFI = 0.988, RMSEA = 0.064) and significant item loadings on the three factors.

Study 3 confirms the three-factor solution of the brand romance scale and tests its convergent and criterion validities with respect to purchase intention. A survey is conducted, with each respondent evaluating three brands (i.e., a brand they love, a brand they like and a brand they dislike) in terms of brand romance and purchase intention (Putrevu & Lord, 1994). A confirmatory factor analysis using the robust maximum likelihood estimation approach supports the three-factor solution (S-B scaled χ^2 = 129.9319, $p < 0.05$, NFI = 0.977, NNFI = 0.982, CFI = 0.986, RMSEA = 0.068). Tests of validity are conducted.

Study 4 assesses the discriminant and nomological validities of brand romance. A survey is conducted, with respondents being assigned to one of three conditions (i.e., a brand they love, a brand they like and a brand they dislike). In addition to the brand romance scale, they are asked to evaluate the brand they recall using scales on attitude toward the brand (Mitchell & Olson, 1981) and attitudinal brand loyalty (Chaudhuri & Holbrook, 2001). Tests of discriminant and nomological validities are conducted.

Samples

Study 1 involves nine adults in the experience survey. Study 2 is based on a sample of 99 undergraduate students. Study 3 is based on a sample of 112 student respondents. Study 4 uses 500 undergraduate students.

Reliability and validity

The reliability of the brand romance scale is tested in studies 2 and 3. The reported coefficient alpha for the whole scale is 0.954 (study 2) and 0.951 (study 3).

The scale's face validity is checked in study 1, where items are derived through an "experience survey". Respondents provide statements describing their feelings toward a brand in the context of the three dimensions of brand romance (*pleasure, arousal, dominance*).

The convergent and criterion validities of the scale are examined in study 3. To show the scale's convergent validity, an inspection of the factor loadings is carried out; these are all high (the lowest is equal to 0.792) and significant ($p < 0.05$). To demonstrate criterion validity, brand romance is regressed against purchase intention. Results (adjusted R^2 = 0.754; F = 1023.6, p = 0.00) reveal that brand romance is a significant predictor of purchase intention (t = 31,994, p = 0.00).

The discriminant validity of the brand romance scale is tested in study 4. The hypothesized three-factor model is compared with competing models, including the null model and three two-factor models (with, respectively, *pleasure* and *arousal* as one dimension, *pleasure* and *dominance* as one dimension, *arousal* and *dominance* as one dimension). The hypothesized model displays a better fit than all models. A chi-square test with the hypothesized model and the second-best model, that is, the one with *pleasure* and *arousal* treated as one dimension, is also conducted. The test rejects the two-factor model and further supports the three-factor one (SB scaled difference = 28.2715, df = 2, p = 0.00).

Study 4 also checks the nomological validity of the brand romance scale. Using the robust maximum likelihood estimation approach, a second-order model is tested in which brand romance mediates the relationship between brand attitude and brand loyalty. After constraining to 1 the path coefficient from brand romance to brand loyalty, the model reports: S-B scaled χ^2 = 278.1722, df = 16, p = 0.00, NFI = 0.975, NNFI = 0.988 CFI = 0.990, RMSEA = 0.038. Whereas the path coefficient from brand attitude to brand loyalty is not significant (p > 0.05), the path coefficient from brand attitude to brand romance is equal to 0.724, p < 0.05. The effect of brand romance on brand loyalty is assessed through a separate regression analysis (adjusted R^2 = 0.718; F = 1253.235, p < 0.05), which reveals that brand romance is a significant predictor of brand loyalty (t = 35.401, p = 0.00).

Managerial applications

The brand romance scale offers marketers a tool to monitor consumers' attraction toward their brand; it also assesses how much their brand satisfies consumers' needs for stimulation in terms of *pleasure, arousal* and *dominance*. Marketers could relate brand romance with the length of consumer–brand relationships. In new relationships, where brand romance may quickly increase, marketers may want to slow down the process by rationing out novel perspectives, resources and identities in order to lengthen the relationship. On the other hand, in mature relationships, marketers may need to incorporate novel activities so that consumers can continue to be attracted by the brand. This could be done, for example, through re-positioning, creating new brand associations, changing advertising campaigns and so on.

8.4 Brand love (Batra, Ahuvia & Bagozzi, 2012)

Definition of construct

Batra, Ahuvia and Bagozzi (2012) use the notion of prototype to define brand love. For them, the notion of prototype best describes complex phenomena, such as love, that are difficult to define according to rigorous and precise definitions. Prototype-based definitions are fuzzy; they are characterized by uncertain boundaries and often include not only elements of the phenomenon itself but also its antecedents and outcomes. The brand love prototype includes seven core components of brand love itself: *self-brand integration, passion-driven behaviours, positive emotional connection, long-term relationship, positive overall attitude valence, attitude certainty and confidence (strength)* and *anticipated separation distress*. In addition to these core elements, the brand love prototype includes one antecedent, that is, *quality beliefs*, and one outcome, that is, *brand loyalty, word of mouth and resistance to negative information*.

Scale description

The brand love prototype includes scales to measure brand love, its antecedent and its consequences. The scales are comprised of 84 items grouped in 16 first-order dimensions, some of which are also grouped in second-order dimensions.

170 Consumers' emotions toward the brand

The first-order dimensions of brand love are *current self-identity* (eight items), *desired self-identity* (three items), *life meaning and intrinsic rewards* (six items) and *attitude strength 1* (seven items), grouped in the second-order dimension called "self–brand integration"; *willingness to invest resources* (six items), *passionate desired to use* (six items) and *things done in the past* (three items), grouped in the second-order dimension called "passion-driven behaviours"; *intuitive fit* (eight items), *emotional attachment* (three items) and *positive affect* (seven items), grouped in the second-order dimension labelled "positive emotional connection"; *long-term relationship* (three items); *anticipated separation distress* (four items); *attitude valence* (eight items); and *attitude strength 2* (five items).

The scale that measures the antecedent of brand love refers to *high quality* (three items). Those that measure the consequences of brand love refer to *loyalty, word of mouth and resistance to negative information* (four items).

All items are rated using 7-point scales anchored at "1 = not at all" to "7 = very much".

TABLE 8.3 Brand love prototype scales

Scale second-order dimension	Scale first-order dimension	Scale item
–	High quality (Antecedent)	• Well-made • Functional quality • Practical
Self-brand integration	Current self-identity	• Says something about who you are • Others seeing you using it get a sense of who you are • Important part of self • Degree of image overlap between brand and self • Personal identity matches brand identity • Important to be one of the people who use this brand • Brand is an important part of self-identity • Brand is a rewarding part of self-identity
	Desired self-identity	• Helps present self to others as the person you want to be • Makes you look like what you want to look • Makes you feel like how you want to feel
	Life meaning and intrinsic rewards	• Makes life meaningful • Makes life worth living • Gives life purpose • Is inherently important • Is more than an investment in future benefit • Experience feelings of desire
	Attitude strength 1: frequent thoughts	• Very often talk to others about it • Very often have thoughts about it • Frequently find myself thinking about it • Frequently find myself thinking about using it • Find that it keeps popping into my head • Feelings toward it are strong • Feel lots of affection toward it

(Continued)

TABLE 8.3 (Continued)

Scale second-order dimension	Scale first-order dimension	Scale item
Passion-driven behaviours	*Willingness to invest resources*	• Have spent lot of time making it fit my needs • Willing to spend lot of money improving and fine-tuning it after buy it • Willing to spend lot of time improving and fine-tuning it after buy it • Have invested lot of time, energy, or money in it • Was willing to spend lot of time shopping to buy it specifically • Have used it often in appropriate occasions
	Passionate desire to use	• Feel myself craving to use it • Feel myself desiring it • Feel a sense of longing to use it • Feeling of wanting toward it • Feeling of desire toward it • Feeling of longing toward it
	Things done in past (involvement)	• Have been involved with it in past • Have done a lot of things with it in the past • Have interacted a lot with it or the company that makes it
Positive emotional connection	*Intuitive fit*	• Feel psychologically comfortable using it • Meets needs perfectly • Natural fit • What I've been looking for • Fits tastes perfectly • Felt right when first encountered it • Now feels right • Strength of feeling of liking
	Emotional attachment	• Feels like old friend • Emotionally connected • Feel a bond
	Positive affect	• Content • Relaxed • Fun • Exciting • Calming • Helps relax • Pleasurable
—	*Long-term relationship*	• Will be using for a long time • Will be part of life for long time to come • Feel sense of long-term commitment
—	*Anticipated separation distress*	• Anxiety • Worry • Fear • Apprehension

(*Continued*)

172 Consumers' emotions toward the brand

TABLE 8.3 (Continued)

Scale second-order dimension	Scale first-order dimension	Scale item
–	Attitude valence	• Satisfaction • Compares well with ideal product • Like/dislike • Positive/negative • Meets expectations • Feelings of liking toward it • Good/bad • Favourable/unfavourable
–	Attitude strength 2: Certainty and confidence	• Certainty of feelings/evaluations • How strongly hold feelings/evaluations • How quickly feelings/evaluations come to mind • Confidence of feelings/evaluations • Intensity of feelings/evaluations
–	Loyalty/ WOM/ resistance (consequence)	• Strength of loyalty • If hear something bad would question it in own mind • Would buy again • Would say positive things about brand to others

Scale development

The scales of the brand love prototype are developed through a series of three studies, of which two are qualitative (studies 1 and 2) and one quantitative (study 3).

Study 1 examines love in situations other than close personal relationships in order to provide the context for brand love. The data collection consists of structured telephone interviews and follow-up in-depth interviews. Respondents are asked about anything they have a close relationship with and that they love apart from people. Interviews are transcribed and coded in a database, and the proportional reduction of loss (PRL; Rust & Coil, 1994) is assessed (equal to 0.87). The initial codes are sorted in groups based on literature and similarity criteria. Seven themes are therefore derived, which represent the major components of love in consumer behaviour.

Study 2 refines the findings from the previous study by focusing specifically on the brands or branded products that people love. In an interview, respondents are asked to complete 21 cards which ask for the names of loved branded products in various categories of meeting specific criteria, then are asked to order the cards from the least to the most loved one and explain the reasons of their choices. Despite most of the cards being about brands, some are not about brands in order to cross-check findings from the previous study. Data collected are analysed in a qualitative way. Ten emergent categories (themes) of brand love are identified, which partially overlap with the findings from study 1.

Study 3 assesses how the components of brand love are organized. An initial set of 84 brand love items is generated by the researchers based on the previous studies and the relevant literature and is then tested in a preliminary study. The data collected in the preliminary study are subjected to an exploratory factor analysis, which reveals 16 factors. Based on studies 1 and 2, of these 16 factors, 14 are viewed as core elements of brand love, 1 as an antecedent (*high quality*) and 1 as a consequence (*loyalty, word of mouth and resistance to negative information*, L/W/R). Items that have the highest loading on these factors and that display satisfactory scale reliabilities are retained, leaving a set of 59 items. In the main study, respondents are asked to pick two brands (a brand they love and a brand they feel neutral about) from the consumer electronics product category and to evaluate them using the 59 items. In addition, they are asked to rate the degree to which they love the brand in an overall sense using two items (see box below).

Overall brand love

- Overall, how much do you love (brand X)?
- Describe the extent to which you feel love toward (brand X).

In data analysis, 2 of the 59 items are dropped based on reliability coefficients. A first-order structural equation model with 14 factors is estimated (RMSEA < 0.06, NNFI > 0.95, CFI > 0.95, SRMR < 0.08); reliability and validity tests are conducted. A second-order model is also estimated where 10 of the 14 factors are reflected in a second-order factor, and they all load on a third-order factor, labelled "brand love"; the model is estimated using both high-brand-love ($\chi^2 = 640.67$, $df = 333$, $p < 0.01$, RMSEA = 0.075, NNFI = 0.97, CFI = 0.98, SRMR = 0.081) and low-brand-love samples ($\chi^2 = 847.14$, $df = 333$, $p < 0.01$, RMSEA = 0.094, NNFI = 0.96, CFI = 0.97, SRMR = 0.069). Additional validity tests are conducted using this model.

Samples

Study 1 uses 70 respondents in the interviews and 10 respondents in the follow-up interviews. Study 2 is based on a sample of 18 university students. Study 3 is based on a sample of 133 undergraduate students in the preliminary study and on a sample of 268 college undergraduates in the main study.

Reliability and validity

Evidence of the reliability and validity of the brand love prototype scales is provided in study 3. Discriminant and validity tests are first conducted using the first-order model of brand love. The analysis shows that all the 14 factors have adequate average variance extracted (> 0.6), composite construct reliability (> 0.7) and discriminant validity (phi coefficient < 1.0 or by the chi-square difference test). The nomological validity is demonstrated by testing the relationships, all positive and significant, among the 14 dimensions of brand love and the two dimensions on its antecedents and consequences; no discriminant validity issues are detected. Multiple group measurement models are employed to show that the high-love-brand factor means are statistically higher ($p < 0.01$) than the low-brand-love factor means on all brand love dimensions, as well as its antecedent and outcome.

Additional validity tests are conducted using the higher-order model of brand love. Using both high- and low-brand-love samples, the nomological validity of the brand love prototype is demonstrated by testing the relationships from the third-order brand love factor to the seven underlying factors (three second-order and four first-order) and from them to their sub-components; all relationships are positive and significant; no discriminant validity issues are detected. The two items of overall brand love are used in the next part of the analysis. A CFA reveals that the correlation between them and the third-order factor of brand love is positive (0.84 and 0.95 respectively) but significantly below 1.00. Using the single-factor measure of overall brand love, it is shown that the brand love prototype adds predictive value compared to a summatory, single-factor measure of brand. In fact, a model in which higher-order brand love predicts L/W/R (high love: $R^2 = 0.61$, low love: $R^2 = 0.63$) performs better than a model in which overall brand love predicts L/W/R (high love: $R^2 = 0.42$, low love: $R^2 = 0.52$) and a model in which *high quality* predicts L/W/R via higher-order brand love (high love: $R^2 = 0.63$, low love: $R^2 = 0.65$) performs better than a model in which *high quality* predicts L/W/R via overall brand love (high love: $R^2 = 0.47$, low love: $R^2 = 0.55$).

Managerial applications

The brand love prototype provided by Batra, Ahuvia and Bagozzi can help managers track to what extent their brand is loved and how this feeling evolves over time. Using the brand love prototype scales, managers can gain insights on how to build love for their brand. The dimensions included in the scale, in fact, represent pathways that managers could follow to build brand love. Specifically, they could facilitate passion-driven behaviours by creating a strong desire to use the brand, to invest resources in it and to interact frequently with it; build brands that symbolize self–brand integration by stressing the brand's ability to connect with life's deeper meanings and important values; create positive emotional connection with the brand by providing the brand with a sense of authenticity from its origins, history, founders and company culture; create a feeling of anticipated separation distress by making the brand valuable and trustable; and establish long-term relationships with consumers by launching loyalty and marketing programs that require frequent and ongoing interaction. Managers could implement various actions along these pathways, based on category- and brand-specific opportunities and constraints.

8.5 A new C-OAR-SE–based measure of brand love (Rossiter, 2012)

Definition of construct

The need for a new measure of brand love is related to the problems that Rossiter identifies about previous measures of brand love, including Carroll and Ahuvia's (2006) first attempt to conceptualize brand love as well as Batra, Ahuvia and Bagozzi's (2012; see this chapter, pp. 169–174) framework of brand love as prototype. In particular, Rossiter identifies two major issues (for a reply to Rossiter's critiques see Ahuvia, Bagozzi & Batra, 2014). First, previous researchers have measured brand love directly without defining it for the respondents, whereas Rossiter defines it as quasi-romantic brand love to distinguish it from love toward a person. Second, previous researchers have used multi-item measures, whereas a single, multi-componential item consisting of one question with binary, not continuous, answer options should be used. Rossiter finds the solution to these problems in a contrastive measure which distinguishes brand love from brand liking, a much weaker feeling which previous researchers did not measure separately. His brand love category is defined by the simultaneous presence of consumers' deep affection for the branded product and separation anxiety anticipated if it were not available.

Scale description

The contrastive measure of brand love consists of a single item with five answer categories representing feelings of hate, disliking, neutrality, liking and love toward the brand. Major brands in a given product category are listed on the left side. Respondents are instructed to read all answer categories first, then select an answer from the five possibilities for each brand. The measure is originally developed in German. An English version is provided by the researcher.

TABLE 8.4 The contrastive measure of brand love

Please tick your overall opinion (evaluation) of each of the following (product category Y) brands. Read all the answers first. Thick one answer for each (product category Y) brand (one answer in each row).

	Hate	Dislike	Neutral	Liking	Love
	I would say that I *hate* this brand	I feel that I *dislike* this brand	I feel *neutral* about this brand – no strong feelings either way	I would not say that I like this brand, but I would say that I *like* it	I would say I feel a deep affection, like *love*, for this brand and I would be really upset if I couldn't have it
Brand 1					
Brand 2					
Brand 3					
Brand . . .					
Brand *n*					

Scale development

Rossiter's measure of brand love is designed by following the principles of the Construct definition, Object classification, Attribute classification, Rater identification, Scale formation, and Enumeration and reporting (C-OAR-SE) method (Rossiter, 2002, 2011). One multi-componential item is generated based on literature and managerial practice. Content validity is assessed in this first stage. It follows a data collection to establish the predictive validity of the scale. Respondents are asked about their feelings of love versus like toward a brand, as well as about their usage rate of the brand and recommendations of the brand to others. Four different product categories representing the quadrants of the Rossiter-Percy grid (Rossiter, Percy & Donovan, 1991) are selected; each respondent evaluates the seven major brands in each of these categories.

Samples

The sample includes 150 male students and 150 female students from a major public university in Germany. A total of 291 of these questionnaires are usable.

Reliability and validity

The content validity of the C-OAR-SE–based, contrastive measure of brand love is established through an expert assessment when the multi-componential item is generated. To establish the predictive validity of the measure, frequency counts and percentages of brand usage and brand recommendation are computed for the brand love category and are compared with the brand linking and neutrality categories. The analysis demonstrates that brand usage and brand recommendation scores are higher for brands rated in the brand love category.

Managerial applications

The measure of brand love designed by Rossiter is intended to replace the multi-item brand love measures previously proposed by the literature (Batra, Ahuvia & Bagozzi, 2012; Carroll & Ahuvia, 2006). The measure also aims to replace overly simplistic approaches sometimes used by marketing research practitioners, who ask consumers directly if they love a given brand and record their answer on a dichotomous scale (yes/no).

8.6 Negative emotions toward brands (Romani, Grappi & Dalli, 2012)

Definition of construct

Romani, Grappi and Dalli (2012, p. 56) define negative emotions toward brands (NEB) as "consumers' negative emotional reactions evoked by the appraisal of brand-related stimuli". The major sources of consumers' negative emotional responses are consumers' appraisals of brand-related stimuli. These stimuli are not directly related to product or service attributes and performance and can originate from both marketer-controlled (e.g., advertising) and non–marketer-controlled (e.g., word-of-mouth) sources of information.

Scale description

The NEB scale includes six first-order dimensions of brand-related negative emotions: *dislike* and *anger* (grouped in the second-order dimension called "NEB_1"); *sadness* and *worry* (grouped in the second-order dimension called "NEB_2"); *embarrassment*; and *discontent*. Each of the six first-order dimensions is measured using three items rated on a 7-point scale, ranging from 1 = "not at all" to 7 = "very much". The authors use the six first-order dimensions to form factor scores for negative emotions toward brands (*dislike, anger,* etc.).

TABLE 8.5 Negative emotions toward brands scale

Scale second-order dimension	Scale first-order dimension	Scale item
NEB_1	Dislike	• Feeling of contempt • Feeling of revulsion • Feeling of hate
	Anger	• Indignant • Annoyed • Resentful
NEB_2	Sadness	• Heartbroken • Sorrowful • Distressed
	Worry	• Threatened • Insecure • Worried
–	Embarrassment	• Sheepish • Ridiculous • Embarrassed
–	Discontent	• Dissatisfied • Unfulfilled • Discontented

Scale development

Before the actual scale development starts, an exploratory qualitative study is conducted in order to understand the types of negative emotions that consumers experience in relation to brands. Participants are instructed to select a brand that could generate a negative emotional response and to provide a detailed report about their reasons for these emotions. These open-ended responses are analysed by two raters with regard to the type of emotions mentioned and the sources of information causing them (marketer-controlled versus non-marketer-controlled).

The actual scale-development process includes five quantitative studies. Study 1 identifies an initial set of negative emotion descriptors (items). Based on the previous exploratory study and the literature review, a set of 106 items is generated. In a survey, respondents are asked to evaluate to which extent each of the 106 items describes their negative emotions toward a brand of their choice. Items with a mean value above 2 are kept and factor analysed using maximum likelihood method and promax rotation. In the resulting solution, items with a loading > 0.5 and a cross-loading < 0.25 are retained. Six factors including 25 items are derived from the analysis and explain 68.4% of the total variance.

Study 2 further examines the structure of negative emotions toward brands and reduces the set of items into a manageable number. Respondents are asked to evaluate a brand of their choice using the 25 items resulting from the previous study. The items are subjected to an exploratory factor analysis using maximum likelihood method and promax rotation. Any item with a loading > 0.5 and a cross-loading < 0.25 is retained; items with a mean rating < 2 are dropped. The final solution reflects the six-factor structure of negative emotions toward brands and includes 18 items. A confirmatory factor analysis (CFA) supports this solution ($\chi^2 = 174.49$, $df = 120$, NNFI = 0.93, CFI = 0.95, RMSEA = 0.04, SRMR = 0.05).

Study 3 confirms the NEB scale's stability using a different sample of respondents and assesses the possible hierarchical relation among the first-order factors representing the construct of NEB. Respondents are asked to rate a brand of their choice using the 18-item NEB scale and Richins's (1997) consumption emotions set (CES), Havlena and Holbrook's (1986) adaptation of Plutchick's (1980) basic emotions scale and Izard's (1977) DES-II scale. These other emotion scales are used for discriminant validity purposes. A CFA confirms the six-factor solution of the NEB scale ($\chi^2 = 285.86$, $df = 120$, NNFI = 0.90, CFI = 0.92, RMSEA = 0.05, SRMR = 0.05). Different CFA models are then tested, including one with a single first-order factor, one with six uncorrelated first-order factors and one with six first-order factors, four of which reflect two second-order factors (NEB1 and NEB2); this latter model has the best fit ($\chi^2 = 309.84$, $df = 136$, NNFI = 0.90, CFI = 0.91, RMSEA = 0.05, SRMR = 0.06). Likelihood-ratio tests show that the four constructs (NEB1, NEB2, embarrassment and discontent) are different dimensions. Construct validity tests are conducted next.

Study 4 examines the predictive validity of the NEB scale compared to the CES scale. Respondents are asked to choose a brand that can generate negative emotional responses and to rate it using the NEB and CES scales, as well as measures on brand switching (adapted from Bougie, Pieters & Zeelenberg, 2003), negative word of mouth (adapted from Bougie, Pieters & Zeelenberg, 2003) and consumer complaining (adapted from Zeelenberg & Pieters, 2004). Predictive validity tests are conducted.

Study 5 further examines the predictive validity of specific negative emotions included in the NEB scale. Respondents are assigned to a "recall emotion" condition for a total of six conditions corresponding to the six NEB scale dimensions.

Respondents are asked to identify a brand that evokes the assigned negative emotion, report the reasons for their negative emotion toward this brand and complete scales on NEB, brand switching, negative word of mouth and consumer complaining. ANOVA and a step-down analysis using MANOVA are employed to test the differential effects of negative emotions on consumer behaviour.

Samples

The exploratory qualitative study uses 115 consumers. Study 1 is based on a sample of 106 undergraduate and graduate students. Study 2 is based on a sample of 227 undergraduate and graduate students. Study 3 employs 421 ordinary consumers. Study 4 employs 146 ordinary consumers. Study 5 employs 1,217 ordinary consumers. All studies involve Italian individuals.

Reliability and validity

The reliability of the NEB scale is shown is study 3, when the final list of items is identified. All factors report a Cronbach's alpha coefficient greater than 0.70. The stability of the six-factor structure is demonstrated by employing a different sample of respondents (ordinary consumers instead of students).

The construct validity of the NEB scale is also verified in study 3 through the multi-trait multi-method matrix (MTMM). The CFA for the MTMM consists of five traits (*anger, dislike, embarrassment, worry* and *sadness*) and two methods (the NEB scale as method 1 and measures selected from Richins (1997), Havlena and Holbrook (1986) and Izard (1977) as method 2). The *discontent* factor is not included in the MTMM given the lack of alternative measures available to form an indicator for the second method. The CFA model of MTMM reports $\chi^2 = 19.82$, $df = 14$, $p = 0.14$, NNFI = 0.99, CFI = 1.00, RMSEA = 0.03 and SRMR = 0.02. This model is compared to the trait-only model, and the analysis reveals that it performs better (delta $\chi^2 = 58.6$, $df = 11$, $p < 0.01$). Construct validity is therefore tested using the trait-method-error model. It is shown that all traits achieve convergent validity as all factor loadings for traits are statistically significant, ranging from moderate to high in magnitude; random error variances and method variance range from very low to moderate in magnitude. All traits also achieve discriminant validity because the correlation plus 2 standard errors between each pair is below 1, with $p < 0.05$.

The predictive validity of the NEB scale is tested in studies 4 and 5. Study 4 tests the predictive validity of the NEB scale in comparison with the CES scale. The analysis shows that the NEB scale is superior to the CES scale in predicting negative word of mouth (delta $\chi^2 = 34.03$, $df = 3$, $p < 0.05$) and brand switching (delta $\chi^2 = 10.02$, $df = 3$, $p < 0.05$), whereas it is equivalent to the CES scale in predicting consumer complaining (delta $\chi^2 = 0.75$, $df = 3$, $p > 0.05$). Study 5 tests the predictive validity of the NEB dimensions using the same negative behavioural outcomes. An ANOVA performed on each behavioural response among the different recalled emotions shows that consumer complaining ($F(5, 1208) = 17.16$,

$p < 0.001$) is elicited primarily by *anger*; negative word of mouth ($F(5, 1207) = 65.63$, $p < 0.001$) is elicited primarily by *dislike* and *anger*; and brand switching ($F(5, 875) = 41.20$, $p < 0.001$) is elicited primarily by *dislike*, *anger* and *discontent*. These results are largely supported by a step-down analysis using MANOVA, which demonstrates that effects on behaviour are due to the mediating role of negative emotions.

Managerial applications

The NEB scale represents a tool that managers could use to assess and track consumers' negative emotions toward their brand and to understand how to deal with situations when negative consumer behaviours arise from negative emotions toward the brand. Through the use of the scale, in fact, managers could examine whether these behaviours need to be addressed and the appropriate countermeasures to adopt. Managers could also use the NEB scale to evaluate consumers' negative emotions toward competitive brands and provide their consumers with new components of the brand; these components could also be used as important elements for oppositional brand loyalty, in order to reduce the chance that their consumers will buy products from competing brands.

8.7 Romantic brand jealousy (Sarkar & Sreejesh, 2014)

Definition of construct

Sarkar and Sreejesh (2014) move from the assumption that brand love alone is not sufficient to motivate consumers, as in many cases, consumers' feelings of love toward a brand are not as deep as interpersonal love. They advance the idea that consumers are also motivated by what they call "romantic brand jealousy". That is, "a complex of thoughts and feelings that follow threats to self-esteem generated by a romantically loved and esteemed brand in the mind of a romantic brand lover who does not possess the brand currently due to some constraint, after seeing another person (rival) using the same brand" (p. 25). They believe that romantic brand jealousy can arise only with respect to highly esteemed and luxury brands.

Scale description

The romantic brand jealously scale includes three items which are evaluated on a 5-point Likert scale from 1 = "strongly disagree" to 5 = "strongly agree".

TABLE 8.6 Romantic brand jealousy scale

Scale item

- I feel really hurt when I see that others are using the brand and I don't have it
- I feel very possessive about the brand when I see that others are using the brand and I don't have it
- The thought that others are using the brand and I don't have it always haunts me

Scale development

The romantic brand jealously scale is developed through four studies.

Study 1 generates 20 scale items using semi-structured interviews. Respondents are asked to describe their feelings about any loved brand that they do not possess but see others using.

Study 2 consists of item editing and purification. Following a face validity check with experts, the set of items is reduced to 13. These items are administered to a sample of respondents, who are instructed to use them to rate a brand of their choice that they love but cannot buy for some reason. Four items are deleted because of item-to-total correlation < 0.40. The remaining nine items are common factor analysed using oblique rotation. Because of loading < 0.40, six items are deleted, leaving a set of three romantic brand jealously items.

Study 3 tests the convergent and discriminant validities of the scale. Respondents are asked to rate a brand they love but do not own for some reasons on the following, in addition to romantic brand jealously items: self-esteem (adapted from Truong & McColl, 2011); brand love and self-expressiveness (adapted from Carroll & Ahuvia, 2006); purchase intention (adapted from Yoo & Donthu, 2001; see Chapter 11, pp. 228–233); and active brand engagement (adapted from Bergkvist & Bech-Larsen, 2010). Common factor analysis using oblique rotation is used to demonstrate the scale's validity.

Study 4 further tests the validity of the scale in relation to self-esteem, self-expressiveness, brand love, brand jealously, purchase intention and active engagement. The scales included in the questionnaire and the instructions provided to respondents are the same as in the previous study. Confirmatory factor analysis is used in data analysis to provide evidence of nomological validity and further support to convergent and discriminant validities.

Samples

Study 1 is based on a sample of 25 informants belonging to a high-income group residing in various metropolitan cities; they are owners of premium car brands and are selected from a database provided by various car dealers. Study 2 employs a panel of psychology professors and a convenience sample of 65 respondents belonging to a high-income group selected from a dataset provided by various car dealers. Study 3 is based on a sample of 170 premium car owners; contact information is provided by car showrooms in metropolitan cities. Study 4 collects data using a quota-sampling procedure with car types and geographic locations as selection criteria; questionnaires are administered face to face. All samples include respondents belonging to the high economic class. All studies are conducted in India.

Reliability and validity

The convergent and discriminant validities of the romantic brand jealously scale are checked in study 3. The following is reported to support such validities. Romantic brand jealously items are factor analysed together with items on self-esteem, self-expressiveness, brand love, purchase intention and active engagement. All items load on the corresponding factors (loadings > 0.40), without any overlap. Inter-factor correlations are positive and significant ($p < 0.05$). Romantic brand jealously reports a composite reliability of 0.87 and an average variance extracted (AVE) of 0.63.

The scale's convergent and discriminant validities are tested in study 4. The AVE associated with romantic brand jealously is 0.63, and its composite reliability is > 0.77. A discriminant validity check is performed by comparing the AVE of all constructs (self-esteem, self-expressiveness, brand love, purchase intention, active engagement) with the squared correlation between each pair of constructs. The correlation between brand jealousy and any other of these constructs range from 0.46 (with purchase intention) to 0.92 (with self-expression).

The nomological validity of the romantic brand jealously scale is examined in study 4 with respect to the same constructs used to demonstrate convergent and discriminant validities. Structural equation modelling is used to estimate a model in which brand jealousy is determined by both self-esteem and brand love (which is determined by self-expressiveness), and brand jealously, in turn, determines purchase intention and active engagement. An alternative model measuring direct effects from brand love to purchase intention and from brand love to active engagement is considered. This model, however, is discarded because it is less parsimonious and not significantly different from the hypothesized one ($\chi^2 = 3{,}225.67$, $df = 397$, $p = 0.00$, NFI = 0.91, CFI = 0.92, SRMR = 0.041, RMSEA = 0.053; delta $\chi^2 = 6.25$, delta $df = 2$).

Managerial applications

Marketers are encouraged to create romantic brand jealousy in the minds of their potential customers, in addition to brand love. Romantic brand jealousy can motivate consumers toward the purchase of a brand and can engage them in an active way. Consumers' self-esteem, which represents one of the antecedents of brand jealousy, could be used as a psychographic segmentation variable. The other two antecedents of brand self-expressiveness and brand love can be increased through *ad hoc* marketing communications. To induce brand jealousy, marketers can leverage its antecedents or the feeling of jealousy itself, which could be increased through, for example, advertising strategies.

8.8 Academic focus

- Rossiter (2012) found that brand love drastically varies across product categories, as consumers seem to have a brand that they love rather than like, especially for high-involvement products. One dissertation could compare different types of product categories, for example, categories offering functional versus experiential versus symbolic benefits (Park, Jaworski & MacInnis, 1986). Using one of the brand love frameworks

presented in the chapter, the dissertation may investigate how brand love and its dimensions change across these product categories.
- So far, brand love has been examined in relation to consumer brands mainly. In a dissertation, one may verify how brand love frameworks can be applied to another field: destination branding, higher education and sports branding are a few examples.
- Scholars have shown the relationship between brand love and behavioural outcomes such as brand loyalty and positive word of mouth (e.g., Batra, Ahuvia & Bagozzi, 2012). A dissertation could further explore how brand love is related to behavioural outcomes that lead to brand equity (for brand equity conceptualizations and measurements, see Chapter 11).
- The study of how brand love evolves over time is in its infancy (Langner, Bruns, Fischer & Rossiter, 2014). One dissertation may track not only the general love feeling over time, but also how its different components evolve over time. For instance, Albert, Merunka and Valette-Florence's (2009) as well as Batra, Ahuvia and Bagozzi's (2012) frameworks could be used to that purpose.
- One dissertation may investigate the antecedents of consumer negative emotions. For example, the dissertation could compare the different role that brand image (see Chapter 1) versus brand experience (see Chapter 7) has in determining negative consumer emotions.

8.9 Managerial focus

- **Why is it important that consumers love your brand?**
  One of the major appeals of brand lovers is that they become brand advocates who will amplify the marketer's message. According to Nielsen (www.nielsen.com/us/en/insights/reports/2013/global-trust-in-advertising-and-brand-messages.html), 84% of consumers say they trust recommendations from friends and family above all forms of advertising. Companies are investing a lot in communication and loyalty programs to create strong relationships with consumers, but are they efficient enough to make consumers love their brands, since a majority of customers do not care about this? It is important for managers to identify passionate consumers and to understand the drivers of their passion in order to help foster similar feelings among the brand's customer base at large and increase the performance of marketing actions. The brand love scales included in this chapter can allow managers to identify these consumers who are really brand passionate and measure the intensity of their emotion toward the brand to predict their advocacy behaviour.

- **Do you consider brand love a new criterion to use in your segmentation?**
  Nowadays, consumers are always expecting interaction with brands because technology allows them to do so. Nevertheless, the ways brands communicate to new consumers, loyal consumers or brand lovers cannot be the same. By clearly identifying brand lovers, managers can gain deep insight into the motivations of that specific group of consumers. This can help determine what messages and content communicate in order to deepen the relationship with them and reinforce their advocacy efforts. It is also interesting to understand what the brand lovers are doing to help others experience the brand in order to define specific marketing programs. Brand love can therefore be a new segmentation criterion which can be used to improve the performance of marketing strategies.
- **Have you checked the impact of your social media campaign on brand love?**
  If your brands have many "likes" on Facebook or Twitter, it does not mean that your brands receive brand love. It is quite amazing to think that in a virtual world, consumers love brands which help them enhance their identity and are in sync with their fundamental life values. Social media campaigns should enhance a brand's ability to express the consumer's identity and connect with life values which are considered as important for that individual (Batra, Ahuvia & Bagozzi, 2012). Managers should develop social media campaigns which are able to emphasize some positive life values such as sharing, enjoyment, kindness and honesty in order to reach the heart of the consumers. Just think about one of the latest viral campaigns orchestrated by Nike in order to enhance positive emotion. The brand set up a pitch invasion by a small child in South Africa who wanted to meet his hero Neymar, the golden boy of Brazilian football. The Nike endorser kindly took selfies with the boy as well as "protecting" him from the security men. The video spread the positive values of Nike to people and Nike customers all over the world. The scale developed by Albert, Merunka and Valette-Florence (2009) can be used to evaluate the efficiency of a social media campaign in enhancing the consumer's feeling of love toward the brand.
- **Is your brand subjected to brand love by teenagers?**
  Teenagers are volatile consumers, and furthermore they are in the process of constructing their own identities. Adolescents like to belong to groups and communities in which they can instantly share ideas, pictures, videos and experiences. Indeed, these groups offer teenagers both identity and self-esteem. Young people follow brands, particularly the fashionable ones, which can reinforce their identity by reflecting who they are. The brands also increase their social integration by making them feel good about themselves. Teenagers can have a high level of interaction with their favourite brands and be very participative among brand communities,

> resulting in their becoming real brand ambassadors to their peers. Therefore, it could be interesting for managers to identify the teenagers who are brand lovers in order to develop specific actions toward them.
> - **Have you checked that your consumers haven't got negative feelings about your brand?**
> It is commonly admitted that it costs six to seven times more to acquire a new customer than keep an old one, so it is really important not to deceive consumers. Negative feelings toward brands may occur because of negative consumption experiences or misfit between the brand image and consumer's identity or between the brand values and consumer's beliefs (Dalli, Romani & Gistri, 2006; Lee, Motion & Conroy, 2009). These negative feelings may have negative effects on brand image, brand reputation and brand equity. Therefore, it is important for managers to control and minimize the risk of negative reputation, especially as the online environment may amplify these negatives effects. In general, managers are used to track the brand image or the associations linked to the brand but do not particularly track the negative emotions toward the brand. The scale developed by Romani, Grappi and Dalli (2012) can be used to understand which negative emotions are felt by consumers and the intensity of those feelings in order to take preventive actions.

References

Ahuvia, A., Bagozzi, R. P., & Batra, R. (2014). Psychometric vs. C-OAR-SE measures of brand love: a reply to Rossiter. *Marketing Letters*, 25 (2), 235–243.

Albert, N., Merunka, D., & Valette-Florence, P. (2009). The feeling of love toward a brand: concept and measurement. *Advances in Consumer Research*, 36, 300–307.

Bagozzi, R. P., Gopinath, M., & Nyer, P. (1999). The role of emotions in marketing. *Journal of the Academy of Marketing Science*, 27 (2), 184–206.

Batra, R., Ahuvia, A., & Bagozzi, R. P. (2012). Brand love. *Journal of Marketing*, 76 (2), 1–16.

Bergkvist, L., & Bech-Larsen, T. (2010). Two studies of consequences and actionable antecedents of brand love. *Journal of Brand Management*, 17 (7), 504–518.

Bougie, R., Pieters, R., & Zeelenberg, M. (2003). Angry customers don't come back, they get back: the experience and behavioral implications of anger and dissatisfaction in services. *Journal of the Academy of Marketing Science*, 31 (4), 377–393.

Carroll, B., & Ahuvia, A. (2006). Some antecedents and outcomes of brand love. *Marketing Letters*, 17 (2), 79–89.

Chaudhuri, A., & Holbrook, M. B. (2001). The chain of effects from brand trust and brand affect to brand performance: the role of brand loyalty. *Journal of Marketing*, 65 (2), 81–93.

Churchill, G. A., Jr. (1979). A paradigm for developing better measures of marketing constructs. *Journal of Marketing Research*, 16 (1), 64–73.

Dalli, D., Romani, S., & Gistri, G. (2006). "Brand dislike: representing the negative side of consumer preferences," *Advances in Consumer Research*, 33, eds. Connie Pechmann and Linda Price, Duluth, MN: Association for Consumer Research, pp. 87–95.

Donovan, R. J., & Rossiter, J. R. (1982). Store atmosphere: an environmental psychology approach. *Journal of Retailing*, 58 (Spring), 34–57.

Edell, J., & Burke, M. (1987). The power of feelings in understanding advertising effects. *Journal of Consumer Research*, 14 (3), 421–433.

Havlena, W. J., & Holbrook, M. B. (1986). The varieties of consumption experience: comparing two typologies of emotion in consumer behaviour. *Journal of Consumer Research*, 13 (3), 394–404.

Holbrook, M. B., & Batra, R. (1987). Assessing the role of emotions as mediators of consumer responses to advertising. *Journal of Consumer Research*, 14 (3), 404–420.

Izard, C. E. (1977). *Human emotions*. New York, NY: Plenum Press.

Langner, T., Bruns, D., Fischer, A., & Rossiter, J. R. (2014). Falling in love with brands: a dynamic analysis of the trajectories of brand love, *Marketing Letters*. doi:10.1007/s11002-014-9283-4

Laros, F.J.M., & Steenkamp, J.B.E.M. (2005). Emotions in consumer behavior: A hierarchical approach. *Journal of Business Research*, 58 (10), 1437–1445.

Lee, M.S., Motion, J., & Conroy, D. (2009). Anti-consumption and brand avoidance. *Journal of Business Research*, 62 (2), 169–180.

Mitchell, A. A., & Olson, J. C. (1981). Are product attribute beliefs the only mediator of advertising effects on brand attitude? *Journal of Marketing Research*, 18 (3), 318–332.

Park, C. W., Jaworski, B., & MacInnis, D. J. (1986). Strategic brand concept-image management. *Journal of Marketing*, 50 (4), 135–145.

Patwardhan, H., & Balasubramanian, S. K. (2011). Brand romance: a complementary approach to explain emotional attachment toward brands. *Journal of Product & Brand Management*, 20 (4), 297–308.

Plutchik, R. (1980). *Emotion: A psychoevolutionary synthesis*. New York: Harper & Row.

Putrevu, S., & Lord, K. P. (1994). Comparative and noncomparative advertising: attitudinal effects under cognitive and affective involvement conditions. *Journal of Advertising*, 23 (2), 77–91.

Richins, M. L. (1997). Measuring emotions in the consumption experience. *Journal of Consumer Research*, 24 (2), 127–146.

Romani, S., Grappi, S., & Dalli, D. (2012). Emotions that drive consumers away from brands: measuring negative emotions toward brands and their behavioral effects. *International Journal of Research in Marketing*, 29 (1), 55–67.

Romaniuk, J. (2013). Viewpoint: What's (brand) love got to do with it? *International Journal of Market Research*, 55 (2), 185–186.

Rossiter, J. R. (2002). The C-OAR-SE procedure for scale development in marketing. *International Journal of Research in Marketing*, 19 (4), 305–335.

Rossiter, J. R. (2011). Marketing measurement revolution: the C-OAR-SE method and why it must replace psychometrics. *European Journal of Marketing*, 45 (11/12), 1561–1588.

Rossiter, J. R. (2012). A new C-OAR-SE-based content-valid and predictively valid measure that distinguishes brand love from brand liking. *Marketing Letters*, 23 (2), 905–916.

Rossiter, J. R., Percy, L., & Donovan, R. J. (1991). A better advertising planning grid. *Journal of Advertising Research*, 31 (5), 11–21.

Rust, Roland T., & Cooil, Bruce. (1994). Reliability measures for qualitative data: Theory and implications. *Journal of Marketing Research*, 31, 1–14.

Sarkar, A., & Sreejesh, S. (2014). Examination of the roles played by brand love and jealousy in shaping customer engagement. *Journal of Product & Brand Management*, 23 (1), 24–32.

Truong, Y., & McColl, R. (2011). Intrinsic motivations, self-esteem, and luxury goods consumption. *Journal of Retailing and Consumer Services*, 18 (6), 555–561.

Yoo, B., & Donthu, N. (2001). Developing and validating a multi-dimensional consumer-based brand equity scale. *Journal of Business Research*, 52 (1), 1–14.

Zeelenberg, M., & Pieters, R. (2004). Beyond valence in customer dissatisfaction: a review and new findings on behavioral responses to regret and disappointment in failed services. *Journal of Business Research*, 57 (4), 445–455.

9
ATTACHMENT TO THE BRAND

9.1 Overview

Attachment is a well-established concept in psychology. Attachment is defined by developmental psychologist Bowlby (1969) as an emotional bond between a person (e.g., an infant) and another person (e.g., infant's mother). Because of the motivational and behavioural implications that attachment has, such as the willingness to stay close to the attachment figure and the distress experienced when separation from this figure occurs (Bowlby, 1969), marketing researchers have shown interested in this concept. Marketing researchers have extended the area of applicability of attachment and have postulated that attachment can exist not only toward another person but also toward a brand. They have also shown that attachment to the brand is significantly related to various behavioural intentions and actual behaviours (for a review, see Park, MacInnis & Priester, 2006).

The measurement of attachment has concerned marketing researchers since the first studies centred on this topic and has evolved together with the notion of brand attachment itself. The first conceptualizations and measurement scales looked at brand attachment from a purely emotional point of view. In these works, attachment to the brand is considered an emotional type of attachment that consumers may develop with respect to a brand. That is the case of Lacœuilhe (2000)'s *attachment à la marque* scale and Thomson, MacInnis and Park's (2005) consumers' emotional attachment to the brand scale. A more articulated view of brand attachment is instead proposed by Park, MacInnis, Priester, Eisingerich and Iacobucci (2010) with their brand attachment scale. These researchers go beyond attachment as a purely emotional construct. They posit that brand attachment includes not only an emotional component but also brand–self cognition, thoughts and autobiographical brand memories.

Attachment has also been investigated in negative terms – what psychology literature has called "detachment", a concept studied in the context of interpersonal

188 Attachment to the brand

relationship dissolution (Duck, 1982). Similarly, in brand management, the concept of detachment has been used to investigate the psychological state of a consumer following the weakening or breaking of a relationship with a brand to which the consumer was previously attached. Perrin-Martinenq (2004) proposes a measurement scale to capture this state of detachment with a brand.

9.2 *Attachement à la marque*/Attachment to the brand (Lacœuilhe, 2000)

Definition of construct

Attachment to the brand is defined by Lacœuilhe (2000) as a psychological construct which reflects the presence of an affective relationship between the consumer and the brand. This relationship can be described as durable and stable and is characterized by psychological proximity between the consumer and the brand; if broken, this relationship can lead to a harmful separation for the consumer. Attachment to the brand is also defined as an evolving concept, as it is likely to change over the life of an individual: the same individual can be attached to a brand during his/her adolescence and detached from this brand once he/she is adult, because the values of the brand are not aligned with him/her anymore.

Scale description

The attachment to the brand scale includes five items. Items are measured on Likert scales.

TABLE 9.1 *Attachement à la marque*/Attachment to the brand scale

Scale Item
• *J'ai beaucoup d'affection pour cette marque*
• *L'achat de cette marque me procure beaucoup de joie, de plaisir*
• *Je trouve un certain réconfort à acheter ou posséder cette marque*
• *Je suis très lié à cette marque*
• *Je suis très attiré par cette marque*

Scale development

The attachment to the brand scale has been developed in accordance with Churchill (1979b). After having defined the construct that the scale measures, the first step to develop the scale consists of the item generation and selection. Three sources are used to that aim, that is, the review of the relevant literature, in-depth interviews and projective techniques. An initial pool of 40 items is generated and submitted to a panel of brand experts. Based on their feedback, 25 items are retained.

A first data collection is conducted to further purify the set of items. A series of exploratory factor analysis using principal component analysis results in a unidimensional solution explaining more than 60% of the total variance and with eight items having a loading > 0.70. The other items are eliminated based on the output of the analysis and qualitative assessment.

A second data collection is conducted to validate this solution. Participants receive one of three product categories (tights, feminine deodorants and laxatives) and are asked questions on attachment to the brand; for validity purposes, they are also asked questions on perceived risk (Laurent & Kapferer, 1986), perceived difference among brands (derived from Jain & Srinivasan, 1990; Zaichkowsky, 1985), brand involvement (Strazzieri, 1994), brand sensitivity (Laurent & Kapferer, 1986), brand typicality (Ladwein, 1994) and brand engagement (Amine, 1994, 1996). The five items on attachment to the brand are subjected to a new exploratory factor analysis using principal component analysis, which leads to rejection of three items on attachment and to retention of a five-item solution explaining 60.3% of total variance (all items have loadings between 0.74 and 0.81). An exploratory factor analysis on each of the three product categories corroborates these findings. A confirmatory factor analysis is performed to further support the five-item solution. This analysis reports an adequate fit of the model (GFI = 0.992, AGFI = 0.976, RMR = 0.035, RMSEA = 0.032) and t-values > 2, $p < 0.05$, for each scale item. Reliability and validity tests are finally performed.

Samples

Item generation is conducted thanks to the help of 15 consumers. The first data collection is based on a convenience sample of 120 participants. The second data collection employs 311 participants who are selected from a panel from Sécodip.

Reliability and validity

Aggregate data on three product categories are used to test the scale reliability and validity. The internal consistency of the scale is examined through Cronbach's alpha and Jöreskog's rho, which report good scores (respectively, 0.83 and 0.89).

Trait validity is examined through tests of convergent and discriminant validities. Evidence of convergent validity is provided by showing that the average variance extracted is equal to 0.51 and that all items have loadings which are significant at $p < 0.05$. The scale's discriminant validity is demonstrated with respect to perceived risk, perceived difference among brands, brand involvement, brand sensitivity and brand typicality. It is shown that the average variance extracted is higher than the square of the correlations between attachment to the brand and any other constructs. Using chi-square tests, it is also shown that the model with unconstrained factors performs better than the models where the correlation between attachment to the brand and any other constructs is fixed to one.

The predictive validity of the scale is demonstrated with respect to engagement. Structural equation model analysis shows that attachment to the brand is the best predictor of engagement ($\beta = 0.450$, $t = 4.64$) compared to perceived risk, perceived difference among brands and brand sensitivity.

Managerial applications

The use of the scale can help managers better understand the relationship between their consumers and brands. By encouraging attachment to their brands, managers can stimulate consumers' engagement and loyalty toward their brands so consumers are less attracted by other brands when promotional activities are available. Attachment to the brand results from the perception of a fit between the consumer and the brand as the consumer uses the brand to build and communicate his/her identity to others. Communication activities, which spread the values of the brands, should therefore be planned carefully.

9.3 Brand detachment (Perrin-Martinenq, 2004)

Definition of construct

Perrin-Martinenq (2004, p. 1007) defines brand detachment as "the psychological state of distance with regard to a brand, resulting from the weakening or the dissolution of the affective bond existing between the consumer and the brand". As such, brand detachment assumes the pre-existence of a consumer–brand relationship in which the consumer feels some degree of attachment to the brand. It is a unidimensional construct, characterized by an affective and cognitive nature. This means that detached consumers are consumers who have a weak or null affective link with the brand in which they are not interested anymore.

Scale description

The brand detachment scale consists of one dimension and six items. Of these items, one is reverse coded. All items must be evaluated using a 7-point Likert scale, where 1 = "completely disagree" and 7 = "completely agree".

TABLE 9.2 Brand detachment scale

Scale item
• I no longer pay attention to this brand
• I no longer think about this brand
• I am no longer attracted by this brand
• I no longer pay any special attention to this brand
• I no longer like this brand
• I am interested by what this brand offers*

Note: *indicates the item is reverse coded.

Scale development

The brand detachment scale is developed in accordance with Churchill (1979b, 1995) and other methods of analysis (Peter, 1981). The brand detachment scale is developed through a questionnaire survey, preceded by an item-generation and refinement phase. The initial pool of brand detachment items is generated based on a literature review and is refined thanks to the contribution of experts. In the survey, respondents are asked to think about a brand from which they are detached in one of four product categories (clothing, cars, cosmetics and hi-fi) and to rate it using scales on brand detachment, brand sensitivity (Laurent & Kapferer, 1992), involvement in product category (Strazzieri, 1994), brand commitment (Cristau, 2001), consideration of the brand (one-item measure: "Do you still think about this brand when you buy the product?") and repeated buying behaviour (adapted from Odin, 1998). A series of exploratory and confirmatory factor analyses allows the researchers to identify one dimension for brand detachment inclusive of six items. The final exploratory factor analysis explains 59.3% of the total variance; factor loadings range from 0.709 to 0.823. The confirmatory factor analysis supports the solution previously identified ($\chi^2 = 26.825$, $df = 9$, $p < 0.001$, RMR = 0.070, GFI = 0.978, RMSEA = 0.069, AGFI = 0.949, CFI = 0.982). Different types of scale validity are tested.

Samples

The study is based on a convenience sample of 434 individuals.

Reliability and validity

The reliability of the brand detachment scale is tested through the alpha coefficient (equal to 0.86) and the rho coefficient of Jöreskog (equal to 0.88). The face validity of the brand detachment items is examined in the item-generation and refinement phase, thanks to the experts. Convergent validity is checked through the computation of the average variance extracted for the construct, which is equal to 0.51. Discriminant validity is examined with respect to brand sensitivity and involvement in product category. Exploratory factor analysis with varimax rotation shows that the three constructs load on a different factor. Finally, to show the scale's nomological validity, a series of regression analyses is conducted. Results show that brand detachment has a negative influence on repeated buying behaviour (standardized beta = −0.543, $p < 0.0001$) and consideration of the brand (standardized beta = −0.618, $p < 0.0001$). The influence of brand detachment on brand commitment cannot be evaluated, as the psychometric properties of the brand commitment scale are not satisfactory.

Managerial applications

The brand detachment scale can be used to better understand the weakening of the relationship between consumers and the brand. As brand detachment indicates the imminence of the relationship dissolution, managers can use the scale to detect possible risky situations and react promptly before the final dissolution of the relationship takes place. As brand detachment is not the same as strong negative affective states toward the brand, such as rejection, the recovery of the relationship is still possible.

9.4 Consumers' emotional attachment to brands (Thomson, MacInnis & Park, 2005)

Definition of construct

The conceptualization of consumers' emotional attachment (EA) to brands is developed by referring to Bowlby's (1979, 1980) work on attachment in the field of psychology. Attachment is defined as an "an emotional-laden target specific bond between a person and a specific object" (Thomson, MacInnis & Park, 2005, pp. 77–78); in this case the object is the brand. EA to brands is a multi-dimensional construct consisting of three dimensions, which are related to one another: *affection*, which describes consumers' warm feelings toward a brand; *passion*, which reflects consumers' intense and aroused feelings toward a brand; and *connection*, which refers to consumers' feelings of being joined with the brand.

Scale description

The EA scale includes the following dimensions and items: *affection* (four items), *connection* (three items) and *passion* (three items). Respondents are asked to indicate to which extent the items describe their feelings toward a brand using a 7-point scale from 1 = "describes poorly" to 7 = "describes very well". Items can be summed and averaged within each dimension to form dimension scores (e.g., *passion* score) or can be summed and averaged over all the 10 items to from an overall EA score.

TABLE 9.3 Emotional attachment scale

Scale dimension	Scale item
Affection	• Affectionate
	• Loved
	• Peaceful
	• Friendly
Connection	• Attached
	• Bonded
	• Connected
Passion	• Passionate
	• Delighted
	• Captivated

Scale development

The EA scale is developed through a series of five studies following the procedure suggested by Churchill (1979a, 1979b).

Study 1 generates an initial pool of items that reflect consumers' EA to brands. To that aim, respondents are asked to identify a brand to which they are emotionally attached and to indicate the extent to which the items listed describe their typical feelings toward that brand; they are also asked to indicate any other emotions not included in the original list. Items with mean rating < 4.0 along the 7-point Likert scale used to record answers are dropped. The reduced set of items is revised by experts; additional items judged as non-emotional are dropped, leaving a pool of 35 items.

Study 2 further reduces the items generated in study 1. Respondents are asked to think about a brand to which they are strongly emotionally attached and to evaluate it using the 35 items. Items not rated by 10% of respondents are removed, as well as the items with a mean rating below the scale midpoint and limited variance ($SD < 1.5$). The remaining items are subjected to a series of exploratory factor analyses with oblique rotation. The output of the analysis is a three-factor solution with eigenvalues > 1.0 and including 10 items.

Study 3 confirms the stability of the scale using a different sample of respondents and assesses its factorial structure (first-order versus second-order). Respondents are asked to think of a brand to which they had some degree of emotional attachment and to complete the 10-item EA scale. Confirmatory factor analyses are conducted to compare three models of EA: a model where all items load on a single factor ($\chi^2 = 156.3$); one with three uncorrelated first-order factors loading on a second-order factor ($\chi^2 = 102.8$); and one with three correlated first-order factors loading on a second-order factor ($\chi^2 = 66.7$). Based on the chi-square statistics, the latter model is considered the best one.

Study 4 assesses the convergent validity of the EA scale. To ensure variance in the EA score, respondents are asked to think of a brand to which they have either weak or strong attachment and to complete scales on EA and four attachment behaviours, including proximity, security, safety and separation distress (adapted from Hazan & Shaver, 1994; Hazan & Zeifman, 1999). Reliability tests are conducted, and convergent validity is tested using structural equation models.

Study 5 tests the convergent, discriminant and predictive validities of the EA scale. Again, to ensure variance in the EA score, respondents are asked to evaluate a brand to which they are either weakly, moderately or strongly attached and to complete a series of scales. In addition to the EA scale, the scales in the questionnaire cover brand attitude favourability (Batra & Stayman, 1990), satisfaction (Mano & Oliver, 1980), involvement (Zaichowsky, 1985), brand loyalty (adapted from Sirgy, Johar, Samli & Clairborne, 1991) and willingness to pay a premium price (developed by the researchers). Reliability tests are conducted. The scale's validities are assessed through exploratory factor analysis and structural equation models.

Samples

Study 1 employs 68 students and two independent judges. Study 2 is based on a sample of 120 undergraduate and graduate students. Study 3 is based on a sample of 65 undergraduate and graduate students. Study 4 is based on a sample of 184 undergraduate students. Study 5 uses 179 non-student respondents solicited at a science museum and outside a restaurant.

Reliability and validity

The reliability of the EA scale is tested in studies 2 and 3. The coefficient alpha score is computed for the global EA scale by averaging dimension scores. The coefficient is equal to 0.77 in study 2 and 0.88 in study 3 and is equal to or higher than 0.87 in study 4.

The scale's convergent and discriminant validities are tested in studies 4 and 5. In study 4, convergent validity is shown by relating EA to four attachment behaviours. A structural equation model (χ^2 = 38.6, CMIN/df = 3.50, NFI = 0.97, RFI = 0.95, CFI = 0.98) where the three EA dimensions predict the four behaviours via a second-order construct of global EA indicates that EA is related to proximity (γ = 0.92, p < 0.01), securement (γ = 0.91, p < 0.01), safety (γ = 0.88, p < 0.01) and separation distress (γ = 0.95, p < 0.01). The analysis checks another model (χ^2 = 299.8, CMIN/df = 49.97, NFI = 0.78, RFI = 0.22, CFI = 0.78), discarded because of a worse fit, which assumes that the three EA dimensions independently predict the four behaviours. Convergent validity is checked again in study 5, together with discriminant validity. Discriminant validity is tested by an exploratory factor analysis with oblique rotation, which shows that EA items load on a different factor from related constructs (involvement, satisfaction/loyalty, brand attitude favourability and dissatisfaction). Evidence of convergent validity is given by the correlations between EA and the factors obtained from this factor analysis – correlations which are positive and significant but moderate in size.

Predictive validity is tested in study 5 using structural equation models. A structural equation model where the three EA dimensions predict the four behaviours via a second-order construct indicates that EA predicts brand loyalty (γ = 0.54, p < 0.01) and premium price (γ = 0.43, p < 0.01). This model (χ^2 = 138.4, CMIN/df = 2.82, NFI = 0.97, RFI = 0.95, CFI = 0.98) presents a better fit than another one (χ^2 = 137.4, CMIN/df = 2.92, NFI = 0.91, RFI = 0.87, CFI = 0.94) where the three EA dimensions predict brand loyalty and premium price directly. The last model estimated shows that EA is a predictor of involvement, dissatisfaction and attitude favourability (γ equal to, respectively, 0.23 and 0.25, with ps < 0.01) even when other antecedents are introduced (loyalty/satisfaction and premium price). These results are supported by hierarchical regression analyses, which reveal that EA is a predictor of both brand loyalty (β = 0.14, p < 0.02) and price premium (β = 0.25, p < 0.01).

Managerial applications

The EA scale can be used to measure the consumers' emotional attachment to brands. Managers may be interested in consumers' emotional attachment to brand to appraise the strength of the relationship between consumers and their brands.

9.5 Brand attachment (Park, MacInnis, Priester, Eisingerich & Iacobucci, 2010)

Definition of construct

Brand attachment is defined by Park, MacInnis, Priester, Eisingerich and Iacobucci (2010) as the strength of the bond connecting the brand with consumers' self. Brand attachment consists of two dimensions: *brand–self connection*, which refers to the cognitive and emotional connection between the brand and the consumer, and *brand prominence*, which indicates the perceived ease and frequency with which brand-related thoughts and feelings come to the consumer's mind. Both aspects are important in defining brand attachment. Whereas brand–self connection is the core of brand attachment as it reflects the bond between the consumer and the brand, brand prominence measures the strength of such a bond. In contrast to Thomson, MacInnis and Park (2005; see this chapter, pp. 192–195), Park, MacInnis, Priester, Eisingerich and Iacobucci's conceptualization of brand attachment goes beyond consumer emotions toward the brand. According to them, in fact, emotions are important but not central to their conceptualization of attachment, as brand attachment is more than purely emotions; it also includes brand–self cognition, thoughts and auto-biographical brand memories. Park, MacInnis, Priester, Eisingerich and Iacobucci also highlight that brand attachment is different from attitude strength because of the different nature of affect, type of strength, valence and relationship with time.

Scale description

The scale includes four items, two for each dimension (*brand-self connection* and *brand prominence*). Items are evaluated on 11-point Likert scales from 0 = "not at all" to 10 = "completely".

TABLE 9.4 Brand attachment scale

Scale dimension	Scale item
Brand-self connection	• To what extent is (brand X) part of you and who you are?
	• To what extent do you feel personally connected to (brand X)?
Brand prominence	• To what extent are your thoughts and feelings toward (brand X) often automatic, coming to mind seemingly on their own?
	• To what extent do your thoughts and feelings toward (brand X) come to your mind naturally and instantly?

Scale development

In study 1, a set of 10 items, 5 for each dimension (*brand-self connection* and *brand prominence*), is generated by the authors. The items are evaluated by a sample of participants with respect to three brands. Exploratory factor analyses using oblique factor rotation reduce the items to eight. Based on factor loadings and reliability tests, the set of items is further reduced to four (two for each dimension).

Study 2 supports the two-factor solution of brand attachment and verifies the scale's convergent and discriminant validities. Respondents are asked to rate the Apple iPod brand on items on brand attachment, separation distress and brand attitude strength. Confirmatory factor analyses (CFAs) support the two-factor solution: the CFA where the two factors of brand attachment correlate ($r = .37$; $\chi^2(3) = 18.37$) fits the data better than the CFA where the two factors are forced to be perfectly correlated ($\chi^2(4) = 223.11$), based on chi-square change (delta $\chi^2(1) = 204.74$, $p < 0.001$). Evidence of convergent and discriminant validities of brand attachment is provided with respect to brand attitude strength and separation distress. The structural equation models testing the scale's validity further support the structure of brand attachment, as the fit of the second-order model of attachment ($\chi^2(10) = 11.50$) is significantly better than the first-order model ($\chi^2(12) = 85.00$), based on chi-square difference (delta $\chi^2(2) = 73.50$, $p < 0.001$).

Study 3 replicates the previous study using a different brand. Respondents are asked to rate the Nike shoe brand in terms of brand attachment, separation distress, brand attitude strength and intention to perform 10 types of behaviours (i.e., buying the brand for oneself; recommending the brand to others; switching from the brand to another; using products with the brand's logo; buying the brand for others; paying a price premium; defending the brand when others speak poorly about it; waiting for brand to become available; always buying latest brand model when it becomes available; spending money, time and energy to participate in activities to promote the brand) varying in perceived difficulty. CFAs further support the two-factor solution for brand attachment: the CFA where the two factors correlate ($r = 0.67$; $\chi^2(1) = 3.84$, $p < 0.05$) fits the data better than the CFA where the two factors are forced to be perfectly correlated ($\chi^2(2) = 48.70$, $p < 0.001$), based on the chi-square test (delta $\chi^2(1) = 44.86$, $p < 0.001$). Convergent and discriminant validities are demonstrated with respect to brand attitude strenght and the 10 types of behaviours.

Study 4 is conducted in collaboration with a European bank and considers actual behaviour instead of behavioural intentions. Because of the new country involved, the quantitative study is preceded by telephone interviews, which are conducted to discuss the meaning to reduce item ambiguity, and a pre-test of the questionnaire, where respondents are asked to point out ambiguity in responding to individual questions. Minor word changes are made to ensure question clarity. In the quantitative study, the questionnaire, sent by mail, includes questions on brand attachment, brand attitude strength and separation distress. The following are used as dependent variables: actual purchase, measured by summing the sales of all investment products over the six months after the survey; brand purchase share, measured by asking respondents to indicate how many banks they are using in addition to the surveyed one; and need share, measured by asking respondents to indicate the extent to which they use the surveyed bank for all their financial services. Past purchase in the previous six months, gender and relationship length are used as controls. Data analyses further support the convergent, discriminant and predictive validities of the brand attachment scale.

Samples

Study 2 is based on a sample of 108 undergraduate marketing students; the survey is administered in a group setting (30 to 40 students per group). Study 3 is based on a sample of 141 undergraduate marketing students. Study 4 uses a sample of 2,000 customers randomly selected from one of the firm's branch networks: of them, 41 are randomly selected for the telephone interviews and 52 are randomly selected for the pre-test; in the quantitative study, 701 customers return the questionnaire, and the number of usable responses is 697 (34.85% effective response rate). Studies 1 to 3 are conducted in the United States, whereas study 4 is conducted in a European country.

Reliability and validity

The reliability of the brand attachment scale is examined through the Cronbach's alpha. In study 1, the coefficient alpha for the two-item *brand-self connection* scale is equal to 0.92, 0.90 and 0.86 for the three brands surveyed; the coefficient alpha for the two-item *brand prominence* scale is equal to 0.91, 0.90 and 0.89, respectively. In study 2, the two-item *brand-self connection* scale displays a correlation of 0.91, whereas the two-item *brand prominence* scale presents one of 0.71.

Convergent, discriminant and predictive validities of the brand attachment scale are provided in studies 2, 3 and 4. In study 2, to show that brand attachment and brand attitude strength are related but distinct, two CFAs are conducted. The CFA where both constructs are allowed to correlate ($r = 0.66$; $\chi^2(3) = 3.80$) fits the data better than the CFA where the factors are forced to be perfectly correlated ($\chi^2(4) = 27.70$), based on chi-square change (delta $\chi^2(1) = 23.90$, $p < 0.001$). With regard to separation distress, regression analysis reveals that brand attachment dimensions independently predict separation distress: two main effects are found (for *brand-self connection*: $\gamma = 0.50$, $F(1, 104) = 15.6$, $p < 0.001$; for *prominence*: $\gamma = 0.63$, $F(1, 104) = 11.4$, $p < 0.001$), with no significant interaction ($F(1, 104) = 0.02$). Moreover, structural equation models show that brand attachment is a stronger predictor of separation distress than brand attitude strength, both in the model where attachment is represented as first-order (for attachment: $\gamma = 0.74$; for attitude: $\gamma = 0.27$, $z = 3.94$, $p < 0.001$) and second-order construct (for attachment: $\gamma = 0.98$; for attitude: $\gamma = 0.02$; $z = 4.39$, $p < 0.001$), with the latter model best fitting the data based on chi-square difference (delta $\chi^2(2) = 73.50$, $p < 0.001$). As a further proof of discriminant validity, all items load on distinct factors in factor analysis with minimal cross-loadings (loadings between 0.78 and 0.99, cross-loadings between 0.03 and 0.18).

In study 3, to show the convergent and discriminant validities of brand attachment compared to brand attitude strength, two CFAs are conducted. The CFA where attachment and attitude are let free to correlate ($r = .80$; $\chi^2(3) = 5.10$, $p > 0.05$) fits the data better than the one where the two constructs are forced to be perfectly correlated ($\chi^2(4) = 53.40$, $p < 0.001$), based on the chi-square difference (delta $\chi^2(1) = 48.30$, $p < 0.001$). Predictive validity is demonstrated with regard to the 10 different behaviours, which are classified in three groups based on their degree of perceived difficulty to be performed. Structural equation models show that brand attachment better predicts intentions for most difficult behaviours ($\gamma = 0.81$, $p < 0.001$) than brand attitude strength ($\gamma = 0.05$, $p > 0.05$; $z = 3.87$, $p < 0.01$); it also better predicts moderately difficult behaviours ($\gamma = 0.52$, $p < 0.01$) than brand attitude strength ($\gamma = 0.47$, $p < 0.01$; $z = 2.91$, $p < 0.01$). Both brand attachment ($\gamma = 0.45$, $p < 0.01$) and brand attitude strength ($\gamma = 0.46$, $p < 0.01$) are strong predictors of least difficult behaviours ($z = 0.07$, $p > 0.05$). The last analysis compares the predictive power of two attachment models, one with both dimensions (*brand–self connection* and *brand prominence*) and one with only *brand–self connection*. The results show no significant difference in the one-component versus the two-component brand attachment measure's predictive ability of behaviours: most difficult to perform ($\gamma = 0.84$ and 0.82, $p < 0.001$, respectively), moderately difficult to perform ($\gamma = 0.87$ and 0.82, $p < 0.001$, respectively) and least difficult to perform ($\gamma = 0.82$ and 0.77, $p < 0.001$, respectively); the difference in coefficients and model fit (delta $\chi^2(7) = 10.62$; delta $\chi^2(5) = 5.31$; delta $\chi^2(11) = 6.90$; $p > 0.05$, respectively) is not significant.

In study 4, the validities of the brand attachment scale are demonstrated through a series of analyses, including both attachment and attitude strength as possible predictors of actual types of behaviours. Analyses show that brand attachment significantly predicts actual purchase behaviour ($\gamma = 0.14$, $p < 0.01$), whereas brand attitude strength does not ($\gamma = 0.05$, $p > 0.05$; $z = 2.44$, $p < 0.01$); brand attachment is a stronger predictor of brand purchase share ($\gamma = 0.65$, $p < 0.001$) than brand attitude strength ($\gamma = 0.21$, $p < 0.001$; $z = 8.86$, $p < 0.001$); and brand attachment is a stronger predictor of brand need share ($\gamma = 0.83$, $p < 0.001$) than strong brand attitudes ($\gamma = 0.26$, $p < 0.001$; $z = 11.86$, $p < 0.001$). These effects are verified even after accounting for past behaviour, relationship length and gender. Additional analyses compare brand attachment as consisting of two factors (*brand–self connection* and *brand prominence*) versus only one factor (*brand-self connection*) and show that the model including attachment as a two-factor construct has more predictive power (for actual purchase behaviour: $\gamma = 0.11$ versus $\gamma = 0.18$, $ps < 0.001$, respectively, delta $\chi^2(8) = 49.83$, $p < 0.001$; for brand purchase share: $\gamma = 0.64$ versus $\gamma = 0.20$, $ps < 0.001$, respectively, delta $\chi^2(8) = 56.40$, $p < 0.001$; for brand need share: $\gamma = 0.82$ versus $\gamma = 0.29$, $ps < 0.001$, respectively; delta $\chi^2(8) = 49.20$, $p < 0.001$).

Managerial applications

Brand attachment, including its two components of *brand-self connection* and *brand prominence*, has proved to be associated with behavioural intentions and actual behaviours more strongly than brand attitude strength. Using the proposed scale, managers could incorporate brand attachment in their evaluation matrices to assess consumer–brand relationships. Through brand attachment, they could have a deeper understanding of how current brand management efforts are related to future sales.

9.6 Academic focus

- Similarly to what has been done for attitudes, which have been examined in relation to children (Pecheux & Derbaix, 1999; see Chapter 6, pp. 134–136) and adolescents (Derbaix & Leheut, 2008a, 2008b; see Chapter 6, pp. 137–139), a dissertation may investigate brand attachment with respect to young consumers. How do young consumers attach to brands? How can this attachment be described? What are the differences between adults' and young consumers' attachments to brands?
- Brand attachment has been examined in relation to various behavioural intentions and actual behaviours (Lacœuilhe, 2000; Park, MacInnis, Priester, Eisingerich & Iacobucci, 2010; Thomson, MacInnis & Park, 2005). Marketing researchers have also hypothesized an impact of brand attachment on the equity of brands (Park, MacInnis & Priester, 2006). A dissertation may test this hypothesis, either focusing on brand attachment as a purely emotional (Lacœuilhe, 2000; Thomson, MacInnis & Park, 2005) or as both affective and cognitive (Park, MacInnis, Priester, Eisingerich & Iacobucci, 2010) construct and considering one of the frameworks that have been developed with regard to brand equity (see Chapter 11).
- Brand attachment could be studied in relation to the techniques that managers could use to stimulate it. For example, by adopting one of the frameworks proposed in the chapter, how do different communication tools impact overall brand attachment as well as its components?

200 Attachment to the brand

- Brand detachment represents an emerging concept in brand management literature, as studies on this concept are still scarce. One dissertation may be interested in further developing this concept by taking into account its antecedents. It may be interesting, for example, to relate brand detachment to brand relationship quality (Kim, Lee & Lee, 2005; see Chapter 10, pp. 213–215). One could ask, "How does brand relationship quality, as well as its components, impact brand detachment in the context of consumer–brand relationship dissolution?" or "Which components of brand relationship quality have the strongest impact on brand detachment in the context of consumer–brand relationship dissolution?"
- Another dissertation may be concerned not only with the antecedents but also with the outcomes of brand detachment. For example, one may want to relate brand detachment to negative consumer emotions toward brands (Romani, Grappi & Dalli, 2012; see Chapter 8, pp. 176–180) and answer the question, "How does brand detachment relate to negative consumer emotions toward brands?" One, for instance, may want to understand the extent to which negative consumer emotions toward a brand lead to brand detachment. Once the consumer is detached from a brand, one may examine the extent to which other negative consumer emotions are felt and the type of these emotions.

9.7 Managerial focus

- **Have you checked the attachment to your brand in comparison to the attachment to your competitors' brands?**
  Brand attachment consists of a strong emotional connections (Lacœuilhe, 2000; Thomson, MacInnis & Park, 2005) between a consumer and a brand. As this link gets stronger and stronger, consumers become less vulnerable to competitors' actions. They will have preference for the brand and will engage in a strong relationship with the brand. Measuring the level of attachment to your brand in comparison to competitive brands can be a good indicator of behavioural intentions and the continuity of the relationship. Consumers who are highly attached should have particular attention in order to feel privileged, as they are also ambassadors for the brand (Park, MacInnis, Priester, Eisingerich & Iacobucci, 2010). Therefore, it is important to identify them and define specific marketing programs in order to make them recommend your brand.
- **Do you measure the brand attachment of your followers?**
  A recent study in the UK conducted by Kantar Media (www.kantarmedia.co.uk/news-views/our-latest-news/social-media-targeting-know-your-

audience/) indicates that more than half of Britain's adult population engaged in social media have low influence for brands, and only 10% are more valuable for marketers. Many managers develop different activities in order to increase the number of fans and likes. Nevertheless, the consumers who click on "like" for the brand because of an attractive games or promotions do not always have a strong emotional connection with the brand. It is therefore interesting to evaluate if the followers are really attached to the brand. The brand attachment scale developed by Park, MacInnis, Priester, Eisingerich and Iacobucci (2010) can be useful to measure the brand attachment of the followers by evaluating both the self-identification and connection with the brand as well as the prominence of the brand in consumers' minds. Marketers can use the level of attachment as criteria of segmentation in order to enhance the contribution of attached consumers in terms of purchase, participation and level of influence toward others.

- **Does your communication campaign increase attachment to the brand?**
The performance of your communication campaign is generally assessed with indicators such as increase of brand awareness, market penetration, brand image and brand loyalty. Considering the importance of the emotional bond which represents brand attachment, it could be interesting to monitor the brand attachment created and enhanced by a communication campaign; this could complement more cognitive measures traditionally used. To illustrate, the Nespresso brand has used for many years a saga campaign with George Clooney as ambassador. This long-standing Nespresso brand ambassador has been recently supported by Matt Damon or Jean Dujardin as other protagonists of their TV saga. It could be relevant to measure how this strategy impacts the brand attachment.

- **Have you checked the attachment to your brand before deciding to replace a local brand with a global brand?**
Many marketers decide to replace small local brands with strong global brands in order to optimize the profitability of their brand portfolio. Nevertheless, local brands benefit from a positive image and have built a strong consumer-brand relationship. Consumers are attached to their local brands, which can be sometimes perceived as being part of the history of the country. Brand attachment may reduce the acceptance of the brand change and create resistance to change. On the other hand, if attached consumers are informed about the change, they can become real ambassadors of the change (Pauwels-Delassus et al., 2014). Therefore, it is important to measure the level of brand attachment before the change, in order to communicate specifically to this target and inform them about the future change.

- **You have identified a lack of brand performance; have you checked that your consumers are not in the detachment process?**
  The market share of your brand is declining; consumers are more sensitive to competitors' sales promotions and find private labels quite attractive. Managers should check if the brand still has key points of differentiation which remain appealing for consumers and if consumers are not abandoning the brand. The brand detachment scale (Perrin-Martinenq, 2004) can be useful to evaluate if consumers have still a positive relationship with the brand. Identifying the consumers who are in a detachment process is important in order to define specific actions to keep their emotional connection, as it is commonly accepted that it costs five time more to acquire a new consumer than to retain an existing one.

References

Amine, A. (1994). Implication du consommateur et fidélité aux marques. *Cahiers de Recherche*, 235, DMSP.

Amine, A. (1996, September). Brand loyalty, product importance and consumer expertise: some empirical evidence about their relationships. In I. Balderjahn & E. Vernette (eds.), *French-German Workshop Proceedings*, Potsdam, Germany.

Batra, R., & Stayman, D. M. (1990). The role of mood in advertising effectiveness. *Journal of Consumer Research*, 17, 203–214.

Bowlby, J. (1969). *Attachment and loss. Vol. 1, Attachment*. New York, NY: Basic Books.

Bowlby, J. (1979). *The making and breaking of affectional bonds*. London: Tavistock.

Bowlby, J. (1980). *Loss: sadness and depression*. New York, NY: Basic Books.

Churchill, G. A., Jr. (1979a). *Marketing research: Methodological foundations*. Hinsdale, IL: Dryden Press.

Churchill, G. A., Jr. (1979b). A paradigm for developing better measures of marketing constructs. *Journal of Marketing Research*, 16, 64–73.

Churchill, G. A., Jr. (1995). *Marketing research: methodological foundations*. Fort Worth, TX: Dryden Press.

Cristau, C. (2001). *Définition, mesure et modélisation de l'attachement à une marque avec deux composantes: la dépendance et l'amitié vis-à-vis d'une marque*. Thèse de doctorat en Sciences de Gestion, Université d'Aix-Marseille.

Derbaix, C., & Leheut, É. (2008a). Adolescents: implication envers les produits et attitude envers les marques (French). *Recherche et Applications en Marketing*, 23 (2), 37–66.

Derbaix, C., & Leheut, É. (2008b). Adolescents: involvement in product categories and attitude toward brands. *Recherche et Applications en Marketing (English edition)*, 23 (2), 37–64.

Duck, S. (1982). *Personal relationships 4: dissolving personal relationships*. London: Academic Press.

Hazan, C., & Shaver, P. R. (1994). Attachment as an organizational framework for research on close relationships. *Psychological Inquiry*, 5 (1), 1–22.

Hazan, C., & Zeifman, D. (1999). Pair bonds as attachments. In J. Cassidy & P. R. Shaver (eds.), *Handbook of attachment*. New York, NY: Guilford, 336–354.

Jain, K., & Srinivasan, N. (1990). A empirical assessment of multiple operationalizations of involvement. *Advances in Consumer Research*, 17, 594–602.

Kim, H. K., Lee, M., & Lee, Y. W. (2005). Developing a scale for measuring brand relationship quality. *AP-Asia Pacific Advances in Consumer Research*, 118–126.

Lacœuilhe, J. (2000). L'attachement à la marque: proposition d'une échelle de mesure. *Recherche et Applications en Marketing*, 15 (4), 61–77.

Ladwein, R. (1994). Le jugement de typicalité dans l'évaluation de l'extension de marque, *Recherche et Applications en Marketing*, 9 (2), 1–18.

Laurent, G., & Kapferer, J.-N. (1986). Les profils d'implication. *Recherches et Application en Marketing*, 1, 41–57.

Laurent, G., & Kapferer, J.-N. (1992). *La sensibilité aux marques: marches sans marques, marches a marques.* Paris: Les Editions d'Organisation.

Mano, H., & Oliver, R. L. (1993). Assessing the dimensionality and structure of the consumption experience: Evaluation, feeling and satisfaction. *Journal of Consumer Research*, 20, 451–466.

Odin, Y. (1998). *Fidélité et inertie: clarification conceptuelle et test empirique.* Doctoral thesis in management science, Université Pierre Mendes France, Grenoble.

Park, C. W., MacInnis, D. J., & Priester, J. (2006). Brand attachment: constructs, consequences, and causes. *Foundations & Trends in Marketing*, 1 (3), 191–230.

Park, C. W., MacInnis, D. J., Priester, J. Eisingerich, A. B., & Iacobucci, D. (2010). Brand attachment and brand attitude strength: conceptual and empirical differentiation of two critical brand equity drivers. *Journal of Marketing*, 74 (6), 1–17.

Pauwels-Delassus, V., Leclercq-Vandelannoitte, A., & Mogos Descotes, R. (2014). La résistance au changement de nom de marque: ses antécédents et ses conséquences sur le capital de marque. *Management International*, 18 (3), 45–59.

Pecheux, C., & Derbaix, C. (1999). Children attitude toward the brand: a new measurement scale. *Journal of Advertising Research*, 39 (4), 19–27.

Perrin-Martinenq, D. (2004). The role of brand detachment on the dissolution of the relationship between the consumer and the brand. *Journal of Marketing Management*, 20 (9), 1001–1023.

Peter, J. (1981). Construct validity: a review of basic issues and marketing practices. *Journal of Marketing Research*, 18 (2), 133–145.

Romani, S., Grappi, S., & Dalli, D. (2012). Emotions that drive consumers away from brands: Measuring negative emotions toward brands and their behavioral effects. *International Journal of Research in Marketing*, 29 (1), 55–67.

Sirgy, M. J., Johar, J. S., Samli, A. C., & Claiborne, C. B. (1991). Self-congruity versus functional congruity: Predictors of consumer behavior. *Journal of the Academy of Marketing Science*, 19, 363–375.

Strazzieri, A. (1994). Mesurer l'implication durable vis-à-vis du produit indépendamment du risque perçu. *Recherche et Applications en Marketing*, 9 (1), 73–91.

Thomson, M., MacInnis, D. J., & Park, C. W. (2005). The ties that bind: measuring the strength of consumers' emotional attachments to brands. *Journal of Consumer Psychology*, 15 (1), 77–91.

Zaichkowsky, J. L. (1985). Measuring the involvement construct. *Journal of Consumer Research*, 12 (December), 341–352.

10
CONSUMER–BRAND RELATIONSHIPS

10.1 Overview

Following the emergence of the relationship paradigm in marketing (Morgan & Hunt, 1994), the notion of relationship started to be studied in the field of brand management at the end of the 1990s. It is thanks to the work of Susan Fournier (1998), who draws from marketing and psychology literature, that a theory of consumer–brand relationships is formalized. In particular, Fournier (1998) proposes to look at brands as relationship partners and develops a typology of possible relationships that can be established between consumers and brands. Subsequent work has further articulated consumer–brand relationships, especially by focusing on specific relationship types and relationships of different valence (Fournier & Alvarez, 2013; Fournier, Breazeale & Fetscherin, 2013; Park, Eisingerich & Park, 2013). The relevance of this brand relationship perspective relates to the fact that it enhances the understanding of the roles of brands in consumers' lives.

In this chapter, we report six measurement scales pertaining to the relationships between consumers and brands. Two of these scales view consumer–brand relationships on a general level. The brand relationship quality scale from Kim, Lee and Lee (2005) is concerned about the level of quality characterizing the relationships between consumers and brands. It can be used in the case of product brands as well as service brands, provided that some modifications are taken into account. The scale developed by Veloutsou (2007), called the brand-relationship scale, evaluates the communication between the brand and the consumer, as well as the emotional experience and exchange occurring between these two subjects. According to the researcher, these are the two key aspects that should be taken into account when dealing with consumer–brand relationships.

The other scales presented in the chapter focus on particular aspects of the consumer–brand relationship. The scale developed by Odin, Odin and Valette-Florence

(2001) is related to brand loyalty, traditionally considered a fundamental condition to establish relationships between consumers and brands that are both satisfying for the consumer and profitable for the company. In their framework, brand loyalty is considered as repeating purchasing behaviour under conditions of strong brand sensitivity, meaning that consumers attach great importance to brands in their choice and are involved in the product category.

The remaining three scales are centred on brand trust. All these scales are based on a complex conceptualization of brand trust, as they view brand trust as consisting of various components. Gurviez and Korchia's (2002) scale, called *mesure multidimensionnelle de la confiance dans la marque* and originally developed in French, considers brand trust as a consumer's belief that the brand is credible, integral and benevolent. The brand trust scale developed by Delgado-Ballester, Munuera-Alemán and Yagüe-Guillén (2003) considers brand trust as a brand's reliability and brand-related intentions. Finally, Li, Zhou, Kashyap and Yang's (2008) brand trust scale relies on a conceptualization of brand trust as consisting of different levels: overall brand trust on a general level and the specific dimensions of competence and benevolence which contribute to overall brand trust.

10.2 Brand loyalty (Odin, Odin & Valette-Florence, 2001)

Definition of construct

Brand loyalty can be characterized as the repurchase of a same brand under conditions of strong perceived differences between brands and strong involvement for the repurchased brand (Filser, 1994). The level of sensitivity to brand (Kapferer & Laurent, 1983) can be used to distinguish loyalty from inertia, which corresponds to repeat purchasing without a real motive for the chosen brand. Therefore, Odin, Odin and Valette-Florence (2001) consider brand loyalty as repeating purchasing behaviour accompanied by strong brand sensitivity. They do not refer to a real behaviour but the consumer's perception of his/her own repeat purchasing behaviour, focusing on degrees of loyalty rather than on an evaluation of loyalty versus disloyalty.

Scale description

The scale is composed of four items which are evaluated on a 6-point Likert scale ranging from 1 = "totally disagree" to 6 = "totally agree".

TABLE 10.1 Brand loyalty scale

Scale item
• I am loyal to only one brand of (product category Y)
• During my next purchase, I will buy the same brand of (product category Y) as the last time
• I always buy the same brand of (product category Y)
• Usually, I buy the same brand of (product category Y)

Scale development

The brand loyalty scale is developed in accordance with Churchill (1979). The scale development process consists of a preliminary study, which is used to specify the construct of brand loyalty and generate items issued from the literature, from group interviews and from experts. A set of 18 items is generated and then integrated in a questionnaire for the first quantitative research. The category of jeans is selected for the first data collection, based on a pre-test showing that this type of product has a large variety in terms of brand sensitivity and repeat purchasing behaviour. Four items are selected after a series of confirmatory factor analyses.

A second data collection is conducted in order to evaluate the reliability and the validity of the scale with a questionnaire including the brand loyalty items and also other items used in the involvement scale of Kapferer and Laurent (1983) to evaluate the perceived risk and the brand sensitivity. Two groups of respondents are extracted from the data according to their level of brand sensitivity after performing a K-means cluster analysis on one item adapted from Kapferer and Laurent's (1983) brand sensitivity scale.

Samples

The sample of the first data collection is composed of 109 undergraduate students. The second data collection uses a convenience sample of 334 individuals. The sample is split into one group of brand-sensitive consumers ($N = 209$) and one group of brand insensitive consumers ($N = 102$).

Reliability and validity

The reliability of the brand loyalty scale is tested through a series of factor analyses using maximum likelihood estimation (RMSEA = 0.10, γ = 0.950, GFI = 0.987, AGFI = 0.935, NFI = 0.995) and bootstrap asymptotically free estimation (RMSEA = 0.097). In both analyses, the rho coefficient of Jöreskog is equal to 0.96 and student t-tests on each parameter show that all of them are significant at $p < 0.01$.

The content validity of the scale is assured with the precautions taken for the generation and the purification of the list of items in the preliminary study (large literature review, qualitative interviews with experts and consumers).

With respect to trait validity, considering that the measure is unidimensional, discriminant validity is not assessed. Convergent validity is evaluated through confirmatory analysis by using student t-test to evaluate the significance of the loadings. All lambda parameters are statistically significant. The shared variance between the latent construct and its measures is higher than 0.50.

The nomological validity of the brand loyalty scale is established using the two dimensions of perceived risk (risk importance and risk probability). A multi-group analysis is used to investigate the structural model on the two different groups of respondents (strong brand sensitivity group/weak brand sensitivity group). Parameters are estimated through both the maximum likelihood and the bootstrap maximum likelihood methods. The results indicate a good adequation of data to the specified model (ML method: RMSEA = 0.053, γ = 0.979; bootstrap ML method: RMSEA = 0.043). The two dimensions of risk influence brand loyalty significantly and positively (γ = 0.260 and 0.265, respectively), but do not influence consumer purchase inertia.

Managerial applications

An increasing number of companies are developing tools that can contribute to relationship development, aiming to increase consumer loyalty. This brand loyalty scale allows them to measure the consumers' perception of their degree of loyalty and to make a distinction between real loyalty and purchase inertia. This four-item scale can easily be integrated in a study to evaluate the impact of marketing actions such as communication campaigns or consumer loyalty.

10.3 *Mesure multidimensionnelle de la confiance dans la marque*/Multi-dimensional measure of brand trust (Gurviez & Korchia, 2002)

Definition of construct

The researchers (Gurviez & Korchia, 2002) conceptualise brand trust under three dimensions: *crédibilité* (credibility), *intégrité* (integrity) and *bienveillance* (benevolence). The *crédibilité* dimension corresponds to the consumer's perception of the brand expertise and know-how in satisfying consumers' needs regarding functional characteristics. The *intégrité* dimension concerns the honesty of the brand in fulfilling its promise. The *bienveillance* dimension corresponds to the consumer's belief that the brand is durably consumer oriented and is guided by long-term consumer's interests before its own short-term interest.

Scale description

The brand trust measure consists of three dimensions and eight items. The *crédibilité* and *intégrité* dimensions contain three items each. The *bienveillance* dimension contains two items. Items are evaluated on a 5-point scale ranging from "completely strongly disagree" (= 1) to "strongly agree" (= 5). The scale is developed in French.

TABLE 10.2 *Mesure multidimensionnelle de la confiance dans la marque*/Multi-dimensional measure of brand trust

Scale dimension (English translation)	Scale item
Crédibilité (Credibility)	• Les produits de cette marque m'apportent de la sécurité • J'ai confiance dans la qualité des produits de cette marque • Acheter des produits de cette marque, c'est une garantie
Intégrité (Integrity)	• Cette marque est sincère vis-à-vis des consommateurs • Cette marque est honnête vis-à-vis de ses clients • Cette marque montre de l'intérêt pour ses clients
Bienveillance (Benevolence)	• Je pense que cette marque renouvelle ses produits pour tenir compte des progrès de la recherche • Je pense que cette marque cherche continuellement à améliorer ses réponses aux besoins des consommateurs

Scale development

The scale development process is developed through a qualitative study and three quantitative data collections.

The qualitative study understands consumers' conceptualization of brand trust, as the literature review indicates the absence of consensus regarding the dimensionality of trust. In-depth interviews are conducted with consumers and orient the conceptualization of trust under three dimensions in coherence with Rempel, Holmes and Zanna's (1985) work. Based on the literature review and the qualitative interviews, 14 items are selected and classified under the three dimensions.

The first quantitative study consists of a pre-test in which respondents are asked to evaluate the 14 items toward a perfume brand they feel the closest to. A reliability analysis is conducted, and results indicate satisfactory Cronbach's coefficient alpha for each of the three dimensions.

In the second quantitative study, respondents are asked to evaluate the items toward a perfume brand they feel the closest to. An exploratory factor analysis with varimax rotation is conducted and allows the researchers to eliminate six items because they are either too strongly connected to two of the three dimensions or, on the contrary, too weakly connected to these dimensions. The three dimensions explain 63.36 % of the total variance with, respectively, 36.69% of total variance explained for *credibility*, 14.16% for *integrity* and 12.51% for *benevolence*.

In the third quantitative study, respondents are asked to evaluate their trust and engagement toward a brand from another category of product with a high level of awareness (Coca-Cola). The engagement measure consists of three items issued from the scale developed by Le Roux, Chandon and Strazzieri (1997). A confirmatory factor analysis is performed using AMOS 4. Results support the three-factor solution of brand trust (χ^2 = 55.199 with df = 17 and p = 0; GFI = 0.985; RMSEA = 0.049; SRMR = 0.024; TLI = 0.983; CFI = 0.990). The scale's construct validity is assessed by analysing whether brand trust influences brand engagement.

Samples

The sample of the first quantitative study consists of 62 women. The sample of the second quantitative study is composed of 300 women. The sample of the third quantitative study consists of 937 respondents, of which 63% are students and 37% are business executives. All three samples are convenience samples.

Reliability and validity

The reliability and validity of the scale are tested using the third data collection.

The scale's reliability is examined through the Jöreskog's rho associated with each dimension. The coefficient is equal to 0.87 for *credibility* and *integrity* and 0.77 for *benevolence*.

The validity is tested with respect to convergent, discriminant and predictive validities. Convergent validity is checked by the ρVC (or AVE), which should be higher than 0.5. The ρVC is equal to 0.69 for *credibility* and *integrity* and 0.63 for *benevolence*.

The discriminant validity is demonstrated as the square root of the AVE of each dimension (0.831 for *credibility*; 0.829 for *integrity*; 0.795 for *benevolence*; 0.822 for *engagement*) is larger than the correlation of each dimension with any other dimension including engagement (0.586 between *integrity* and *credibility*; 0.344 between *benevolence* and *credibility*; 0.469 between *benevolence* and *integrity*; 0.620 between engagement and *credibility*; 0.520 between engagement and *integrity*; and 0.364 between engagement and *benevolence*). These results indicate that the three dimensions of trust are distinctive dimensions and are also distinctive from engagement.

The predictive validity is examined by testing the interaction between trust and engagement, which is theoretically a consequence of brand trust. This analysis also tests the formative structure of trust and identifies the relative importance of each dimension. Following a bootstrap procedure, the results confirm that all structural paths are significant ($p < 0.03$) and that *credibility* is the dimension which influences the most trust, whereas *benevolence* the least (γ between *credibility* and trust equal to 0.713; γ between *integrity* and trust equal to 0.294; γ between *benevolence* and trust equal to 0.171). Finally, the results confirm the formative nature of trust and the influence of trust on engagement (γ between trust and engagement equal to 0.657), which confirms the scale's predictive validity.

Managerial applications

This multi-dimensional brand trust scale helps managers better understand and measure the trust relationship between consumers and the brand, in order to build long-term brand relationships. The scale allows them to evaluate the impact of specific marketing actions on each dimension of brand trust. In a crisis context, for instance, the credibility of the brand may be negatively impacted, and this scale can be particularly useful to track the credibility dimension of brand trust. The scale can also be used to measure the impact of corporate social responsibility programs on the benevolence dimension and on a long-term construction of brand trust.

10.4 Brand trust (1) (Delgado-Ballester, Munuera-Alemán & Yagüe-Guillén, 2003)

Definition of construct

Brand trust is conceptualised by the researchers as "the confident expectations about the brand's reliability and intentions in situations entailing risk to the consumer" (Delgado-Ballester, Munuera-Alemán & Yagüe-Guillén, 2003, p. 37). Brand trust is a multi-dimensional construct containing a *reliability* dimension and an *intentions* dimension. *Reliability* corresponds to the consumer perception that the brand fulfils its promise and satisfies consumers' needs. The *intentions* dimension concerns the consumers' belief that the brand is guided by positive intentions toward consumers' interests in any kinds of situation.

Scale description

The brand trust scale (BTS) consists of two dimensions and eight items. Each dimension, that is, *reliability* and *intentions*, contains four items each. Items are evaluated on a 5-point scale ranging from 1 = "completely disagree" to 5 = "completely agree".

TABLE 10.3 Brand trust scale

Scale dimension	Scale item
Reliability	• (Brand X) is a brand name that meets my expectations • I feel confidence in (brand X) brand name • (Brand X) is a brand name that never disappoints me • (Brand X) brand name guarantees satisfaction
Intentions	• (Brand X) brand name would be honest and sincere in addressing my concerns • I could rely on (brand X) brand name to solve the problem • (Brand X) brand name would make any effort to satisfy me • (Brand X) brand name would compensate me in some way for the problem with the (product Y)

Scale development

The brand trust scale is developed in accordance with the process suggested by Churchill (1979). To start, a literature review and personal interviews are conducted to generate a first set of 16 items. These are then submitted to a panel of experts in order to check their relevance. Experts are asked to assign the items to one of the conceptualized brand trust dimensions. Items that are correctly classified by at least four experts are retained, leaving a set of 13 items for the quantitative phase.

In the questionnaire, respondents are asked to refer to the brand of deodorant they use and rate it on the 13 items. The sample is then split into two samples for the analysis, the first half (calibration sample) being used to develop the scale and the second half (validation sample) to validate the results.

An item analysis allows the researchers to retain 12 items which satisfy the item retention criteria. Items with corrected item-to-total correlations below 0.35 on the hypothesized dimension are eliminated, as well as items with no statistically significant correlation with the total score for each dimension. A subsequent principal components factor analysis results in two components, which account for 62% of the total variance. Each of the 12 items has a loading exceeding 0.6 on its hypothesized factor, and its convenience to the analysis is supported by the measure of sample adequacy above 0.8. A series of confirmatory factor analyses is then performed using the correlation matrix as input via LISREL 8.3 maximum likelihood method. After removing four items based on modification indexes, as they cause poor fit, the two-factor model of brand trust with eight items reaches a good fit ($\chi^2(19)$ = 23.70 (p = 0.21); GFI = 0.96; RMSEA = 0.034; SRMR = 0.042; CFI = 0.99; NFI = 0.96; NNFI = 0.99). Convergent and discriminant validities are established through additional analyses.

In order to validate the scale, the second half of the sample is used and completed with a new data collection. Respondents are asked to report their consumption experience of a shampoo brand and rate the brand on the eight-item brand scale; they are also asked about their overall satisfaction (Oliver, 1997; Spreng, Mackenzie & Olshavsky, 1996) and brand loyalty (Bloemer & Kasper, 1995; Dick & Basu, 1994). A measurement model is estimated, and the results confirm the two-factor structure with acceptable model fits for both validation samples (deodorant validation sample: χ^2 = 44.93; GFI = 0.95; SRMR = 0.053; CFI = 0.95; NFI = 0.91; NNFI = 0.92; shampoo validation sample: χ^2 = 59.24; GFI = 0.95; SRMR = 0.041; CFI = 0.95; NFI = 0.93; NNFI = 0.93). Using only data related to shampoo brands, the construct validity of brand trust is assessed by analysing whether brand trust correlates significantly with overall satisfaction and brand loyalty.

Samples

Personal interviews are conducted with six consumers, and the panel of experts includes five marketing faculty. The sample used for the quantitative study is composed of 272 individuals who are consumers of deodorants. The new data collection is composed of 127 consumers of shampoo. Both quantitative data collections are conducted by a marketing research firm, which administers the questionnaire by telephone to random samples of consumers.

Reliability and validity

The reliability of the scale is checked with the calibration dataset through different tests which provide satisfactory indices: composite reliability (equal to 0.87 for *reliability* and 0.86 for *intentions*), average variance extracted (equal to 0.63 for *reliability* and 0.61 for *intentions*), corrected item-to-total correlations (ranging from 0.52 to 0.70 for *reliability* and from 0.54 to 0.71 for *intentions*) and coefficient alpha estimates (equal to 0.81 for *reliability* and 0.83 for *intentions*). The reliability of the scale is confirmed in the two validation samples. Composite reliability indices are satisfactory (deodorant sample: equal to 0.84 for *reliability* and 0.86 for *intentions*; shampoo sample: equal to 0.95 for *reliability* and 0.85 for *intentions*), as well as the average variance extracted (AVE) values for both dimensions (equal to 0.59 for *reliability* and 0.61 for *intentions* in the deodorant sample; equal to 0.84 for *reliability* and 0.59 for *intentions* in the shampoo sample). The coefficient alphas are also above the recommended levels (the *reliability* dimension: alpha of 0.7304 in the deodorant sample and of 0.9034 in the shampoo sample; the *intentions* dimension: alpha of 0.8307 in the deodorant sample and of 0.7913 in the shampoo sample).

Convergent and discriminant validities are established using the calibration sample. The convergent validity is confirmed, as the parameter estimates for all items are 10 to 20 times as large as the standard errors, all items load on their hypothesized dimensions, and the estimates are positive and significant ($p < 0.01$). The discriminant validity is demonstrated through three different procedures which confirm the relevance of the distinction of the two dimensions: (1) confidence intervals around estimates ($\varphi 21 = [0.21; 0.53]$); (2) chi-square difference test between constrained ($\chi^2 = 68.20$ with 20 df) and unconstrained models ($\chi^2 = 23.70$ with 19 df); and (3) comparison between AVE and the squared correlation (*reliability*: $0.62 > 0.31^2$; *intentions*: $0.61 > 0.31^2$).

The construct validity of the BTS is further assessed by showing that brand trust correlates significantly with overall satisfaction and brand loyalty. This analysis is performed using structural equation modelling and the shampoo validation sample. Results show that overall satisfaction explains a substantial amount of the variance of brand trust, as the square multiple correlations (SMC) for *reliability* is equal to 0.77 and for *intentions* is equal to 0.20. Furthermore, brand trust is positively related to brand loyalty, explaining more than half of its variance (SMC = 0.85).

Managerial applications

The BTS provides a useful tool to assess brand trust. Measuring brand trust can contribute to enhancing the consumer's brand relationship, as trust is positively related to brand satisfaction and loyalty. The BTS scale can be used to evaluate the impact of communication and merchandising strategies on trust, which can influence consumer loyalty and therefore improve brand performance and brand equity. The BTS can also be used in case of unexpected problems with a product or a service to check the evolution of trust after the event.

10.5 Brand relationship quality (Kim, Lee & Lee, 2005)

Definition of construct

Kim, Lee and Lee (2005) develop the conceptualization of brand relationship quality using the service marketing literature, studies on product management and the work of Fournier (1998) on consumer–brand relationships. They theorize brand relationship quality (BRQ) as a multi-dimensional construct consisting of: *self-connective attachment*, which refers to the involvement of the brand in one's self-concept and image; *satisfaction*, which indicates consumers' overall evaluation based on long-term experience of purchasing and consuming a brand; *behavioural commitment*, which refers to consumers' willingness not to switch to other alternative brands; *trust*, which indicates consumers' perception that the brand performs its role in an effective way; and *emotional intimacy*, which is intended as an affective tie that consumers develop with the brand.

Scale description

The BRQ scale is developed for both product and service brands. The BRQ includes the dimensions of *self-connective attachment, satisfaction, behavioural commitment, trust* and *emotional intimacy*. The number of items in the scale, however, changes slightly based on the brand type: the product brand-related BRQ scale consists of 19 items, whereas the service brand-related BRQ scale includes 20 items. The dimensions of *self-connective attachment, satisfaction* and *emotional intimacy* present the same items for the two brand types. *Behavioral commitment* presents three items in both scales, but one item changes depending on the brand type. *Trust* presents three items for product brands and four for service brands.

TABLE 10.4 Brand relationship quality scale

Scale dimension	Scale item
Self-connective attachment	• I am intrigued by this brand because it shows who I want to be • This brand goes so well with my lifestyle that I would feel empty without it • Since this brand shows who I am, I would feel empty without it • I like this brand because it makes me feel more special than other people
Satisfaction	• This brand is exactly what I want • I don't regret choosing this brand • I really like this brand • Using this brand is a good experience for me • The performance of this brand is better than expected • I really enjoy using this brand

(*Continued*)

TABLE 10.4 (Continued)

Scale dimension	Scale item
Behavioural commitment	• I don't have to consider other brands because I have this one • I want to keep using this brand • I want to maintain a long-term commitment with this brand[b] • I enjoy my relationship with this brand, so I want to keep buying it[a]
Trust	• This brand always cares about the consumer's needs • This brand keeps its promises • Whatever happens, I believe that this brand would help me • This brand works hard for my well-being[b]
Emotional intimacy	• I am familiar with this brand • This brand makes me feel comfortable • This brand fits me naturally

Note: Items without any superscript are included in both the product and service brand scales. Superscript [a] indicates the item is included in the product-related scale only, whereas superscript [b] indicates the item is included in the service-related brand scale only.

Scale development

By following the procedure proposed by Churchill (1979), Kim, Lee and Lee conduct two pilot studies and one main study to develop the BRQ scale.

The first pilot study consists of face-to-face in-depth interviews that investigate the dimensionality of the scale. Respondents are asked to choose a favourite brand and to describe the elements that contribute to the quality of their relationship with that brand. The dimensions of relationship quality offered by interviewees are consistent across age and gender, although differences are found based on the type of brand mentioned (product or service). The second pilot study consists of the revision of a list of items on BRQ derived from the literature. Items are administered to a sample of respondents, who are asked to choose and rank the five items that best explain the determinants of BRQ. The two pilot studies result in 31 items.

In the main study, respondents are asked to choose one of the categories proposed (three product-related and three service-related), to identify their favourite brand in these categories and to rate the items with these brands in mind. Exploratory and confirmatory analyses are performed separately for product and service brands. Exploratory analyses reveal five dimensions in both cases, and items with a loading < 0.6 are deleted. A measurement model is built with the remaining items. Because of unsatisfactory fit (product brands: GFI = 0.84, AGFI = 0.79, SRMR = 0.059, NFI = 0.80; service brands: GFI = 0.86, AGFI = 0.82, SRMR = 0.049, NFI = 0.86), some items are deleted and the model is re-estimated in order to obtain a satisfactory output (product brands: GFI = 0.92, AGFI = 0.89, SRMR = 0.047, NFI = 0.91; service brands: GFI = 0.92, AGFI = 0.89, SRMR = 0.045, NFI = 0.91).

Samples

The first pilot study includes four respondents for three age groups. The second pilot study includes 40 respondents among marketing professional and university students. The main study includes 361 respondents, of which 53.8% are students.

Reliability and validity

Reliability and validity are verified in the main study for product and service brands separately. With regard to reliability, all dimensions report a Cronbach's alpha > 0.8 and a composite reliability > 0.6. Convergent validity is established for all dimensions, as t-values of all factor loadings > 2.00. Discriminant validity is checked by testing the null hypothesis, assuming all constructs to be the same (correlation between them = 1); discriminant validity is established, as all correlation coefficients are not equal to 1 at a 95% confidence level.

Managerial applications

The BRQ scale provides insights about the dimensions on which brand managers and marketers should focus in their consumer research and brand strategies in order to improve the quality of the relationship between consumers and their brand. The research by Kim, Lee and Lee identifies *self-connective attachment* as the most important factor in BRQ. Therefore, managers need to find ways to reflect consumers' desired or ideal self-images when they develop strategies for establishing and nourishing consumer–brand relationships that last in time.

10.6 Dimensions of the product-brand and consumer relationship (Veloutsou, 2007)

Definition of construct

Brand relationships are theorized as relationships that consumers form with brands. Brand relationship is a multi-dimensional concept, as it has two dimensions: *two-way communication* and *emotional exchange*. The former indicates that brand relationships are characterized by an interaction between the consumer and the brand. Both the consumer and the brand can be senders and receivers: consumers are not only willing to receive information about the brands but also to provide feedback to the brand if required. The latter dimension of brand relationships indicates the presence of a psychological link between consumers and brands. Consumers perceive a sense of closeness to the brand, toward which they develop feelings of comfort and enjoyment.

Scale description

The brand relationship scale assesses the strength of the relationship between the consumer and the brand. It includes 11 items, of which 6 belong to the dimension of *two-way communication* and 5 belong to the dimension of *emotional exchange*. All items are expressed in a positive form except for one in the *two-way communication* dimension, which is reverse-coded. Items are measured on a 7-point Likert scale from 1 = "strongly disagree" to 7 = "strongly agree".

TABLE 10.5 Brand relationship scale

Scale dimension	Scale item
Two-way communication	• I want to be informed about my preferred (product category Y) brand • I am more willing to learn news about my preferred brand of (product category Y) than for other brands • I listen with interest to info about my favourite (product category Y) brand • If leaflets are sent to me from my preferred (product category Y) brand, I get annoyed* • I will be willing to be informed about my preferred brand of (product category Y) in the future • I am willing to give feedback to the manufacturer of my preferred (product category Y) brand
Emotional exchange	• I care about the developments relevant to my preferred brand of (product category Y) • My preferred brand of (product category Y) and I complement each other • My preferred brand of (product category Y) is like a person with whom I am close to • Both my preferred brand of (product category Y) and I benefit from our link • Over time my preferred brand of (product category Y) becomes more important to me

Note: *indicates the item is reverse coded.

Scale development

Eight steps are employed in developing the brand relationship scale. In step 1, the relevant literature is reviewed. Step 2 consists in interviews which investigate the existence and dimensions of brand relationships. Respondents are asked to describe their feelings toward brands they have either a very positive or very negative relationship with. A content analysis is performed on the material collected. In step 3, a list with dimensions and items representing the brand relationship construct is generated based on the literature review and the interviews.

Step 4 consists of a series of focus groups, which support the brand relationship dimensions found in the previous step and are used to finalize the brand relationship items. Participants are asked to evaluate the extent to which each of the previously generated items is relevant for describing the specific dimension using a 5-point scale (1 = "not relevant" and 5 = "very relevant"). The data collected are content analysed, which results in the formulation of 18 items. The product category to use in the next step is also identified. The 18-item scale is subjected to a pilot test in step 5. Thirteen of the original items are retained based on results.

Step 6 represents the primary data collection of the study. The data collected are factor analysed using principal component analysis with varimax rotation. The analysis shows two factors with an eigenvalue > 1.0, explaining 65.75% of total variance. The first factor, which relates to various communicational issues, explains 56.5% of the total variance and includes six items with loadings of 0.66 or above. The second factor is about the closeness between the consumer and the brand; it explains 9.3% of the total variance and presents five items with loading of 0.70 or above. Two items with loadings < 0.70 are removed, leaving the scale with 11 items. In steps 7 and 8, the reliability and validity of the scale are assessed.

Samples

Step 2 consists of interviews with 10 students. Step 4 consists of three focus groups of five participants each; participants have different demographic profiles. Step 5 involves 20 female students from a Scottish university. Step 6 is based on 277 usable responses; respondents are selected from marketplaces and near a university campus over a period of six months.

Reliability and validity

Reliability is tested for both dimensions of the brand relationship scale in step 7. The Cronbach's alpha is 0.897 for the dimension of *two-way communication* and 0.896 for *emotional exchange*. Inter-correlations of the items are all greater than 0.40 and significant at $p < 0.001$. Item-to-total correlation is greater than 0.50.

The validity of the brand relationship scale is tested from step 1 to step 4 for content validity and in step 7 for the convergent and discriminant validities. The discriminant validity of the scale is demonstrated through the inter-correlations of the items. Convergent validity is supported by the correlation of the two brand relationship dimensions (Pearson correlation = 0.71, $p < 0.001$).

Managerial applications

The brand relationship scale can be used by companies to assess the strength of the relationship between their customer base and their brands. The strength of the relationship that consumers form with brands can be used by companies as an indicator of the equity of their brands. The scale also provides guidance to companies that would like to enhance the relationships between their customer base and their brands. Companies should develop brands that consumers want to interact with in terms of both communication and feelings.

10.7 Brand trust (2) (Li, Zhou, Kashyap & Yang, 2007)

Definition of construct

Li, Zhou, Kashyap and Yang (2007) take a different approach from that of previous research, including Chaudhuri and Holbrook (2001), Delgado-Ballester,

Munuera-Alemán and Yagüe-Guillén (2003; see this chapter, pp. 210–212) and Lau and Lee (1999), which treat brand trust as a first-order construct. Following Jarvis, MacKenzie and Podsakoff (2003), who suggest that brand trust should be specified as a second-order factor formed by lower-level dimensions, the researchers conceptualize brand trust as a multi-dimensional construct of a higher level of abstraction relative to its various dimensions. The researchers believe that brand trust can exist at different levels: overall trust in brand and trust in specific aspects of the brand (i.e., competence and benevolence), which contribute to overall brand trust. The researchers thus advance a reflective-formative model of brand trust where overall trust is specified as a second-order factor that is determined by first-order factors of *competence* and *benevolence* (formative indicators), with each construct (*overall trust*, *competence* and *benevolence*) being measured using reflective indicators.

Scale description

The scales developed by Li, Zhou, Kashyap and Yang includes a global scale of brand trust and a multi-dimensional scale of brand trust. Whereas the former is made up of three items, the latter consists of two dimensions, that is, *competence* and *benevolence*, which contain four and five items, respectively. All items are measured on Likert scales.

TABLE 10.6 Global measure of brand trust

Scale dimension	Scale item
Overall trust	• I have no doubt this brand can be trusted • This brand is trustworthy • I trust this brand

TABLE 10.7 Multi-dimensional scale of brand trust

Scale dimension	Scale item
Competence	• This brand does a good job • I expect this brand to deliver on its promise • I am confident in this brand's ability to perform well • The quality of this brand has been very consistent
Benevolence	• This brand has good intentions towards its customers • This brand will respond constructively if I have any product-related problems • This brand would do its best to help me if I had a problem • This brand cares about my needs • This brand gives me a sense of security

Scale development

The scale-development process starts with an item-generation phase. An initial set of items is generated thanks to psychology and business literature and in-depth interviews. Interviewees are asked to provide statements of either a trusted or a distrusted brand for one of three product categories (laptop computers, shampoo and athletic shoes). Statements with higher frequency of mention are selected and converted into potential items. The deriving set of items is screened by the researchers, then assessed by two pools of experts. The first pool of experts is asked to judge how each item is representative of the central construct using a 3-point scale (1 = "clearly representative", 2 = "somewhat representative" and 3 = "not at all representative"). Only items evaluated as at least "somewhat representative" are retained. The second pool of experts is asked to rate the remaining items following the same procedure, except that they are also asked to compare their results after rating the items independently. Twenty-six items are generated this way.

It follows an item-purification phase conducted both in the United States and China. A Chinese version of the items is prepared following a translation and back-translation process. Participants are asked to think of a shampoo brand they trust and then answer the questions with reference to such a brand. Data collected are combined and submitted to an exploratory factor analysis, which reveals three factors. Items that do not load on any factors or have high loadings on more than one factor are eliminated. Another exploratory factor analysis is conducted for the U.S. and Chinese samples separately. Eleven items that have high loading in one sample but not in the other are excluded. These analyses leave 15 items. To further purify the items, additional analyses are conducted on the aggregate sample. Items with item-to-total correlation > 0.35, an inter-item correlation > 0.20 and a factor loading > 0.50 are retained. These additional analyses result in a set of 12 items.

The next phase validates the scale to measure brand trust and its dimensions. A second data collection is conducted in multiple cities in China. Participants are administered a questionnaire containing the 12 items on brand trust, as well as measures on purchase loyalty (Chaudhuri & Holbrook, 2001) and materialism (Richins, 2004) as filler items. Six products (detergent, beer, digital camera, laptop computer, car and wireless phone service), identified through a pre-test, are used in this study. In the pre-test, respondents are asked to evaluate various products in terms of their involvement level and the importance of a brand name in making a purchase of that product type. The six products are selected based on these ratings, along with considerations on the heterogeneity of products selected (goods and services) and purchase frequency.

Data collected in the study are analysed using LISREL 8.53 to test the plausibility of the hypothesized model. Such a model includes overall brand trust as a second-order factor, which is determined by both formative indicators (the multidimensional scale consisting of the *competence* and *benevolence* dimensions) and reflective measures (the global scale). The model performs as follows: $\chi^2 = 183.71$, $df = 51$, $p = 0.00$, $\chi^2/df = 3.60$, GFI = 0.98, CFI = 0.99, NFI = 0.99, AGFI = 0.97, RMSEA = 0.044, $p = 0.92$). A competing model where the direction of the causal relationship is reversed is also tested ($\chi^2 = 190.50$, $df = 52$, $p = 0.00$, $\chi^2/df = 3.66$, GFI = 0.98, CFI = 0.99, NFI = 0.99, AGFI = 0.97, RMSEA = 0.045, $p = 0.90$). The basic model performs slightly better, so the competing model is rejected. Reliability and validity tests complement the analysis.

Samples

The item generation involves a sample of 45 respondents with different demographic profiles; interviews are conducted by students from a marketing research class at a mid-sized state university in the northeastern United States. The item generation involves also a panel of eight faculty members at different institutions in Hong Kong and the United States, as well as three MBA students at a medium-sized U.S. university used as judges. The item purification involves 92 business students at a medium-sized U.S. university and 101 business students at a major university in Beijing. The scale validation is based on a pre-test with 88 students and a study with 1,343 Chinese consumers recruited by a professional research firm in China using the central location test approach.

Reliability and validity

Evidence of reliability is provided in the item purification (through Cronbach's alphas) and scale validation (composite reliability) phases. Alpha coefficients are equal to 0.82 (*competence*), 0.80 (*benevolence*) and 0.71 (*overall trust*). Composite reliability scores are equal to 0.85 (*competence*), 0.86 (*benevolence*) and 0.78 (*overall trust*).

The brand trust scales' validity is examined with respect to different types. Content validity is demonstrated by comparing the coding of three judges. The inter-judge agreement is equal to 82%, and items for which judges cannot reach an agreement are excluded from subsequent analysis.

Convergent validity is shown by testing two CFA models: one with the two dimensions of brand trust, the other one with *overall trust*. Both models have a reasonable fit. All factor loadings are high (between 0.62 and 0.81) and significant (*t*-values from 18.16 to 26.67). All but two squared multiple correlations exceed 0.50. The average variance extracted is equal to 0.585 (*competence*), 0.516 (*benevolence*) and 0.540 (*overall trust*).

Concurrent and discriminant validities are demonstrated through a model with *overall trust* and its dimensions being specified as unanalysed. The model has a reasonable fit ($\chi^2 = 119$, $df = 26$, $p < 0.01$, RMSEA = 0.05, NFI = 0.99, CFI = 0.99, GFI = 0.98 and AGFI = 0.97). It is shown that (1) the correlation between the two dimensions is not too high (standardized correlation = 0.70); (2) the correlation between the two dimensions and *overall trust* is positive and significantly high (standardized correlation of 0.81 between overall trust and *competence* and 0.79 between *overall trust* and *benevolence*); and (3) these correlations are significantly less than unity.

Nomological validity is finally examined. Purchase loyalty is added to the basic model and is specified as a consequence of *overall trust* ($\chi^2 = 305.87$, $df = 73$, $p = 0.00$,

$\chi^2/df = 4.19$, GFI = 0.97, CFI = 0.99, NFI = 0.99, AGFI = 0.95, RMSEA = 0.049, $p = 0.63$). In this model, the sign of both path coefficients remains unchanged, and a considerable part of the variances of purchase loyalty is explained by the model ($R^2 = 0.38$). Purchase loyalty is also added to the competing model. This model also has a reasonable fit ($\chi^2 = 312.47$, $df = 74$, $p = 0.00$, $\chi^2/df = 4.22$, GFI = 0.97, CFI = 0.99, NFI = 0.99, AGFI = 0.95, RMSEA = 0.049, $p = 0.60$). However, it explains a smaller portion of variances ($R^2 = 0.35$) and reports a higher Akaike Information Criterion (AIC = 374.47 versus 237.71 of previous model).

Managerial applications

The scale developed by Li, Zhou, Kashyap and Yang allows managers to measure brand trust either directly, using the global scale, or indirectly, measuring the two dimensions of brand trust (*competence* and *benevolence*). Managers can therefore assess *overall trust* as well as the strength of the dimensions related to it and understand how much these dimensions contribute to overall trust. Knowing this can provide guidance on how to better build and enhance consumers' trust toward a brand. If *competence* is stronger, managers should focus on improving competence and promote the brand accordingly. If, on the contrary, *benevolence* is the most important dimension of brand trust, managers should stress the goodwill of the brand.

10.8 Academic focus

- It is not a rare situation when a brand launches an initiative, such as a new marketing campaign, a new product version or the use of a new celebrity endorser, that consumers do not believe is consistent with the brand's history, heritage and identity. In a dissertation, one may investigate how consumer–brand relationships are affected by perceptions of inauthenticity related to different brand cues (see Chapter 4). Various different dimensions of authenticity could be examined with respect to the outcomes produced.
- Brand crisis can have a negative impact on brand trust and brand image (e.g., Johar, Birk & Einwiller, 2010). A dissertation may investigate how one specific type of brand crisis impacts brand trust (Delgado-Ballester, Munuera-Allemán & Yagüe-Gillén, 2003; Li, Zhou, Kashyap & Yang, 2008) and/or brand loyalty (Gurviez & Korchia, 2002; Odin, Odin & Valette-Florence, 2001). What are the dimensions that are affected the most? What are the ones that are affected the least? Which ones can be restored more easily? These are examples of questions the dissertation may try to answer.
- One dissertation may be interested in analysing possible sources of consumer–brand relationships and comparing their relative

importance. Brand experience (see Chapter 7) and brand personality (see Chapter 3) may be examples of possible antecedents. The dissertation could therefore try to understand how different types of brand experiences (sensory, affective, intellectual, social and relational) and brand personality profiles (sincere, exciting, competent, sophisticated and rugged) shape consumer–brand relationships. Consumers' characteristics such as need for cognition (Cacioppo & Petty, 1982), need for affection (Maio & Esses, 2001) or personalities may be considered as well, as they may significantly moderate the effect from brand experiences and brand personality to consumer–brand relationships.
- In another dissertation, one may want to focus on consumer–brand relationships in online and offline environments. The dissertation could examine, for example, consumer–brand relationships that are born, developed and mature exclusively in online versus offline environments. What are the peculiarities of these relationships? How do they differ from one another? These are examples of research questions one may address. Alternatively, the dissertation could analyse the different contributions of online versus offline marketing communication tools. What do new online marketing activities bring to consumer–brand relationships? What about traditional offline marketing activities? These are other examples of research questions that could be investigated.
- There is evidence in literature that, in B2B markets, consumer–brand relationship is a source of industrial brand equity (Arquardt, 2013). A dissertation may consider other types of industries, such as sports or touristic industries, and analyse how consumer–brand relationship relates to, respectively, sports brand equity (Bauer, Sauer & Schmitt, 2005; see Chapter 11, pp. 242–245) or destination brand equity (Konecnik & Gartner, 2007).

10.9 Managerial focus

- **Have you examined the quality of the relationship between your brand and your consumers?**
  Brand managers are focused on loyalty programs because loyal consumers generate repeated purchases and are brand ambassadors. When retailers launch a loyalty card, usually their main concern is to maximize the number of cardholders within the shortest amount of time or acquire a given number of holders (Demoulin & Zidda, 2009). Nevertheless, in order to enhance the efficiency of loyalty programs, it is essential to check the quality of the relationship with consumers. The scales included in the chapter allow managers to better understand the drivers of brand

loyalty. Managers cannot build strong loyalty programs without gaining consumer trust, brand trust being one of the main antecedents of loyalty (Chaudhuri & Holbrook, 2001). The brand must provide confidence to consumers, as it should be perceived as credible and reliable.

- **Have you checked the consumers' trust toward your brand in a cross-channel environment?**
Brand trust plays an important role in determining a consumer's purchase behaviour in store but even more when consumers buy online. Trust is a dynamic process, and it takes time for consumers to trust brands online, considering the security and privacy risks which may be associated with online purchases. It is therefore important that consumers feel positive emotions when visiting a website and that the brand reassures them regarding its intention to keep its promises. Building initial trust is important when consumers visit the website for the first time, because their trust may determine whether they will visit the site again and can also influence the brand trust across channels. Brand trust can also be influenced by word of mouth, the quality of information and the online brand experience. It is therefore important to track overall trust in a cross-channel environment.

- **You have faced a crisis; have you checked the evolution of brand trust after this event?**
All brands, even strong brands such as Coca-Cola, Nike, Quick and so on, may become victims of a crisis. These situations can become more serious due to the use of social media, which allows consumers to inform others and express their opinions quickly. Nevertheless, trusted brands receive more empathy from consumers due to the mutual confidence that has been created over time. It is therefore important to monitor brand trust regularly in order to be sure that brands survive a possible crisis and receive consumer comprehension. In the event of a crisis, managers should develop a good communication strategy in order to be transparent, to reassure and to preserve consumers' trust in the brand. Furthermore, during and after this event, it is very important to analyse social media traffic and measure the evolution of brand trust over time to verify whether the brand has regained consumers' confidence.

- **Before changing a brand name or other key elements of the brand, have you checked consumer brand trust and brand loyalty?**
Changing a brand name is a very risky decision, potentially nullifying many years of sustained investment and damaging the brand equity (Muzellec & Lambkin, 2006). Replacing the brand might disturb the consumers' brand relationship; nevertheless, if the change is made progressively and if consumers are informed properly, brand trust and

> brand loyalty can be transferred to the replacement brand (Pauwels-Delassus & Mogos Descotes, 2013). Therefore, tracking brand trust and brand loyalty is crucial when conducting a brand change in order to check if the brand trust and loyalty are effectively transferred to the new brand. Managers can define specific actions in order to reassure consumers and make them feel more confident regarding the substitution.
>
> - **Is your brand loyalty affected by your social media strategy?**
>   Social media is an ideal environment for businesses to reach their customers, while others believe brands crash an environment that is supposed to be for people and their friends (Fournier & Avery, 2011; Kaplan & Haenlein, 2010). Nevertheless, social media can hurt brand image in cases of negative buzz even though consumers who trust the brand may be less sensitive to negative word of mouth. Therefore, brand trust plays a key role in enhancing the effects of social media. By enhancing brand communities through social media and facilitating information sharing, the social link among communities will be higher. The self-connection with the community will be enhanced, which will also increase the brand trust and brand loyalty (Laroche, Habibi & Richard, 2013). Measuring brand trust and brand loyalty can therefore provide useful indications about the performance of your social media strategy.

References

Arquardt, A. (2013). Relationship quality as a resource to build industrial brand equity when products are uncertain and future-based. *Industrial Marketing Management*, 42 (8), 1386–1397.

Bauer, H. H., Sauer, N. E., & Schmitt, P. (2005), Customer-based brand equity in the team sport industry: Operationalization and impact on the economic success of sport teams. *European Journal of Marketing*, 39 (5/6), 496–722.

Bloemer, J., & Kasper, H. (1995). The complex relationship between consumer satisfaction and brand loyalty. *Journal of Economic Psychology*, 16 (2), 311–329.

Cacioppo, J. T., & Petty, R. E. (1982). The need for cognition. *Journal of Personality and Social Psychology*, 42 (1), 116–131.

Chaudhuri, A., & Holbrook, M. B. (2001). The chain of effects from brand trust and brand affect to brand performance: the role of brand loyalty. *Journal of Marketing*, 65 (April), 81–93.

Churchill, G. A., Jr. (1979). A paradigm for developing better measures of marketing constructs. *Journal of Marketing Research*, 16 (February), 64–73.

Delgado-Ballester, E., Munuera-Alemán, J. L., & Yagüe-Guillén, M. J. (2003). Development and validation of a brand trust scale. *International Journal of Market Research*, 45 (1), 35–53.

Demoulin, N., & Zidda, P. (2009). Drivers of customers' adoption and adoption timing of a new loyalty card in the grocery retail market. *Journal of Retailing*, 85 (3), 391–405.

Dick, A.S., & Basu, K. (1994). Customer loyalty: toward an integrated conceptual framework. *Journal of Academy of Marketing Science*, 22 (2), 99–113.

Filser, M. (1994). *Le comportement du consommateur*. Dalloz, France: Collection précis de Gestion.

Fournier, S. (1998). Consumers and their brands: Developing relationship theory in consumer research. *Journal of Consumer Research*, 24 (March), 343–373.

Fournier, S., & Alvarez, C. (2013). Relating badly to brands. *Journal of Consumer Psychology*, 23 (2), 253–264.

Fournier, S., & Avery, J. (2011). The uninvited brand. *Business Horizon*, 54, 193–207.

Fournier, S., Breazeale, M., & Fetscherin, M. (eds.). (2013). *Consumer–brand relationships: theory and practice*. New York, NY: Routledge.

Gurviez, P., & Korchia, M. (2002). Proposition d'une échelle de mesure multidimensionnelle de la confiance dans la marque. *Recherche et Applications en Marketing*, 17 (3), 41–61.

Jarvis, C.B., MacKenzie, S.B., & Podsakoff, P.M. (2003). A critical review of construct indicators and measurement model misspecification in marketing and consumer research. *Journal of Consumer Research*, 30 (2), 199–218.

Johar, G., Birk, M., & Einwiller, S. (2012). How to save your brand in the face of crisis. *MIT Sloan Management Review*, 51 (4), 7–64.

Kapferer, J.-N., & Laurent, G. (1983). *La sensibilité aux marques: un nouveau concept pour gérer les marques*. Paris: Fondation Jour de France pour la Recherche en Publicité.

Kaplan, A.M., & Haenlein, M. (2010). Users of the world, unite! The challenges and opportunities of social media. *Business Horizons*, 53, 59–68.

Kim, H.K., Lee, M., & Lee, Y.W. (2005). Developing a scale for measuring brand relationship quality. *AP-Asia Pacific Advances in Consumer Research*, 118–126.

Konecnik, M., & Gartner, W.C. (2007). Customer-based brand equity for a destination. *Annals of Tourism Research*, 34 (2), 400–421.

Laroche, M., Habibi, M.R., & Richard, M.O. (2013). To be or not to be in social media: how brand loyalty is affected by social media? *International Journal of Information Management*, 33, 76–82.

Lau, G.T., & Lee, S.H. (1999). Consumers' trust in a brand and the link to brand loyalty. *Journal of Market Focused Management*, 4 (4), 341–370.

Le Roux, A., Chandon, J.-L., & Strazzieri, A. (1997). Une analyse confirmatoire de la mesure d'implication durable PIA. *Actes du Congrès International de l'AFM*, 13, Toulouse, 958–986.

Li, F., Zhou, N., Kashyap, R., & Yang, Z. (2008). Brand trust as a second-order factor. An alternative measurement model. *International Journal of Market Research*, 50 (6), 817–839.

Maio, G.R., & Esses, V.M. (2001). The need for affect: Individual differences in the motivation to approach and avoid emotions. *Journal of Personality*, 69, 583–614.

Morgan, R.A., & Hunt, S.D. (1994). The commitment-trust theory of relationship marketing. *Journal of Marketing*, 58 (July), 20–38.

Muzellec, L., & Lambkin, M.C. (2006). Corporate rebranding: the art of destroying, transferring and recreating brand equity? *European Journal of Marketing*, 40 (7/8), 803–824.

Odin, Y., Odin, N., & Valette-Florence, P. (2001). Conceptual and operational aspects of brand loyalty – an empirical investigation. *Journal of Business Research*, 53, 75–84.

Oliver, R.L. (1997) *Satisfaction: a behavioral perspective on the consumer*. Boston, MA: McGraw-Hill.

Park, C.W., Eisingerich, A.B., & Park, J. (2013). Attachment-aversion (AA) model of customer-brand relationships. *Journal of Consumer Psychology*, 23 (2), 229–248.

Pauwels-Delassus, V., & Mogos Descotes, R. (2013). Brand name change: can trust and loyalty be transferred? *Journal of Brand Management*, 20 (8), 656–669.

Rempel, J. K., Holmes, J. G., & Zanna, M. P. (1985). Trust in close relationships. *Journal of Personality and Social Psychology*, 49 (1), 95–112.

Richins, M. L. (1994). Valuing things: the public and private meanings of possessions. *Journal of Consumer Research*, 21 (December), 504–521.

Spreng, R. A., Mackenzie, S. B., & Olshavsky, R. W. (1996). A reexamination of the determinants of consumer satisfaction. *Journal of Marketing*, 60 (July), 15–32.

Veloutsou, C. (2007). Identifying the dimensions of the product-brand and consumer relationship. *Journal of Marketing Management*, 23 (1–2), 7–26.

11
BRAND EQUITY

11.1 Overview

The interest in brand equity started to manifest in the 1980s and grew in the 1990s, with the results that, today, brand equity represents a well-established concept in marketing (Christodoulides & de Chernatony, 2010). Brand equity reflects the importance that brands have for consumers, companies, organisations, channel distributions and the financial markets. Brand equity is considered, according to the Marketing Science Institute definition, "a set of associations and behaviours on the part of a brand's consumers, channel members and parent corporation that enables a brand to earn greater volume or greater margins than it could without the brand name and, in addition, provides a strong, sustainable and differential advantage" (Srivastava & Shocker, 1991). From a consumer's perspective, brand equity refers to the value added to a product due to the presence of the brand (Farquhar, 1989) which induces favourable impressions and attitudes toward the brand. The difference in consumer response due to the brand name provides incremental utility or added value thanks to price premium and positively influences company's long-term profitability (Srivastava & Shocker, 1991). Therefore, marketing managers develop strategies in order to enhance brand equity and need to optimise their brand portfolio in a global environment.

While the theoretical debate on brand equity was moving forward, researchers started being concerned about the measurement of this concepts (for a review, see Christodoulides & de Chernatony, 2010). To operationalize brand equity, researchers mainly have referred to two main frameworks: Keller's (1993) and Aaker's (1991). Keller (1993) conceptualises brand equity under brand knowledge including two components: brand awareness and brand image. Aaker (1991) conceptualises brand equity with five main dimensions: brand awareness, perceived quality, brand associations, brand loyalty and other brand assets which are in general omitted as not related to consumers. Among the seven scales presented in this chapter to measure brand equity, four of them have their roots in these two frameworks. The cross-national consumer-based brand equity scale (Buil, de Chernatony & Martinez, 2008) is derived from Aaker's model, whereas the customer-based equity in the team sports industry scale (Bauer, Sauer & Schmitt, 2005) builds upon Keller's framework. The multi-dimensional customer-based brand equity scale developed by Yoo and Donthu (2001) and the customer-based brand equity scale developed by Netemeyer and co-authors (2004) are based on both Aaker's and Keller's conceptualizations.

The other three scales that are included in the chapter take a different perspective. The consumer-based brand equity scale proposed by Vázquez, del Río and Iglesias (2002) considers brand equity in terms of the utilities obtained by a consumer from the brand following its purchase. The measurement scale of online retail/service brand equity (Christodoulides, de Chernatony, Furrer, Shiu & Abimbola, 2006) differs from the classical approach in incorporating more emotional or experiential assets, which are co-created through the interaction between consumers and brands. Finally, the employee brand equity scale from King, Grace and Funk (2012) looks at brand equity from an employee's perspective and evaluates the differential effect that brand knowledge has on employee behaviour.

11.2 Multi-dimensional consumer-based brand equity (Yoo & Donthu, 2001)

Definition of construct

Consumer-based brand equity is defined by Yoo and Donthu (2001, p. 1) as "consumers' different response between a focal brand and an unbranded product when both have the same level of marketing stimuli and product attributes". Drawing from the brand equity framework of Aaker (1991, 1996a) and Keller (1993), the researchers conceptualize multi-dimensional brand equity (MBE) as consisting of *brand loyalty, brand awareness, perceived quality* of brand and *brand associations. Brand loyalty* refers to the tendency of consumers to be loyal to a given brand and is reflected in their intention to buy the brand. *Brand awareness* relates to the ability of consumers to recognize a brand and recall its product category. *Perceived quality* is about consumers' judgement of the overall excellence and superiority of a brand. *Brand associations* indicate anything in consumers' memory that is linked with a brand.

Scale description

The MBE scale comprises 10 items representing the three dimensions of *brand loyalty, perceived quality* and *brand awareness/associations*, the latter of which combine brand awareness and brand associations. *Brand loyalty* encompasses three items, *perceived quality* contains two items and *brand awareness/associations* regroups five items, of which two concern brand awareness and three relate to brand associations. All items are measured using a 5-point Likert scale anchored at 1= "strongly disagree" and 5 = "strongly agree".

Items can be combined to form either an MBE index or a composite MBE. To compute the MBE index, the weights of the dimensions need to be summed up; the weight of a dimension is obtained by dividing the path coefficient of that dimension by the sum of the three path coefficients. The composite MBE score can be obtained from a simple sum of the mean scores of the three dimensions.

TABLE 11.1 Multi-dimensional consumer-based brand equity scale

Scale dimension	Scale item
Brand loyalty	• I consider myself to be loyal to (brand X) • (Brand X) would be my first choice • I will not buy other brands if (brand X) is available at the store
Perceived quality	• The likely quality of (brand X) is extremely high • The likelihood that (brand X) would be functional is very high
Brand awareness/ associations	• I can recognize (brand X) among other competing brands[a] • I am aware of (brand X)[a] • Some characteristics of (brand X) come to my mind quickly[b] • I can quickly recall the symbol or logo of (brand X)[b] • I have difficulty in imagining (brand X) in my mind*[b]

Note: *indicates the item is negatively phrased and reverse coded; [a] indicates the item refers to brand brand awareness, whereas [b] indicates the item refers to brand associations.

Scale development

The MBE scale is developed thanks to a multi-step study including the definition of the construct, an item-generation phase, an item-purification phase and finally a main study to validate the set of items which constitute the final brand equity measure. In so doing, an etic approach is followed by the researchers, who develop their MBE scale in multiple cultures simultaneously (Korean, Korean American and American). The two countries selected for the study, South Korea and the United States, show an adequate range of cultural variation based on Hofstede's (1991) model.

In the item-generation phase, a pool of 48 scale items is generated based on the literature review and is then reduced to 22 items after a screening by the researchers. Twelve brands from three different categories of consumer goods are selected in order to have products with high brand equity, high familiarity and difference in price range, frequency of purchase, consumers' product involvement and consumption situation. The three categories used as stimuli are film or cameras, athletic shoes and colour television sets.

A quantitative pilot study is conducted next to further purify the scale items. The questionnaire is first developed in English and then translated into Korean through a translation and back-translation process involving different experts. Respondents from South Korea and the United States are involved in this study.

Four brands of athletic shoes are used as brand stimuli, and a different version of the questionnaire is prepared for each brand surveyed. Reliability analysis is used to select the items for the main study: only those with a Cronbach's coefficient of at least 0.70 are retained; if items contribute similarly to Cronbach's alpha, the one with the weaker coefficient is dropped. Seventeen items result from this study.

The main study is conducted with Korean, Korean American and American samples. Twelve brands from the three product categories are used as stimuli. Each questionnaire is about one brand; in addition to MBE scale items, the questionnaire includes measures generated by the researchers on purchase intention (see box below), brand attitude (see box below), product category involvement, brand and product category experience (see box below). Answers to all these measures are reported on 5-point Likert scales, except for brand and product experience (yes/no questions).

Purchase intention

- I would like to buy (brand X)
- I intend to purchase (brand X)

Attitude toward the brand

- Very bad/Very good
- Very nice/Very awful*
- Very attractive/Very unattractive*
- Very desirable/Very undesirable*
- Extremely likable/Extremely unlikable*

Note: * indicates the item is reverse coded.

Brand and product category experience

- Have you ever bought any brand of (product category Y)?
- Have you ever bought (brand X)?
- Do you currently use/own any brand of (product category Y)?

The data are analysed at individual, multi-group and pooled levels. The individual analysis identifies the common items and dimensions in each of the three samples. Fourteen items are selected based on reliability scores across samples. Exploratory factor analysis reveals that only three factors out of four (*perceived quality, brand loyalty* and *brand awareness/brand associations*) are consistently found in each sample. Confirmatory factor analysis through LISREL 8 maximum likelihood method is performed to further examine the dimensionality of brand equity. A comparison between two four-dimensional models, one where the correlation between awareness/associations is set free, the other one where this correlation is constrained to 1, is conducted. Results indicate that awareness and associations have to be combined due to lack of discriminant validity between the two (the squared correlation between awareness and associations is greater than their AVE). Other comparisons are conducted with any other three-dimensional model and with the one-dimensional model, but the three-dimensional model combining awareness and associations performs better than all of them (Americans: χ^2 = 533.09, df = 74, SRMR = 0.061, GFI = 0.87, AGFI = 0.82, CFI = 0.93, IFI = 0.93; Korean Americans: χ^2 = 317.81, df = 74, GFI = 0.87, AGFI = 0.82, CFI = 0.91, IFI = 0.92; Koreans: χ^2 = 273.59, df = 74, SRMR = 0.054, GFI = 0.94, AGFI = 0.92, CFI = 0.95, IFI = 0.95).

The multi-group analysis examines the factorial invariance of the 14 items across the three samples. A comparison between an unconstrained model, where the factor variance is specified to vary across cultures, and a constrained model, where the factor variance is constrained to be the same, is conducted. Results (delta χ^2 = 91.24, df = 28, p < 0.0001) indicate that the factor structure is not invariant across cultures with the 14 items. To locate the source of inequality, a partial measurement invariance test is conducted. The invariance of each factor loading is tested by declaring the loading alone to be invariant across samples. The χ^2 difference test with the unconstrained model (χ^2 = 1124.49, df = 222) reveals that the metric inequivalence occurs because of four items. After deleting these items, in a new comparison between the unconstrained model and the constrained model with the 10 items, the χ^2 difference test is not significant (delta χ^2 = 31.01, df = 20, p > 0.05).

The pooled analysis identifies culture-free universal dimensions of brand equity. The cross-cultural validity of the 10 items is checked by an individual-level, multi-cultural factor analysis. After a double-standardization procedure (within-subject and within-culture), the data are pooled across cultures and analysed. As in the individual analysis, different measurement models (four-, three- and one-dimensional) are examined for the 10 items, and chi-square difference test are performed. Results confirm that the three-dimensional model combining awareness and associations is the best one (χ^2 = 326.19, df = 32, SRMR = 0.042, GFI = 0.96, AGFI = 0.93, CFI = 0.96 and IFI = 0.96).

Samples

The pilot sample is composed of 414 undergraduate university students, of whom 218 are from South Korea and 196 from the United States. The main study is conducted with a sample of a total of 1,530 undergraduate students at major universities in South Korea and in the United States. Of them, 650 are Korean participants in South Korea, 350 are Korean Americans in the United States and 650 are Americans in the United States.

Reliability and validity

The content validity of the MBE items is ensured in the item-generation phase, when the initial pool of items is evaluated for conformity to the theoretical definitions and redundancy.

The reliability of the final, 10-item MBE scale is established in the multi-group analysis. Reliability is reported to be equal to 0.88, 0.86 and 0.87 *for brand loyalty* among Americans, Korean Americans and Koreans, respectively; 0.81, 0.77 and 0.84 for *perceived quality* among Americans, Korean Americans and Koreans, respectively; and 0.90, 0.86 and 0.86 for *brand awareness/associations* among Americans, Korean Americans and Koreans, respectively.

The construct validity of the MBE scale is established in relation to purchase intention and attitude toward the brands. The analysis shows a high correlation between MBE and purchase intention (correlations equal to 0.66, 0.70 and 0.55 with $p < 0.0001$ for Americans, Korean Americans and Koreans, respectively) as well as between MBE and brand attitude (correlations equal to 0.72, 0.71 and 0.50 with $p < 0.0001$ for Americans, Korean Americans and Koreans, respectively).

The convergent validity of the MBE scale is checked using the MBE index and a four-item unidimensional measure of overall brand equity (OBE; see box below), which is developed using the same respondents. The reliability of the OBE scale is of 0.90, 0.89 and 0.90 for Americans, Korean Americans and Koreans, respectively. The correlation between the OBE scale and the MBE index is equal to 0.60, 0.63 and 0.59 ($p < 0.0001$) for Americans, Korean Americans and Koreans, respectively, thus supporting the convergent validity of the MBE.

Overall brand equity (OBE)

- It makes sense to buy (brand X) instead of any other brand, even if they are the same
- Even if another brand has the same features as (brand X), I would prefer to buy (brand X)
- If there is another brand as good as (brand X), I prefer to buy (brand X)
- If another brand is not different from (brand X) in any way, it seems smarter to purchase (brand X)

Managerial applications

Given the importance of brand equity for managers, the MBE and OBE scales provide two useful tools to evaluate and track the long-term performance of the brand. The 10-item MBE scale provides managers with a better understanding of the effectiveness of the brand among the different dimensions of brand equity. Thus, managers can better identify the drivers of brand strength and point out brand weaknesses. By tracking the performance of their brands with MBE scales, managers can prioritize their efforts and allocate their resources more efficiently on specific brand equity dimensions in order to improve their brand equity over time. These measures can also be useful in examining the performance of specific brand strategies such as brand extension or co-branding by measuring the equity of the co-brands and the parent brand before or after the brand extension. Finally, these scales can be useful to assess the value of the brand for licensing or sales purposes.

11.3 Consumer-based brand equity (Vázquez, del Río & Iglesias, 2002)

Definition of construct

Consumer-based brand equity (CBBE) is conceptualised by the researchers under the lens of utilities obtained by the consumer from the brand following its purchase. It is defined as "the overall utility that the consumer associates to the use and consumption of the brand; including associations expressing both functional and symbolic utilities" (Vázquez, del Río & Iglesias, 2002, p. 28). Consistently with Keller (1993, 1998) and Park and Srinivasan (1994), the researchers consider that the product as well as the brand can contribute to both types of utilities to consumers, although it is reasonable that the functional utility derives from the product, whereas the symbolic utility arises from the brand. CBBE is therefore conceptualized as consisting of different utilities associated with the product and the brand: *product functional utility*, which is directly linked to product tangible attributes; *product symbolic utility*, which relates to aesthetic product characteristics; *brand name functional utility*, which refers to the guarantee provided by the brand; and the *brand name symbolic utility*, which relates to the capacity of the brand in meeting psychological and social needs.

Scale description

This scale measures the brand equity through the measurement of four dimensions (second-order constructs), eight sub-dimensions (first-order constructs) and 21 items. The scale is developed with specific reference to the sports shoes sector. The *product functional utility* dimension consists of three sub-dimensions: "comfort" (three items), "safety" (four items) and "duration" (one item). The *product*

234 Brand equity

symbolic utility dimension includes the sub-dimension of "aesthetics", which is measured with two items. The *brand name functional utility* dimension includes the sub-dimension of "guarantee" and is measured with three items. The *brand symbolic utility* dimension consists of three sub-dimensions: "social identification" (four items), "status" (two items) and "personal identification" (two items). All items are measured on an 11-point Likert scale ranging from 0 = "strongly disagree" to 10 = "strongly agree".

TABLE 11.2 Consumer-based brand equity scale

Scale dimension (second-order dimension)	Scale sub-dimension (first-order dimension)	Scale item
Product functional utility	• Comfort	• Flexibility • Weight • Size
	• Safety	• Foot protection-care • Sensation when walking • Sole absorption/perspiration • Grip
	• Duration	• Duration
Product symbolic utility	• Aesthetics	• Design/aesthetic line • Colours
Brand name functional utility	• Guarantee	• Brand that continuously improves features • Brand that is trustworthy • Brand of excellent quality
Brand name symbolic utility	• Social identification	• Brand in fashion • Brand used by friends • Reputed brand • Leading brand
	• Status	• The use of the brand is a prestige symbol • Brand recommended by famous people
	• Personal identification	• Brand you particularly like/find attractive • Brand in keeping with your lifestyle

Scale development

In accordance with Churchill (1979) and Deng and Dart (1994), the development of the scale follows a research process in eight steps.

Step 1 consists of the literature review in order to specify the brand equity construct. Based on this, step 2 allows the researchers to identify the four key dimensions associated to brand utilities. Step 3 consists of the generation of items representing these four brand utilities. A pool of items is generated based on four information sources: examination and adaptation of the main scales published for the measurement of brand utilities, two focus groups with sports shoes users, in-depth interviews with distributors and the consultation of secondary data such as specialised journals and studies on the sector. Step 4 allows the researchers to refine the scale by submitting the constituted list of items to a group of experts and by pre-testing the items in order to finalize the item wording. This step leads to a pool of 22 items.

Step 5 comprises the data collection by means of face-to-face interviews, accompanied by survey questionnaire administration. Each respondent is asked to evaluate a maximum of two brands on the 22 CCBE items; questions on price premium, which is defined as the amount consumers would pay more for the brand in comparison with others, and recommendation of the brand are also included in the questionnaire for validity purposes. In total, six brands of athletic shoes are investigated in the survey. These brands are identified through a pre-test in which respondents are asked to indicate, on a list of 28 brands, the ones they used and knew the most.

The next steps consist of assessments of the reliability (step 6), convergent and discriminant validities (step 7) and nomological validity (step 8) of the scale. EQS program is used to perform a series of confirmatory factor analysis. Results show that a one-factor model produces unsatisfactory goodness-of-fit indexes (NNFI, NFI, GFI, AGFI and CFI are below the minimum level of 0.9 and the RMSEA is over 0.1), whereas an eight-factor model presents a good fit to the data (S-B χ^2 = 847.91, df = 162, $p < 0.01$, NNFI = 0.913, NFI = 0.923, GFI = 0.939, AGFI = 0.912, CFI = 0.933, RMSEA = 0.060 and AIC = 985.914). One item is dropped from the scale in the process, leaving the CBBE scale with 21 items. The reliability, convergent and discriminant validities of the eight factors are examined. A four-factor, second-order model is then estimated, and all indexes indicate a satisfactory fit except the S-B chi-square due to the large sample size (S-B χ^2 = 136.62, $p < 0.01$, NNFI = 0.921, NFI = 0.961, GFI = 0.971, AGFI = 0.919, CFI = 0.968, RMSEA = 0.093). The reliability, convergent and discriminant validities of the four second-order factors are examined before proceeding with the test of the nomological validity of the CBBE scale in relation to price premium and recommendation of the brand.

Samples

The study is based on a sample of 1,054 consumers who bought sports shoes in the last two years and are users of the brands being studied. The sample is representative of the national population of Spain in terms of age and gender and results in 1,000 valid questionnaires.

Reliability and validity

The reliability of the CBBE scale is established in step 6. Composite reliability coefficients of the eight sub-dimensions ("comfort", "safety", "duration", "aesthetics", "guarantee", "social identification", "status" and "personal identification") are over 0.6, ranging from 0.635 to 0.837. Composite reliability is also computed for two of the four dimensions containing more than one dimension (*product functional utility* and *brand name symbolic utility*) and is equal to 0.737 and 0.846, respectively.

The content validity of the CBBE scale items is assured through steps 1, 2, 3 and 4, where shoe users, distributors and other experts are used to complement the literature review for generating and refining the scale items.

The convergent and discriminant validities of the scale are verified in step 7. The convergent validity of the eight first-order dimensions is supported by the lambda standardised parameters that relate each variable to the corresponding factors, as they are all significant (t-values > 22.015) and reach values over 0.5. The discriminant validity of the eight sub-dimensions is supported by the confidence intervals of the correlations between these sub-dimensions, which do not include the value of 1. The same criteria are used to verify the convergent and discriminant validities of the four second-order dimensions.

The nomological validity of the CBBE scale is checked in step 8 by analysing the causal relationship existing between the four second-order dimensions and two observable variables: price premium and consumer's willingness to recommend the brand to others. A causal model is estimated, and results show that *brand name functional utility* and *brand name symbolic utility* have a positive and significant influence on price premium (parameters equal to 0.10 and 0.16, respectively, with $ps < 0.05$); *product symbolic utility, brand name functional utility* and *brand name symbolic utility* have a positive and significant influence on recommendation of the brand (parameters equal to 0.11, 0.28 and 0.31, respectively, with $ps < 0.05$).

Managerial applications

This scale provides managers with the possibility of measuring brand equity through the perspective of utility that consumers associate to the use and consumption of the brand, including both functional and symbolic utilities related to the brand and the product. This measure can help managers from sport shoes companies identify the source of brand equity and orient their marketing programs in terms of the brand utilities they wish to improve. They can evaluate each of the four macro-dimensions and decide on which one to focus. In the sports shoes market, it is noted that brand name utilities are particularly important. The interest of this scale also resides in the consideration of operational associations related to the product as well as to the brand that the manager can measure and decide to strengthen specifically or simultaneously to generate an optimized communication message. The consideration of each of the macro-dimensions and dimensions can offer managers an efficient tool to optimize their segmentation and better orient their differentiation strategy.

11.4 Facets of customer-based brand equity (Netemeyer *et al.*, 2004)

Definition of construct

Brand equity is considered by Netemeyer *et al.* (2004) the "value added" to the product, associated by the consumer with a brand name. This "value added" is a function of several facets. The facets of customer-based brand equity (CBBE) considered by the researchers are the common core or primary facets defined in Aaker's framework (Aaker, 1996a) and Keller's model (Keller, 1993), namely *perceived quality (PQ)*, *perceived value for the cost (PVC)*, *uniqueness* and *willingness to pay a price premium*, which are seen as the strongest predictors of purchase intent and purchase behaviour. *Perceived quality* is defined as the customer's judgment of the overall brand performance and superiority of the brand relative to other brands (Aaker, 1996b; Keller, 1993; Zeithaml, 1988). *Perceived value* for the cost is considered the customer's overall assessment of the utility of the brand based on perceptions of the benefit gained in relation to the cost (money, time and effort; Kirmani & Zeithmal, 1993). *Uniqueness* is defined as the degree to which customers consider how distinct the brand is relative to competitors. *Willingness to pay a price premium* is defined as the amount a customer is willing to pay for a same offer of a preferred brand compared to the one of another brand.

Scale description

The CBBE scale developed by the researchers contains three facets or dimensions: the *PQ/PVC* facet, which is measured with eight items (four reflecting *PQ* and four reflecting *PVC*); the *uniqueness* facet, which contains four items; and the *willingness to pay a price premium* facet, which is also measured with four items. All items are evaluated on a 7-point Likert scale ranging from "strongly disagree" to "strongly agree", except for one item from the *willingness to pay a price premium* facet. To rate the item, "I am willing to pay ____ % more for (brand name) brand over other brands of (product)", respondents can choose among the following options: 0%, 5%, 10%, 15%, 20%, 25%, 30% or more.

TABLE 11.3 Customer-based brand equity scale

Scale dimension	Scale item
Perceived quality/ perceived value for the cost	• Compared to other brands of (product category Y), (brand X) is of very high quality • (Brand X) is the best brand in its product class • (Brand X) consistently performs better than all other brands of (product category Y) • I can always count on (brand X) brand of (product category Y) for consistent high quality

(Continued)

TABLE 11.3 (Continued)

Scale dimension	Scale item
	• What I get from (brand X) brand of (product category Y) is worth the cost. • All things considered (price, time and effort), (brand X) brand of (product category Y) is a good buy • Compared to other brands of (product category Y), (brand X) is a good value for the money • When I use a (brand X) brand of (product category Y), I feel I am getting my money's worth
Uniqueness	• (Brand X) is "distinct" from other brands of (product category Y) • (Brand X) really "stands out" from other brands of (product category Y) • (Brand X) is very different from other brands of (product category Y) • (Brand X) is "unique" from other brands of (product category Y)
Willingness to pay a price premium	• The price of (brand X) would have to go up quite a bit before I would switch to another brand of (product category Y). • I am willing to pay a higher price for (brand X) brand of (product category Y) than for other brands of (product category Y) • I am willing to pay _____ % more for (brand X) brand over other brands of (product category Y) • I am willing to pay a lot more for (brand X) than other brands of (product category Y)

Scale development

In accordance with Bearden and Netemeyer (1998) and Haynes, Nelson and Blaine (1999), the scale development starts with qualitative procedures prior to the main studies. Two consumer focus groups are conducted in order to choose product categories and brands for the main study. Participants are asked scaled and open-ended questions about brands in 10 product categories with high rate of purchase containing both weak and strong brands. Based on these two focus groups, the literature review and the researchers' judgement, 65 items are generated. The list of items is then judged by marketing professors and is reduced to 37 items based on the representativeness of the items for each facet.

A pre-test study is conducted next in order to further reduce the number of items. Respondents are asked to complete a take-home survey, where they have to rate the 37 CBBE items with respect to four brands (Coca-Cola, Crest, Levi's and Nike) in four product categories, of which two are relatively frequently purchased (cola and toothpaste) and two are infrequently purchased nondurables (jeans and athletic shoes). Responses are analysed via principal components and item analyses. Items with consistently low (< 0.50) or very high factor loading (> 0.95), low or very high item-to-total correlation and high correlation with another item in the same facet are considered for deletion. The procedure allows the researchers to retain 23 items, with acceptable levels of factor loadings and item-to-total correlations.

The first study consists of a survey to refine the CBBE measure and obtain initial estimates of its psychometric properties. In addition to the 23 CBBE items, the questionnaire contains single-item measures on brand awareness, brand familiarity, brand popularity, brand purchase intent and past percentage of brand purchases (adapted from Aaker, 1996b; Agarwal & Rao, 1996; Cobb-Walgreen, Ruble & Donthu, 1995). Three brands (two strong, one weak) are evaluated in each of the four categories mentioned. An iterative approach including both quantitative and qualitative judgement is adopted in data analysis. For each brand, a four-factor CBBE model is estimated using LISREL 8 covariance structure modelling. The first iteration results in the deletion of four items with consistently high within- and/or across-factor correlated measurement errors and low or very high completely standardized within-factor loadings unless they show high face validity. The second iteration results in the deletion of two more items with high cross-loadings, leaving 17 CBBE items. Although the four CBBE facets exhibit internal consistency, a correlation in the range from 0.93 to 0.99 is found between *PQ* and *PVC* for 11 of 12 brands. The lack of discriminant validity between these two facets is showed by the most stringent test of discriminant validity, which is unsuccessful.

The second study further examines the dimensionality of CBBE and establishes the scale's reliability and validity. The survey includes 18 CBBE items: one item for *uniqueness* is added to the list of 17 items in order to have at least four items per facet. The survey contains other measures on organizational associations, brand image consistency (see box below), brand purchase intent and past percentage of brand purchase, which are developed by the researchers and are included for assessing the nomological validity of the CBBE scale. Three brands (Coca-Cola, Reebok and Levi's) are chosen for their high degree of familiarity and use. Responses are subjected to confirmatory factor analyses using LISREL 8. For each brand, a four-factor model is estimated. Two items with high cross-loadings are dropped. Correlation between *PVC* and *PQ* facets is still high across brands (0.90 or above), and no evidence of discriminant validity is found between them through formal tests. These results lead to the decision of forming a combined *PQ/PVC* factor. The three-factor model is then estimated for each brand and provides good fit indexes (NNFI and CFI estimates are above 0.90; RMSEA estimates range from 0.07 to 0.10).

Brand image consistency

- (Brand X) brand of (product category Y) has a rich history
- (Brand X) brand of (product category Y) has a strong brand image
- (Brand X) brand of (product category Y) has a consistent brand image
- Over the years, (brand X) of (product category Y) has a maintained a strong image
- Over time, (brand X) brand has been very consistent in what it stands for

The third study extends the scale validation process by examining CBBE in relation to actual brand purchase behaviour thanks to a survey conducted in collaboration with a supermarket. Two brands are evaluated (Coca-Cola and a local brand of coffee) by shoppers at home, and the purchase buying act is controlled by checking the grocery store receipt of their next purchases of any coffee and cola from the store. The three-factor models fit the data better for the cola brand (CFI = 0.93, NNFI = 0.92, RMSEA = 0.11) than the coffee brand (CFI = 0.89, NNFI = 0.87, RMSEA = 0.14). A MANOVA follows up ANOVAs used to assess mean differences on the CBBE facets between two groups of respondents: those who purchase the cola/coffee brand and those who do not purchase it in the next store visit. This analysis is used to establish the "known-group" validity of the scale.

The fourth study consists in a multiple-time-period study to test the predictive validity of the CBBE scale with respect to brand purchase behaviour. All participants complete the main survey, where they evaluate three fast-food restaurants on the CBBE scale. At the end of each week for the next five weeks following the initial survey, participants are asked to provide behavioural data regarding the frequency of their visits to the three fast-food restaurants. The three-factor measurement model is estimated for each brand using covariance structure modelling via LISREL 8 (CFI between 0.91 and 0.94, NNFI between 0.89 and 0.93, RMSEA between 0.9 and 0.10). After aggregating behavioural data on brand purchases, the predictive model is estimated via structural equation methodology.

Samples

The pre-test is conducted with a sample of 44 MBA students.

Study 1 is based on four samples of nonstudent adults from a southeastern city who are collected by undergraduate marketing students. Two hundred surveys are given out, and usable responses obtained from the four sample range from 138 to 154 participants (return rates between 69% and 77%).

Study 2 is based on a sample of 186 nonstudent adults from a southeastern city collected by students through a similar procedure as study 1. Two hundred fifty surveys are given out, for an effective response rate of 74.4%.

Study 3 uses a sample of shoppers contacted at the entrance of a supermarket. Two hundred fifty shoppers are given the questionnaires; of them, 101 return the survey, for an effective response rate of 41%; of them, 77 respondents provide behavioural data.

Study 4 is conducted with a sample of undergraduate business students at a major state university. Two hundred two students take the main survey; of them, 167 (response rate = 83%) report behavioural data for all the five weeks.

All studies are conducted in the United States.

Reliability and validity

The content validity of the CBBE scale is established through measurement pre-tests, including focus groups of consumers, item evaluation by marketing professors and a survey.

The scale's internal consistency is tested in studies 2, 3 and 4. Across CBBE facets and across brands, the alpha coefficient is reported to range from 0.87 to 0.96 in study 2, from 0.89 to 0.95 in study 3 and from 0.85 to 0.94 in study 4. The average variance extracted estimates are reported to be all above 0.50 in study 2 and to range from 0.67 to 0.77 in study 3.

Evidence of discriminant validity of the three-factor model is assessed in studies 2 and 4. In study 2, the square of the parameter estimate between pairs of constructs is less than the average variance extracted estimates of the two constructs all but in one instance (the correlation between the facets of *PQ/PVC* and *willingness to pay a price premium*). The same test is used in study 4, and results support the discriminant validity of the three dimensions.

Nomological validity is tested in studies 1 and 2. The analysis in study 1 shows that (1) CBBE facets are correlated with brand purchase intent and past percentage of brand purchases (68 significant correlations over 72); (2) the correlation between CBBE facets with, respectively, brand purchase intent and past percentage of brand purchases for other brands are negative or nonsignificant (all 144 correlations); and (3) CBBE facets are correlated with brand awareness, brand familiarity and brand popularity (141 significant correlations over 144). These results are confirmed in study 2.

"Known-group" validity is tested in study 3. MANOVA/ANOVA results show that all mean scores for the CBBE facets are significantly higher for respondents who purchase the brand (cola brand: *PQ/PVC* = 47.81, *uniqueness* = 23.69, *price premium* = 17.40; coffee brand: PQ/PVC = 47.67, *uniqueness* = 23.96, *price premium* = 18.62) compared to respondents who do not purchase them (cola brand: *PQ/PVC* = 39.11, *uniqueness* = 19.06, *price premium* = 11.87; coffee brand: PQ/PVC = 35.93, *uniqueness* = 19.33, *price premium* = 10.92).

The predictive validity of the CBBE scale is established in study 4. The predictive model estimated includes the *PQ/PVC* and *uniqueness* facets as direct antecedents of the *willingness to pay a price premium* facet, which in turn directly affects brand purchase behaviour. Results indicate an acceptable level of fit across brands (CFI range from 0.93 to 0.94, NNFI from 0.89 to 0.93 and RMSEA between 0.9 and 0.10). Furthermore, across brands, all directional paths are significant (coefficient between 0.20 and 0.69); *PQ/PVC* and *uniqueness* explain between 59% and 68% of the variance in *willingness to pay a price premium*; and *willingness to pay a price premium* explains between 13% and 26% of the variance in the purchase behaviour.

Managerial applications

According to Netemeyer *et al.* (2004), in comparison to other CBBE scales, this measure presents the advantages of retaining several facets which are the most predictive of key brand-related response variables. Given the brevity of the measures, managers can easily integrate this scale in tracking studies to monitor brand performance. The predictive characteristic of the scale allows managers to evaluate the brand in terms of financial strength by estimating purchase intent and therefore financial return. The applicability across product categories and brands allows manager to track brand performance across varied products categories in order to evaluate, for instance, the performance of brand-extension strategies.

11.5 Customer-based brand equity in the team sports industry (Bauer, Sauer & Schmitt, 2005)

Definition of construct

Bauer, Sauer and Schmitt (2005) extend the notion of customer-based brand equity to the team sports industry. The importance of the brand in this industry has increased over the last years: nowadays, in fact, the strength of a sport team brand depends not only on the sport athletic success but also on the management of the brand. The brand equity in team sports (BETS) model developed by Bauer, Sauer and Schmitt takes its roots from Keller's (1993) brand equity conceptualization, which considers brand knowledge the central driver of brand equity and is constituted of two dimensions: brand awareness and brand image. The BETS model is also based on Gladden and Funk's (2001) notion of brand associations in team sports, which offers a framework for brand image with specific reference to the sports sector. Therefore, brand equity in the sports industry is conceptualized as a multi-dimensional construct containing four dimensions: *awareness, product-related brand attributes, non–product-related brand attributes* and *brand benefits*.

Scale description

The BETS scale is composed of four dimensions (*awareness, product related brand attributes, non–product-related brand attributes and brand benefits*) and 14 items. The *awareness* dimension is operationalized through two indicators, that is, brand recognition and brand familiarity. The *product-related attributes* dimension consists of four items directly related to the athletic aspects of the competition, while the *non–product-related attributes* dimension is concerned with further non-athletic characteristics of the brand such as the logo or the stadium atmosphere. The *brand benefits* dimension is operationalized with four items pertaining to fan identification, interest of family and friends, nostalgia and escape from daily routine. The majority of items are measured on a 7-point Likert scale with the endpoints "totally agree" and "do not agree at all".

TABLE 11.4 Brand equity in team sports scale

Scale dimension	Scale item
Awareness	• Recognition • Familiarity
Product-related brand attributes	• Athletic success • Star player(s) • Coach • Management

(*Continued*)

TABLE 11.4 (Continued)

Scale dimension	Scale item
Non product-related brand attributes	• Logo • Stadium • Stadium atmosphere • Regional importance
Brand benefits	• Fan identification • Interest of family and friends • Nostalgia • Escape

Scale development

The scale development starts with the operationalization of the BETS, based on existing research. BETS is operationalized as brand awareness, following Keller's (1993) consumer-based brand equity conceptualization, and brand image, according to Gladden and Funk's (2001) brand associations framework. Items are derived from these models and are modified in order to fit the current context of research, that is, German team sports. This results in a BETS model including two dimensions, five factors and 16 items.

An online survey is conducted next in order to test the psychometric properties of the scale. The generated questionnaire is first pre-tested by a small sample. Test respondents are asked to indicate potential problems in terms of clarity and understanding of the items. Their feedback is used to finalize the items. The final questionnaire is presented online and programmed to randomly assign each respondent a soccer team from the 18 major German league teams of the 2003/2004 season. In addition to the BETS scale, respondents are asked to complete two measures developed by the researchers about the level of expertise of soccer and a direct measure of brand equity ("The team under investigation is a strong brand"), as well as other measures derived from the literature on purchase intention, price insensitivity and loyalty toward the assigned brand.

The hypothesized BETS model is subjected to various multivariate analyses. First, analyses are performed separately for brand *awareness* and brand image dimensions. One item is dropped from the awareness dimension, based on exploratory and confirmatory factor analyses as well as item-to-total correlations. Similarly, one item is removed from the brand image dimension. The four-factor, 14-item model deriving from these analyses is then tested. Results show satisfactory goodness-of-fit measures (GFI = 0.990; AGFI = 0.986; SRMR = 0.047; χ^2/df = 886.11/73). The scholars point out that the goodness-of-fit measures have to be evaluated with care, as the dataset does not show a normal distribution. Nevertheless, LISREL offers the opportunity of using an estimation technique appropriate for non-normally distributed data. The model is factor analysed using the ML estimator. Although the AGFI of 0.893 falls slightly short of the required level of 0.9, the rest of the results verify the model.

Overall, the analyses show that the *awareness* dimension explains a small part of the variance. To further test the importance of the *awareness* component of BETS, the sample is split based on consumer expertise (low-expertise and high-expertise samples). Various CFA models are then estimated. The whole sample model (M1) and the low-expertise sample model (M2) produce good results; however, awareness remains the dimension of least importance as demonstrated by a second-order factor loading of 0.63 compared to factor loadings of 0.81 to 0.85 for the other three factors in M1. Furthermore, in the low-expertise group, the brand familiarity indicator is relatively more important than the recognition indicator as compared to the high-expertise group ($\Delta = 0.43$ versus $\Delta = 0.14$).

Samples

The sample used for the pre-test is composed of 14 individuals. The sample used in the survey is composed of 1,594 respondents, with a large proportion of males (91.6%) due to the selected sport (soccer). The whole sample is divided into low-expertise group ($n = 397$) and high-expertise group ($n = 1,197$).

Reliability and validity

Various indicators are provided by the researchers to support the reliability and validity of the BETS model. The following are based on EFA results: item-to-total-correlations are above 0.37; Cronbach's alpha are equal to 0.45 (*awareness*), 0.82 (both *product-related* and *non–product-related attributes* dimensions) and to 0.85 (*brand benefits*); all factor loadings are greater than 0.60; AVE scores are equal to 9.56% (*awareness*), 19.58% (*product-related attributes*), 18.38% (*non-product-related attributes*) and to 20.90 (*brand benefits*). Indicators based on CFA results include: composite reliability, which is equal to 0.63 (*awareness*), 0.82 (both *product-related* and *non-product-related attributes* dimensions) and to 0.85 (*brand benefits*); factor loadings, which go from 0.16 (*recognition*) to 0.83 (*familiarity*); t-values of factor loadings, which are all greater than 9.24; and AVE scores, equal to 0.49 (*awareness*), 0.54 (both *product-related* and *non-product-related attributes*) and 0.59 (*brand benefits*).

Tests of different types of validity are conducted. Content validity is established through a quantitative test; a structural equation model is estimated, where BETS is related to the direct measure of brand equity. The scale's discriminant validity is shown by following the Fornell/Larcker criterion (Bagozzi et al., 1991), which calls for smaller associations between indicators assigned to different factors than between those that belong to the same factor. Finally, the nomological validity of the BETS scale is demonstrated through CFA results, which confirm that BETS has positive and significant effects on purchase intention ($\gamma = 0.77$, t-value = 101.64, SMC = 0.59), price insensitivity ($\gamma = 0.65$, t-value = 79.46, SMC = 0.42) and loyalty ($\gamma = 0.75$, t-value = 94.94, SMC = 0.56).

Managerial applications

The potential of football club brands has emerged powerfully in recent years. Nowadays, football stars are as popular as Hollywood actors worldwide, and this phenomenon has led to an increase in the value of the club brand. Large investments and sponsorships have placed football brands in people's minds underlining the importance of intangible assets and immaterial goods that team sport brands represent economically. Thanks to this BETS scale, managers can track the management of their sport team brand and focus on specific actions to enhance concrete items when the brands are less successful. Indeed, sport team brand performance depends not only on the athletic success or awareness of the brand but also on cash flows (via merchandise revenues, sponsoring, TV rights . . .) generated by different stakeholder groups, such as corporate sponsors or fans going to the stadium who feel part of the club or occasional fans. This scale can also be used when exploiting new markets. A good example of this could be teams that employ Asian footballers in order to increase their brand awareness and brand equity in that particular part of the world.

11.6 The equity of online brands (Christodoulides, de Chernatony, Furrer, Shiu & Abimbola, 2006)

Definition of construct

Christodoulides *et al.* (2006) study brand equity in relation to the online environment, which presents unique characteristics compared to the offline context and focus on online retail/service (ORS) brands. Considering the change induced by the Internet, which allows brands and consumers to interact one another, ORS brand equity is conceptualised by the researchers as a relational type of intangible asset that is co-created through the interaction between consumers and the online brand. ORS brand equity is a five-dimensional construct. The *emotional connection* dimension refers to the affinity between consumers and ORS brands. The *online experience* dimension reflects how users experience the brand online. The *responsive service nature* dimension refers to the customer service response and interaction. The *trust* dimension reflects the brand's reliability and intentions. The *fulfilment* dimension provides the connection between the online and offline experiences by focusing on customer satisfaction regarding the delivery.

Scale description

The ORS brand equity scale consists of 12 items and five correlated dimensions. The *emotional connection* and the *online experience* dimensions encompass three items each, whereas *responsive service nature, trust* and *fulfilment* are measured with two items each. All items are evaluated using 7-point Likert scales anchored at 1 = "strongly disagree" and 7 = "strongly agree". The weights of the dimensions, which can be obtained by dividing the path coefficient of one dimension by the sum of the path coefficients of all the other dimensions, can be summed to create an ORS brand equity index.

TABLE 11.5 Online retail/service brand equity scale

Scale dimension	Scale item
Emotional connection	• I feel related to the type of people who are (brand X)'s customers • I feel like (brand X) actually cares about me • I feel as though (brand X) really understands me
Online experience	• (Brand X)'s website provides easy-to-follow search paths • I never feel lost when navigating through (brand X)'s website • I was able to obtain the information I wanted without any delay
Responsive service nature	• (Brand X) is willing and ready to respond to customer needs • (Brand X)'s website gives visitors the opportunity to "talk back" to (brand X)
Trust	• I trust (brand X) to keep my personal information safe • I feel safe in my transactions with (brand X)
Fulfilment	• I got what I ordered from (brand X)'s website • The product was delivered by the time promised by (brand X)

Scale development

The development of the ORS brand equity scale is based on the iterative procedures suggested by Churchill (1979) and Gerbing and Anderson (1998). To identify the content domain of ORS brand equity, the first step of this scale development includes a comprehensive literature search on brand equity and online marketing. In order to enhance the understanding of this new construct, two exploratory qualitative studies (studies 1 and 2) are performed. A third study is then conducted with an online survey to purify and validate the final scale.

Specifically, study 1 consists of an experience survey with semi-structured in-depth interviews with brand experts. Content analysis is performed on the interview transcripts. Inter-coder reliability is established through an independent coder. The coefficient of agreement is equal to 82.2%, which is considered acceptable, and discrepancies are resolved through discussion. The analysis of the transcripts suggests that ORS brand equity has five dimensions: *emotional connection, online experience, responsive service nature, trust* and *fulfilment*.

Study 2 comprises two focus groups with consumers in order to further explore the concepts that emerged from the expert interviews and generate items to cover the constructs. An initial pool of 59 items is generated based on these results.

Study 3 is based on a web-based questionnaire developed to collect data and sent via personalised email. Respondents are asked to rate the ORS brand equity items, as well as measures on overall brand equity (adapted from Yoo & Donthu, 2001; see this chapter, pp. 228–233), attitude toward the ORS brand (adapted from Bruner, James & Hensel, 2001), consistent image (adapted from Loiacono, Watson &

Goodhue, 2002) and purchase intention (Graeff, 1997). Before starting the data analysis, the sample is randomly split in half: the first half is used to develop the ORS brand equity scale, whereas the second half is used to validate the results.

In particular, using the first half of the sample, item-to-total correlations are computed for the ORS brand equity items, and those with a correlation lower than 0.30 are dropped. A series of exploratory factor analyses is performed. Items with loadings < 0.45 are dropped, as well as items with loadings > 0.45 on more than one factor; single-item factors are also excluded from the analysis. The EFA analysis is repeated, and items with loadings less than 0.67 are deleted. The resulting five-factor, 18-item solution is submitted to a CFA in LISREL, which shows a poor fit. Items with high modification indices or residuals are removed, as well as items with significant cross-loadings. Through a series of iterative procedures, a final 12-item ORS brand equity model is supported by good values of fit (S-B χ^2 = 55.59 (p = 0.11), df = 44, GFI = 0.93, AGFI = 0.88, CFI = 0.94, IFI = 0.95, NNFI = 0.92). Item loadings range from 0.59 to 0.96, and all t-values are greater than 6.45.

A CFA is performed in LISREL using the second half of the sample. Results indicate a satisfactory fit (S-B χ^2 = 38.11 (p = 0.72), df = 44, GFI = 0.96, AGFI = 0.93, CFI = 1.00, IFI = 1.00, NFI = 1.00), with item loadings ranging from 0.59 to 0.90 and all t-values greater than 6.80. A higher-order ORS brand equity model is also estimated, where the five brand equity dimensions are related to a higher-order factor. Causal paths of this higher-order model are used to compute the weight of each dimension in order to create an index of ORS brand equity. The ORS brand equity index is equal to 0.21 (the mean of *emotional connection*) + 0.18 (the mean of *online experience*) + 0.18 (the mean of *responsive service nature*) + 0.20 (the mean of *trust*) + 0.23 (the mean of *fulfilment*). Reliability and validity tests are conducted using measures of overall brand equity, attitude toward the ORS brand, consistent image and purchase intention.

Samples

Study 1 is undertaken in the UK with 16 experts. Study 2 includes two groups of eight members of the MBA programme at the University of Birmingham. Study 3 is based on a sample of 375 Internet shoppers and is split in half for the analyses. The first half includes 188 respondents, while the second half includes 187 respondents.

Reliability and validity

The internal consistency of the scale is evaluated in study 3 with LISREL results. Composite reliability estimates are equal to 0.88 for *emotional connection*, 0.83 for *online experience*, 0.66 for *responsive service nature*, 0.85 for *trust* and 0.86 for *fulfilment* in the second sample; 0.90 for *emotional connection*, 0.90 for online experience, 0.75 for *responsive service nature*, 0.78 for trust and 0.77 for *fulfilment* in the first sample.

The content validity of the ORS brand equity scale is established using experts and consumers in the exploratory studies 1 and 2. All other validities are demonstrated in study 3 using the second half of the sample. The scale's criterion validity is assessed by correlating the ORS brand equity index to the overall brand equity measure. The two scales are correlated at 0.51 ($p < 0.01$). Convergent validity is confirmed, with results of AVE exceeding 0.5 for the five factors (0.71 for *emotional connection*, 0.63 for *online experience*, 0.50 for *responsive service nature*, 0.74 for *trust* and 0.76 for *fulfilment*).

The discriminant validity among the five dimensions of ORS brand equity is established with three tests. First, the AVE for each factor is higher than the squared pairwise correlations between factors, which range from 0.01 (*emotional connection* and *fulfilment*) to 0.46 (*emotional connection* and *responsive service nature*). Second, the pairwise correlations between all pairs of factors are significantly smaller than 1; this is tested by building a 95% confidence interval around each correlation. Third, the five-factor ORS brand equity model is compared to alternative measurement models with fewer factors, and χ^2 difference tests are conducted. The smallest χ^2 difference is 443.50 ($p < 0.001$), suggesting that treating the individual dimensions as distinct factors is superior to collapsing the dimensions.

The scale's construct validity is further assessed by examining the relationship between ORS brand equity and attitude toward the ORS brand, consistent image and purchase intention. The correlation of the ORS brand equity index with the constructs is significant at the 0.01 level (0.63 with attitudes toward the ORS brand, 0.35 with purchase intention and 0.45 with consistent image). Similarly, the correlation between individual ORS brand equity dimensions and the three constructs is consistent and significant.

Managerial applications

Brand equity becomes an integral component of marketing performance measurement. Nevertheless, the Internet environment has completely changed the ways in which brand equity is created online and managed by marketers. This ORS brand equity provides managers with a tool to track the development of the brand equity in an online environment. By assessing individual dimensions of ORS brand equity, marketers are able to identify areas of strength and weakness and focus their strategy on specific dimensions to reinforce their equity. The ORS brand equity scale can assist marketers in making decisions and managing their brand cross-channel.

11.7 Cross-national consumer-based brand equity (Buil, de Chernatony & Martinez, 2008)

Definition of construct

Although several scales have been developed in literature to measure consumer-based brand equity (CBBE), the researchers (Buil, de Chernatony & Martinez, 2008) highlight the need for improving the measurement of brand equity. Indeed, some of the existing scales include single-item measures for brand equity dimensions such as brand awareness, which represent a limitation in data analysis. Furthermore, most existing scales have been validated in one country only, whereas the researchers stress the importance of brand equity measures that are valid across cultures and that can be applied in more than one country. To develop their conceptualization of CBBE, the researchers draw on Aaker's framework (1991), which identifies *brand awareness, brand associations, perceived quality* and *loyalty* as the core dimensions of brand equity. *Brand awareness* refers to the ability of a consumer to recall and recognise the brand and to consumers' familiarity with the brand. *Perceived quality* corresponds to consumers' perception about the product's excellence. *Brand loyalty* refers to the tendency of consumers to be loyal to a given brand and is reflected in their intention to buy the brand. They expand brand associations and further articulate them in *perceived value, brand personality* and *organisational associations*. Their cross-national CBBE, therefore, consists of six dimensions, which are consistent in different countries.

Scale description

The cross-national CBBE scale includes six dimensions and 21 items. The *brand awareness* dimension is measured with five items which capture recall, recognition and familiarity with the brand. The *perceived quality* dimension is measured using four items. The *brand loyalty* dimension is assessed with three items. The dimensions of brand associations include *perceived value associations* (measured by three items), *brand personality associations* (two items) and *organisational associations* (three items). Each item is measured with a 7-point Likert-type scale where 1 = "strongly disagree" and 7 = "strongly agree".

TABLE 11.6 Cross-national consumer-based brand equity

Scale dimension	Scale item
Brand awareness	• I am aware of (brand X)
	• When I think of (product category Y), (brand X) is one of the brands that comes to mind
	• (Brand X) is a brand of (product category Y) I am very familiar with
	• I know what (brand X) looks like
	• I can recognise (brand X) amongst other competing brands of (product category Y)
Perceived quality	• (Brand X) offers very good quality products
	• (Brand X) offers products of consistent quality
	• (Brand X) offers very reliable products
	• (Brand X) offers products with excellent features

(Continued)

TABLE 11.6 (Continued)

Scale dimension	Scale item
Brand loyalty	• I consider myself to be loyal to (brand X) • (Brand X) would be my first choice when considering (product category Y) • I will not buy other brands of (product category Y) if (brand X) is available at the store
Brand associations – perceived value	• (Brand X) is good value for money • Within (product category Y), I consider (brand X) a good buy • Considering what I would pay for (brand X), I would get much more than my money's worth
Brand associations – brand personality	• (Brand X) has a personality • (Brand X) is interesting • I have a clear image of the type of person who would use (brand X)
Brand associations – organisational associations	• I trust the company which makes (brand X) • I like the company which makes (brand X) • The company which makes (brand X) has credibility

Scale development

The cross-national CBBE scale is developed through a data collection in the UK and Spain, two countries which present cultural differences according to Hofstede's (1984) framework. The questionnaire includes measures of brand awareness (derived from Netemeyer et al., 2004; Yoo, Donthu & Lee, 2000), perceived quality (derived from Pappu, Quester & Cooksey, 2005, 2006), brand loyalty (derived from Yoo, Donthu & Lee, 2000), perceived value (derived from Aaker, 1996a; Lassar, Mittal & Sharma, 1995; Netemeyer et al., 2004), brand personality (derived from Aaker, 1996a) and organizational associations (derived from Aaker, 1996a; Pappu, Quester & Cooksey, 2005, 2006). The product categories and brands in the questionnaire are selected using the "Best global brand ranking" of Interbrand. Two strong and mature brands are selected in four different categories (soft drinks, sportswear, consumer electronics and cars). Eight different versions of questionnaires are used in total (one per brand in both countries). The questionnaire is administered in English in the UK and in Spanish in Spain; a correct translation is ensured through a back-translation process.

Data analysis starts with an evaluation of the baseline model in each country. After assessing the reliability of the CBBE measures, an exploratory factor analysis using principal components analysis with varimax rotation is performed. Results indicate that the measures are reliable and that the corresponding items load on a single factor (the explained variance exceed 60 per cent in each case) except for the associations items, which load on more than one factor. The dimensionality of brand associations is further investigated in both countries. Different measurement models (one-, two- and three-dimensional) are estimated using CFA and are compared based on the S-B χ^2, other values of fit and their psychometric properties. Results indicate that brand associations are best represented by a three-dimensional model in both countries. The six-factor CBBE measurement model is then subjected to a confirmatory factor analysis in each sample using EQS 6.1. Results indicate adequate fit indices (UK: χ^2 = 407.49, df = 155, p < 0.001; NFI = 0.917, NNFI = 0.935, CFI = 0.947, IFI = 0.947, RMSEA = 0.064; Spain: χ^2 = 415.20, df = 155, p < 0.001; NFI = 0.888, NNFI = 0.909, CFI = 0.926, IFI = 0.927, RMSEA = 0.063). Reliability and validity analyses are conducted. Competing models are estimated, but their fit is not as good as the six-factor model. The final part of the analysis verifies the configural and metric invariance of the CBBE scale.

Samples

A non-student sample is collected in both the UK and Spain. The samples have similar size and demographic structure in each country and are composed of consumers selected using quota sampling by age and gender. Four hundred eleven valid questionnaires are collected in each country.

Reliability and validity

The convergent validity of each factor is verified based on factor loadings, which are significant with values above 0.5. Composite reliability (CR) and average variance extracted (AVE) indices are above 0.6 in the UK and Spain. Discriminant validity is also supported in both countries, as none of the confidence intervals around the correlation estimate between any two factors contains a value of 1.

To test for configural invariance, a multi-group analysis of the baseline models for the UK and Spain is conducted. The fit of the six-factor measurement model is acceptable (UK: S-B χ^2 = 407.49, df = 155, p = 0.000; NFI = 0.917, NNFI = 0.935, CFI = 0.947, IFI = 0.947, RMSEA = 0.064; Spain: S-B χ^2 = 415.20, df = 155, p = 0.000; NFI = 0.888, NNFI = 0.909, CFI = 0.926, IFI = 0.927, RMSEA = 0.063), indicating a consistent factor structure across the two countries. Metric invariance is tested by constraining the factor pattern coefficients to be equal across both countries. The results indicate that there is a non-significant increase in the S-B χ^2 between the unconstrained model S-B χ^2 = 822.83, df = 300, p = 0.000; NFI = 0.902, NNFI = 0.922, CFI = 0.936, IFI = 0.937, RMSEA = 0.064) and the constrained model (S-B χ^2 = 835.36, df = 324, p = 0.000; NFI = 0.901, NNFI = 0.925, CFI = 0.936, IFI = 0.937, RMSEA = 0.063) (delta S-B χ^2 = 13.26, delta df = 14, p > 0.05). These results suggest that metric invariance of the brand equity scale is supported across the two countries.

Managerial applications

In an international environment, marketers must manage their brands globally and need metrics which can be compared across countries. Given the fact that this consumer-based brand equity scale has been validated cross-nationally, managers can use the same scale to measure brand equity in each country. They can directly compare the results in order to build efficient international strategies and improve the global brand equity. Managers can also identify more clearly on which dimension to focus in order to improve the position of the brand in each country and also adapt the strategy locally if needed.

11.8 Employee-based brand equity (King, Grace & Funk, 2012)

Definition of construct

King, Grace and Funk (2012) examine brand equity from an employee perspective & define employee brand equity (EBE) as "the differential effect that brand knowledge has on an employee's response to internal brand management" (King, Grace & Funk 2012, p. 269). Internal brand management focuses on the role of the employee in delivery the promise of the brand. Therefore, EBE reflects employees' willingness to participate and contribute to brand success. EBE is conceptualized with three dimensions: *brand consistent behaviour, brand endorsement* and *brand allegiance*. The *brand consistent behaviour* dimension considers the coherence of employees' behaviours with the brand's values. The *brand endorsement* dimension refers to the extent to which an employee is willing to say positive things and recommend the organization (brand) to others. The *brand allegiance* dimension considers the desire of the employees to maintain their relationship with the organization and can be viewed as the future intention of employees to remain with the organization (brand).

Scale description

The EBE scale includes three dimensions and 11 items. The *brand endorsement* and *brand allegiance* dimensions are measured with four items each, whereas the *brand consistent behaviour* dimension is measured with three items. All items are presented as declarative statements enabling respondents to answer them on 7-point Likert scales, ranging from "strongly disagree" to "strongly agree".

TABLE 11.7 Employee brand equity scale

Scale dimension	Scale item
Brand endorsement	• I say positive things about the organisation (brand X) I work for to others • I would recommend the organisation (brand X) I work for to someone who seeks my advice • I enjoy talking about the organisation (brand X) I work for to others • I talk positively about the organisation (brand X) I work for to others

(Continued)

Brand equity 253

TABLE 11.7 (Continued)

Scale dimension	Scale item
Brand allegiance	• I plan to be with the organisation (brand X) I work for, for awhile • I plan to be with the organisation (brand X) I work for 5 years from now • I would turn down an offer from another organisation (brand X) if it came tomorrow • I plan to stay with the organisation (brand X) I work for
Brand consistent behaviour	• I demonstrate behaviours that are consistent with the brand promise of the organisation I work for • I consider the impact on my organisation's brand before communicating or taking action in any situation • I show extra initiative to ensure that my behaviour remains consistent with the brand promise of the organization I work for

Scale development

The scale-development process is guided by the work of Campbell and Fiske (1959), Churchill (1979) and DeVellis (2003) and is carried out over four phases.

Phase 1 consists of a literature search and in-depth interviews conducted with employees in service-based industries. The interviews reveal three dominant themes in EBE, which serve as guides for item generation. Items relating to *brand endorsement* are adapted from word-of-mouth scales, and those about *brand allegiance* are adapted from existing intention-to-stay scales. As *brand consistent behaviour* is a slightly new concept, items for this dimension are developed by the researchers. The resulting 20 items cover the three dimensions of EBE and are submitted to a panel of experts for refinement. These are asked to rate each item as either "not at all representative", "somewhat representative" or "clearly representative" of the conceptualized dimensions. All items are judged as clearly representative by the majority and are therefore retained. The qualitative feedback provided by the experts results in the rewording of some items and the development of three new ones.

Phase 2 consists of an exploratory phase for item purification. It is based on a quantitative data collection in which respondents are asked to rate the 23 EBE items on 7-point Likert scales. A principle components factor analysis using oblique rotation is performed and results in a six-factor solution that explains 71% of the variance. Item-to-total correlations are examined, and items with a correlation < 0.4 are considered for possible deletion, similarly to items with low loading (< 0.50) or high cross-loading (> 0.4). A new factor analysis is conducted and results in a three-factor solution, with 12 items explaining 73% of the variance.

Phase 3 involves a confirmatory phase to further purify the 12 items resulting from the previous phase. A survey is distributed to a broader sample of service employees. The three-factor EBE model is estimated using AMOS 17.0 with maximum likelihood estimation. Two confirmatory factor analyses are conducted. The first CFA leads to the deletion of one item, which exhibits a factor loading

< 0.50. The second CFA, run with 11 items, provides acceptable results: $\chi^2 = 87.71$, $df = 41$, $p = 0.00$, GFI = 0.95, NFI = 0.94, TLI = 0.95, CFI = 0.96 and RMSEA = 0.06. All factor loadings range from 0.69 to 0.87. The three-factor model is compared to alternative models, namely one-factor and two-factor ones, which perform worse (respectively, chi-square difference = 387.8 with 3 df and chi-square difference = 207.5 with 2 df). Reliability and validity analyses are conducted.

Phase 4 validates the EBE scale using a different sample of respondents (nonstudents). The questionnaire contains 11 EBE items, as well as eight items measuring role clarity and five items measuring brand commitment derived from King and Grace (2010). The three-factor, 11-item EBE model is estimated using AMOS 17.0 with maximum likelihood estimation. The fit for the measurement model is good with $\chi^2 = 122.2$, $df = 41$, $p = 0.00$, GFI = 0.95, NFI = 0.96, TLI = 0.97, CFI = 0.98 and RMSEA = 0.07. The parameter estimates and the accompanying t-test of significance for the relationships between each scale item and its intended construct are significant ($p < 0.01$). The standardized regression coefficients for each construct range from 0.68 to 0.92. Standardized residuals for each scale item do not exceed ±1.68, below the 2.57 ceiling.

Samples

The scale-development process involves four separate data collections and a total of 752 respondents based in Australia. Phase 1 is conducted with a sample of 22 service employees (management and front-line employees). The samples used for phases 2 and 3 are, respectively, composed of 86 and 273 university students who are currently employed in a service-related industry. The sample of phase 4 comprises 371 service employees obtained from a national database; the sample contains entry-level, middle-level and senior-level management respondents.

Reliability and validity

The internal consistency of the final EBE scale is tested in phases 3 and 4. Composite reliability is equal to 0.93 in both phases, whereas AVE is equal to 57.3% in phase 3 and to 75% in phase 4.

The content and face validities of EBE items are established by using in-depth interviews with service employees to generate items and an expert panel to judge the items.

The construct and convergent validities of the EBE scale are demonstrated in phase 3. Construct validity is established through the CFA, whereby the goodness-of-fit estimates for the measurement model are above the recommended levels (see earlier). Convergent validity is evaluated by the strength and significance of the loadings (t-values > 0.20), the AVE (> 0.50) and the construct reliability (> 0.70).

The discriminant validity between the three EBE factors of the EBE scale is established in phase 3, where chi-square difference tests between each pair of factors are conducted. Constrained and unconstrained models of each pair of factors are compared. Results show that the unconstrained models are significantly better than the constrained models (*brand endorsement/brand allegiance*: delta χ^2 = 5.9, 1 *df*; *brand endorsement/brand consistent behaviour*: delta χ^2 = 20.6, 1 *df*; *brand allegiance/brand consistent behaviour*: delta χ^2 = 47.7, 1 *df*).

Discriminant validity is tested again in phase 4, but this time between the EBE scale and the two related scales of role clarity and brand commitment. Both chi-square difference tests between EBE and, respectively, role clarity and brand commitment reveal that unconstrained models are significantly better than constrained models (EBE/role clarity: delta χ^2 = 15.8, 1 *df*; EBE/brand commitment: delta χ^2 = 87.2, 1 *df*), providing evidence of discriminant validity between these constructs.

The nomological validity of the EBE scale is established in phase 4 by examining the relationships among EBE, role clarity and brand commitment in a structural equations model. The results confirm the scale's nomological validity, as EBE is significantly influenced by role clarity (β = 0.23) and brand commitment (β = 0.79). The relationship between role clarity and brand commitment is also significant (β = 0.76). The R^2 obtained for EBE and brand commitment are significant at 0.96 and 0.59 respectively.

Managerial applications

By assessing brand equity from an employee perspective, this EBE scale provides managers an indication of employees' willingness to participate in and contribute to the brand's success. The EBE scale allows managers to assess the employees' pro-brand behaviour through three distinct dimensions: *brand endorsement, brand allegiance* and *brand consistent behaviour*. EBE is a valuable scale to evaluate the effectiveness of internal brand management activities and can enhance employee understanding of their important role as brand ambassadors in delivering the brand promise. The EBE scale can provide useful insight with respect to employees' behaviour prior to undertaking significant brand-related marketing actions, such as repositioning, to verify if the employee will be a good ambassador for the new brand strategy.

11.9 Academic focus

- One dissertation may want to connect employee brand equity (King, Grace & Funk, 2012) with one of the frameworks of consumer-based brand equity presented in the chapter. One may investigate to what extent overall employee brand equity and its specific dimensions affect overall consumer-based brand equity and its specific dimensions. Service brands should be taken into account in this dissertation, given the importance that employees have in this context. Online retailer brands (Christodoulides *et al.*, 2006) could be an example.
- Building brand equity in online environments is an emerging topic (Christodoulides *et al.*, 2006). One dissertation may investigate how different social media can be used by companies to build the equity of

their brands. Possible moderators such as consumer age and gender may be included in the analysis.
- Marketing communications can be used to build brand equity (Keller, 1998). A recent paper, for instance, shows how attending different types of branded events increases the equity of these brands through brand experiences and, to some extent, brand attitudes (Zarantonello & Schmitt, 2013). A dissertation may build on that paper and include other variables that may mediate the relationship between brand equity before attending an event and brand equity after attending an event. Otherwise, one may consider other types of communication tools instead of event marketing.
- One dissertation may focus on the link between overall brand image (see Chapter 1) or specific brand associations (see Chapter 2) and brand equity. In case, for instance, of a brand crisis, how does a negative brand image influence brand equity dimensions? Or how do negative brand associations influence brand equity dimensions? These are examples of questions the dissertation may try to answer.
- The performance of a brand in a market is also linked to the image of the company itself. According to Porter and Claycom (1997), a strong corporate brand image helps to achieve a competitive advantage and encourages repeat purchases, leading to higher levels of performance. One dissertation may investigate the impact of corporate brand image on brand equity.

11.10 Managerial focus

- **Do you really track your brand equity or do you only evaluate short-term indicators?**
  Brand equity is a strong influencer of critical business outcomes such as market share or sales. Nevertheless, measuring only short-term indicators such as willingness to pay premium price, awareness and market share provides only a partial vision of the brand performance. Nowadays, brand managers need brand equity measures which help them evaluate and track the long-term performance of the brand. By understanding the relationship between marketing-mix activities and brand equity (Yoo, Donthu & Lee, 2000), managers can distinguish brand-building activities from brand-harming activities and evaluate the efficacy of marketing programs over time. The scales which have been presented in this chapter allow marketing practitioners to track the performance of their brands and identify drivers of brand strength and sources of weaknesses in comparison to other brands. Therefore, with these measures, managers can prioritize their efforts, allocate their resources, optimize their

actions and evaluate the efficacy of brand-building programs in terms of return on investment from a long-term perspective.
- **Have you checked the equity of the different brands of your portfolio before deciding to replace one brand with another one?**
Nowadays, changing a brand name has become a frequent phenomenon. Several well-known examples of brand name change are Allegheny Airlines-US Air, Raider-Twix or Marathon-Snickers. More recently, Marie Thumas to Bonduelle, Bio to Activia, Champion to Carrefour Market. Nevertheless, changing a brand name represents a risky decision, which may alter the performance of the company (Pauwels-Delassus & Mogos Descotes, 2013). When an international brand manager wants to optimise the brand portfolio by replacing a small local brand with a global brand, the brand equity measure can be used to check the level of brand equity of each brand before the change. Indeed, if the local brand has a high level of brand equity or if the global brand is not strong enough in this particular country, the change should be conducted more progressively in order to manage successfully the brand substitution.
- **Does this new brand extension really increase your brand equity?**
In order to enhance brand equity, managers may decide to extend the brand to another category or to build an alliance with another brand. In general, marketing practitioners monitor the performance of the new brand extension or co-brand in order to check if it is successful. Nevertheless, it is also important to track the impact of these strategies on the parent brand and evaluate its return of investment. Tracking brand equity before and after the extension or the co-branding can provide useful insights to evaluate if these strategies increase the brand equity and verify if it does not impact negatively the parent brands.
- **Have you identified a relevant brand equity measure to track internationally the performance of your brand?**
In case of the management of an international brand portfolio, the consumer-based brand equity scales developed by Yoo and Donthu (2001) and Buil, de Chernatony and Martinez (2008) which have been validated cross-nationally could be useful tools to evaluate brand equity in each country in a consistent way, in order to compare the performance of the brand internationally. Using the same measure worldwide, managers can prioritize action plans and invest more in some country where the brand has a weaker position. They can also evaluate if it is needed to invest more on specific strategic dimensions in some countries in order to have the same level on these key dimensions worldwide.
- **Have you checked if your online channel increases your brand equity?**
The online retail/service brand equity (Christodoulides *et al.*, 2006) is an up-to-date scale which can be useful to check if the online channel

> enhances brand equity. Indeed, the online environment allows brands and consumers to have more interactions, which should enhance the relationship with the brand. Nevertheless, if consumers encounter difficulties searching for information and finding the right product or if they are disappointed regarding the delivery, the online channel may influence negatively the brand equity.

References

Aaker, D. A. (1991). *Managing brand equity*. New York, NY: Free Press.
Aaker, D. A. (1996a). Measuring brand equity across products and markets. *California Management Review*, 38 (3), 102–120.
Aaker, D. A. (1996b). *Building strong brands*. New York, NY: Free Press.
Agarwal, M. K., & Rao, V. (1996). An empirical comparison of consumer-based measures of brand equity. *Marketing Letters*, 7 (3), 237–247.
Bagozzi, R. P., Yi, Y., & Phillips, L. W. (1991). Assessing construct validity in organizational research. *Administrative Science Quarterly*, 36, 421–458.
Bauer, H. H., Sauer, N. E., & Schmitt, P. (2005). Customer-based brand equity in the team sport industry: Operationalization and impact on the economic success of sport teams. *European Journal of Marketing*, 39 (5/6), 496–722.
Bearden, W. O., & Netemeyer, R. G. (1998). Chapter one: introduction. In W. O. Bearden & R. G. Netemeyer (eds.), *Handbook of marketing scales* (2nd ed.). Thousand Oaks, CA: Sage, 1–14.
Bruner, G. C., II, James, K. E., & Hensel, P. J. (2001). *Marketing scale handbook*. Chicago, IL: American Marketing Association.
Buil, I., de Chernatony, L., & Martinez, E. (2008). A cross-national validation of the consumer-based brand equity scale. *Journal of Product and Brand Management*, 17 (6), 384–392.
Campbell, D. T., & Fiske, D. W. (1959). Convergent and discriminant validation by the multitrait-multimethod matrix. *Psychological Bulletin*, 56, 81–105.
Christodoulides, G., & de Chernatony, L. (2010). Consumer based brand equity conceptualization and measurement: a literature review. *International Journal of Market Research*, 52 (1), 43–66.
Christodoulides, G., de Chernatony, L., Furrer, O., Shiu, E., & Abimbola, T. (2006). Conceptualising and measuring the equity of online brands. *Journal of Marketing Management*, 22, 799–825.
Churchill, G. A., Jr. (1979). A paradigm for developing better measures of marketing constructs. *Journal of Marketing Research*, 16 (February), 64–73.
Cobb-Walgreen, K. J., Ruble, C. A., & Donthu, N. (1995). Brand equity, brand preference, and purchase intent. *Journal of Advertising*, 24 (Fall), 25–41.
Deng, S., & Dart, J. (1994). Measuring market orientation: a multi-factor, multi-item approach. *Journal of Marketing Management*, 10, 725–742.
DeVellis, R. F. (2003). *Scale development: theory and applications* (2nd ed.). Thousand Oaks, CA: Sage.
Farquhar, P. H. (1989). Managing brand equity. *Marketing Research*, 1 (September), 24–33.
Gerbing, D. W., & Anderson, J. C. (1998). An updated paradigm for scale development incorporating unidimensionality and its assessment. *Journal of Marketing Research*, 25 (2), 186–192.
Gladden, J., & Funk, D. (2001). Understanding brand loyalty in professional sport: examining the link between brand associations and brand loyalty. *International Journal of Sports Marketing and Sponsorship*, 3 (2), 67–94.

Graeff, T. R. (1997). Consumption situations and the effects of brand image on consumers' brand evaluations. *Psychology & Marketing*, 14 (1), 49–70.

Haynes, S. N., Nelson, K., & Blaine, D. (1999). Psychometric issues in assessment research. In P.C. Kendall, J.N. Butcher, & G. Holmbeck (eds.), *Handbook of research methods in clinical psychology*. New York, NY: Wiley, 125–154.

Hofstede, G. (1984). *Culture's consequences: international differences in work-related values*. Newbury Park, CA: Sage.

Hofstede, G. (1991). *Cultures and organizations: Software of the mind*. London: McGraw-Hill.

Keller, K. L. (1993). Conceptualizing, measuring and managing customer-based brand equity. *Journal of Marketing*, 57 (January), 1–22.

Keller, K. L. (1998). *Strategic brand management: building, measuring and managing brand equity*. Upper Saddle River, NJ: Prentice-Hall.

King, C., & Grace, D. (2010). Building and measuring employee-based brand equity. *European Journal of Marketing*, 44 (7/8), 938–971.

King, C., Grace, D., & Funk, D. C. (2012). Employee brand equity: scale development and validation. *Journal of Brand Management*, 19 (4), 268–288.

Kirmani, A., & Zeithmal, V. A. (1993). Advertising, perceived quality, and brand image. In D. A. Aaker & A. Biel (eds.), *Brand equity and advertising*. Hillsdale, NJ: Lawrence Erlbaum Associates, 143–161.

Lassar, W., Mittal, B., & Sharma, A. (1995). Measuring customer-based brand equity. *Journal of Consumer Marketing*, 12 (4), 11–19.

Loiacono, E. T., Watson, R. T., & Goodhue, D. L. (2002). WebQual: A measure of website quality. Winter Marketing Educators' Conference, Austin, TX, pp. 432–438.

Netemeyer, R.G., Krishnan, B., Pullig, C., Wang, G., Yagci, M., Dean, D., Ricks, J., & Wirth, F. (2004). Developing and validating measure of facets of customer-based brand equity. *Journal of Business Research*, 57 (2), 209–224.

Pappu, R., Quester, P.G., & Cooksey, R. W. (2005). Consumer-based brand equity: improving the measurement empirical evidence. *Journal of Product and Brand Management*, 14 (3), 143–154.

Pappu, R., Quester, P.G., & Cooksey, R. W. (2006). Consumer-based brand equity and country-of-origin relationships. *European Journal of Marketing*, 40 (5/6), 696–717.

Park, C.S., & Srinivasan, V. (1994). A survey-based method for measuring and understanding brand equity and its extendibility. *Journal of Marketing Research*, 31 (May), 271–288.

Pauwels-Delassus, V., & Mogos Descotes, R. (2013). Brand name change: Can trust and loyalty be transferred? *Journal of Brand Management*, 20, 656–669.

Porter, S.S., & Claycomb, C. (1997). The influence of brand recognition on retail store image. *Journal of Product and Brand Management*, 6, 373–384.

Srivastava, R. K., & Shocker, A. D. (1991). *Brand equity: a perspective on its meaning and measurement*. Marketing Science Institute, Report No. 91–124, Cambridge, MA.

Vázquez, R., del Río, A. B., & Iglesias, V. (2002). Consumer-based brand equity: development and validation of a measurement instrument. *Journal of Marketing Management*, 18, 27–48.

Yoo, B., & Donthu, N. (2001). Developing and validating a multidimensional consumer-based brand equity scale. *Journal of Business Research*, 52, 1–14.

Yoo, B., Donthu, N., & Lee, S. (2000). An examination of selected marketing mix elements and brand equity. *Journal of the Academy of Marketing Science*, 28 (2), 195–211.

Zarantonello, L., & Schmitt, B. (2013). The impact of event marketing on brand equity. *International Journal of Advertising*, 32 (2), 255–280.

Zeithaml, V. A. (1988). Consumer perceptions of price, quality, and value: a means-end model and synthesis of evidence. *Journal of Marketing*, 52 (July), 2–22.

12
CONSUMER DISPOSITIONS TOWARD BRANDS

12.1 Overview

In addition to scales assessing consumers' perceptions, responses and evaluations about specific brands described in the previous chapters, the marketing literature offers scales assessing consumers' dispositions toward brands. Consumers' dispositions toward brands are general tendencies, inclinations or propensities characterizing consumers in their approach toward brands in general. Consumers' dispositions toward brands do not vary across brands but vary across consumers. This means that these scales are not intended to be used to measure brand-specific aspects but dispositions to brands in general.

Among the five scales presented in this chapter, two of them, namely the brand dependence scale (Bristow, Schneider & Schuler, 2002) and the brand relevance in category (BRiC) scale (Fischer, Volckner & Sattler, 2010), focus on the role of the brand in purchase-decision situations. Specifically, the brand dependence scale (Bristow, Schneider & Schuler, 2002) refers to a consumers' tendency to use brand names when making purchase decisions. Similarly, the BRiC scale (Fischer, Volckner & Sattler, 2010) reflects the perceived importance that brands have in decision making compared to other criteria such as price.

The meanings of branded products scale (Strizhakova, Coulter & Price, 2008) relates to how consumers derive meanings from brands in general. The scale allows researchers to understand the tendency of consumers to use brand names to form their perceptions of quality of products, build their identities, express their personal values and keep traditions going. This scale is validated in cross-cultural contexts involving developing and developed countries and is intended to be used in such contexts. The application of this scale can clarify how consumers in a given country use branded products to build brand meaning.

Moving from the assumption that consumers may have a special connection with their favourite brands, as these brands reflect an important part of their identity, the brand engagement in self-concept (BESC) scale (Sprott, Czellar & Spangenberg, 2009) takes into account the relationship between brands and consumers' selves and reflects consumers' propensity to use brands to build their self-concepts. The scale allows researchers to understand the differences across consumers in terms of their tendency to construe their self-concept using their favourite brands.

Finally, the brand schematicity scale (Puligadda, Ross & Grewal, 2012), reflects the general importance that brands have for consumers and how consumers use brand-related information. Some consumers attribute great importance to brands, and they organize, interpret and retrieve consumption-related information at the brand-level, whereas other consumers do not pay attention to the brand and organize consumption-related information on other levels, such as the product. The brand schematicity scale allows researchers to understand how consumers approach brands under this angle.

12.2 Brand dependence (Bristow, Schneider & Schuler, 2002)

Definition of construct

Brand dependence refers to consumers' tendency to use (or "depend on") brand names when making purchase decisions. Brand dependence is defined as a tendency rather than an attitude, as it refers to consumer behaviour toward purchasing the product rather than consumer affect about the product itself.

Scale description

The brand dependence scale consists of seven items, which are measured on a 6-point Likert scale where 1 = "strongly disagree", 2 = "disagree", 3 = "slightly disagree", 4 = "slightly agree", 5 = "agree" and 6 = "strongly agree". Items can be summated to form an overall brand dependence score.

TABLE 12.1 Brand dependence scale

Scale item
• When it comes to buying (product category Y), I rely on brand names to help me choose among alternative products
• I would be more likely to purchase (product category Y) that had a well-known brand name
• Brand name would play a significant role in my decision of which (product category Y) to purchase
• When faced with deciding among two or more brands of (product category Y), I depend on the brand name of each product to help me make a choice
• If faced with choosing between two (product category Y) with similar features, I would select the better known brand name
• The brand name of (product category Y) is important to me when deciding which product to purchase
• Regardless of what features a competing brand of (product category Y) may offer, I would buy the brand of (product category Y) that I most trust

Scale development

The development process for the brand dependence scale includes two phases: the "domain specification and item generation" and the "scale purification".

In the "domain specification and item generation" phase, a set of seven items capturing consumers' dependence on brand names is generated through discussions among researchers and the involvement of students.

In the "scale purification" phase, a sample of respondents is asked to answer the scale on brand dependence and one on brand disparity (see box below), which is created by the researchers and included for validity purposes. Two product categories are selected for the questionnaire (blue jeans and personal computers) because of the likelihood that the respondents have made a purchase in these categories and have, therefore, experience and knowledge of evaluating the various brands available. Items from the two scales are factor analysed using principal component analysis with varimax rotation. Data analysis conducted without any constraint reveals two factors explaining 64.4% (blue jeans) and 65.2% (personal computers) of total variance. Brand dependence and brand disparity items load highly on their corresponding factor: loadings are included between 0.633 and 0.874 for brand dependence and from 0.574 to 0.872 for brand disparity. Reliability analyses and validity tests are finally performed.

Brand disparity

- There is really no difference among different brands of (product category Y)
- The primary difference between various brands of (product category Y) is price
- Regardless of brand name, most (product category Y) are the same
- I can't think of any major differences among the different brands of (product category Y)

Samples

The first phase, related to domain specification and item generation, is based on a sample of 40 college students. The second phase, aimed at scale purification, involves a sample of 208 college students, of whom 103 rate blue jeans and 105 rate personal computers.

Reliability and validity

The general face validity of the brand dependence scale is examined in the "domain specification and item generation" phase by administering the scale to a student sample.

Scale reliability and other types of validity are tested in the "item purification" phase. To check reliability, Cronbach's alpha is computed for the two product categories separately. The coefficient is equal to 0.91 for blue jeans and 0.92 for personal computers. Item-to-total correlations range from 0.550 to 0.826.

To provide evidence of convergent and discriminant validities, the researchers conduct an unconstrained exploratory factor analysis, which shows that brand dependence and brand disparity items load highly on their corresponding factor only. Construct validity is demonstrated by showing that brand dependence and brand disparity, which are two distinct but related constructs, are positively correlated to one another ($r = 0.203$ for blue jeans and $r = 0.210$ for computers, both $ps < 0.05$).

Managerial applications

The brand dependence scale can assist brand managers to examine the degree of consumers' dependence on brand names for product categories within their sphere of responsibility in order to better understand the specificity of these categories compared to others. The scale can also be used by brand managers as a segmenting variable to profile consumers: highly brand dependents versus non-dependent consumers of some product, who could then be described in socio-economic terms. Other suggested applications of the brand dependent scale include family branding, co-branding and global branding contexts, as well as cross-cultural country differences.

12.3 Meanings of branded products (Strizhakova, Coulter & Price, 2008)

Definition of construct

The concept of meanings of branded products refers to the meanings that consumers associate with branded products as a collective (rather than the meaning of an individual brand, such as Coca-Cola or Apple). Branded product meanings are derived by consumers from various sources, including advertising, third-party sources and personal experience. Branded product meanings cover seven dominant branded product meanings: quality, which corresponds to the quality signals provided by the branded products; self-identity, which refers to the idea of branded products as symbols of the self; group-identity, which considers the associations with other users or owners of the brand that are possible thanks to branded products; status, which refers to the price-related meanings that connote social class and condition; values, which evaluates the specific values associated by consumers with branded products which may influence their choice; family traditions, which refers to family usage/intergenerational influence of branded products; national traditions, which reflects ethnic national identification related to branded products.

Scale description

The meanings of branded products scale is composed of six first-order dimensions (*quality, self-identity, group-identity, status, values* and *traditions*) and 32 items. *Quality* is measured by five items. *Self-identity, group-identity* and *status* are measured by five indicators each and are grouped into the second-order dimension called "personal identity". *Traditions* covers aspects of family traditions (five items) and national traditions (four items) items. *Values* is measured by three items. Each item is evaluated on a 7-point Likert scale (1 = "strongly disagree"; 7 = "strongly agree"). Item scores within a dimension can be summed and averaged to form a dimension mean score.

TABLE 12.2 Meanings of branded products scale

Scale second-order dimension	Scale first-order dimension	Scale item
–	Quality	• A brand name is an important source of information about the durability and reliability of the product • I can tell a lot about a product's quality from the brand name • I use brand names as a sign of quality for purchasing products • I choose brands because of the quality they represent • A brand name tells me a great deal about the quality of a product
Personal identity	Self-identity	• I choose brands that help to express my identity to others • The brands I use communicate important information about the type of person I am • I use different brands to express different aspects of my personality • I choose brands that bring out my personality • My choice of a brand says something about me as a person
	Group identity	• Using brands can help me connect with other people and social groups • I buy brands to be able to associate with specific people and groups • I feel a bond with people who use the same brands as I do • By choosing certain brands, I choose who I want to associate with • My choice of a brand says something about the people I like to associate with
	Status	• I avoid choosing brands that do not reflect my social status* • I use brands to communicate my social status • I choose brands that are associated with the social class I belong to • The brands I use reflect my social status • I communicate my achievements through the brands I own and use

(*Continued*)

TABLE 12.2 (Continued)

Scale second-order dimension	Scale first-order dimension	Scale item
–	Values	• I choose brands because I support the values they stand for • I buy brands that are consistent with my values • My choice of brand is based on the company's values
–	Traditions	• I buy brands because they are an important tradition in my household[a] • I use brands that my family uses or have used[a] • I use brands that remind me of my family[a] • I buy brands in order to continue family traditions[a] • I buy brands that my parents buy/have bought[a] • I use brands that reflect my national heritage[b] • I prefer brands associated with my national heritage[b] • I avoid brands because they do not fit with my national heritage[b] • I choose brands because they are part of national traditions[b]

Note: [a]indicates an item that describes family traditions, whereas [b]indicates an item that describes national traditions.

Scale development

The meanings of branded products scale is developed using an adapted etic approach (Burgess & Steenkamp, 2006; Douglas & Craig, 2006) in order to validate the scale across multiple countries.

The scale development starts with item generation and refinement. Twenty-four exploratory interviews are conducted in the United States, Ukraine and Romania in order to understand the range of meanings of branded products across countries and to identify words and phrases to be used to develop equivalent measures of branded product meaning across countries. The protocol of the interview is translated consistently across English, Russian and Romanian languages. Informants are invited to discuss their favourite brands in different product categories in an open way in order to allow various branded product meanings to emerge; they are later prompted about specific meanings identified in the literature. These interviews result in the generation of 56 items covering quality, self-identity, group-identity, status, personal values, family traditions and national traditions.

A pre-test in the United States is conducted next, where responded are asked to assess each of the 56 items. A principal component analysis (PCA) is conducted for each set of branded product meanings. A new PCA is then conducted on the five items with the highest loadings from the initial PCA. The percent of variance explained in the PCAs range from 59% (national traditions) to 79% (status). Reliability analysis is finally conducted for the five items associated with each of the seven dimensions.

The following part of the scale-development process consists in a data collection in the United States, Romania, Ukraine and Russia. The researchers use standard translation practices to translate and back-translate the questionnaire into Russian (for the Russian and Ukrainian samples) and Romanian. The questionnaire included the 35 branded product meanings scale items, questions about awareness, use of specific brand-name products and demographic questions. A clarification of the product–brand distinction is provided at the beginning of the survey with an information sheet presenting definitions of product/brand terms and examples.

In data analysis, a multi-group confirmatory factor analysis (CFA) is conducted using AMOS 7.0 with the seven derived latent factors. The results indicate an acceptable fit of the model for multi-country samples (χ^2/df ratio = 3.14, CFI = 0.84, TLI = 0.83, RMSEA < 0.03, Hoelter = 843 at p = 0.05). Considering the correlations among *self-identity*, *group-identity* and *status* (0.82–0.93 range) and the correlations between family traditions and national traditions (0.72–0.98 range), a four-factor model is examined. The four factors are *quality, values, traditions* (comprising items on family and national traditions) and personal identity as a second-order construct consisting of *self-identity, group-identity* and *status* dimensions. This four-factor model has a fit similar to that of the previous model (χ^2/df ratio = 3.05, CFI = 0.84, TLI = 0.83, RMSEA < 0.03, Hoelter = 845 at p = 0.05). After examining the modification indices and identifying items with possible sources of co-variation, three items are dropped. The re-specified four-factor model with 32 items reports an acceptable fit (χ^2/df ratio = 2.56, CFI = 0.90, TLI = 0.89, RMSEA < 0.03, Hoelter = 1036 at p = 0.05). Multi-group CFAs are then performed to assess cross-national configural, metric and scalar invariance.

Comparisons of latent factor means for branded product meanings by country and z-tests are finally carried out. *Quality* is identified as the significantly (p < 0.001) most important branded product meaning in both developed and developing markets (M_{US} = 5.54, M_{UA} = 4.96, M_{RU} = 4.84, M_{RO} = 5.60). Identity-related meanings are significantly (p < 0.001) stronger in developed countries (M_{US} = 3.60) than in developing countries (M_{UA} = 3.22, M_{RU} = 3.15, M_{RO} = 3.13). *Values* meanings are significantly more important (p < 0.001) in Romania (M_{RO} = 4.47) than in Ukraine (M_{UA} = 4.11), the United States (M_{US} = 3.86) and Russia (M_{RU} = 3.71). Furthermore, *traditions* meanings are significantly lower (p < 0.001) than the other meanings in each country (M_{US} = 3.08, M_{UA} = 2.66 M_{RO} = 2.48, M_{RU} = 2.23).

Samples

Participants in the studies are young adults aged from 18 to 29 years to ensure that study participants in the developing countries of Ukraine, Romania and Russia are familiar with the concept of branded products. Qualitative interviews are conducted with 24 informants (eight informants per each of the three countries:

United States, Ukraine and Romania). The pre-test is taken by 120 undergraduate consumer behaviour students in the United States. A sample of 1,261 university students participate in the survey: 218 in the United States, 287 in Romania, 464 in Ukraine and 292 in Russia.

Reliability and validity

The cross-national invariance, reliability and discriminant validity of the meaning of branded products scale are tested using data from the survey.

The scale's invariance is established through tests of configural invariance, metric invariance and scalar invariance. The configural invariance is verified by multiple criteria: the acceptable fit of the CFA measurement model (see p. 266); the factor loadings, which are all significantly different from zero in each country; and the discriminant validity of the constructs, which is verified through the correlations between them. These correlations range from 0.10 to 0.61 in the United States, from 0.22 to 0.67 in Romania, from −0.02 to 0.57 in Ukraine, from −0.03 to 0.67 in Russia and from 0.05 to 0.57 in the pooled data. Coefficient alpha estimates of reliability range from 0.78 to 0.94 in the United States, from 0.78 to 0.92 in Romania, from 0.65 to 0.89 in Ukraine, from 0.66 to 0.91 in Russia and from 0.72 to 0.91 in the pooled data. These results confirm configural invariance.

Measurement metric invariance is assessed by constraining each factor loading to be equal across countries and by comparing the fit of the equal-factor model with that of the unconstrained model. The analysis indicates that 29 items are metrically invariant. The CFA for the measurement model with 29 invariant loadings reports a good fit (χ^2/df ratio = 2.53, CFI = 0.90, TLI = 0.89, RMSEA < 0.03, Hoelter = 1047 at p = 0.05). Although the chi-square difference between this model and the unconstrained one is significant (delta χ^2 with 92 df = 168.44, p < 0.001), fit indexes are almost identical to those for the configural model, thus establishing partial measurement metric invariance. Structural metric invariance is then assessed by fixing the loadings of the latent factors of *self-identity*, *group-identity* and *status* on the second-order factor of personal identity to be equal across countries. The CFA reports a good fit (χ^2/df ratio = 2.58, CFI = 0.89, TLI = 0.89, RMSEA < 0.03, Hoelter = 1027 at p = 0.05), and no significant change in the fit indexes compared to the configural model (delta $\chi^2(112)$ = 335.75, delta CFI = −0.01, identical TLI and RMSEA).

Scalar invariance is finally tested for metrically invariant items. After setting the intercepts to be equal across samples, the analyses indicate that 22 of the 29 metrically invariant loadings exhibit scalar invariance. CFA results for the model with 22 and 29 items that exhibit scalar and metric invariance, respectively, and three latent factors that exhibit metric and scalar invariance show a good fit (χ^2/df ratio = 2.58, CFI = 0.89, TLI = 0.89, RMSEA < 0.03, Hoelter = 1025 at p = 0.05) and a slight deterioration in fit parameters from the configural model (delta $\chi^2(200)$ = 567.03; delta CFI = −0.01, identical TLI and RMSEA).

Managerial applications

The meanings of branded products scale is particularly relevant in cross-cultural contexts including both developed and developing countries. The application of this scale provides global marketing managers with indications about how consumers in a given country attribute meanings to branded products. If included in longitudinal data collections, the scale can also provide information about the evolution of branded product meanings with evolving consumer culture (especially for developing countries). Global marketing managers interested in launching their brands or products in new markets can use the scale to understand the relative importance of each branded product meaning and adapt marketing and communication strategies consistently.

12.4 Brand engagement in self-concept (Sprott, Czellar & Spangenberg, 2009)

Definition of construct

Brand engagement in self-concept (BESC) is defined as "an individual difference representing consumers' propensity to include important brands as part of how they view themselves" (Sprott, Czellar & Spangenberg, 2009, p. 92). BESC is not about the connection between consumers and a specific brand but describes a general tendency of consumers to construe their self-concept using their favourite brands.

Scale description

The (BESC) scale includes eight items. Items are measured on a 7-point Likert scale anchored by 1 ("strongly disagree") and 7 ("strongly agree"). Items can be summated to form an overall BESC score.

TABLE 12.3 Brand engagement in self-concept scale

Scale item
• I have a special bond with the brands that I like
• I consider my favourite brands to be a part of myself
• I often feel a personal connection between my brands and me
• Part of me is defined by important brands in my life
• I feel as if I have a close personal connection with the brands I most prefer
• I can identify with important brands in my life
• There are links between the brands that I prefer and how I view myself
• My favourite brands are an important indication of who I am

Scale development

The process to develop and validate the BESC scale follows standard procedures (Nunnally & Bernstein, 1994) and is articulated in three parts: scale development, nomological validity and five validation studies.

In the scale development, items are generated through a review of the literature on branding and self-concept. This initial set of 36 items is brought to 32 items after a screen by a pool of scholars. A study is conducted to further reduce the set of items. Factor analysis resulted in a final BESC scale consisting of eight items.

Four data collections are then conducted to test the scale's nomological validity with respect to relational-interdependent self-construal (RISC; Cross, Bacon & Morris, 2000); independent and interdependent self-construal (Singelis, 1994); collective self-esteem (Luhtanen & Crocker, 1992); self-concept clarity (Campbell et al., 1996); self-esteem (Rosenberg, 1965); satisfaction with life (Diener et al., 1985); material values (Richins, 2004); self-deception and impression management (Paulhus, 1998); and the interpersonal Bem sex-role inventory (Brems & Johnson, 1990).

Five validation studies are conducted to show how BESC affects consumer behaviour.

Study 1 is about BESC and self–brand associations in consumer memory. Using the IAT (implicit associations test) including the most/least favourite brands entered by each participant, the study uses correlation analysis and demonstrates that higher levels of BESC are associated with stronger brand associations in memory ($r = 0.30$, $p < 0.01$).

Study 2 deals with BESC and brand possessions in consumer pantries. Participants are asked to think about their personal belongings in the campus room and to write down the brand names of those items. Correlation analysis indicates that BESC is positively associated with recall of brand names associated with material possessions ($r = 0.35$, $p < 0.01$).

Study 3 looks at BESC, incidental brand exposure and recall. Participants are shown pictures featuring people in casual outfits displaying brand names and logos and are asked about their first impressions, overall attitudes and brand names recalled. Through correlation analysis, this study provides evidence that higher levels of BESC are associated with more brand names recalled ($r = 0.43$, $p < 0.01$).

Study 4 examines BESC and attitudes toward overtly branded products. Participants are randomly assigned to two conditions (brand visibility: brand logo presence versus absence for two clothing products). After viewing pictures, participants are asked about their product and brand attitudes. Regression analysis using product attitudes as dependent variable and BESC, brand attitude and brand visibility and their interactions as independent variables shows that, if brand attitudes are positive and the brand is visible, higher levels of BESC are associated with more favourable product attitudes (BESC × brand attitudes × brand visibility is significant at $p < 0.05$ for two different brands).

Study 5 deals with BESC and patterns of brand loyalty, namely price (study 5a) and time (study 5b) insensitivity. In study 5a, participants are randomly assigned to two pricing conditions (high-priced versus low-priced new product) and are asked to complete the same product attitudes scale used in study 4 and to answer one question on purchase intention. Regression analysis using BESC, price and their interaction as independent variables and product attitudes and purchase intention as dependent variable shows that higher levels of BESC are associated with more favourable product attitudes and purchase intentions for highly priced products (BESC × price is significant at $p < 0.01$ with product attitudes and at $p < 0.05$ with purchase intention).

In study 5b, participants are assigned to one of three conditions related to waiting time of their favourite brand (one versus three versus six months) and asked about their willingness to wait for the brand to market a new product rather than buying a competitor's. Regression analysis using willingness to wait for the favourite brand as dependent variable and BESC, waiting time and their interaction as independent variable shows that higher levels of BESC are associated with greater willingness to wait for the favourite brands for the three-month and six-month conditions (BESC × time conditions is significant at $p < 0.05$).

Samples

The scale development uses nine scholars and 430 undergraduate students. Nomological validity is demonstrated through four data collections of, respectively, 279, 199, 107 and 398 undergraduate students. Study 1 is based on a sample of 106 undergraduate students. Study 2 is based on a sample of 56 students. Study 3 is based on a sample of 42 students. Study 4 is based on a sample of 153 undergraduate students. Study 5a uses 62 participants, whereas study 5b uses 126 undergraduate students.

Reliability and validity

Evidence of the BESC scale reliability is provided throughout several of the conducted studies. Cronbach's alpha is computed to indicate the scale's internal consistency. It reports scores of 0.94 (scale development), 0.93 (study 1), 0.92 (studies 3 and 4), 0.91 (study 5a) and 0.93 (study 5b). Intertemporal reliability ranges from 0.62 to 0.78 (scale development).

The scale's discriminant validity is demonstrated in the nomological validity portion of the paper. The correlation between BESC and other measures is non-significant, apart from RISC ($r = 0.15$, $p < 0.01$) and material values ($r = 0.42$, $p < 0.05$). Because of the high correlation between BESC and material values, a confirmatory factor analysis is conducted and indicates that BESC and materialism are distinct constructs. Further evidence of discriminant validity is provided in study 2. Although BESC and the material value scale are correlated ($r = 0.35$, $p < 0.01$), BESC is predictive of the number of brands possessed beyond the effect attributable to material values: materialism is not significantly correlated with the number of brands possessed ($p = 0.28$), and the correlation between BESC and the number of brands possessed is significant after controlling for material values ($r = 0.36$, $p < 0.01$).

The predictive validity of the scale is demonstrated in studies 1 to 5. BESC is shown to be positively related with IAT scores (study 1), number of brands possessed (study 2) and brand names recalled (study 3); product attitudes if brand attitudes are positive and the brand is visible (study 4); product attitudes and purchase intention for highly priced products (study 5a); willingness to wait for the favourite brand (study 5b).

Managerial applications

The applications of the BESC scale suggested by the authors address the company's brand as well as the competitors'. The BESC scale can be used in addition to other criteria to further investigate the brand's current target segments so that the company can achieve a better understanding of its consumers and adapt communication strategies accordingly. For segments of consumers with high levels of BESC, managers should also consider how these consumers build connections not only with their own brand but also with competing brands. Managers should actively consider how to incorporate their brands in high–BESC consumers' self-concept and how to inhibit competing brands from building such connections.

12.5 Brand relevance in category (Fischer, Völckner & Sattler, 2010)

Definition of construct

Brand relevance in category (BRiC) is a consumer-oriented construct which measures the perceived overall influence of brands on consumer decision making in a given product category. This role that brands have is relative, as consumers may take into account other criteria than the brand (for example, the price) when making their purchasing decision. BRiC is also defined at the product category level, not the brand level: this means that it does not vary across brands, but it varies across product categories. Important antecedents of BRiC, at the consumer level, include two brand functions: *risk reduction*, which refers to the contribution of the brand in reducing the consumer subjective risk of making a purchase mistake (functional benefit) and *social demonstrance*, which refers to the use that consumers make of brands to project their self-image (symbolic function).

Scale description

Fischer, Völckner and Sattler (2010) develop a scale for the BRiC construct itself and its antecedents, that is, *risk reduction* and *social demonstrance*. Each construct includes 4 items, for a total of 12 items. Given that the BRiC metric is defined at the category level, items refer to all brands in a specific product category. Items are evaluated using a 7-point Likert scale with 1 = "strongly disagree" and 7 = "strongly agree" as anchors.

TABLE 12.4 Brand relevance in category and antecedents scales

Construct	Item
Brand relevance in category	• When I purchase a product in the given category, the brand plays – compared to other things – an important role • When purchasing, I focus mainly on the brand • To me, it is important to purchase a brand-name product • The brand plays a significant role as to how satisfied I am with the product

(Continued)

TABLE 12.4 (Continued)

Construct	Item
Antecedent: Risk reduction function	• I purchase mainly brand-name products because that reduces the risk of aggravation later • I purchase brand-name products because I know that I get good quality • I choose brand-name products to avoid disappointments • I purchase brand-name products because I know that the performance promised is worth its money
Antecedent: Social demonstrance function	• To me, the brand is indeed important because I believe that other people judge me on the basis of it • I purchase particular brands because I know that other people notice them • I purchase particular brands because I have much in common with other buyers of that brand • I pay attention to the brand because its buyers are just like me

Scale development

To develop the scales on BRiC and its antecedents, the researchers start with a literature review and a pre-test consisting of a focus group with scholars and practitioners for comprehension, logic and relevance of the items. Based on their feedback, the items are modified and are submitted to a panel of academic experts for face and content validity. This check results in a set of 19 items.

A first data collection is conducted in order to purify the scales. Based on confirmatory factor analysis and Cronbach's alpha, items with a reliability score or item-to-total correlation below 0.40 are discarded. Items with lowest contribution to coefficient alpha are also discarded, leaving four items per construct.

A second data collection is conducted in five countries (France, Japan, Spain, UK and the United States) in order to establish the generalizability of the scale and to assess its validity. Twenty product categories covering fast-moving consumer goods (FMCG), consumer durable, services and retailers are included, and a uniform data collection procedure is used (online survey). Items included in the survey are translated through a translation and back-translation procedure. In addition to the BRiC scale, other measures are included in the questionnaire for validity purposes: constant-sum brand importance weight (adapted from Fischer, 2007), willingness to pay a premium price (one-item measure: "I prefer to purchase a brand-name product, even if that means paying an additional price"), brand loyalty (Ailawadi, Neslin & Gedenk, 2001), brand awareness (one-item measure: "I know many brands in the category in question"), brand uniqueness and brand clarity (both adapted from Keller, 1993) and brand likability (Mitchell, 1986). Data from external sources are also collected in order to complement the analyses of validity: conjoint brand importance weight, which is derived from published conjoint studies that include brand as an attribute; advertising expenditure data, which are provided by the COMPUSTAT database; brand equity in the category data, which is taken from the Interbrand website; and U.S. consumer satisfaction index, which is obtained through the ACI reports annual data.

Using a multi-group latent variable modelling approach, a structural equation model (SEM) that links BRiC with brand functions is estimated. The data fit the model well (RMSEA = 0.0355, CFI = 0.988, TLI = 0.983). All factor loadings are significant (t-values > 0.40) and are strongly related to their corresponding construct; also, the two brand functions explain 71.4% of the total variance in BRiC. The scales' reliability, cross-national equivalence and validities are demonstrated. It is also shown that BRiC and its two antecedents significantly vary across product categories, countries and types of good and that gender and age are important moderators of the influence of brand functions on BRiC.

A replication study is conducted in three countries (France, UK and the United States) after two and a half years. Each respondent is asked to provide answers for two product categories randomly chosen from 20 categories. The fit indexes indicate that the multi-group SEM fits the data well (RMSEA = 0.049, CFI = 0.987, TLI = 0.982).

Samples

The pre-test, which consists of a focus group, involves three academics and three practitioners; the expert panel includes three brand management academics. The first data collection uses a sample of 578 graduate students. In the second data collection, 6,168 questionnaires are collected (about 1,200 in each of the five countries), but 399 questionnaires are eliminated because of either a standard deviation < 0.2 or completing time < 6 minutes. The replication study uses a sample of 700 consumers in each country.

Reliability and validity

The reliability of BRiC and its antecedents (i.e., *risk reduction* and *social demonstrance* functions) is checked using data from the second data collection and from the replication study. The internal consistency of the three constructs is demonstrated through multiple criteria: individual item reliabilities range from 0.553 to 0.784 in the pooled dataset (five countries), the average variance extracted (AVE) estimates range from 0.405 to 0.508, composite reliabilities range from 0.731 to 0.805 and coefficients alpha from 0.900 to 0.928. The BRiC stability over time is demonstrated in the replication study. Data are correlated with those from the second data collection across the three countries and exhibit a correlation of 0.938 ($p < 0.05$; $N = 60$).

The validity of BRiC and its antecedents is demonstrated using data from the second data collection.

A test of discriminant validity for the two BRiC antecedents is conducted. Each of the shared variance estimates at the country level and the pooled sample level (0.508 and 0.475 in the pooled sample) exceeds the square root of the corresponding phi coefficient (0.201).

The cross-national equivalence is established with regard to configural, metric and scalar invariance across the three constructs. To demonstrate configural invariance, it is checked that all factor loadings are statistically significant in the five-country samples and exhibit a similar pattern of loadings. Partial metric and scalar invariance for the data are proved by comparing common information criteria and fit indexes. Both information criteria (delta Bayesian information criterion = −41.10; delta consistent Akaike information criterion = −41.10) and fit indexes ($RMSEA_{free}$ = 0.036, $RMSEA_{restricted}$ = 0.035, TLI_{free} = 0.983, $TLI_{restricted}$ = 0.983) do not change or even improve when invariance restrictions are imposed.

The construct validity of BRiC is assessed using both surveyed measures and external data. Evidence of convergent validity is given by showing that the correlations between BRiC and constant-sum brand importance weight and conjoint brand importance weight are high and significant: respectively, 0.567 and 0.540 ($ps < 0.05$). Nomological validity is demonstrated by showing the positive and significant correlations between BRiC and, respectively, willingness to pay a premium price (correlation = 0.655, $p < 0.05$), brand loyalty (correlation = 0.781, $p < 0.05$), advertising expenditures (correlation = 0.417, $p < 0.10$) and brand equity in the category (correlation = 0.521, $p < 0.10$).

Discriminant validity is tested with regard to multi-item measures (brand uniqueness, brand clarity, brand likability), single-item measures (brand awareness and consideration set size) and a measure taken from an external source (U.S. consumer satisfaction index). For multi-item measures, proof of discriminant validity is given by showing that the AVE of each construct ($AVE_{brand\ uniqueness}$ = 0.444, $AVE_{brand\ clarity}$ = 0.496, $AVE_{brand\ likability}$ = 0.614) exceeds the squared correlation of each construct with BRiC (equal to 0.304, 0.191 and 0.119 for brand uniqueness, brand clarity and brand likability, respectively; $ps < 0.10$). Squared correlations with BRiC are low for single-item measures (equal to 0.151 and −0.002 for brand awareness and consideration set size, respectively; $ps < 0.10$) and non-significant for the external derived measure of U.S. customer satisfaction index ($p > 0.10$).

Managerial applications

The BRiC scale allows managers to determine the relevance of the brand in a given product category (BRiC scale). The scale can be used, in addition to managerial expertise, to revise budget allocation decisions as well as to evaluate new categories of consumer segments in advance. Managers need to understand how to react to differences in BRiC across product categories and/or countries. In higher-BRiC markets, for example, brand expenditures tend to be higher, as the brand is a key driver in consumers' decision making. In these markets, therefore, managers should ensure enough resources for the brand; otherwise they may have to deal with lower market shares and lower profits.

12.6 Brand schematicity (Puligadda, Ross & Grewal, 2012)

Definition of construct

Brand schematicity is defined as a generalized consumer propensity or predisposition toward brands as a representation of consumers' information processing approach. As such, brand schematicity is not a consumer inclination toward a specific brand. Brand schematicity can vary across different consumers. Consumers with high brand schematicity, or "brand schematic consumers", attend to, organize, interpret and use information at the level of a brand node (Keller, 1998). They give importance to the brand and structure brand-related information around this node. Consumers with low brand schematicity or "brand aschematic" consumers do not pay attention to the brand and organize information at other levels (e.g., product attribute).

Scale description

The brand schematicity scale contains 10 items, 4 of which are reverse coded. Responses have to be coded on a 9-point scale anchored at 1 = "disagree completely" and 9 = "agree completely". Respondents' scores on the 10 items can be summated and averaged in order to obtain a composite score of brand schematicity.

TABLE 12.5 Brand schematicity scale

Scale item
• I couldn't care less what brands people around me are using*
• Product features are more important than brand names in my buying decisions*
• When I go shopping, I am always scanning the environment for brand names
• Brands are not at all important to me*
• Brand name considerably influences my buying decisions
• I like to surround myself with recognizable brand names at home
• When I am considering products, the brand name is more important to me than any other information
• Brands are important to me because they indicate social status
• The brand name is the least important information to me when I am considering a product*
• I keep abreast of the brands people around me are using

Note: *indicates the item is reverse coded.

Scale development

The brand schematicity scale is developed and validated through seven studies. Studies 1 and 2 develop the brand schematicity scale. In study 1, a set of 14 scale items is generated based on literature and exploratory qualitative research (two focus groups and 10 in-depth interviews). A first quantitative data collection is then conducted. Based on a first exploratory factor analysis (EFA; principal component with direct oblimin rotation), three items with high cross-loadings are removed. A new EFA reveals one factor with eigenvalue greater than 1.0 that explains 53% of total variance; corrected item-to-total correlations are greater than 0.50, and inter-item correlations are satisfactory. A confirmatory factor analysis (CFA) is performed on the retained items specifying one factor ($\chi^2(44)$ = 174.28, RMSEA = 0.09, NFI = 0.95, NNFI = 0.95 and CFI = 0.96). After removing one item because of poor loading, a new CFA shows an improved fit ($\chi^2(35)$ = 131.75, RMSEA = 0.09, NFI = 0.96, NNFI = 0.96 and CFI = 0.97) and item loadings greater than 0.55. Reliability tests are conducted.

The resulting 10-item brand schematicity scale is administered in study 2, together with a single-item brand schematicity scale ("I think I am very brand centric") for convergent validity purposes. An EFA reveals one factor with eigenvalue greater than 1.00 explaining 52% of total variance; corrected item-to-total correlations are greater than 0.50, and inter-item correlations are satisfactory. A CFA shows a satisfactory fit ($\chi^2(35)$ = 104.71, RMSEA = 0.10, NFI = 0.94, NNFI = 0.94 and CFI = 0.96). Loadings from completely standardized solutions are greater than 0.50. Reliability and convergent validity are demonstrated.

Study 3 validates the brand schematicity scale using response time. Participants complete two tasks in counterbalanced order: in one, they are asked to respond to the brand schematicity scale; in the other one, they are shown 10 brand logos from different product categories and are asked to type the related brand name. In addition to response time, errors made are recoded. Convergent validity is established in the analysis.

Study 4 relates brand schematicity with correlated constructs, using four different samples. In addition to brand schematicity, participants are asked about self-esteem (Rosenberg, 1965), susceptibility to normative influence (SNI; Bearden, Netemeyer & Teel, 1989) (sample 1); need for cognition (Cacioppo, Petty & Kao, 1984) (sample 2); materialism (Richins & Dawson, 1992) and social comparison orientation (Gibbons & Buunk, 1999) (sample 3); need to evaluate (Jarvis & Petty, 1996), concern for appropriateness (Lennox & Wolfe, 1984) and brand engagement in self-concept (Sprott, Czellar & Spangenberg, 2009; see this chapter, pp. 268–271) (sample 4). Correlations between constructs are computed: brand schematicity correlates significantly with SNI (r = 0.45, p < 0.01), NFC (r = –0.32, p < 0.01), materialism (r = 0.59, p < 0.01) and concern for appropriateness (r = 0.32, p < 0.01). Discriminant validity tests are conducted.

Studies 5 and 6 test the predictive validity of the brand schematicity scale with respect to brand extension evaluations. Study 5 is modelled after Park, Milberg and Lawson (1991). It uses a 2 (brand schematicity: low versus high) × 2 (brand: Timex versus Rolex) ×2 (brand concept consistency: low versus high) ×2 (product feature similarity: low versus high) mixed design, where the former two factors are between subjects and the latter two factors are within subjects. Each participant evaluates 4 out of 12 products as possible extensions of the assigned brand. A pre-test supports that the original brand concepts are still contemporaneous and that the 12 extension products prompt functions or prestige perceptions. Participants' brand extension evaluations are recoded on a three-item scale. Analyses of covariance (ANCOVA) are conducted to show the predictive validity of the brand schematicity scale.

Study 6 uses response time as a measure of brand schematicity to ensure that responding to the brand schematicity scale does not increase brand-related thoughts. Similar to study 3, participants complete the 10 response-time items measuring brand schematicity and, similar to study 5, a computer version of the brand extension evaluation task employing a binary scale for each item (left key = unfavourable, right key = favourable). Differently from study 5, this study employs one brand and manipulates only brand concept consistency, with high product similarity for all conditions. Each respondent evaluates three products as possible extensions of the Rolex brand. ANCOVAs are performed to show the predictive validity of response time as an indicator of brand schematicity.

Study 7 establishes the schematic nature of brand schematicity by examining memory structures using a card-sort method. Participants are given 16 cards, each displaying a unique combination of four attributes (i.e., brand, flavour, price and size) of snack chips. Participants are asked to sort the cards according to their preference, complete the brand schematicity scale and write their thoughts about three products. Based on ratings for the brand and flavours obtained in a pre-test with an independent sample, cards are ranked in order of the importance of brand information they indicate. Each participant's top eight picks indicate the importance of brand information for that participant. Open-ended responses are also categorized by an independent coder as brand-related or attribute-related, and the ratio of brand-related to total thoughts is computed. Data analysis shows that the importance of brand information is correlated negatively with brand schematicity ($r = -0.39$, $p < 0.001$) and that brand-related to total thoughts are correlated positively with brand schematicity ($r = 0.44$, $p < 0.0001$).

Samples

To develop the scale, studies 1 and 2 use, respectively, 312 and 60 students. To validate the scale, study 3 employs a sample of 60 students. Study 4 is based on four independent samples which include, respectively, 64, 62, 114 and 104 participants. Study 5 uses 119 students in the main study and 51 students in the pre-test. Study 6 uses 85 students. Study 7 is based on a sample of 59 students. All students are undergraduate students from a large northeastern university in the United States.

Reliability and validity

The brand schematicity's reliability and validities are checked throughout the scale-development process.

With regard to reliability, study 1 reports that both composite reliability (CR) and Cronbach's alpha are greater than 0.90. Study 2 reports a CR = 0.90 and an alpha = 0.89. Study 3 reports a reliability of 0.87.

With regard to validity, study 2 demonstrates convergent validity using the correlation between the 10-item and the 1-item scales on brand schematicity ($r = 0.80$, $p < 0.0001$); the significant t-values > 7.00 associated with item loadings; and the average variance extracted (AVE) equal to 0.51. Further evidence of convergent validity is provided in study 3 using response time. It is shown that the correlation between brand schematicity and response time is of −0.30 ($p < 0.05$). Two CFA models are also compared: one in which the latent factor measured by the 10-item brand schematicity scale is allowed to correlate with the factor measured by the response time and the other in which the two latent factors are specified as uncorrelated; the former model reports a significantly better fit ($\chi^2(2) = 645.84$, $p < 0.001$). It is finally shown that the error rate is negatively correlated with the brand schematicity scale, although not significantly ($p > 0.05$).

Evidence of discriminant validity is provided in study 4. AVE is reported to be greater than 0.50 in three over four samples (equal to, respectively, 0.53, 0.57, 0.55 and 0.44). AVE is also reported to be greater than the square of the correlations of brand schematicity with self-esteem and SNI (AVE = 0.53 > $r^2 = 0.04$ and $r^2 = 0.20$, respectively); NFC (AVE = 0.57 > $r^2 = 0.10$); materialism and social comparison orientation (AVE = 0.74 > $r^2 = 0.35$ and $r^2 = 0.006$, respectively); need to evaluate, concern for appropriateness and BESC (AVE = 0.67 > $r^2 = 0.008$, $r^2 = 0.10$ and $r^2 = 0.01$, respectively).

The predictive validity of the brand schematicity scale is demonstrated in studies 5 and 6. Study 5 shows that brand schematicity moderates the influence of brand concept consistency but not that of product feature similarity on brand extension evaluations. An ANCOVA, conducted using brand concept consistency as within-subject factor and brand schematicity as covariate, shows a significant interaction between brand schematicity and brand concept consistency ($F(1, 236) = 8.40$, $p < 0.004$). Further, an ANCOVA conducted using product feature similarity as within-subject factor and brand schematicity as covariate reveals that product feature similarity increases extension evaluations ($F(1, 236) = 8.29$, $p < 0.01$), but brand schematicity has no moderating influence ($F(1, 236) = 0.002$, $p > 0.9$), thus showing the predictive validity of brand schematicity.

Study 6 supports the moderating role of brand schematicity in the relationship between brand concept consistency and brand extension evaluations using unobtrusive measures of brand schematicity. An ANCOVA, conducted using brand concept consistency as between-subjects factor and response time as covariate, indicates a main effect of brand concept consistency ($F(1, 78) = 8.605$, $p < 0.005$) and an interaction between response time and brand concept consistency ($F(1, 78) = 4.568$, $p < 0.04$). Regression analysis confirms these findings.

Managerial applications

The researchers suggest marketers use the brand schematicity scale mainly for segmentation purposes. Classifying consumers based on their brand schematicity score could allow brand managers to better formulate advertising strategies such that brand-schematic consumers are interested in brand information, whereas brand-aschematic consumers are more sensitive to messages centred on product attributes.

12.7 Academic focus

- A dissertation may be interested in understanding how brand dependence (Bristow, Schneider & Schuler, 2002) is influenced by consumer value orientation. One could argue, for example, that consumers high on certain values, such as materialism (Richins, 1994; Richins & Dawson, 1992), tend to be more dependent on brand names in their purchasing decisions. The dissertation could therefore try to answer the following research question: "How do consumer value orientations (e.g., materialism) influence consumers' dependence on brands in their decision-making processes?"
- A dissertation may be interested in focusing on branded product meanings in developing countries. In their work, Strizhakova, Coulter and Price (2008) identify four cross-national key meanings of branded products and show some differences in their importance in the developing countries of Romania, Ukraine and Russia. However, developing countries around the world are very different from each other (e.g., developing countries in Latin America, Southern Asia and Africa). The dissertation could adopt a classification of developing countries based on economic (e.g., GDP/capita) and/or cultural (de Mooij & Hofstede, 2010; Inglehart & Welzel, 2005) factors and examine the differences in the way consumers attribute meanings to branded products.
- Sprott, Czellar and Spangenberg (2009) investigate how high–BESC consumers behave toward their favourite brands and show that high–BESC consumers not only associate themselves with their favourite brands but also distance themselves from brands that are not part of who they are. Therefore, following the suggestions of these researchers, one dissertation may investigate the relationship between consumer self-concept and the least favourite brands. How do the least favourite brands define one's self-concept in comparison to the most favourite brands? This is an example of a research question a dissertation may try to investigate.

- Building on the work of Fischer, Völckner and Sattler (2010), a dissertation may further explore brand relevance in category (BRiC) in a cross-cultural context. In particular, the dissertation could examine the role of cultural and economic differences for explaining country differences in BRiC. To take into account cultural and economic differences between countries, the framework outlined by Inglehart and Welzel (2005) could be used.
- Puligadda, Ross and Grewal (2012) argue that the extant literature on consumer–brand relationships (see Chapter 10) is dominated by a brand-centred perspective. For example, relationships between consumers and brands can be affected by elements such as brand personality and brand transgressions (Aaker, Fournier & Brasel, 2004), which are external to the consumer. Following Puligadda, Ross and Grewal's argument, one dissertation may complement this brand-centred perspective with a consumer-centred one. The dissertation could investigate the influence that consumer factors, such as brand schematicity, have on this relationship. Does brand schematicity moderate the effects of marketer activities on the consumer–brand relationship? This is an example of a question the dissertation may try to answer.

12.8 Managerial focus

- **Have you thought about using brand schematicity as a criterion of segmentation?**
  Consumer behaviour can vary because consumers are processing and organizing information about brands differently. Some consumers are really focused on product characteristics and do not pay attention to the brand, whereas others will select a product just because of the brand and what it means to them. Because consumers vary based on their predispositions to brands, brand managers could use brand schematicity as a criterion of segmentation in order to maximize the effectiveness of their marketing program (Puligadda, Ross & Grewal, 2012). Indeed, brand-schematic consumers will be influenced by advertising that promotes the brand and by the opinions of others, whereas brand aschematic consumers will be more sensitive to messages centred on product attributes.
- **Do you consider brand dependence when developing your private label?**
  Brand dependence corresponds to the tendency to use brand names when making purchase decisions. Brand managers who are in charge of the development of private labels could use brand dependence as a

segmenting variable to identify people who are highly brand dependent and the ones who are low-dependent consumers. Indeed, low-dependent consumers will not consider brand names when making purchase decisions and will be less loyal to national brands. Therefore, as private labels provide good value-for-money products, targeting this low-dependent consumers with coupons, for instance, will likely be efficient to enhance sales and interact with those consumers.

- **Have you checked the relevance of your brand extension in the new category?**
Before deciding on a brand extension, it is really important to check the perceived overall influence of brands on consumer decision making in a given product category. Indeed, if the relevance of brands in a given category is low, consumers may not consider the brand in their purchase decision. On the other hand, if brand relevance is high, the fact that consumers already appreciate the parent brand in another category could facilitate the introduction of the brand extension in this category. By using the BRiC scale (Fischer, Völckner & Sattler, 2010), managers can have a better understanding of the risks and the opportunities when considering a brand extension strategy.

- **You are launching a new branded product/brand in a developing country. What factors should you consider to plan your communication campaign?**
In addition to traditional usage and attitudes or brand image studies, global marketing managers could use the scale developed by Strizhakova, Coulter and Price (2008) to understand how consumers in specific countries attribute meaning to branded products. Is quality more important to them then personal values? Are traditions important to them? Do they pay attention to how brands are related to their personal identities? By answering these questions, managers can have some precious indications about the factors to highlight in their communications campaign.

- **Do you consider brand engagement in self-concept as segmentation criteria for your luxury brand?**
Luxury brand provides in comparison to other brands more psychological benefices such as social identity and self-esteem (Vigneron & Johnson, 1999). The BESC scale developed by Sprott, Czellar and Spangenberg (2009) can therefore be relevant in addition to other criteria of segmentation in the luxury market. For instance, many luxury brands such as Pierre Cardin, Burberry and so on tend to offer more accessible products, such as accessories and sunglasses. It could be interesting to use the BESC scale to identify the consumers who are using their favourite brands to construe their self-concept in order to target them more specifically with these new products and to adapt communication strategies accordingly.

References

Aaker, J., Fournier, S., & Brasel, S. (2004). When good brands do bad. *Journal of Consumer Research*, 31 (1), 1–16.

Ailawadi, K. L., Neslin, S. A., & Gedenk, K. (2001). Pursuing the value-conscious consumer: store brands versus national brand promotions. *Journal of Marketing*, 65 (January), 71–89.

Bearden, W. O., Netemeyer, R. G., & Teel, J. E. (1989). Measurement of consumer susceptibility to interpersonal influence. *Journal of Consumer Research*, 15 (4), 473–481.

Brems, C., & Johnson, M. E. (1990). Reexamination of the Bem sex-role inventory: the interpersonal BSRI. *Journal of Personality Assessment*, 55 (3–4), 484–498.

Bristow, D. N., Schneider, K. C., & Schuler, D. K. (2002). The brand dependence scale: measuring consumers' use of brand name to differentiate among product alternatives. *Journal of Product and Brand Management*, 11 (6/7), 343–356.

Burgess, S. M., & Steenkamp, J.-B.E.M. (2006). Marketing renaissance: How research in emerging markets advances marketing science and practice. *International Journal of Research in Marketing*, 23 (4), 337–356.

Cacioppo, J. T., Petty, R. E., & Kao, C. F. (1984). The efficient assessment of need for cognition. *Journal of Personality Assessment*, 48 (3), 306–307.

Campbell, J., Trapnell, P. D., Heine, S. J., Katz, I. M., Lavallee, L., & Lehman, D. R. (1996). Self-concept clarity: measurement, personality correlates, and cultural boundaries. *Journal of Personality and Social Psychology*, 70 (1), 141–156.

Cross, S. E., Bacon, P. L., & Morris, M. L. (2000). The relational-interdependent self-construal and relationships. *Journal of Personality and Social Psychology*, 78 (4), 791–808.

Diener, E., Emmons, R. A., Larsen, R. J., & Griffin, S. (1985). The satisfaction with life scale. *Journal of Personality Assessment*, 49 (1), 71–75.

Douglas, S. P., & Craig, C. S. (2006). On improving the conceptual foundations of international marketing. *Journal of International Marketing*, 14 (1), 1–22.

Fischer, M. (2007). Valuing brand assets: a cost-effective and easy-to-implement measurement approach. *MSI Report No. 07–107*. Marketing Science Institute.

Fischer, M., Völckner, F., & Sattler, H. (2010). How important are brands? A cross-category, cross-country study. *Journal of Marketing Research*, 47 (5), 823–839.

Gibbons, F. X., & Buunk, B. P. (1999). Individual differences in social comparison: development of a scale of social comparison orientation. *Journal of Personality & Social Psychology*, 76 (1), 129–142.

Inglehart, R. F., & Welzel, C. (2005). *Modernization, cultural change, and democracy: the human development sequence*. New York, NY: Cambridge University Press.

Jarvis, W.B.G., & Petty, R. E. (1996). The need to evaluate. *Journal of Personality & Social Psychology*, 70 (1), 172–194.

Keller, K. L. (1993). Conceptualizing, measuring, and managing customer-based brand equity. *Journal of Marketing*, 57 (January), 1–22.

Keller, K. L. (1998). *Strategic brand management: Building, measuring and managing brand equity*. Upper Saddle River, NJ: Prentice-Hall.

Lennox, R. D., & Wolfe, R. N. (1984). Revision of the self-monitoring scale. *Journal of Personality and Social Psychology*, 46 (6), 1349–1364.

Luhtanen, R., & Crocker, J. (1992). A collective self-esteem scale: self-evaluation of one's collective identity. *Personality & Social Psychology Bulletin*, 18 (3), 302–318.

Mitchell, A. A. (1986). The effect of verbal and visual components of advertisements on brand attitudes and attitude toward the advertisement. *Journal of Consumer Research*, 13 (June), 12–24.

de Mooij, M., & Hofstede, G. (2010). The Hofstede model: Applications to global branding and advertising strategy and research. *International Journal of Advertising*, 29 (1), 85–110.

Nunnally, J. C., & Bernstein, I. (1994). *Psychometric theory*. New York, NY: McGraw-Hill.

Park, C. W., Milberg, S., & Lawson, R. (1991). Evaluation of brand extensions: the role of product feature similarity and brand concept consistency. *Journal of Consumer Research*, 18 (2), 185–193.

Paulhus, D. L. (1998). *Manual for the balanced inventory of desirable responding*. Toronto: Multi-Health Systems.

Puligadda, S., Ross, W. T., & Grewal, R. (2012). Individual differences in brand schematicity. *Journal of Marketing Research*, 49 (1), 115–130.

Richins, M. L. (1994). Valuing things: the public and private meanings of possessions. *Journal of Consumer Research*, 21 (December), 504–521.

Richins, M. L. (2004). The material values scale: Measurement properties and development of a short form. *Journal of Consumer Research*, 31 (June), 209–219.

Richins, M. L., & Dawson, S. (1992). A consumer values orientation for materialism and its measurement: scale development and validation. *Journal of Consumer Research*, 19 (3), 303–316.

Rosenberg, M. (1965). *Society and the adolescent self-image*. Princeton, NJ: Princeton University Press.

Singelis, T. M. (1994). The measurement of independent and interdependent self-construals. *Personality & Social Psychology Bulletin*, 20 (5), 580–591.

Sprott, D., Czellar, S., & Spangenberg, E. (2009). The importance of a general measure of brand engagement on market behavior: development and validation of a scale. *Journal of Marketing Research*, 46 (1), 92–104.

Strizhakova, Y., Coulter, R. A., & Price, L. L. (2008). The meanings of branded products: a cross-national scale development and meaning assessment. *International Journal of Research in Marketing*, 25, 82–93.

Vigneron, F., & Johnson, L. W. (1999). A review and a conceptual framework of prestige-seeking consumer behavior. *Academy of Marketing Science Review*, 1 (1), 1–15.

13
BRAND ORIENTATION

13.1 Overview

The concept of brand orientation emerges in the literature at the beginning of the 1990s, thanks to the work of Urde (1994). Brand orientation represents a complementary approach to the traditional market orientation (Urde, Baumgarth & Merrilees, 2013); it has been described as a managerial approach that puts brand building at the centre of marketing strategy. Various different definitions of brand orientation have been provided in the literature (for a review, see Gromark & Melin, 2011). One of the first and most quoted definitions describes brand orientation as "an approach in which the processes of the organisation revolve around the creation, development, and protection of brand identity in an ongoing interaction with target customers with the aim of achieving lasting competitive advantages in the form of brands" (Urde, 1999, pp. 117–118).

In more recent years, brand orientation has been examined in relation to contexts, such as non-profit, B2B and tourism, that have traditionally been less interested in brands and brand management. The pressure of competition and the complexity of environments that characterize these contexts nowadays, however, have forced companies and organizations to turn to branding to improve their competitiveness. In light of these developments, some researchers have applied the notion of brand orientation to contexts like these and have developed measurement scales to capture the brand orientation of companies and organizations within these contexts. The chapter includes these scales.

More specifically, in light of the increasing importance of branding in the non-profit sector (Hankinson 2001, 2002), Ewing and Napoli (2005) highlight the need that non-profit organizations have to become more "business-like". They propose a non-profit brand orientation scale that can be used by non-profit organizations from any industry to assess the organization's focus on internal and external activities to build and sustain strong brands in the marketplace.

Similarly, Baumgarth (2010) focuses on the B2B sector, where the brand concept has been less applied compared to B2C marketing. The researcher advances a B2B brand orientation scale that companies in this sector can use to assess and improve their brand orientation. In support of this, the researcher provides evidence of the benefits associated with the inclusion of the B2B brand orientation scale in the company's strategies; benefits related to the positive association between brand orientation and market performance.

Finally, Hankinson (2012) follows the significant growth of place branding, in particular of places as tourism destinations, and looks at the brand orientation framework from the perspective of tourism destinations. By taking into account the factors that determine the success of destination brand management (Hankinson, 2009), the researcher develops a destination brand orientation scale that organizations can include in their strategies to improve their performance.

13.2 Multi-dimensional non-profit brand orientation (Ewing & Napoli, 2005)

Definition of construct

Ewing and Napoli (2005) bring the notion of brand orientation into the non-profit sector. Non-profit brand orientation (NBO) is defined by them as "the organization wide process of generating and sustaining a shared sense of brand meaning that provides superior value to stakeholders and superior performance to the organization" (p. 842). NBO can be considered a reflection of both internal and external activities of non-profit organizations, activities that are necessary to build strong brands. NBO is a multi-dimensional construct, consisting of the following dimensions: *interaction*, which refers to the ability of the non-profit organization to respond to the changes in the environment and the stakeholders' needs; *orchestration*, which relates to the ability of the non-profit organization to implement activities of integrated marketing communication to both internal and external stakeholders; and *affect*, which refers to the ability of a non-profit organization to understand the attitudes and feelings of stakeholders toward itself.

Scale description

The NBO scale includes three dimensions and 12 items: *interaction*, which is measured through 5 items; *orchestration*, which is also measured through 5 items; and *affect*, which is measured through 2 items. To complete the scale, respondents are asked to rate the degree to which a given non-profit organization is currently engaged in the activity described in the items. Responses can be provided on 7-point scales where 1 = "to a very little extent" and 7 = "to a very great extent". Composite measures of *interaction*, *orchestration* and *affect* can be computed by averaging the corresponding items. A composite score of the NBO can also be computed by averaging all the 12 items of the scale.

TABLE 13.1 Multi-dimensional non-profit brand orientation scale

Scale dimension	Scale item
Interaction	• Invests adequate resources in product/service improvements that provide better value to our stakeholders • Keep "in touch" with our stakeholders' needs • Focus on creating a positive product/service experience for our stakeholders • Keep "in touch" with current market conditions • Have a system in place for getting stakeholders' comments to the people who can instigate change
Orchestration	• Design our integrated marketing activities to encourage consumers directly to use our products/services • Design our integrated marketing activities to encourage our suppliers, distributors and other key stakeholders to promote our products/services to consumers • Ensure that managers within the organization are aware of all of the marketing activities that involve the brand • Develop marketing programs that send consistent messages about our brand to our stakeholders • Create a brand/sub-brand structure that is well thought out and understood by our staff
Affect	• Develop detailed knowledge of what our stakeholders dislike about the brand • Develop detailed knowledge of what our stakeholders like about the brand

Scale development

To develop the NBO scale, the researchers first generate a pool of 37 items using the "brand report card" framework developed by Keller (2000). These items are assessed by two marketing academics and then examined in three focus groups, where participants are asked to comment on the clarity of each item and its relevance to their organization. This refinement stage leads to remove seven items considered irrelevant to the non-profit context.

Two data collections take place afterwards. The first data collection is used to purify the pool of items. Respondents are asked to evaluate their non-profit organization in relation to the 30 NBO items. After assessing for non-response bias, a reliability analysis is conducted. Items with a corrected item-to-total correlation < 0.40 (first round of analysis) and a corrected item-to-total correlation < 0.50 (second round of analysis) are removed. This analysis leads to deletion of additional 14 items. The remaining 16 items are subjected to a principal component analysis with varimax rotation. It emerges as a three-factor solution with eigenvalues > 1.00 explaining 66% of total variance.

The second data collection is used to confirm the factor structure and assess the scale validity. In this case, respondents are asked to evaluate their non-profit organization not only using the NBO scale but also on market orientation items (adapted from Narver & Slater, 1990), two subjective measures of organization performance (ability to better serve stakeholders compared to competitors and ability to serve short- and long-term objectives) and an overall brand management effectiveness scale (measured as "not effective", "somewhat effective", "very effective"). A confirmatory factor analysis is conducted through structural equation modelling. The analysis shows an acceptable fit ($\chi^2(51) = 58.69$, $p = 0.214$, RMR = 0.93, AGFI = 0.917 and CFI = 0.992) supporting the three-factor, 12-item solution previously identified. Reliability and validity tests are conducted to validate the scale.

Samples

The item-generation stage includes three focus groups with 10 to 12 senior managers each. The two following data collections are conducted via mail. In the first data collection, 1,300 questionnaires are distributed and 233 usable questionnaires are returned (response rate = 19.2%). In the second data collection, 1,000 questionnaires are sent out and 170 usable questionnaires are returned (response rate = 20.9%). Respondents in both data collections include chief executive officers or equivalent from non-profit organizations identified through a simple random sampling technique; these non-profit organizations are representative of the 12 sectors included in the *International Classification of Non-Profit Organizations* (Sargeant, 1999). All studies are conducted in Australia.

Reliability and validity

The reliability of the NBO scale is examined using data from both collections. Data from the first data collection is used to compute the coefficient alpha, which is equal to 0.917. Data from the second data collection is used to compute the composite reliability (CR) and average variance extracted for each of the three dimensions: CR is equal to 0.76 (*interaction*), 0.83 (*orchestration*) and .91 (*affect*), whereas AVE is equal to 0.51 (*interaction*), 0.60 (*orchestration*) and 0.84 (*affect*).

The validity of the scale is examined through several tests. Face validity is examined using two marketing academics at the beginning of the process. All other types of validities are verified using data from the second data collection.

Convergent validity is demonstrated by showing that the AVE of each factor is > 0.50. Discriminant validity is proved by showing that the AVE for each factor is greater than the squared correlation between that factor and any other factor in the model. Discriminant validity is also proved in relation to market orientation. Principal component analysis with varimax rotation reveals a six-factor solution, accounting for 67% of total variance, where the majority of NBO and market orientation items load on different factors (the sixth factor includes one NBO and one market orientation item, whereas all the other factors include either NBO or market orientation items).

The nomological validity of the NBO scale is tested using the two subjective measures of organization performance: the organization's ability to better serve stakeholders compared to competitors and the organization's ability to serve short- and long-term objectives. A regression analysis with each measure is conducted with NBO as independent variable. Both regression models are significant (adjusted R^2 = 0.305 and 0.327, respectively, ps < 0.001). The analysis shows that the *interaction* (std. β = 0.436 and 0.412, respectively, ps < 0.001) and *orchestration* dimensions (std. β = 0.197, p < 0.001 and 0.154, p < 0.05, respectively) are significant predictors of both constructs, whereas the *affect* dimension predicts only the organization's ability to serve short- and long-term objectives (std. β = 0.098, p < 0.10).

The scale's criterion validity is proved by showing that NBO behaves as expected in relation to overall brand management effectiveness. A regression analysis (adjusted R^2 = 0.567, p < 0.001) shows that all three NBO dimensions are significant predictors (std. β = 0.245 for *interaction*, 0.454 for *orchestration* and 0.191 for *affect*, ps < 0.001). Overall brand management effectiveness is also used to prove the NBO scale's content validity. A one-way ANOVA is performed between the mean scores of each NBO dimension and respondents' ratings of the overall brand management effectiveness. The analysis shows a positive relation among the overall rating and the three NBO dimensions, meaning that the higher the overall effectiveness of the organization's brand management practices, the higher the average rating of the individual NBO dimensions.

Finally, the generalizability of the scale across non-profit organizations in different sectors is verified through a variance component analysis using the maximum likelihood method. Results show that the differences in brand orientation are not due to the sector in which a non-profit organization operates but to the respondent/organization and the items/dimensions used to measure NBO. Moreover, the G-coefficient for comparing brand orientation across non-profit organizations is equal to 0.838; the G-coefficients for comparing brand management practices within a non-profit organization are equal to 0.996, if the object of measurement is the items, and 0.976, if the object of measurement are the NBO dimensions.

Managerial applications

The NBO scale helps non-profit managers improve the performance of their organization. Through its three dimensions, the scale highlights the importance for managers of being aware of the needs of the organization's stakeholders and how these change (*interaction*); coordinating all the organization's brand-related activities in order to maximize market awareness and performance (*orchestration*); and developing an understanding of what aspects of the organization's brand are most liked and disliked by stakeholders (*affect*). The extent to which each of these issues is taken into account by the organization provides an indication about its current brand management practices. Besides using the NBO scale to guide the organization's internal and external activities, non-profit managers could use it to benchmark current brand management practices, that is, to compare their practices against those of other organizations operating in a range of non-profit sectors. This could help managers identify the strengths and weaknesses of their organization and use this information to enhance their relative performance.

13.3 Brand orientation in the business-to-business sector (Baumgarth, 2010)

Definition of construct

Brand orientation is defined by Baumgarth (2010) as a specific type of marketing orientation, and business-to-business (B2B) brand orientation refers to a specific sector. Building on the corporate culture model developed by Schein (1992), the author conceptualizes B2B brand orientation as consisting of four layers, that is, *value*, *norms*, *artefacts* and *behaviours*. The *value* layer refers to the extent to which the brand is incorporated in the firm's strategy development. The *norms* layer refers to the extent to which regulations and institutions influence the basic operations of brand management. The *artefacts* layer refers to the degree to which tangible symbols (e.g., uniforms, logo), which reflect the brand positioning, are used by the firm. The *behaviours* layer refers to the extent to which concrete actions and communications are undertaken in support of the brand. These four layers are related to each other in a causal way, according to which *value* determines *norms*, *norms* determine *artefacts* and *behaviours*, *artefacts* determine *behaviours*.

Scale description

The scale includes four layers, or dimensions, for a total of 16 items: the *value* dimension comprises 5 items, the *norms* dimension consists of 4 items, the *artefacts* dimension includes 3 items and the *behaviours* dimension is made of 4 items. Items are measured on a 5-point Likert scale and can be summarized into a 0% to 100% index following the procedure suggested by Hadwich (2003).

TABLE 13.2 B2B brand orientation scale

Scale dimension	Scale item
Value	• In our company, brand decisions are discussed and decided at the top management level • Our brand is differentiated toward the brands of our competitors • We take care that our brand positioning remains essentially the same over a long time period • We take care that our branding is constant over a long time period • We also invest in our brand in times of scarce financial resources

(*Continued*)

TABLE 13.2 (Continued)

Scale dimension	Scale item
Norms	• In all brand communications, we pay explicit attention to the integration of all communication methods • Our company has a detailed written specification of the brand positioning • Brand managers have the competence and authority to succeed with the positioning of our brand internally • We check regularly whether or not our brand is different from the profiles of competing brands
Artefacts	• Our stands at trade fairs reflect our brand • We conduct regular meetings about the status-quo of our brand • "Stories" in our company reflect the positioning of our brand
Behaviours	• We invest in image advertising • We teach our employees about the brand • We instruct new employees about the positioning of our brand • We conduct regularly market research studies of our brand

Scale development

The development of the B2B brand orientation scale starts with preliminary qualitative research in order to generate an initial set of items on the conceptualized B2B brand orientation dimensions and to evaluate the relationships among them. Qualitative research into internal branding of three companies is conducted and is complemented with secondary data available from them (i.e., companies' presentations, advertisements and manuals) as well as with scales from the literature. The set of items is then reduced thanks to discussions with academic researchers and managers. The resulting set includes 19 items covering the four dimensions.

The main study is conducted next. The questionnaire, which is pre-tested, includes the B2B brand orientation scale, measures on market and economic performance and questions about company characteristics (number of employees, turnover, industry sector, ownership). In data analysis, a non-response bias check is conducted and differences between early and late respondents are found with respect to one variable ($p < 0.05$); the majority of variables is not affected. Using PLS, a measurement model is then tested with the four dimensions of B2B brand orientation operationalized as formative constructs. Three items are discarded, as their weight is < 0.01; all other items have a weight > 0.01. The next part of the analysis tests a structural model of B2B brand orientation. Results show that the *values* dimension has an effect on the *norms* dimension (std. β = 0.638, R^2 = 40.8%, Q^2 = 0.25); the *norms* dimension has an effect on the *artefacts* dimension (std. β= 0.727, R^2 = 52.8%, Q^2 = 0.26); the *artefacts* (std. β = 0.522) and *norms* (std. β = 0.332, R^2 = 63.4%, Q^2 = 0.42) dimensions have an effect on the *behaviours* dimension (all $ps < 0.01$). Tests of the scale's validity are finally conducted.

Samples

The preliminary research involves three companies, two academic researchers and three managers. In the main study, 981 top managers working for German B2B companies are identified through a commercial database; 268 of them return completed questionnaires, and 261 of them are usable (return rate = 26.6%).

Reliability and validity

The B2B brand orientation predictive and criterion validities are tested. Results reveal that B2B brand orientation has a positive effect on market performance (std. $\beta = 0.400$, $R^2 = 16.6\%$, $Q^2 = 0.08$), which in turn has a positive effect on economic performance ($\beta = 0.572$, $R^2 = 24.0\%$, $Q^2 = 0.14$; all $ps < 0.01$). Using t-tests, differences on all four B2B brand orientation dimensions are found between successful versus unsuccessful companies ($ps < 0.01$); the two groups are identified on the basis of the median of their market performance index.

Managerial applications

The B2B brand orientation scale, with its four layers or dimensions, offers managers practical guidelines. The scale can be used as a tool for diagnosing brand's strengths and weaknesses in relation to brand-oriented values, norms, behaviours and artefacts. The scale can also be used as a tool for planning future activities to develop the brand orientation of a B2B company. Specifically, managers should first promote the brand-oriented *values* which characterize the firm. Then, they should formulate and disseminate brand-oriented *norms* (for example, through manuals and positioning statements) and brand-oriented *artefacts* (for example, using architecture and livery). Finally, they should implement brand-oriented *behaviours* (for example, through control procedures, effectiveness measurements and brand-centred advertising).

13.4 Brand orientation in the context of destination branding (Hankinson, 2012)

Definition of construct

Hankinson (2012) applies the notion of brand orientation to tourist organizations. Building on his previous work (Hankinson, 2009), the researcher conceptualizes destination brand orientation (DBO) as a multi-dimensional construct including five dimensions: *brand culture*, which refers to the extent to which a destination marketing organization develops and implements its brand values; *departmental coordination*, which refers to the extent to which departmental processes are centred around the brand; *brand communication*, which refers to the degree to which the destination marketing organization communicates with a wide range of stakeholders; *brand reality*, which refers to the degree to which brand associations are embedded in the reality of the brand, that is, the consumer experience of the brand; and *brand partnership*, which refers to the degree to which the destination marketing organization is engaged in building strong partnerships to deliver long-term economic, social and environmental value. Hankinson also conceptualizes DBO as an antecedent of brand performance and as a consequence of brand leadership.

Scale description

The DBO scale includes five dimensions, for a total of 18 items: *brand culture*, *departmental condition* and *brand communications* are measured by 3 items each, whereas *brand reality* is measured by 5 items and *brand partnership* by 4 items. Items are evaluated on a 6-point Likert scale anchored at 1 = "strongly disagree" and 6 = "strongly agree".

TABLE 13.3 Destination brand orientation scale

Scale dimension	Scale item
Brand culture	• Brand understood by staff • Brand well thought of by staff • Managers aware of brand activities
Departmental coordination	• Communication between marketing and other departments about branding • Regular team meetings at senior level • Coordinated business processes around brand development
Brand communications	• Consistency across internal and external brand communications • Focus on awareness • Focus on brand values
Brand reality	• Brand embedded in reality • Positive brand experience • Invest resources in product improvements that provide better value for customers • Branding starts with communications through to the customer experience • Staff live the brand
Brand partnership	• Compatibility with brand values • Send consistent messages • Regular meetings • Encouraging partners to promote brand

Scale development

The DBO scale-development process starts with item generation. A first set of items is derived from a literature review, then is assessed through a round of personal interviews. The revised set of items is shown to a panel of marketing academics and, after having integrated their feedback, is assessed in a final round of interviews. Items on brand leadership, the antecedent of DBO, are generated by the author (see box below), whereas items on brand performance, the consequence of DBO, are derived from the literature (Wong & Merrilees, 2007).

> **Brand leadership**
>
> - Senior management has a good understanding of what is necessary to build a strong brand
> - Top management has led the development of the brand values
> - It is our CEO who sets the strategic vision for the brand
> - Top management has actively tried to align the culture of the organisation with the brand values
> - Our CEO is able to speak to senior managers in other organisations to open doors and make things happen

It follows a quantitative data collection in which respondents are asked to evaluate their organization in terms of the DBO items. Data are analysed in two steps using PLS path modelling. Step 1 builds a measurement model in order to assess the constructs. As two DBO dimensions (*departmental condition* and *brand communications*) are defined as formative, no formal test is conducted on them; the assessment is carried out based on qualitative judgment based on relevant theory. For the other three dimensions (*brand culture, brand reality* and *brand partnership*), only items with a loading > 0.70 are retained. This analysis leads to discarding 16 items among formative and reflective constructs. DBO antecedent and consequence are also analysed, and all items report a loading > 0.70. Reliability and validity tests are conducted. In step 2, a structural model is built to assess the relation between DBO and its antecedent and consequence. The model ($R^2 = 38\%$) shows a significant relation between brand leadership and DBO (path coefficient = .639, $p < 0.001$) and between DBO and brand performance (path coefficient = .507, $p < 0.001$).

Samples

The item-generation phase uses 25 senior managers from destination marketing organizations and five marketing academics. Questionnaires are sent to 450 chief executive officers and directors of a variety of destination marketing organizations in the UK (national tourist boards, regional tourist boards, cities, county councils, borough councils, district councils and others); of these, 90 usable questionnaires are returned (response rate = 20%).

Reliability and validity

The face validity of the DBO items is tested with in-depth interviews with managers and academics.

Reliability, convergent and discriminant validities of the scale are tested only for reflective factors (*brand culture, brand reality* and *brand partnership*). Reliability is examined by composite reliability, which is equal to 0.907 for *brand culture*, 0.909

for *brand reality* and 0.858 for *brand partnership*. Convergent validity is tested through the computation of AVE, which is equal to 0.76 for *brand culture*, 0.66 for *brand reality* and 0.60 for *brand partnership*. Finally, discriminant validity is verified by showing that the square root of the AVE of each factor (between 0.775 and 0.872) is greater than the correlation between this factor and any other factor in the model (between 0.347 and 0.721).

All these tests are also conducted for the antecedent and consequence of DBO, showing satisfactory results.

Managerial applications

The DBO scale represents a toolkit that managers can use to develop and evaluate destination brands. The scale highlights the activities, both internal and external, that should be undertaken to develop DBO. Internally, managers should be aware of the marketing activities in support for the brand, and the organization should ensure their departments support the brand's development. Externally, the organization should be able to build affiliation with the destination brand in partner organizations and should ensure that the brand promise is embedded in the reality of what a destination has to offer. The DBO scale can also be used as a tool for benchmarking activities against other destination brands.

13.5 Academic focus

- The topic of brand orientation has been recently investigated in relation with the higher education sector (Casidy, 2014), politics (O'Cass & Voola, 2011), churches (Mulyanegara, 2011), small firms (Hirvonen & Laukkanen, 2014) and retail banking (Wallace, Buil & de Chernatony, 2011), among others. In a dissertation, one may be willing to test the applicability of Ewing and Napoli's (2005), Baumgarth's (2010) and/or Hankinson's (2012) frameworks to these emerging contexts.
- One dissertation may focus on one of the frameworks of brand orientation proposed in the chapter (Baumgarth, 2010; Ewing & Napoli, 2005; Hankinson, 2012). For example, if one considers the non-profit brand orientation construct (Ewing & Napoli, 2005), it may be worth investigating how brand orientation impacts brand image in non-profit organizations (Michel & Rieunier, 2012; see Chapter 1, pp. 18–21). Or, if one takes into account B2B brand orientation (Baumgarth, 2010), one may explore how brand orientation impacts brand personality in a B2B context (Herbst & Merz, 2011; see Chapter 3, pp. 73–75).
- Recent studies (e.g., Hirvonen, Laukkanen & Reijonen, 2013) have examined the impact of brand orientation on brand performance and included moderators such as firm age, firm size, branding know-how, customer

type, industry type and market life cycle. A dissertation may be interested in exploring the relationship between brand orientation and brand performance in B2B, non-profit, or tourist destination contexts by including other possible moderators that are relevant in these contexts.
- One dissertation may analyse the brand orientation of an organization in relation to the value that such organization has for its employees. The organization's brand orientation, as conceptualized in Baumgarth (2010), Hankinson (2012) and/or Ewing and Napoli (2005), could be therefore related to employee-based brand equity (King, Grace & Funk, 2012; see Chapter 11, pp. 252–255).
- A dissertation may want to merge the internal perspective, mainly focused on employees, with the external perspective, mostly related to end consumers. In such a dissertation, one may investigate the extent to which the relationship between brand orientation and consumer outcome variables is mediated by employee-related aspects. As consumer outcome variables, one may consider brand loyalty (Odin, Odin & Valette-Florence, 2001; see Chapter 10, pp. 205–207) or brand relationship quality (Kim, Lee & Lee, 2005; see Chapter 10, pp. 213–215). As employee-related aspects, one may consider their satisfaction or loyalty toward the brand/organization for which they work (King, Grace & Funk, 2012).

13.6 Managerial focus

- **Why should companies measure brand orientation?**
Many companies use various metrics to understand how their brand is performing, how the brand is perceived by their consumers and how the consumer is engaged with the brand in order to implement actions and better align the brand with overall business objectives. Nevertheless, it is also important to evaluate internally how effectively the managers communicate the value proposition to employees, how the brand's values are perceived and if there are necessary resources to achieve organizational goals. Measuring brand orientation can provide a good understanding of the degree to which the organization values brands and is oriented toward building brand capabilities in order to improve the performance of the company in delivering the value proposition.
- **Have you checked whether the values perceived by your consumers are shared internally?**
Brand perceptions influence how customers think and determine whether they will purchase the product, recommend the company to others, or choose the competitor. The way the customer perceives your company

can be influenced by any kind of touchpoints such as communication and website but also company visit and meeting with employees. Therefore it is important that all managers, not just the marketing department, are aware of the promise of the brand and its image and act in order to truly deliver this value proposition. The B2B brand orientation scale developed by Baumgarth (2010) can help evaluate the degree to which the company is informed and oriented toward building brand capabilities.

- **Do your managers have a clear understanding of your customer value proposition?**
  Company performance is closely linked to the clarity and differentiating value proposition that the company offers to its customers and the way it is orchestrated internally. But when managers are asked to explain their vision about the customer value proposition, the answers are generally centred on products and services and not on the value they create. With a good understanding of customers' expectations and a clear comprehension of the core competencies, the history, the culture and the unique expertise in providing a product or a service, companies are more able to have a distinctive value proposition. Customer value proposition is more than a brand statement; it captures the unique value the company provides in a clear and concise way in order to make customers understand it and respond to it. A brand orientation measure such as Baumgarth's (2010) can help evaluate the internal understanding of the perception of the actions which are orchestrated internally in order to enhance the customer value proposition.

- **Have you checked whether the perception of your non-profit organization is coherent among stakeholders?**
  Brand image of non-profit organizations plays a key role for donors by influencing their charitable giving (Michel & Rieunier, 2012). The way donors perceive the organisation can be influenced by any kind of contacts such as communication, website or interactions with employees from the charity. Therefore, it is important to evaluate if the external perception of the organisation is shared among stakeholders and well-orchestrated within the organization. The non-profit brand orientation scale (Ewing & Napoli, 2005) can be useful for evaluating the current brand management practices and guide the organization's internal and external activities in order to provide superior value to stakeholders and superior performance to the organization.

- **How do you manage your brand internally?**
  Brand management and brand equity are most often considered from a customer or a financial perspective. Nevertheless, it would be an oversight for managers to ignore the importance of internal brand management in enhancing equity. Developing a strong brand promise

> is not just having an appealing statement on your website; it should really guide company practices and starts with all employees. Indeed, employees play a key role in delivering the promise which will be perceived by consumers. Internal branding is therefore important in order to make sure that employees have a clear understanding of the brand promise and are enthusiastic in making this promise real. Organizations are increasingly encouraging employees to embrace their role as brand ambassadors (de Chernatony & Cottam, 2006). Measuring the internal brand orientation perception can provide good indicators to improve the internal brand management.

References

Baumgarth, C. (2010). "Living the brand": brand orientation in the business-to-business sector. *European Journal of Marketing*, 44 (5), 653–671.

Casidy, R. (2014). Linking brand orientation with service quality, satisfaction, and positive word-of-mouth: evidence from the higher education sector. *Journal of Nonprofit & Public Sector Marketing*, 26 (2), 142–161.

de Chernatony, L., & Cottam, S. (2006). Internal brand factors driving successful financial services brands. *European Journal of Marketing*, 40 (5/6), 611–633.

Ewing, M. T., & Napoli, J. (2005). Developing and validating a multidimensional nonprofit brand orientation scale. *Journal of Business Research*, 58 (6), 841–853.

Gromark, J., & Melin, F. (2011). The underlying dimensions of brand orientation and its impact on financial performance. *Journal of Brand Management*, 18, 394–410.

Hadwich, K. (2003). *Beziehungsqualität im relationship marketing*. Wiesbaden: Gabler.

Hankinson, G. (2009). Managing destination brands: establishing a theoretical foundation. *Journal of Marketing Management*, 25 (1/2), 97–115.

Hankinson, G. (2012). The measurement of brand orientation, its performance impact, and the role of leadership in the context of destination branding: an exploratory study. *Journal of Marketing Management*, 28 (7/8), 974–999.

Hankinson, P. (2001). Brand orientation in the top 500 fundraising charities in the UK. *Journal of Product & Brand Management*, 10 (6), 346–360.

Hankinson, P. (2002). The impact of brand orientation on managerial practice: a quantitative study of the UK's top 500 fundraising managers. *International Journal of Non-Profit and Voluntary Sector Marketing*, 7 (1), 30–44.

Herbst, U., & Merz, M. A. (2011). The industrial brand personality scale: Building strong business-to-business brands. *Industrial Marketing Management*, 40 (7), 1072–1081.

Hirvonen, S., & Laukkanen, T. (2014). Brand orientation in small firms: an empirical test of the impact on brand performance. *Journal of Strategic Marketing*, 22 (1), 41–58.

Hirvonen, S., Laukkanen, T., & Reijonen, H. (2013). The brand orientation–performance relationship: an examination of moderation effects. *Journal of Brand Management*, 20 (8), 623–641.

Keller, K. L. (2000). The brand report card. *Harvard Business Review*, 78 (1), 147–156.

Kim, H. K., Lee, M., & Lee, Y. W. (2005). Developing a scale for measuring brand relationship quality. *AP-Asia Pacific Advances in Consumer Research*, 118–126.

King, C., Grace, D., & Funk, D. C. (2012). Employee brand equity: scale development and validation. *Journal of Brand Management*, 19 (4), 268–288.

Michel, G., & Rieunier, S. (2012). Nonprofit brand image and typicality influences on charitable giving. *Journal of Business Research*, 65, 701–707.

Mulyanegara, R. (2011). The role of brand orientation in church participation: an empirical examination. *Journal of Nonprofit & Public Sector Marketing*, 23 (3), 226–247.

Narver, J.C., & Slater, S.F. (1990). The effect of a market orientation on business profitability. *Journal of Marketing*, 54 (4), 20–35.

O'Cass, A., & Voola, R. (2011). Explications of political market orientation and political brand orientation using the resource-based view of the political party. *Journal of Marketing Management*, 27 (5/6), 627–645.

Odin, Y., Odin, N., & Valette-Florence, P. (2001). Conceptual and operational aspects of brand loyalty: An empirical investigation. *Journal of Business Research*, 53, 75–84.

Sargeant, A. (1999). *Marketing management for nonprofit organizations*. Oxford: Oxford University Press.

Schein, E.H. (1992). *Organizational culture and leadership* (2nd ed.). San Francisco, CA: Jossey-Bass.

Urde, M. (1994). Brand orientation: a strategy for survival. *Journal of Consumer Marketing*, 11 (3), 18–32.

Urde, M. (1999). Brand orientation: a mindset for building brands into strategic resources. *Journal of Marketing Management*, 15 (1–3), 117–133.

Urde, M., Baumgarth, C., & Merrilees, B. (2013). Brand orientation and market orientation: from alternatives to synergy. *Journal of Business Research*, 66 (1), 13–20.

Wallace, E., Buil, I., & de Chernatony, L. (2011). Within-role, extra-role and anti-role behaviours in retail banking. *International Journal of Bank Marketing*, 29 (6), 470–488.

Wong, H.Y., & Merrilees, B. (2005), "A brand orientation typology for SMEs: a case research approach", *Journal of Product & Brand Management*, Vol. 14 No. 3, 155–162.

AUTHOR INDEX

Aaker, D. A. 6, 26, 27, 28, 30, 108, 116, 227, 228, 237, 239, 249, 250
Aaker, J. 13, 14, 43, 44, 48, 51, 56, 58, 59, 60, 62, 63, 66, 70, 73, 75, 76, 77, 81, 82, 84, 87, 88, 150, 152, 280
Abimbola, T. 228, 245, 255, 257
Agarwal, M. K. 239
Ahuvia, A. 162, 169, 174, 175, 176, 181, 183, 184
Ailawadi, K. L. 272
Alba, J. W. 99
Albarracín, D. 130
Albert, N. 162, 163, 183, 184
Alden, D. L. 112, 116, 126, 127
Algesheimer, R. 154, 155
Allen, C. T. 81
Allison, N. K. 85
Alvarez, C. 204
Ambroise, L. 43, 77
Amine, A. 189
Andersen, K. 13
Anderson, J. C. 16, 147, 246
Armstrong, G. 6
Arquardt, A. 222
Askegaard, S. 130
Aurier, P. 38
Avery, J. 224
Azar, S. L. 44, 84

Backhaus, K. 75
Bacon, P. L. 269
Bagozzi, R. P. 130, 162, 169, 174, 175, 176, 183, 184, 241
Balasubramanian, S. K. 162, 166

Balmer, J. M. T. 10
Bamossy, G. 130
Barak, B. 62, 64
Barbaranelli, C. 13, 14
Bashaw, R. E. 38
Bastien, V 112
Basu, K. 211
Batra, R. 112, 116, 126, 127, 162, 169, 174, 175, 176, 183, 184, 193
Bauer, H. H. 38, 222, 228, 242
Baumgarth, C. 22, 284, 289, 294, 295, 296
Bearden, W. O. 16, 123, 238, 276
Beasley, F. M. 38
Beatty, S. 132
Bech-Larsen, T. 181
Belch, G. E. 155
Bem, S. L. 62
Benet-Martínez, V. 44, 48
Bennett, R. 18
Bergeron, J. 95
Bergkvist, L. 181
Bernam, W. H. 105
Bernstein, I. 268
Berry, L. L. 11
Beverland, M. B. 92, 100, 107, 108
Bhat, S. 64
Birk, M. 221
Blaine, D. 238
Bloemer, J. 211
Bogoloma, S. 21
Boland, W. A. 141
Bougie, R. 178
Boush, D. M. 109
Bowlby, J. 187, 192

Author index

Brakus, J. J. 95, 144, 148, 152, 157, 158
Brasel, S. 280
Breazaele, M. 142, 204
Brems, C. 269
Bristol, T. 38
Bristow, D. N. 260, 261, 279
Broniarcyk, S. M. 99
Brown, S. 92
Brown, T.K.J. 34
Bruhn, M. 92, 93, 107, 108
Bruner, G. C. II 6, 130, 246
Bruns, D. 183
Buil, I. 126, 228, 248, 257, 294
Burgess, S. M. 265
Burke, M. 162
Burton, S. 130, 131
Bush, V. D. 22, 44, 56, 75
Buunk, B. P. 276

Cacioppo, J. T. 222, 276
Campbell, D. T. 122, 147, 253
Campbell, J. 269
Caprara, G. V. 13, 14
Caravella, M. 93, 96, 107, 109
Carroll, B. 175, 176, 181
Casidy, R. 294
Cegarra, J. J. 19
Chaiken, S. 134, 137
Chandon, J. L. 142, 208
Chang, Y. 112, 122, 126, 127
Charry, K. 140
Chaudhuri, A. 63, 168, 217, 219, 223
de Chernatony, L. 7, 15, 21, 24, 126, 228,
    248, 257, 227, 228, 245, 255, 257, 294,
    297
Ching Hsing, L. 126
Chiu, H.-C. 140
Chon, K.-S. 63
Christodoulides, G. 7, 15, 21, 24, 126, 227,
    228, 245, 255, 257
Chumpitaz Cáceres, R. 140
Chun, R. 10, 11
Churchill, G. A., Jr. 16, 28, 32, 35, 54, 67,
    84, 105, 114, 121, 134, 137, 164, 188,
    191, 192, 206, 211, 214, 234, 246, 253
Cialdini, R. B. 38
Claiborne, C. B. 63, 193
Claycomb, C. 256
Cobb-Walgreen, K. J. 239
Coleman, D. 7, 15, 21, 24
Connell, P. M. 141
Conroy, D. 185
Cooil, B. 172
Cook, T. D. 147
Cooksey, R. W. 250

Cooper, L. G. 13
Correia, A. L. 87
Cottam, S. 297
Cousin, A. 140
Cova, B. 145
Cova, V. 145
Craig, C. S. 265
Cristau, C. 191
Crocker, J. 269
Crocker, K. E. 155
Cronin, J. J. 60
Crosno, J. L. 44, 80
Cross, S. E. 269
Curran, M. T. 99
Czellar, S. 206, 261, 268, 276, 279, 281

Da Silva, R. V. 7, 10, 11, 21
Dacin, P. A. 34
Dalli, D. 163, 176, 185, 200
Dart, J. 234
Davies, G. 10, 11
Dawar, N. 99
Dawson, S. 276, 279
De Luquet, M. 126
De Wulf, K. 43, 66, 69
Dean, D. 228, 237, 241, 250
Decoopman, I. 140
del Río, A. B. 228, 233
Delgado-Ballester, E. 38, 102, 205, 210,
    217, 221
Demoulin, N. 222
Deng, S. 234
Derbaix, C. 130, 134, 135, 137, 140, 141,
    199
DeVellis, R. F. 16, 253
Dholakia, U. M. 154, 155
Dick, A. S. 211
Dickinson, S. J. 92, 100, 107, 108
Diener, E. 269
Dionísio, P. 154
Dodds, W. B. 117
Donovan, R. J. 162, 176
Donthu, N. 150, 160, 181, 228, 239, 246,
    250, 256, 257
Dorfman, P. 126
Douglas, S. P. 265
Duck, S. 188

Eagly, A. 134, 137
Edell, J. 162
Ehrenberg, A.S.C. 43, 126
Einwiller, S. 221
Eisingerich, A. B. 187, 195, 199, 200, 201,
    204
Ekinci, Y. 44, 59, 87

Emmons, R. A. 269
Erickson, L. M. 141
Esses, V. M. 222
Ewing, M. T. 284, 285, 294, 295, 296

Farquhar, P. H. 7, 227
Farrelly, F. 92, 100, 107, 108
Feick, L. 121
Ferrandi, J.-M. 43, 53, 77
Fetscherin, M. 204
Filser, M. 205
Fischer, A. 183
Fischer, M. 260, 271, 272, 280, 281
Fiske, D. W. 122, 253
Fornell, C. 79, 152
Fosse-Gomez, M. H. 40, 140, 142
Fournier, S. 26, 204, 213, 224, 280
Francisco-Maffezzolli, E. 157
Freling, T. H. 44, 80
Funk, C. L. 13
Funk, D. 27, 30, 32, 242, 243
Furrer, O. 228, 245, 255, 257

Gabriel, H. 18
Garolera, J. 44, 48
Garretson, J. A. 130, 131
Gartner, W. C. 222
Gedenk, K. 272
Gentina, E. 140, 142
Gerbing, D. W. 16, 147, 246
Geuens, M. 43, 66, 69
Ghuman, M. K. 21, 24, 26, 34, 38, 39
Gibbons, F. X. 276
Gilbert, F. W. 22, 44, 56, 75
Gilmore, J. H. 92
Gistri, G. 185
Gladden, J. 27, 30, 32, 242, 243
Glasman, L. R. 130
Golden, L. L. 85
Goldman, B. M. 104, 105
Goodhue, D. L. 247
Gopinath, M.
Grace, D. 228, 252, 255, 295
Graeff, T. R. 247
Grappi, S. 163, 176, 185, 200
Gray, E. R. 10
Grayson, K. 92
Grewal, D. 63, 117
Grewal, R. 261, 275, 280
Grewe, G. 140
Griffin, S. 269
Grohmann, B. 44, 62, 84
Gromark, J. 284
Grossbart, S. 155
Guneri, B. 44, 70, 87

Guo, L. 38
Gurviez, P. 205, 207, 221
Guzmán, F. 7, 13, 21

Habibi, M. R. 224
Hadwich K. 289
Haenlein, M. 224
Han, C. M. 116
Han, D. 63
Hanges, P. 126
Hankinson, G. 284, 285, 291, 292, 294, 295
Harris, L. 6
Hausman, A. 95
Havlena, W. J. 179
Haynes, S. N. 238
Hazan, C. 193
Heath, T. B. 99
Heine, S. J. 269
Heinrich, D. 92, 93, 107, 108
Helmreich, R. 62
Henard, D. H. 44, 80
Hensel, P. J. 6
Hensel, P. J. 6, 130, 246
Herbst, U. 44, 73, 294
Herr, P. M. 7
Herrmann, A. 154, 155
Higie, R. A. 121
Hirschman, E. C. 144
Hirvonen, S. 294
Hofstede, G. 38, 116, 229, 250, 279
Hogg, M. 130
Holbrook, M. B. 63, 144, 162, 168, 179, 217, 219, 223
Holden, S. 38
Holmes, J. G. 208
Holmes, J. H. 155
Horbunluekit, S. 60
Hosany, S. 44, 59, 60, 87
Hota, M. 140
House, R. 126
Hoyer, W. D. 87
Hsieh, M. H. 7, 22, 23
Hsieh, Y.-C. 140
Huang, H. 87
Hui, C. H. 50
Hunt, K. A. 38
Hunt, S. D. 204
Hunter, E. D. 117

Iacobucci, D. 187, 195, 199, 200, 201
Iglesias, V. 228, 233
Ilicic, J. 92, 104, 108
Inglehart, R. F. 279, 280
Iyer, R. 113
Izard, C. E. 178, 179

Jain, K. 189
James, J. D. 27, 30, 38
James, K. E. 6, 130, 246
Jarvis, C. B. 218
Jarvis, W.B.G. 276
Javidan, M. 126
Jaworski, B. 6, 182
Joachimsthaler, E. 108
Johar, G. 221
Johar, J. S. 193
Johnson, L. W. 112, 118, 126, 12, 128, 281
Johnson, M. E. 269
Juster, F. T. 81

Kalwani, M. U. 81
Kangun, N. 155
Kao, C. F. 276
Kapferer, J.-N. 43, 87, 112, 127, 189, 191, 205, 206
Kaplan, A. M. 224
Kaplan, M. D. 44, 70, 87
Kashyap, R. 38, 205, 217, 218, 221
Kasper, H. 211
Kassarijian, H. H. 13
Katz, I. M. 269
Keller, K. L. 6, 26, 27, 28, 43, 87, 112, 116, 157, 227, 228, 233, 237, 242, 243, 256, 272, 275, 286
Kent, R. J. 81
Kernis, M. H. 104, 105
Kim, C. K. 63
Kim, H. K. 200, 204, 213, 214, 215, 295
Kim, H. S. 158
Kim, J. K. 158
King, C. 228, 252, 255, 295
King, C. W. 121
Kirmani A. 102, 237
Kirton, M. A. 38
Ko, Y. J. 112, 122, 126, 127
Koebel, M.-N. 88
Koenig, H. F. 145, 158, 159, 160
Koll, O. 38
Konecnik, M. 222
Korchia, M. 205, 207, 221
Kotler, P. 6
Kozinets, R. 92
Krishnan, B. 228, 237, 241, 250
Krohmer, H. 87
Kurtulus, K. 44, 70, 87

Labrecque, L. I. 89
Lacoeuilhe, J. 187, 188, 199, 200
Ladwein, R. 88, 189
Lamb, C. W. 26, 27, 39, 40
Lambkin, M. C. 223

Langner, T. 183
Larcker, D, F. 79
Laroche, M. 95, 224
Laros, F.J.M. 162
Larsen, R. J. 269
Lassar, W. 250
Lau, G. T. 218
Laukkanen, T. 294
Laurent, G. 189, 191, 205, 206
Lavallee, L. 269
Lawson, R. 276
Le Roux, A. 208
Leal, C. 154
Leclercq-Vandelannoitte, A. 200
Lee, D. 158
Lee, M. 200, 204, 213, 214, 215, 295
Lee, M. S. 185
Lee, S. 250, 256
Lee, S. H. 218
Lee, Y. W. 200, 204, 213, 214, 215, 295
Leheut, É. 130, 137, 140, 141, 142, 199
Lehman, D. R. 269
Leigh, J. H. 29
Leigh, T. 92
Lennox, R. D. 276
Li, F. 38, 205, 217, 218, 221
Lichtenstein, D. R. 121, 130, 131, 132
Lin, C.-C. 140
Lindeman, M. 68
Locander, W. B. 29
Loiacono, E. T. 246
Loken, B. 109
Lord, K. P. 102, 168
Louie, T. A. 99
Low, G. S. 26, 27, 39, 40
Lueg, E. 142
Luhtanen, R. 269
Lutz, R. J. 155

MacInnis, D. J. 6, 150, 182, 187, 192, 195, 199, 200, 201
MacKenzie, S. B. 155, 211, 218
Maehle, N. & Shneor, R. 87
Maio, G. R. 222
Malär, L. 87
Mangleburg, T. F. 63
Mann, B.J.S. 21, 24, 26, 34, 38, 39
Mano, H. 193
Marchetti, R. 54
Martin, W. 132
Martinec, R. 92
Martinez, E. 126, 228, 248, 257
McAlexander, J. H. 145, 158, 159, 160
McCarthy, M. S. 99
McColl, R. 181

Author index 303

McDougall, G.H.G. 95
McNeal, J. U. 130
Melin, F. 284
Meng, X. 38
Mercer, A. A. 95
Merrilees, B. 284, 292
Merunka, D. 19, 162, 163, 183, 184
Mervis, C. 19
Merz, M. A. 44, 73, 294
Meyers-Levy, J. 99
Michaelidou, N. 126
Michel, G. 7, 18, 22, 24, 39, 160, 294, 296
Milberg, S. 276
Milberg, S. J. 99
Milne, G. R. 89
Mitchell, A. A. 105, 168, 272
Mitchell, V. 87
Mittal, B. 250
Mogos Descotes, R. 40, 200, 224, 257
Monroe, K. B. 117
de Mooij, M. 279
Morgan, R. A. 204
Morris, M. L. 269
Moschis, G. P. 121
Motion, J. 185
Moutinho, L. 154
Muehling, D. D. 155
Muller Prado, P. 157
Mullet, G. M. 85
Mulyanegara, R. 294
Muncy, J. A. 113, 126
Munuera Alemán, J. L. 38, 205, 210, 218, 221
Muzellec, L. 223

Nakanishi, M. 13
Napoli, J. 92, 100, 107, 108, 284, 285, 294, 295, 296
Narver, J. C. 287
Nebenzahl, I. D. 117
Neijens, P. 140
Nelson, K. 238
Neslin, S. A. 272
Netemeyer, R. G. 16, 123, 121, 130, 131, 132, 228, 237, 238, 241, 250, 276
Newsom, J. T. 38
Ngobo, P.-V. 38
Nguyen, H. T. 93, 96, 107, 109
Nunnally, J. C. 268
Nyer, P. 162
Nyffenegger, B. 87
Nysveen, H. 145, 151, 152, 157, 158

O'Cass, A. 294
Odin, N. 38, 204, 205, 221, 295

Odin, Y. 38, 191, 204, 205, 221, 295
Olbrich, R. 140
Oliver, R. L. 11, 26, 95, 150, 152, 193, 211
Olshavsky, R. W. 211
Olson, J. C. 105, 168
Olson, J. M. 130
Ong, B. S. 60
Osgood, C. E. 84

Pappu, R. 250
Parasuraman, A. 11
Park, C. S. 233
Park, C. W. 6, 150, 182, 187, 192, 195, 199, 200, 201, 204, 276
Park, J. 204
Park, J.-O. 63
Park, S.-B. 63
Patterson, M. 10
Patwardhan, H. 162, 166
Paulhus, D. L. 269
Pauwels-Delassus, V. 40, 200, 224, 257
Peabody, D. 78
Pecheux, C. 130, 134, 135, 140, 141, 199
Pedersen, P. E. 145, 151, 152, 157, 158
de Pelsmacker, P. 140
Percy, L. 176
Pereira, R.L.G. 87
Perrin-Martinenq, D. 188, 190, 202
Peter, J. 191
Peters, C. 92
Petty, R. E. 222, 276
Phillips, L. W. 241
Piercy, N. F. 6
Pieters, R. 178
Pine, B. J., Jr. 92
Plinke, W. 75
Plutchik, R. 178
Podsakoff, P. M. 218
Porter, S. S. 256
Priester, J. 187, 195, 199, 200, 201
Puligadda, S. 261, 275, 280
Pullig, C. 228, 237, 241, 250
Putrevu, S. 102, 168

Quester, P. G. 250

Ramachander, S. 116
Ramaswamy, V. 116
Rao, V. 239
Reddy, S. K. 64
Reicheld, F. 26
Reijonen, H. 294
Rempel, J. K. 208
Rese, M. 75
Richard, M. O. 224

Author index

Richins, M. L. 162, 179, 219, 269, 276, 279
Ricks, J. 228, 237, 241, 250
Ridgway, N. 121, 132
Rieunier, S. 7, 18, 22, 24, 294, 296
Riley, F. 21
Ring, L. J. 121
Romani, S. 163, 176, 185, 200
Romaniuk, J. 21, 38, 43, 126, 162
Roper, S. 10, 11
Rosch, E. 19
Rose, G. M. 22, 44, 56, 75
Rosenaum-Elliot, R. 87
Rosenberg M. 269, 276
Ross, S. D. 27, 30, 38
Ross, W. T. 261, 275, 280
Rossiter, J. R. 67, 138, 175, 176, 162, 182, 183
Ruble, C. A. 239
Rueckert, R. W. 22
Ruekert, R. W. 112, 127
Russell, J. A. 60
Rust, R. T. 150, 172

Sahlins, M. D. 154
Samli, A. C. 193
Sargeant, A. 287
Sarkar, A. 162, 180
Sattler, H. 260, 271, 280, 281
Saucier, G. 54
Sauer, N. E. 38, 222, 228, 242
Schäfer, D. 92, 93, 107, 108
Schein, E. H. 289
Schmitt, B. H. 95, 144, 148, 152, 157, 158, 256
Schmitt, P. 38, 222, 228, 242
Schneider, K. C. 260, 261, 279
Schoenmüller, V. 92, 93, 107, 108
Schouten, J. W. 145, 158, 159, 160
Schrader, M. P. 38
Schuler, D. K. 260, 261, 279
Schutz, R.L.A. 87
Semprebon, E. 157
Shabad, G. 13
Shank, M. D. 38
Sharma, A. 250
Sharma, S. 16, 117, 123
Sharp, B. 38
Shaver, P. R. 193
Shelton, J. 92
Sherry, J., Jr. 92
Shimp, T. A. 117
Shiu, E. 228, 245, 255, 257
Shocker, A. D. 22, 112, 127, 227
Sierra, J. J. 145, 154, 158, 159
Sierra, V. 7, 13, 21

Silk, A. J. 81
Singelis, T. M. 269
Singh, S. N. 130
Sirgy, M. J. 63, 193
Skard, S. 145, 151, 157, 158
Slater, S. F. 287
Solomon, M. 130
Spangenberg, E. 206, 261, 268, 276, 279, 281
Spears, N. 34
Spence, J. T. 62
Sperling, M. B. 105
Spiggle, S. 93, 96, 107, 109
Spreng, R. A. 211
Sprott, D. 206, 261, 268, 276, 279, 281
Sreejesh, S. 162, 180
Srinivasan, N. 189
Srinivasan, V. 233
Srivastava, R. K. 22, 112, 127, 227
Stapp, J. 62
Stayman, D. M. 193
Steenkamp, J.-B.E.M. 112, 116, 126, 127, 162, 265
Stern, B. 62, 64
Strazzieri, A. 138, 189, 191, 208
Suci, G. J. 84
Swan, J. E. 95
Syed Alwi, S. F. 7, 10, 21

Tannenbaum, P. H. 84
Taute, H. A. 145, 154, 158, 159
Taylor, S. A. 60
Teel, J. E. 276
Templer, D. I. 121
Terpstra, V. 116
Thomson, M. 105, 150, 187, 192, 199, 200
Tigert, D. J. 121
Trapnell, P. D. 269
Triandis, H. C. 50
Trost, M. R. 38
Truong, Y. 181

Urde, M. 284
Usunier, J.-C. 54

Valette-Florence, P. 38, 43, 53, 77, 162, 163, 183, 184, 204, 205, 221, 295
Vargas, P. 27, 30, 38
Varki, S. 150
Vázquez, R. 228, 233
Veloutsou, C. 204, 215
Venable, B. T. 22, 44, 56, 75
Verkasalo, M. 68
Vigneron, F. 112, 118, 126, 12, 128, 281
Völckner, F. 260, 271, 280, 281
Voola, R. 294

Wallace, E. 294
von Wallpach, S. 38
Wang, G. 228, 237, 241, 250
Wann, D. L. 38
Watson, R. T. 246
Webster, C. M. 92, 104, 108
Weijters, B. 43, 66, 69
Welzel, C. 279, 280
Westbrook, R. A. 95
Weun, S. 132
Wilson, A. M. 38
Wirth, F. 228, 237, 241, 250
Wolfe, R. N. 276
Wong, H. Y. 292

Yagci, M. 228, 237, 241, 250
Yagüe-Guillén, M. J. 38, 205, 210, 218, 221

Yamauchi, K. T. 121
Yang, Z. 38, 205, 217, 218, 221
Yi, Y. 241
Yoo, B. 150, 181, 228, 246, 250, 256, 257
Yurt, O. 44, 70, 87

Zaichkowsky, J. L. 28, 81, 95, 150, 189
Zanna, M. P. 130, 208
Zarantonello, L. 95, 144, 148, 152, 157, 158, 256
Zeelenberg, M. 178
Zeifman, D. 193
Zeithmal V. A. 11, 237
Zhiyong, Y. 95
Zhou, N. 38, 205, 217, 218, 221
Zidda, P. 222
Zimbardo, P. G. 13, 14
Zinkhan, G. M. 29

SCALE INDEX

Active brand engagement scale 181
Adolescents' attitude toward the brand 130, 136–139, 141, 142
Adolescents' involvement in product categories scale 138
Affective destination image, items on 60
Attachement à la marque: *see* attachment to the brand scale
Attachment to the brand scale 187, 188–190
Attitude toward private-label brands scale 130, 131–133
Attitude toward the online retail/service (ORS) brand, measure on 246
Attitudinal brand loyalty scale 63, 168
Authenticity inventory 105

B2B brand orientation scale 285, 289–291, 296
B2B service brand identity scale 7, 13–15, 23
Baromètre de la personnalité de la marque: *see* brand personality barometer
Basic emotions scale 178
Behavioural brand loyalty scale 63
Bem sex role inventory (BSRI) 62, 63, 65
Brand affect scale 63
Brand and product category experience scale 230
Brand as icon of local culture, scale on 116, 117
Brand associations scale 26, 27–30, 39, 40
Brand attachment scale 105, 150, 187, 195–199, 201

Brand attitude favourability scale 193
Brand attitude scale 63, 64, 130, 105, 149, 155, 168, 230
Brand attitude strength, items on 196
Brand authenticity scale 92, 93–96
Brand awareness, measure of 239, 250, 272
Brand clarity, measure on 272
Brand commitment scale 191, 254
Brand credibility scale 102
Brand dependence scale 260, 261–263
Brand detachment scale 188, 190–192, 202
Brand disparity scale 262
Brand engagement in self-concept (BESC) scale 261, 268–271, 276, 281
Brand engagement measure 189, 208
Brand equity, direct measure of 243
Brand experience scale 144, 148–151, 158
Brand extension attitudes scale 99
Brand extension authenticity scale 93, 96–100, 109
Brand extension fit scale: global similarity 98; dimensional similarity 98; relevance 98
Brand familiarity scale 81, 105, 117, 239
Brand fit, measure of 64
Brand image consistency scale 239
Brand image scale 6, 7–10, 22, 23, 95
Brand involvement scale 95, 150, 189
Brand knowledge scale 99
Brand leadership scale 112, 122–125, 127, 293
Brand likability measure on 272
Brand love feeling scale 163–166, 184

Scale index

Brand love scale 162, 169–174, 181
Brand love, contrastive measure of 162, 175–176
Brand loyalty scale 132, 150, 152, 165, 166, 193, 205, 205–207, 211, 250, 272
Brand luxury index scale 112, 118–122, 126, 127, 128
Brand masculinity dimensions scale 44, 84–87
Brand parity scale 113, 113–115
Brand performance, items on 292
Brand personality appeal scale 44, 80–84
Brand personality barometer 43, 77–80
Brand personality scale 14, 43, 44–48, 48, 51, 52, 53, 56, 58, 60, 70, 73, 75, 76, 81, 82, 150, 152, 250
Brand popularity, measure on 239
Brand preference scale 63
Brand purchase intent, measure on 239
Brand relationship quality (BRQ) scale 204, 213–215
Brand relationship quality, indicators of 105
Brand relevance in category (BRiC) scale 260, 271–274, 281
Brand romance scale 162, 163–169
Brand satisfaction scale 95, 152
Brand schematicity scale 261, 275–279; single-item brand schematicity scale 276
Brand sensitivity scale 189, 191, 206
Brand switching scale 179
Brand tribalism scale 145, 154–157
Brand trust scale 63, 102, 165, 205, 210–212, 217–221
Brand trust, global measure of 218
Brand typicality, measure of 189
Brand uniqueness, measure on 272
Brand-relationship scale 204, 215–217

Children's attitude toward the brand 130, 134–136, 141
City brand personality scale 44, 70–73
Cognitive brand loyalty scale 114
Cognitive destination image, items on 60
Collective self-esteem, measure of 269
Concern for appropriateness, measure of 276
Consideration of the brand scale 191
Consistent image, measure on 246
Constant-sum brand importance weight, measure on 272
Consumer complaining scale 179
Consumer ethnocentrism scale 117
Consumer-based brand authenticity scale 92, 100–104

Consumer-based brand equity scale 228, 233–236
Consumer-brand relational authenticity scale 92, 104–107
Consumers' emotional attachment to the brand scale 187, 192–195
Consumption emotions set (CES) scale 178, 179
Corporate brand associations scale 27, 30–34, 38, 39
Corporate character scale 11
Country-of-origin perception, scale on 117
Cross-national consumer-based brand equity scale 228, 248–252, 257
Customer delight scale 150
Customer satisfaction scale 11, 150
Customer-based brand equity scale 228, 237–242
Customer-based equity in the team sports industry scale 228, 242–245

DES-II scale 178
Destination brand orientation scale 285, 291–294
Destination personality scale 44, 59–61
Donation intentions, measure of 19

Emotional attachment scale: *see* consumers' emotional attachment to the brand scale
Employee brand equity scale 228, 252–255
Enduring involvement scale on 121
Extension evaluation, measure of 64

Fashion involvement, scale on 121

Genders of product categories scale 85
General and deal-specific deal proneness, measure on 132
General brand evaluation scale 150, 151

Human and brand personality scale 43, 53–56
Human personality scale 54

Impulsiveness, measure on 133
Independent and interdependent self-construal, measure of 269
Industrial brand personality scale 44, 73–75
Integration in brand community scale 145, 145–148, 159, 160
Intention to recommend, items on 60
Interpersonal Bem sex-role inventory 269
Involvement in product category scale 191
Involvement scale 135, 138, 193, 206

Japanese and Spanish brand personality scales 44, 48–53

Level of expertise of soccer, measure of 243
Likelihood of purchasing the brand, scale on 117
Likelihood of recommendation of the brand scale 64
Likelihood to contribute to a non-profit organization, measure of 58
Loyalty intention, measure on 11
Loyalty toward the brand, measure of 243

Market orientation, items on 287
Masculine and feminine brand personality scale 44, 62–66
Masculinity trait index/femininity trait index 62, 65
Material values, measure of 269
Materialism, measure of 219, 276
Materialistic attitudes, scale on 121
Meanings of branded products scale 260, 263–268, 281
Mesure multidimensionnelle de la confiance dans la marque/multi-dimensional measure of brand trust 205, 207–210
Money-prestige, scale on 121
Multi-dimensional customer-based brand equity scale 228, 228–233, 257
Multi-dimensional non-profit brand orientation scale 284, 285–289, 296
Multi-dimensional scale of brand trust 218

Need for cognition, measure of 276
Need to evaluate, measure of 276
Negative emotions toward brands scale 163, 176–180, 185
Negative word of mouth scale 179
New measure of brand personality 43, 66–69
Non-profit brand image scale 7, 18–21, 22, 23
Non-profit brand personality scale 44, 56–59, 75

Online corporate brand image scale 7, 10–12, 23
Online retail/service (ORS) brand equity index 245, 246, 248
Online retail/service (ORS) brand equity scale 228, 245–248, 257
Organization performance, subjective measure of 287
Organizational associations, measure of 239, 250

Overall brand equity measure 232, 246
Overall brand love scale 173, 174
Overall brand management effectiveness scale 287
Overall satisfaction scale 211

Past percentage of brand purchases, measure on 239
Perceived brand globalness scale 112, 116–118
Perceived brand prestige scale 116
Perceived brand quality scale 116
Perceived difference among brands, measure of 189
Perceived quality, measure of 250
Perceived risk, measure of 189
Perceived usefulness of market information about brands, scale on 114, 115
Perceived value, measure of 250
Personal attributes questionnaire 62
Personal involvement inventory 81
Personnalité humaine et de marque: see human and brand personality scale
Political candidate's brand image scale 7, 15–18
Politician personality scale 14
Price consciousness, measure on 132
Price insensitivity, measure of 243
Price sensitivity to the brand, scale on 114
Price-based prestige sensitivity, scale on 121
Price-quality perception, measure on 132
Product attitudes scale 269
Product category involvement, measure on 230
Proximity scale 193
Purchase intention of the brand scale 63–64
Purchase intention scale 81, 99, 102, 105, 138–139, 168, 181, 230, 243, 247
Purchase likelihood of the extension, measure of 64
Purchase loyalty, measure on 219

Relational-interdependent self-construal, measure of 269
Reliance on internal reference price, measure of 132
Repeated buying behavior scale 191
Repurchase intention 155
Risk averseness, measure on 132
Role clarity, items on 254
Romantic brand jealousy scale 162, 180–182

Scale index

Safety scale 193
Satisfaction scale 193
Satisfaction with life, measure of 269
Security scale 193
Self-concept clarity, measure of 269
Self-deception and impression management, measure on 269
Self-esteem scale 181, 269, 276
Self-expressiveness scale 181
Separation distress scale 105, 193, 196
Service brand experience scale 145, 151–154
Smart-shopper self-perception, measure on 132
Social comparison orientation, measure of 276
Strength of an attachment bond, measure of 105

Susceptibility to normative influence, measure of 276

Team association model (TAM) scale 32, 33
Team brand associations scale 27, 34–37, 38
Typicality of the non-profit organization, measure of 19

U.S. brand personality scale: *see* brand personality scale

Value consciousness, measure on 132

Willingness to pay a premium price, scale on 193, 272
Willingness to recommend scale 99
Word of mouth scale 63, 165, 166

eBooks
from Taylor & Francis
Helping you to choose the right eBooks for your Library

Add to your library's digital collection today with Taylor & Francis eBooks. We have over 45,000 eBooks in the Humanities, Social Sciences, Behavioural Sciences, Built Environment and Law, from leading imprints, including Routledge, Focal Press and Psychology Press.

Choose from a range of subject packages or create your own!

Benefits for you
- Free MARC records
- COUNTER-compliant usage statistics
- Flexible purchase and pricing options
- 70% approx of our eBooks are now DRM-free.

Benefits for your user
- Off-site, anytime access via Athens or referring URL
- Print or copy pages or chapters
- Full content search
- Bookmark, highlight and annotate text
- Access to thousands of pages of quality research at the click of a button.

ORDER YOUR FREE INSTITUTIONAL TRIAL TODAY

Free Trials Available

We offer free trials to qualifying academic, corporate and government customers.

eCollections
Choose from 20 different subject eCollections, including:
- Asian Studies
- Economics
- Health Studies
- Law
- Middle East Studies

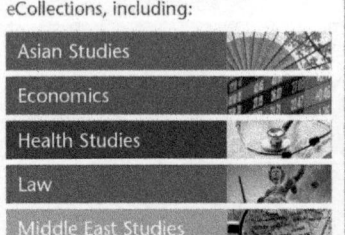

eFocus
We have 16 cutting-edge interdisciplinary collections, including:
- Development Studies
- The Environment
- Islam
- Korea
- Urban Studies

For more information, pricing enquiries or to order a free trial, please contact your local sales team:

UK/Rest of World: **online.sales@tandf.co.uk**
USA/Canada/Latin America: **e-reference@taylorandfrancis.com**
East/Southeast Asia: **martin.jack@tandf.com.sg**
India: **journalsales@tandfindia.com**

www.tandfebooks.com